SECOND EDITION

The General Method of Social Work Practice

A PROBLEM-SOLVING APPROACH

Maria O'Neil McMahon

East Carolina University
Greenville, North Carolina

With a Foreword by Carel B. Germain

PRENTICE HALL
Englewood Cliffs, New Jersey 07632

Library of Congress Cataloging-in-Publication Data

McMahon, Maria O'Neil, 1947-
   The general method of social work practice : a problem-solving
approach / Maria O'Neil McMahon ; with a foreword by Carel B.
Germain. -- 2nd ed.
      p.   cm.
   ISBN 0-13-350380-1
   1. Social work education. 2. Social work education--Curricula.
3. Social service. 4. Holism. I. Title.
HV11.M374 1990
361.3--dc20   89-29977
                                                            CIP

Editorial/production supervision: Lynn Alden Kendall
Interior design: Karen Buck
Cover design: Lundgren Graphics, Ltd.
Manufacturing buyer: Ed O'Dougherty

Printed in the United States of America
10   9   8   7   6   5   4   3   2   1

ISBN 0-13-350380-1

Prentice-Hall International (UK) Limited, *London*
Prentice-Hall of Australia Pty. Limited, *Sydney*
Prentice-Hall Canada Inc., *Toronto*
Prentice-Hall Hispanoamericana, S.A., *Mexico*
Prentice-Hall of India Private Limited, *New Delhi*
Prentice-Hall of Japan, Inc., *Tokyo*
Simon & Schuster Asia Pte. Ltd., *Singapore*
Editora Prentice-Hall do Brasil, Ltda., *Rio de Janeiro*

Definitions used by permission from Webster's Third International Dictionary, © 1986 by Merriam-Webster Inc., publisher of the Merriam-Webster®
dictionaries.

Excerpt from D. G. Norton was first published by the Council on Social Work
Education, and is reprinted here with its permission.

This book is dedicated to
  Carel B. Germain
  Sister Mary Consilia Hannan, R.S.M.
  Sister Mary Joan Cook, R.S.M.
with deep appreciation for their inspiration and assistance

Contents

8 *Evaluation* 244

9 *Termination* 294

10 *Identity and Integration* 328

Foreword to the Second Edition

A serious need in social work is a practice framework for beginning professional practitioners that reflects the distinctions between beginning and advanced practice methods, goals, and skills. Professional values, purpose, and core knowledge are common to both. But despite many helpful attempts to clarify the differences, confusion persists about what the beginning professional social worker "really does" and whether it is "really different" from what the advanced professional social worker "really does."

The General Method of Social Work Practice helps meet that need and reduce that persistent confusion. In developing a framework for the distinctive practice method, goals, and skills for the beginning level worker, Dr. Maria O'Neil McMahon constructs what she calls the "holistic foundation." It comprises selected concepts from general systems theory, ecological ideas, and professional wisdom derived from her experience as a social work educator and practitioner. Incorporating this foundation, students focus their perceptions and conceptions for practice on people and environment as a unitary system. People are regarded as biological and psychological beings engaged in continuous exchanges with their social environments, physical settings, and cultural contexts. This knowledge foundation is broad but is not as developed in depth as it would be at the advanced level.

But the book is not overburdened with theory. It is a how-to book written with the learning needs, concerns, and interests of students in mind. It anticipates their experiences and questions as they begin their methods course and enter the practicum. Not only is it a text for the classroom, it will also be helpful to field instructors in planning appropriate practice experiences. Curriculum developers in foundation social work education will find some organizing principles to use as thematic strands in curriculum design.

Basic social work processes from engagement through evaluation and termination are described and analyzed for individual, family, group, and community work. Skills and techniques associated with each, identified as appropriate for the beginning practitioner, are described and illustrated. Dr. McMahon seeks to enhance the capacities for feeling and thinking, understanding and knowing, caring and doing, in her student readers. Diagrams to clarify concepts, supplemented by imaginative exercises for skills development, support this learning objective. Diverse practice illustrations show how beginning social workers use the General Method to provide services to people experiencing a variety of human predicaments in a variety of environments. Goals set by client and practitioner and the skills of the Method are clearly delineated, and careful attention is paid throughout to the diversity of race and ethnicity, gender, and sexual orientation.

Thus the reader gains clarity about the differences between the two levels of practice and education for practice. The entry-level practitioner learns and applies a general method of working with people and their environments, with limited but significant goals and circumscribed skills of moderate complexity. The beginning worker is skilled in general service provision, in assessing and managing readily amenable and accessible person-environment needs and problems, and in making informed judgments about when to refer more complex or intractable problems to the advanced practitioner.

As the author's analysis and the practice examples show, beginning social workers are prepared to relieve life problems and environmental needs not requiring complex interventions. They provide reassurance, support, and tangible resources; link people to formal and informal helping systems; furnish needed information; and work collaboratively with others in assuring continuity, coordination, and comprehensiveness in basic social welfare services. They are skilled in outreach activities with defined populations in at-risk situations. And their practice in both urban and rural areas spans a variety of institutional bases, including social agencies, health and mental health agencies, schools, industry, housing projects, police precincts, and so on. *The General Method of Social Work Practice* will facilitate the learning of these many professional tasks and skills by the student. It will also meet the interests of the experienced B.S.W. practitioner in ongoing professional development.

Carel B. Germain

Preface to the Second Edition

Since the first edition of this book appeared, several educators in graduate social work programs have recommended that I emphasize in the second edition the valuable use of the text in first-year graduate education as well as in baccalaureate programs. In M.S.W. programs where the foundation for practice is presented from a generalist perspective, it is very appropriate to acquaint students with the problem-solving process identified here as the "General Method." As graduate students study and develop skills in the use of the Method, they may be led to see how their concentrations may build on or incorporate the General Method into advanced practice. In addition to a general problem-solving approach, graduate students may develop more sophisticated modes or methods of intervention, particularly if their identified concentration is in "practice roles or interventive modes" (see *Curriculum Policy Statement* 7.24.4). The holistic conceptualization of the foundation as presented in Chapter 1 offers a clear picture of the essential dimensions of our profession. The basic values, theories, and skills outlined in Diagram 1-5 serve as a comprehensive framework to be extended in depth and scope into an identifiable concentration at the advanced level.

Recently, major efforts have been made to further clarify and refine the meaning of generalist social work. Sixty-two social work educators and practitioners contributed to the development of a definition, which presents generalist social work as a perspective that uses a generic foundation and "incorporates a problem-solving multilevel assessment and methodology" (Schatz and Jenkins, 1987). As did the first edition, the second edition offers a systematic way of viewing the generic foundation for practice and a problem-solving methodology that allows multileveled, differential assessment and modes of intervention.

In addition to its use in graduate and undergraduate social work programs, the text has been found to be very valuable in the orientation and training of workers in public and private human service agencies. For example, in the Department of Social Services of the state of North Carolina, a carefully planned three-tiered training curriculum has been designed, which begins with and builds on the basic foundation and methodology of the General Method. Directors, supervisors, and workers in diverse positions have studied and incorporated the use of the foundation and General Method throughout the system in various ways, including case management, record keeping, supervision, and evaluation.

I have learned also that the text is being used for the development of values, knowledge, skills, and methodology in other human service disciplines, such as criminal justice, counseling, and nursing. As brought out in Chapter 1, various professionals in human services are increasingly recognizing the need to see the client, patient, victim, or accused within the context of his or her life-space environment. With a holistic view of person and problem or need, as presented in this book, the provider can more effectively move forward in the process of service provision.

The central focus of this text is the presentation of a six-stage General Method, which builds on a professional foundation and is used in practice with individuals, groups, families, and communities. Tools, diagrams, examples, and exercises are offered to guide and enrich learning for general practice. Examples are taken from the fields of child welfare, gerontology, public welfare, education, community services, and corrections. A highly praised feature of the text is the ongoing presentation of examples to illustrate a worker's sensitivity to human diversity in each stage of the General Method. A fundamental ecological systems perspective is integrated throughout.

Again, I am deeply grateful to many people who helped to make this text a reality. First of all, for assistance with the writing of the original text, I wish to recognize and thank Dr. Carel B. Germain, Sisters Mary Consilia Hannan and Mary Joan Cook, and the students and faculty of Saint Joseph College, West Hartford, Connecticut. Additional consultants included Emilia E. Martinez-Brawley, Leon W. Chestang, Judith N. O'Brien, Margaret Slowick, Arthur R. LaVoie, and Sister Patricia Cook, R.S.M.

For their enthusiastic reception and application of the text, I am deeply grateful to my friends at East Carolina University; Grambling State University; Cleveland State University; Madonna College, Levonia, Michigan; Mount Mercy College, Cedar Rapids, Iowa; and so very many others. The text was written because of a felt need for such a practice guide. The continued support and appreciation I have received from social workers and educators across the country and from other countries have assured me of the worth of my efforts. I continue to see the work as a beginning response to the need for a holistic conceptualization of the profession of social work, with particular articulation of generalist practice.

1

The Foundation for General Practice: A Holistic View

In my judgment, one of the profession's most important tasks in theory development is the formulation of a way or ways of thinking about social work as a whole. It has always seemed strange to me and somewhat unfortunate that while we have had theory about casework, group work and community organization we have had little, until recently, about social work itself. The serious consequences of this deficiency in the theory of social work is that it has led us to practice as specialists more than as generalists and without a generalist base to anchor our specialties.

—Gordon Hearn[1]

In the present decade, noted social work educators and practitioners have worked diligently at clarifying the educational needs and role expectations for a beginning social work professional.[2] Controversy and confusion have often resulted from the use of such related terms as *basic, core, general,* and *generic* to describe the foundation of social work practice. In addition to the search for appropriate descriptive words, studies have been conducted to identify the specific knowledge, values, and skills that are essential for beginning practice.[3] Even with these components to constitute the base for practice, the search continues for a conceptual framework that will integrate the various dimensions of social work into a unified whole.

Preciseness in identifying and unifying methods, skills, theory, knowledge, values, attitudes, policies, and programs for social work will remain a challenge, owing to the artful and evolving nature of the profession. This book is an attempt to offer a comprehensive conceptualization of content for understanding and describing professional social work practice at the entry level today. The beginning worker is described as a professional who has been socialized into the role of a social work generalist. More specifically, the theoretical and experiential preparation for practice as outlined in this book presents a picture of an ecological generalist: someone who works with a variety of client systems and services, using an ecological perspective and a general method. After presenting a holistic view of the foundation for general practice in the introductory chapter of this book, focus will be given to the general method that is commonly used in the education and practice of beginning social workers.

THE SEARCH FOR HOLISM

In the profession of social work, among the human services, and within the human person, there is a growing expression of a desire for holism. As a concept, *holism* has become increasingly popular in diverse professions since the 1970s. It is currently defined and used from various perspectives. In essence, holism refers to a totality in perspective, with sensitivity to all of the parts or levels that constitute the whole and to their interdependence and relatedness. The terms *health, wholeness,* and *the holy* are often used when describing holism.

The roots of holism may be found in the writings of Jan Smuts,[4] Claude Bernard,[5] Walter Cannon,[6] Kurt Goldstein,[7] Andras Angyal,[8] and others. Smuts introduced holism as a philosophical theory in his book *Holism and Evolution* in 1926. He based the word *holism* on the Greek word *hole,* meaning complete, entire, and whole. Smuts describes the determining factors in nature as "wholes" that are irreducible to the sum of their parts. Focus is on the functional or organic relations between parts and wholes. Evolution in the universe is seen as the recording of the making of wholes.

Bernard (1927) and Cannon (1939) in their work view the human body as a whole and describe the body's capacity to maintain inner balance or equilibrium. A person's "internal environment" is seen as having regulators to cope with external and internal disturbances.

Kurt Goldstein, a neuropsychiatrist, is the major exponent of organismic theory. In this theory, the organism is described as a united whole, with mind and body undifferentiated. Organs and faculties of the body are not independent; what happens to any part has an effect on the whole. Although Goldstein recognizes that the organism is influenced by the environment, he gives predominance to the human organism.

Andras Angyal, who followed Goldstein, said it is impossible to separate the organism from the environment. This would contradict the nature of the whole. Using systems analysis, Angyal conceptualized the "biosphere," which he described as a holistic entity consisting of the two polarities of individual and environment. The two are seen "as aspects of a single reality which can be separated only by abstraction."[9]

From the works of Bernard and Cannon, Goldstein and Angyal, holistic medicine emerged. In the health field, holism is a concept that describes perceptions of the patient, of the environment of the patient, and of the various providers of services. In holistic medicine, emphasis is on health and coping capacities rather than disease and sickness. Helping is defined in terms of managing resources rather than treating illness. The physician is encouraged to look beyond the disease and to take a broader look at the patient. Primarily, holism is seen as an approach for viewing the whole person. For example, Goldwag writes:

> Here, the aim is to understand the living organism as a total entity and to understand its parts as integrated, interdependent, interrelated systems that can be understood by studying the parts, but without losing sight of their relation to the whole organism.[10]

For some health providers, the concept *holistic* or *wholistic* means to see and treat the patient within the environment that surrounds and influences the person. Podolsky writes:

> The term "wholistic," a variant of holistic, signifies that people are treated in the context of their entire environment, including their family situations, social milieu, economic class, and educational attainments, as contrasted with treating only a disease or focusing upon a single complaint.[11]

In addition, a holistic conception has been used to describe a health center where a group of people join their expertise and efforts with a concerted team approach for comprehensive services.

> The City of Health staff also recognizes that no one therapist or single therapy is necessarily the catalyst for healing but rather than a multi-therapeutic approach is the most effective program. With this understanding, the staff works in harmony with one another without the interference of personal ego clouding the attitude of wholeness that prevails.[12]

From this initial overview of the beginnings of holistic theory, it is apparent that early holistic conceptualizations were used predominantly in the field of medicine. Concepts evolved to describe perceptions of the patient, the patient's environment, and the service providers. It is of interest to note that the person recognized as the founder of holistic theory, Jan Smuts, soldier and statesman, was a major advocate of the Commonwealth of Nations and builder of the League of Nations and of the United Nations.[13]

HOLISM IN HUMAN SERVICES

Within the field of human services today, the concept *holism* is commonly applied to consumers of services, their needs, and the services offered. The concept *human services* itself is holistic, in that it draws together professionals and paraprofessionals of diverse backgrounds who are working to meet human needs. The relationship of *human services* to *holistic thinking* is particularly obvious in a contemporary definition that states: "Human services can be defined as an interdisciplinary field encompassing the various concerns related to a person's internal and external environment."[14] Human service workers include those from fields such as mental health, vocational rehabilitation, corrections, welfare, law, child care, social work, housing, education, and physical health.

Professionals and paraprofessionals in human services are growing in the use of a holistic conceptualization of the persons receiving services. The client/patient/consumer is seen holistically when focus is on the whole person—body, spirit, and mind—and on the interdependence of each of the major dimensions of *person*. In addition, the client is not seen in isolation, but within his or her life-space environments. The family, culture, physical surroundings, and society of the individual are seen as essential parts of a holistic view of clients.

In considering the needs of a human being holistically, focus is on the whole hierarchy of needs, and on the necessary and sequential relationship of each. Maslow, for example, identifies the needs of a person as crossing over the physical dimension of person (bodily needs), the intellectual dimension (cognitive needs), and the spiritual dimension (aesthetic needs).[15] With a holistic view of needs, human service workers are aware of the interdependence of needs.

To apply a holistic approach to human services, the interrelationships of various helping professionals with one another and with the family and culture of their clients are highlighted. The need for team building and case coordination and management is seen as basic for effective service. Although certain people with particular needs may come to the attention of individual providers or agencies, holistically minded helpers do not lose sight of the fact that each person is very much a part of other persons, that each need is strongly related to other needs, and that each service can meet neither all the needs of any one person nor one need of all persons. Human service providers are becoming increasingly aware of their dependence on one another within a whole network of human services.[16]

To develop the meaning of holism and its application to human services further, a diagram of the triplex of holism is presented in Figure 1-1. The person with multiple needs is depicted within the immediate environment of family, friends, and community, and all are contained within the larger society with institutions and services. Particular institutions to meet

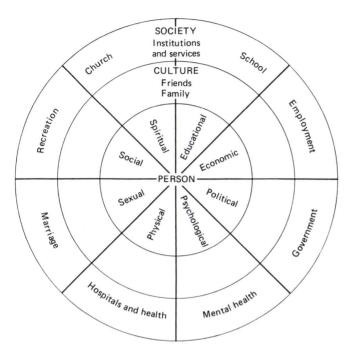

FIGURE 1-1 Holism in Human Services

identified needs are shown with dividing boundary lines that may mark difficult points of passage for the person or family. All of the needs and corresponding institutions are not necessarily felt or used at the same time. They are potential or actual in the cyclical life process of persons in society.

For understanding person and environment, tri-circle diagrams similar to that of Figure 1-1 are frequently used by theorists and practitioners. For example, Kurt Lewin, in his "life-space diagraming," identifies the "person," the "environment," and the extended sphere of reality called the "foreign hull" (see Figure 1-2).[17] Dolores Norton, in her "dual perspective" of practice, depicts the person within a "nurturing system" circumscribed by

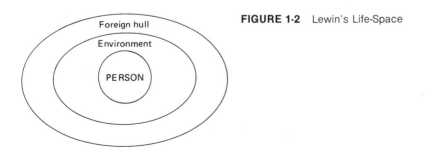

FIGURE 1-2 Lewin's Life-Space

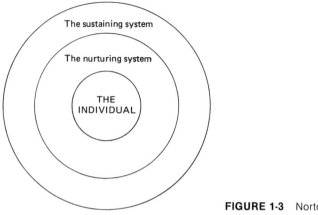

FIGURE 1-3   Norton's Dual Perspective

the "sustaining system" (Figure 1-3).[18] All three holistic perspectives are closely allied to general systems theory and, more specifically, to ecological-systems theory, which will be discussed later in this chapter.

HOLISM IN SOCIAL WORK

Recent writings in social work literature indicate a growing recognition of the value in applying holistic theory to practice. Weick, for example, stresses the "physical" in the person-in-environment paradigm. In addition to a client's internal and external social environments, she sees the need for workers to become more aware of the physical internal and external environments of clients.[19]

Holistic concepts have been used also to describe various aspects of the profession and to describe the whole of social work itself. Certain methodologies and theories have been seen as holistic. For example, in considering different methods of practice, Baer and Federico found that within a generalist approach, emphasis is on a "holistic assessment and intervention at the level of both people and systems."[20] They see general practice as providing a "holistic perspective" of practice situations.

> The generalist or unitary conceptualization with its emphasis on systems and their interactions, appears to be the approach that best helps the student to understand situations from a holistic perspective.[21]

Brieland, Costin, and Atherton concur with Baer and Federico in viewing a generalist method as holistic when they write:

The small voluntary agency finds that it cannot afford a variety of specialists, and the large public agency has learned that to be effective it cannot separate individual and family improvement from societal change. For those who seek the world in holistic terms, the generalist has come to represent a promising solution.[22]

Ecological-systems theory as used in social work practice may be traced back to its roots in holistic theory. Goldstein's work on organismic theory, which had its origin in holistic theory, was a major influence on Bertalanffy in his development of general systems theory. Hearn applied general systems theory to social work, and, as Hearn noted, Gordon extended systems theory to "boundary work."[23] As brought out later in this chapter, boundary work is a bridge to ecological-systems theory in social work practice.

Basically, the focus of ecological-systems theory is on the *interface* where person and environment come together, and the focus of holistic theory is on the *whole*, which is seen as containing and relating to its parts. In holism, central attention has been given to the inner environment of the persons and to "inner balance,"[24] whereas in ecological-systems theory, central attention has moved to the organism and the extended environment and to "adaptive balance."[25] In both "the life model," which is an offspring of ecological-systems theory, and in "holistic health," which is an offspring of holistic theory, there is increasing overlap with the use of such concepts as *coping, stress, transaction, balance,* and *interdependence.*[26]

Later in this chapter, more specific explication and application of ecological-systems theory and of the generalist approach to social work practice will be given. The main point here is that both ecological-systems theory and the generalist approach are currently viewed in practice as holistic. Both are seen as responsive to the expressed need for wholeness in social work today.

With the maturation of the social work profession, it is fitting that social work educators and practitioners are using more complex conceptualizations. The recognition of diversity in unity and the identification of multiple-factor causality have been present in social work practice since its foundation; openness and adaptiveness to theory from other disciplines have also prevailed within the profession. It is timely that social work leaders are calling for a more comprehensive conception of practice, and that they continue to engage in exchanging concepts with other disciplines as they pursue their search for wholeness.

In this book, a holistic conception of social work practice at the entry level will be given. Focus will be on the identification of an ecological theoretical base and a general method of practice to guide the actions of the beginning worker. The incorporation of theoretical and methodological frameworks into a holistic perspective for advanced practice, including the M.S.W. and the independent-practice level, will be left for future works.

THE MEANING OF GENERAL PRACTICE

Social work practice at the entry level is called *general practice.* Within the profession, there is confusion over the use of the concepts *general* and *generic.* Both terms are used frequently to describe social work practice itself or a particular aspect of practice, such as method, knowledge, or skills. An effort has been made in social work to distinguish between the terms, by using *generic* to refer to what is at the core or root of all practice, and by using *general* to mean a little (not necessarily the same) of all of the various parts of the whole. This distinction is erroneous. According to *Webster's Third International Dictionary of the English Language,* the terms *generic* and *general* may be used interchangeably. Both terms refer to what is common or "characteristic of a whole group or class."[27] Both may be used to mean "belonging to the common nature" or "not confined by specialization or careful limitation."[28] Both terms may be used to describe either a group of social work practitioners or a dimension of practice, such as method or theory.

The term *general* appears to be the most commonly used word to describe practice that is "not confined by specialization" and "applicable or relevant to the whole." In general practice, a problem-solving approach is used that is explained in this book and is called the General Method. General practice is solidly based on social systems theory, particularly ecological-systems theory. All practice concentrations may use the method and theory of general practice to some extent.

General practice is taught in undergraduate social work programs accredited by the Council on Social Work Education. It may also be found in the curriculum of graduate programs, along with various concentrations.

A general practitioner is expected to have acquired the foundation of professional knowledge, values, and skills. This foundation is called into action as the worker uses the general method in working with different systems and problems. A more detailed study of the method of general practice will begin in Chapter 2. First, a holistic conception of the foundation for practice will be presented utilizing ecological-systems frameworks.

ECOLOGICAL-SYSTEMS THEORY

A precursor for the application of ecological-systems theory to social work practice may be found in William Gordon's writings on boundary work in social work. Just as ecology concerns itself with the adaptive fit of organisms and their environments, we find that Gordon's seven basic ideas on boundary work constitute extensive consideration of what occurs at the boundary between a system and its environment. Gordon's seven points were summarized by Hearn as follows:

1. Social work has a simultaneous dual focus. It focuses at once upon the person and his situation, upon the system and its environment.

2. It occurs at the interface between the human system and its environment.

3. The phenomenon which occurs at the interface is a transaction between system and environment.

4. Transaction is a matching effort, whose focus is the coping behavior of the organism on the system side, and the qualities of the impinging environment on the environment side.

5. An encounter between the organism and the environment leaves both changed.

6. . . . The best transactions are those which promote the growth and development of the organism while at the same time being ameliorative to the environment, that is, making it a better place for all systems depending upon the environment for their sustenance.

7. . . . Unattended systems proceed relentlessly toward disorder, evenness, high probability, disorganization, randomness, and continuity, or what is technically called a positive increase in entropy. . . . Thus, for growth and development to occur, there has to be a continuous redistribution of entropy between organism and environment.[29]

The similarities between the ideas of Gordon and those of Germain and Gitterman, as they define ecology, may readily be seen.

> Ecology is a science concerned with the relations between living organisms—in this case, human beings and all the elements of their environments. It is concerned with how organisms and environments achieve a goodness-of-fit or adaptive balance and equally important, how and why they sometimes fail to do so.[30]

Rooted in general systems theory, Gordon's work provides the branch for ecological-systems theory to bear fruit in social work.

In ecological-systems theory, the interactions and interdependence between the organism (subsystem) and the environment (macrosystem) are seen as crucial for the survival of both. Any change in one may have a positive or negative effect on the other.[31] The complexity and diversity among people and the various systems that constitute their environments as they exchange and interact continuously for survival is highlighted in this theory.

Ecological-systems theory helps to clarify and to reinforce for social workers the perspective of person in environment. It is not enough to look at people and/or environments. The theory emphasizes the necessary lifeline between the two, at which boundary point most stress or problems occur.

Siporin describes ecological-systems theory as "formulated at a very general conceptual level." He sees that "an ecological perspective gives rich expression to the traditional social work concern with person-situation transaction," and he considers the theory as a "framework" for overviewing practice.[32]

The challenge of using ecological-systems theory to develop frameworks in practice will be taken up in the remainder of this chapter. Using an ecological perspective, frameworks will be delineated for conceptualizing the values, theory, skills, and work environment of general social work practice. All of the frameworks will then be combined into a holistic conception of the foundation for general practice.

AN ECOLOGICAL PERSPECTIVE
OF GENERAL PRACTICE

From the inception of the profession, social workers have looked at human behavior in relation to society. Our earliest pioneers, such as Mary Richmond,[33] stressed the psychosocial nature of the person in his or her environment. At the roots of social work is the belief that any assessment of behavior should necessarily view what a person does in relation to the opportunities, obstacles, and needs that prevail in one's environment. Such a dual focus of person in environment has been described as "ecological."

An ecological perspective of social work practice is one that focuses on the fit and interactions of a person or system in relation to the various environments that are encountered. Carel Germain describes the relationship of ecology with the social work profession as follows:

> Ecology is the science concerned with the adaptive fit of organisms and their environments and with the means by which they achieve a dynamic equilibrium and mutuality. It seems to furnish an appropriate metaphor for a helping profession concerned with the relationships between human beings and their interpersonal and organizational environments with helping to modify or to enhance the quality of transactions between the people and their environments and with seeking to promote environments that support human well-being.[34]

As emphasized by Germain, whether a worker is working directly with a person or with an institution, a social worker is consistently aware of the influence and interdependence of one with the other. The practitioner engaged in policy and planning, as well as the psychotherapist, brings a commitment to the reality and potential of interactions between the person and the environment. At the basis of all professional social work is the belief that constructive change is possible in people and society, but only through mutual responsiveness and cooperation.

The general perspective of person in environment, currently called "ecological," may be used to conceptualize the social worker within the various systems that constitute the environment of social work practice. Gener-

DIAGRAM 1-1   Social Worker and Work Environment from an Ecological Perspective

ECOLOGY

PERSON	IN	ENVIRONMENT

Client systems
  Individuals
  Groups
  Families
  Local neighborhoods
    or communities
	Agency of employment	Client-related resources
		Profession
		Society at large

SOCIAL WORKER

Values
Knowledge
Skills

ally, social workers use knowledge, values, and skills in dynamic interactions with the five major systems of (1) client, (2) agency of employment, (3) client resources, (4) the profession, and (5) society at large (Diagram 1-1). The practitioner generally works within agencies having client systems that may be individuals, groups, families, or communities. The worker works with natural or professional client-related resources or services. In addition, a social worker of high quality is expected to become involved and to demonstrate leadership in society and in the profession.[35]

Although social workers do not all interact with all the systems listed in Diagram 1-1 at one time, generalists are prepared to demonstrate basic competence in working with each of the systems. They practice within the social work environment with a common base of values, knowledge, and skills that may also be diagrammed from an ecological perspective.

VALUES

The values of the social work profession are rooted in (1) a belief in the dignity and worth of every human being, and (2) a recognition of the need for a democratic and caring society. Democratic, as used here, refers to a participatory government in which people directly or through elected officials govern themselves, and in which equality of rights is enforced. These two roots of the profession emphasize person and environment and their interrelatedness. The two fundamental values are intertwined and cannot be viewed as distinct or unequal.

Building on a Judeo-Christian value system, social workers recognize that every human being possesses the potential for greatness but also that human beings are fallible, with needs that include protection and support from the environment. A caring society is not only a resourceful system with open doors but also a vulnerable organization in need of direction and control by responsible individuals. Flowing from a belief in person and the value of a caring society is the commitment of social workers to engage in activities that promote the actualization or potential of both persons and environments. Social workers strive to develop the capacities of individuals and the resources of societies so that together they may achieve the highest quality of life.

Social work values are more clearly understood when they are explained in terms of actions and interactions. Building on the two fundamental values of person and society, social workers have identified basic practice principles and a code of ethics. Whereas the two essential values reflect the ultimate goals of the profession, the principles and code of ethics serve as criteria for directing professional activities that will lead to achieving the goals of the profession. The two essential values of person and society are found at the roots of all of social work practice. The principles and ethics code flow from from the generic values and prescribe appropriate ethical behavior for workers in their work environment.

The basic practice principles, first identified by Felix P. Biestek, S. J., may be conceptualized as individualization, purposeful expression of feelings, controlled emotional involvement, acceptance, nonjudgmental attitude, self-determination, and confidentiality.[36] Although they were initially described as principles for casework, more recent authors have noted the generic nature of these principles for work with systems of any size.[37] Essentially, the principles may be understood as guiding the worker to:

1. Recognize that every client system is unique and deserving of consideration and respect (individualization).
2. Understand the human need to express one's feelings, and the value in this expression as a means of fostering growth (purposeful expression of feelings).
3. Use one's feelings and emotions appropriately for the service of others (controlled emotional involvement).
4. Demonstrate that human beings have a right to be accepted as they are (acceptance).
5. Avoid passing judgments on people (nonjudgmental attitude).
6. Respect the right of clients to choose for themselves as much as possible (self-determination).
7. Keep information obtained from or about clients confidential (confidentiality).

In concurrence with these principles and with a broader scope for guiding practice, there is the Code of Ethics of the National Association of Social Workers. A summary of this code, as adopted by the 1979 NASW Delegate Assembly, reads as follows:

I. THE SOCIAL WORKER'S CONDUCT AND COMPORTMENT AS A SOCIAL WORKER

    A. *Propriety.* The social worker should maintain high standards of personal conduct in the capacity or identity as social worker.

    B. *Competence and Professional Development.* The social worker should strive to become and remain proficient in professional practice and the performance of professional functions.

    C. *Service.* The social worker should regard as primary the service obligation of the social work profession.

    D. *Integrity.* The social worker should act in accordance with the highest standards of professional integrity.

    E. *Scholarship and Research.* The social worker engaged in study and research should be guided by the conventions of scholarly inquiry.

II. THE SOCIAL WORKER'S ETHICAL RESPONSIBILITY TO CLIENTS

    F. *Primacy of Clients' Interests.* The social worker's primary responsibility is to clients.

    G. *Rights and Prerogatives of Clients.* The social worker should make every effort to foster maximum self-determination on the part of clients.

    H. *Confidentiality and Privacy.* The social worker should respect the privacy of clients and hold in confidence all information obtained in the course of professional service.

    I. *Fees.* When setting fees, the social worker should ensure that they are fair, reasonable, considerate, and commensurate with the service performed and with regard for the clients' ability to pay.

III. THE SOCIAL WORKER'S ETHICAL RESPONSIBILITY TO COLLEAGUES

    J. *Respect, Fairness, and Courtesy.* The social worker should treat colleagues with respect, courtesy, fairness, and good faith.

    K. *Dealing with Colleagues' Clients.* The social worker has the responsibility to relate to the clients of colleagues with full professional consideration.

IV. THE SOCIAL WORKER'S ETHICAL RESPONSIBILITY TO EMPLOYERS AND EMPLOYING ORGANIZATIONS

    L. *Commitments to Employing Organizations.* The social worker should adhere to commitments made to the employing organizations.

V. THE SOCIAL WORKER'S ETHICAL RESPONSIBILITY TO THE SOCIAL WORK PROFESSION

    M. *Maintaining the Integrity of the Profession.* The social worker should uphold and advance the values, ethics, knowledge, and mission of the profession.

    N. *Community Service.* The social worker should assist the profession in making social services available to the general public.

    O. *Development of Knowledge.* The social worker should take responsibility for identifying, developing, and fully utilizing knowledge for professional practice.

VI. THE SOCIAL WORKER'S ETHICAL RESPONSIBILITY TO SOCIETY

    P. *Promoting the General Welfare.* The social worker should promote the general welfare of society.[38]

Working within agencies, society, and the profession, with clients and related systems, the social worker draws on the code of ethics and the practice principles of the profession for direction and support. The worker

DIAGRAM 1-2   An Ecological Perspective of Foundation Values for Social Work

	ECOLOGY	
PERSON	IN	ENVIRONMENT
Dignity and worth of every person	Practice principles	Democratic and caring society
	Code of ethics	
	SOCIAL WORKER	

stands at the interface of person and environment with a dynamic value base that is two-sided, including both person and environment. This value base is an essential component of the foundation for all social work practice.

As shown in Diagram 1-2, the ecological perspective provides a framework that indicates the relationship between the *person-in-environment* concept and the basic values of social work. Although the values are listed under the headings of "person" and "environment," in the diagram we find the social worker standing under "in," at the interface where he or she puts into action the principles and code of ethics that flow from the dual values of the profession.

KNOWLEDGE

To carry their commitment into action, social workers need to understand persons and environments and their interdependence. The foundation knowledge base of professional social work is selected for an understanding of behaviors, needs, and goals of human systems within the context of their diverse cultures and environments. More specifically, workers need to know about the various systems that constitute their work environment. These include individuals, groups, families, organizations, institutions, and societies. Social work knowledge includes the study of biology, psychology, sociology, political science, and economics, as well as knowledge of social welfare policies and services. Additional areas include communications, group and family dynamics, and community development.

For intervention to be more than technical activity, the behaviors of the social worker should be directed by careful thought and disciplined knowledge. In addition to gaining knowledge about the profession and social welfare policies and services, social workers study theory, its meaning, and its relevance to practice. An ability to conceptualize and to theorize is expected of professional workers. Knowledge of particular theories that have been found to help explain the person-problem-situation phenomena of social work practice is included in all social work education programs.

Numerous theories are emerging today that may be considered relevant to social work practice. Many theories interrelate, and some duplicate or contradict others. A worker or student may be challenged and perhaps frustrated in trying to see connections or discrepancies among theories. The large amount of contemporary literature may be unmanageable or somewhat overwhelming. A systematic way of organizing and presenting established and developing theory for social workers is needed. A comprehensive framework for viewing various theories under specific headings would assist workers and educators in organizing theories used in social work.

The ecological perspective provides a conceptual framework within which various theories that contribute to the foundation of social work knowledge may be viewed. All theory of relevance to social work may be seen in relation to (1) person, (2) environment, or (3) both in interaction. In Diagram 1-3, relevant theories are classified according to these three options. The three categories are not mutually exclusive. Theories are grouped according to their predominant focus.

To understand the person, a social worker would call on various theories that would collectively provide a comprehensive view of the total person. Theories have been developed in which psychological, physical, social, sexual, intellectual, and spiritual dimensions of the human person have been conceptualized according to subsystems and stages.[39] The common and basic human needs for human development and actualization have been described.

Numerous systems that constitute the environment for each person have been studied and presented in terms of structure, parts, and processes. Theories regarding cultures, economics, politics, organizations, and systems in general have been identified as essential knowledge for social work professionals.

DIAGRAM 1-3   An Ecological Perspective of Foundation Theory for Social Work

PERSON	ECOLOGY IN	ENVIRONMENT
Ego psychology	Role	Organizational theory
Developmental theories	Socialization	Political science
Biological	Behavioral theory	Economic theory
Sexual		
Psychosocial	Communication	Cultural anthropology
Cognitive		
Moral	Stress theory	Systems theory
Spiritual	Ecological-	
Self-actualization	systems theory	
	SOCIAL WORKER	

In the middle category of Diagram 1-3, theories are listed that focus on the interactions that take place as persons and environmental systems interface. The influence of environment on the person is at the center of such theories as role, socialization, behavior modification, stress theory, and ecological theory.

Although Diagram 1-3 does not provide an exhaustive list of all theories used in social work, the categorized theories form a framework for theory building. As a person preparing for practice studies each theory individually, it will be easier to gain a greater sense of the nature of theory if the ecological framework of Diagram 1-3 is kept in mind. The notion of theory and theory building may be understood as the pursuit of truth, and the conception of individual theories as pieces of the puzzle called "truth" may aptly be viewed as depicted in Diagram 1-3. When the pieces (theories) are juxtaposed or merged, a greater understanding or clearer view may be acquired.

Workers need to be able to connect and to converge theories for more appropriate understanding and for application in practice. Diagram 1-3 provides a general overview of the relatedness of different theories. To develop this point further, a more visual expansion of Diagram 1-3 may be demonstrated with the use of Figure 1-1, as presented earlier in this chapter. Building on the profession's early recognition of the need to consider the psychosocial dimensions of person and environment, contemporary theory has been extended to the holistic perspective of the person in the environment, as was shown in Figure 1-1. The inner circle of Figure 1-1 depicts the person with his or her diverse needs. The second circle is the "nurturing system" that includes family, friends, and cultural boundaries. The third circle is the "sustaining system"[40] of institutions and organizations in society.

CASE EXAMPLE

John, 18 years old, has had a difficult time maintaining passing grades in high school, owing to limited cognitive abilities and physical stamina. Because of these limitations, he is unable to help with or eventually to take over the business of his father. This is a role expected of the oldest son according to the culture of the family. John is feeling rejected by his father and relatives. He walked into an outpatient clinic for help.

The worker for this case would need to know cognitive theory and understand the client's culture and physical limitations. Role theory would be useful in assessing the problems (role skills, role expectations, role enactment) within the client-environment situation. Figure 1-4 shows how the worker uses Figure 1-1 and Diagram 1-3 in the application of theory. The lines of the circle in Figure 1-4 are the places where theories under the "in" category of Diagram 1-3 would fall. Role theory is indicated as RT at the

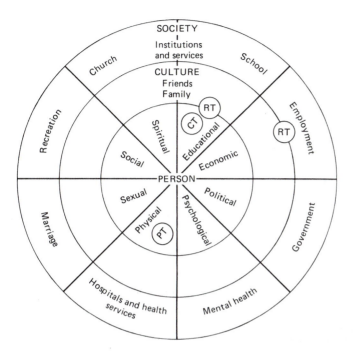

FIGURE 1-4   Use of Theory in Case Example

interfaces between person and family and between family and employment/ society. In the sections within the circles would fall the theories categorized under "person" or "environment" in Diagram 1-3; cognitive theory (CT) is in the "education" section; physiological theory (PT) is in the "physical" section; and theory about culture is in the second circle, "family."

The theories in Diagram 1-3 constitute a foundation for practice from an ecological perspective. This theoretical framework is appropriate for general social work practice. The more advanced worker, with a specialization or concentration in a problem area, field, or population or in a traditional method, would have not only knowledge based on foundation theory, but also extended knowledge of a more complex nature. Additional theory, or greater depth in basic theories, is expected of the advanced worker, particularly as it relates to the area of expertise. For example, the child specialist would have studied more in the area of physical, psychological, or learning abnormalities of children and would have more extensive knowledge of family systems and play therapy.

General practitioners, using the foundation theories as presented in Diagram 1-3, would selectively and collectively apply theory to practice. They would understand the meaning of theory and would grasp the concepts, statements, sources, and application of each of the theories. In addition, with the help of the ecological framework, the generalist would be able to view the relationships and complementarity among the basic theories for collective application and more effective practice. The theories as presented in Diagram 1-3 would support the generalist in using the general social work method that will be presented in the remainder of this book.

SKILLS

Guided by values and knowledge, a social worker executes a series of activities within the framework of a method with client-related systems to achieve identified goals. These activities constitute the skills of the worker. All social workers are trained initially in a broad variety of basic skills (Diagram 1-4). The more sophisticated or specialized worker builds on this base and develops advanced skills for working with particular populations, problems, or environments.

Social workers are known for their use of interpersonal relationships in a helping process. Sensitivity to feeling has been consistently recognized as an essential characteristic of social workers. In addition, problem solving, goal setting, and task defining are commonly identified as central to practice. Through an open, supportive relationship, clients are helped to identify tasks and proceed toward goal accomplishment and problem resolution. In a list of skills for social work practice, obviously, skills for relation-

DIAGRAM 1-4   An Ecological Perspective of Foundation Skills for Social Work

ECOLOGY		
PERSON	IN	ENVIRONMENT
Relationship skills	Problem-solving skills	Political skills
Listening	Problem/need identification	Providing evidence
Responding	Data collection	Bargaining
Guiding	Assessment	Organizing
Paraphrasing	Problem prioritization	Publicizing
Clarifying	Goal setting, planning,	Legal action
Confronting	contracting	Analyzing policies
Referring	Evaluation	Organizing demon-
Feeling/sensing	Termination	strations
	Professional skills	
	Recording/research	
	Workload management	
	Professional speaking/	
	professional writing	
	Teamwork	
	SOCIAL WORKER	

ship and problem solving would be included (in the "person" and "in" columns of Diagram 1-4).

As brought out by Pincus and Minahan, there are times when workers need to bring about change in systems or organizations that are not client systems. They define a "client system" as "people who sanction or ask for the change agent's [worker's] services, who are the expected beneficiaries of service, and who have a working agreement or contract with the change agent." A client system may be an individual, group, family, or community. In addition to working with client systems, a worker often forms "action systems" to bring about changes in "target systems." *Action systems* are formed when a worker joins with others to work with and through them in order to influence a target system and accomplish goals. In identifying causes of problems or sources for meeting needs, workers may find target systems in need of change for goal accomplishment. A *target system* is one that often refuses to accept the change efforts of workers and clients.[41]

The use of relationships or problem-solving skills may be inappropriate and ineffective in work with target systems. This is found to be particularly true in work with large bureaucratic systems. An example of this would be an educational program that rejects minority applicants on the basis of scores on standardized tests known to be biased against certain racial or ethnic groups. Standing at the interface of person and environment, the social worker would need political skills for work with such a target system. In addition to basic supportive and problem-solving skills, therefore, a range of political skills, such as providing evidence, building coalitions, publicizing, bringing legal action, and organizing demonstrations, may be needed ("environment" column, Diagram 1-4).

Besides working with client and target systems, social workers are expected to perform certain activities within agencies and as members of a profession. Skill is expected in record keeping, team building, managing time, and consultation. Research skills, particularly for practice evaluation, are expected also.

The list of skills for fundamental social work practice is lengthy and complex. A framework is needed to provide a comprehensive conceptualization of the different types of skills described. Such a framework would suggest to the worker that a whole array of skills is available for individualized selection, depending on the present situation.

Again, the ecological perspective may be seen as a framework in which to diagram the various essential skills of social workers in general practice today. According to Diagram 1-4, the practitioner would be able to operate with flexibility, using a variety of possible skills. Those skills identified in the diagram indicate the behaviors frequently used by generalist social workers. Numerous additional skills are demonstrated in social work practice. The advanced social worker, in comparison with the beginning generalist worker, would have specialized expertise for work with particular methods, problems, or populations. It would be expected that the graduate worker would have competence in the general skills as well as in more advanced skills for intensive work.

For example, an M.S.W. caseworker's skills range from environmental mobilization to psychotherapy. The caseworker would have the skills of Diagram 1-4 and skills for offering interpretations and enhancing insight. The advanced worker with a concentration in policy and planning would have the foundation skills, augmented by skills in complex program and policy planning and development.

A HOLISTIC CONCEPTUALIZATION
OF THE FOUNDATION OF SOCIAL WORK PRACTICE

Ecological frameworks provide a means for the integration of the foundation of social work practice into a systematic and holistic conceptualization. As demonstrated in Diagram 1-5, the values, theory, and skills for general practice may be perceived collectively under the ecological triplex of "person," "in," and "environment." The social worker is positioned in the center, "where the action is." Change efforts may pull from, or be directed toward, either the person or the environment, depending on the present need. The social worker actualizes the basic dimensions of the profession through dynamic interactions with his or her work environment.

The holistic conceptualization may be viewed as an exciting and needed framework for those involved with beginning practice and education. Graduates of accredited B.S.W. programs, for example, are beginning general practitioners. Frequently, administrators and supervisors in social agencies do not understand or appreciate the competence of baccalaureate-level practitioners from accredited professional programs. The role expectations for baccalaureate practitioners are not sufficiently clear for appropriate case assignments and task distribution. The framework of Diagram 1-5 helps one to understand the parameters of beginning level social work knowledge, values, and skills and serves as a guide for administrators, supervisors, and practitioners.

The holistic conceptualization provides a foundation "to anchor our specialties."[42] It shows the basic parts or dimensions of social work in relation to one another. The worker is in the central column at the point where all of the parts are held in balance for use or redistribution. The General Method of practice, which is set forth in this book, contains various elements depicted in this holistic conception of foundation. The Method pulls from the framework the knowledge, values, and skills as needed in the process of helping (explained further in Chapter 2).

The macroframework of Diagram 1-5 is not conclusive or fixed. It reflects a foundation that is truly general: as *Webster's Third International Dic-*

DIAGRAM 1-5 A Holistic Conceptualization of the Foundation for General Social Work Practice

ECOLOGY

PERSON	IN	ENVIRONMENT

VALUES

Dignity and worth of every person	Practice principles Code of ethics	Democratic, caring society

KNOWLEDGE

Ego psychology
Developmental theories
  Biological
  Sexual
  Psychosocial
  Cognitive
  Moral
  Spiritual
Self-actualization
	Role
	Socialization
	Behavioral theory
	Communication
	Stress theory
	Ecological-systems
	  theory
		Organizational theory
		Political science
		Economic theory
		Cultural anthropology
		Systems theory
		Community resources
		Social policy

SKILLS

Relationship skills
  Listening
  Responding
  Guiding
  Paraphrasing
  Clarifying
  Confronting
  Referring
  Feeling/sensing
	Problem-solving skills
	  Problem/need identifi-
	    cation
	  Data collection
	  Assessment
	  Problem prioritization
	  Goal setting, plan-
	    ning, contracting
	  Evaluation
	  Termination
	Professional skills
	  Recording/research
	  Workload manage-
	    ment
	  Public speaking/pro-
	    fessional writing
	  Teamwork
		Political skills
		  Providing evidence
		  Bargaining
		  Organizing
		  Publicizing
		  Legal action
		  Analyzing policies
		  Organizing demon-
		    strations

WORK ENVIRONMENT

Client systems
  Individuals
  Groups
  Families
  Local neighborhoods
    or communities
	Agency of employment	Client-related resources
		Profession
		Society at large

SOCIAL WORKER IN WORK ENVIRONMENT

tionary defines it, "not confined by specialization or careful limitation."[43] It organizes the content needed for general practice into a comprehensive whole.

CONCLUSION

In conclusion, the need for greater understanding and development at the beginning practice level has led to the study and identification of a holistic conceptualization to describe the foundation of general social work practice. The ecological perspective provides frameworks for comprehending the various systems of the social work environment and the knowledge, values, and skills that constitute the foundation of practice.

The specialist or advanced social worker builds on the identified foundation. Further study is needed to develop and depict the knowledge and skills for each area of concentration in advanced practice. Educators and practitioners at the graduate and postgraduate levels are working toward greater clarification of what constitutes appropriate preparation for advanced practice. It is hoped that the foundation as presented in this chapter will be helpful as a starting point or model for formulating the principles, theory, and methods for each concentration.

As social work generalists interact with a variety of systems, they use a general practice method that activates the foundation knowledge, values, and skills identified in this chapter. An overview of the General Method of social work practice is presented in the next chapter. In the remainder of the book, different phases of the General Method will be addressed.

NOTES

[1]Gordon Hearn, "General Systems Theory and Social Work," in Francis J. Turner, ed., *Social Work Treatment: Interlocking Theoretical Approaches*, 2nd ed. (New York: The Free Press, 1979), p. 350. Copyright 1979 by The Free Press. Reprinted by permission.

[2]Betty L. Baer and Ronald C. Federico, *Educating the Baccalaureate Social Worker*, 2 vols. (Cambridge, Mass.: Ballinger, 1979); Morton L. Arkava and E. Clifford Brennan, eds., *Competency-Based Education for Social Work: Evaluation and Curriculum Issues* (New York: Council on Social Work Education, 1976); and others.

[3]See Baer and Federico, ibid.; Harold L. McPheeters and Robert R. Ryan. *A Core of Competence for Baccalaureate Social Welfare and Curriculum Implications* (Atlanta: Southern Regional Education Board, 1971); Frank M. Lowenberg and Ralph Dolgoff, *Teaching of Practice Skills in Undergraduate Programs in Social Welfare and Other Helping Services* (New York: Council on Social Work Education, 1971).

[4]Jan C. Smuts, *Holism and Evolution* (New York: Macmillan, 1926).

[5]Claude Bernard, *An Introduction to the Study of Experimental Medicine* (New York: Macmillan, 1927).

[6]Walter B. Cannon, *The Wisdom of the Body* (New York: W. W. Norton, 1939).

[7]Kurt Goldstein, *The Organism* (New York: The American Book Company, 1939).

[8]Andras Angyal, *Foundations for a Science of Personality* (New York: Commonwealth Fund, 1941).

[9]Ibid., p. 100.

[10]Elliot M. Goldwag, ed., *Inner Balance: The Power of Holistic Healing* (Englewood Cliffs, N.J.: Prentice-Hall, 1979), p. 18.

[11]M. Lawrence Podolsky, M.D., "Wholistic Medicine: What Is It, Who Practices It, Who Needs It?" *Modern Medicine* (July 15, 1977): 76.

[12]Goldwag, *Inner Balance*, p. 325.

[13]*The Encyclopedia Americana,* International Edition (1981) s.v. "Smuts, Jan Christian."

[14]William Lyon with Bill J. Duke, *Introduction to Human Services* (Reston, Va.: Reston, 1981), p. 16.

[15]Abraham Maslow, *Motivation and Personality*, 2nd ed. (New York: Harper & Row, 1970); and *The Farther Reaches of Human Nature* (New York: Viking, 1971).

[16]Seymour B. Sarason and others, *Human Services and Resource Networks* (San Francisco: Jossey-Bass, 1977).

[17]Kurt Lewin, *Principles of Topological Psychology*, trans. Fritz and Grace Heider (New York: McGraw-Hill, 1936), p. 143.

[18]Dolores G. Norton, *The Dual Perspective: Inclusion of Ethnic Minority Content in the Social Work Curriculum* (New York: Council on Social Work Education, 1978), p. 5.

[19]Ann Weick, "Reframing the Person-in-Environment Perspective," *Social Work* 26, no. 2 (March 1981): 142.

[20]Baer and Federico, *Educating the Baccalaureate,* p. 156.

[21]Reprinted with permission from *Educating the Baccalaureate Social Worker,* Volume II: *A Curriculum Development Resource Guide,* Copyright 1979, Ballinger Publishing Company.

[22]Donald Brieland, Lela B. Costin, and Charles R. Atherton, *Contemporary Social Work: An Introduction to Social Work and Social Welfare* (New York: McGraw-Hill, 1980), p. 146.

[23]Hearn, "General Systems," pp. 338–52.

[24]Goldwag, *Inner Balance.*

[25]Carel Germain and Alex Gitterman, "The Life Model of Social Work Practice," in Francis J. Turner, ed., *Social Work Treatment: Interlocking Theoretical Approaches,* 2nd ed. (New York: The Free Press, 1979), p. 362. Copyright 1979 by The Free Press.

[26]Ibid., pp. 362–64; Goldwag, *Inner Balance*, pp. 10–27.

[27]*Webster's Third International Dictionary of the English Language,* s.v. "generic," "general."

[28]Ibid.

[29]Gordon Hearn, "General Systems," pp. 350, 351.

[30]Germain and Gitterman, "The Life Model," p. 362.

[31]Ibid., p. 302.

[32]Max Siporin, *Introduction to Social Work Practice* (New York: Macmillan, 1975), pp. 151–52. Copyright 1975 by Macmillan Publishing Company.

[33]Mary E. Richmond, *Social Diagnosis* (New York: Russell Sage Foundation, 1917).

[34]Carel B. Germain, "An Ecological Perspective in Casework Practice," *Social Casework* 54 (June 1973): 326.

[35]William J. McGlothlin, *Patterns of Professional Education* (New York: G. P. Putnam's Sons, 1960), p. 2.

[36]Felix P. Biestek, S. J., *The Casework Relationship* (Chicago: Loyola University Press, 1957).

[37]B. J. Picard, *An Introduction to Social Work: A Primer,* 2nd ed. (Homewood, Ill.: Dorsey, 1979).

[38]Copyright 1979, National Association of Social Workers, Inc. Reprinted with permission from *Code of Ethics of the National Association of Social Workers,* as adopted by the 1979 NASW Delegate Assembly, effective July 1, 1980 (excerpts).

[39]Specific references for each theory listed in Diagram 1-3 would be too numerous to identify here.

[40]Dolores Norton, *The Dual Perspective,* p. 5.

[41]Allen Pincus and Anne Minahan, *Social Work Practice: Model and Method* (Itasca, Ill.: Peacock, 1973), p. 63.

[42]Hearn, "General Systems," p. 350.

[43]*Webster's Third New International Dictionary of the English Language,* s.v. "general."

2

The General Method

New configurations of method, a generalist kind of practice, are now emerging that should more accurately translate systemic social work functions into helping procedures.

—Max Siporin[1]

This text focuses on beginning general practice, which is found in baccalaureate social work (B.S.W.) programs or first-year master's social work (M.S.W.) programs. According to the *Curriculum Policy Statement* adopted by the Board of Directors of the Council on Social Work Education in 1982, "The baccalaureate is the first level of professional education for entry into the profession" (6.8), and "in the master's program, the content relating to the professional foundation is directed toward preparing the students for concentration" (6.11). In B.S.W. programs, students are prepared for "generalist practice" (6.9), whereas M.S.W. programs prepare students for "advanced concentrations" (6.12).[2] At the master's level, students build on the liberal arts perspective and the general foundation, as presented in baccalaureate programs, and develop expertise in areas of concentration, which could include advanced general practice.

In 1958, the Commission on Practice of the National Association of Social Workers identified "method" as an essential component of any profession. In their efforts to clarify what constituted "the social work method," they began to identify general characteristics that are found in the traditional social work methods of casework, social group work, and community organization.[3] Perhaps because the profession of social work at the time was composed of workers who mainly practiced one of the traditional methods, there was some hesitancy and resistance to accepting the concept of a general method. Today, there is a growing recognition of the need to develop the conceptualization of a general method in social work practice.

With the rising number of baccalaureate social work programs, the demand for clarifying an appropriate methodology for entry-level workers has increased. Some preliminary efforts have been made to respond to this need.[4] More specific guidelines for action and application of theory to practice at the baccalaureate level are being requested.

In their curriculum-development project, for example, Baer and Federico point out the lack of "specific guides for action"[5] in the generalist approach to practice. They support a generalist conceptualization for baccalaureate-level practice, but they also stress the need for further development in practice methodology.

In his essay on undergraduate social work education, John Meyers also points out the scarcity and inadequacy of literature in the area of method for baccalaureate-level practice. He writes:

> Perhaps the greatest flaw of all exists in the "how to" component, that of practice or methods. With the designation of the term "generalist" for those with entry-level professional preparation, there have been some texts developed for a systems-oriented approach. These are but token contributions to resolving the dilemma of lesser specialization and greater orientation for problem-solving application.[6]

Meyers strongly advocates the writing of additional text materials "to address the generalist practitioner and to provide content to maximize the integration process for practice application."[7]

The curriculum gap identified by Meyers and by Baer and Federico will be addressed in this book. An attempt will be made to further what was begun by the Commission in 1958, and to contribute to social work education with the development of a General Method for social work practice.

THE CURRICULUM OF AN ACCREDITED B.S.W. PROGRAM

What is a "B.S.W."? The B.S.W. is a baccalaureate social worker who practices social work at the entry level of the profession. Any person with a B.A., B.S., or B.S.W. degree, who has completed a baccalaureate social work program in a school accredited by the National Council on Social Work Education, may be called a "B.S.W." Among the many different work settings where B.S.W.'s are employed are hospitals, schools, children's and youth services, vocational rehabilitation programs, community action agencies, human resource departments, nursing homes, public welfare agencies, neighborhood centers, criminal justice programs, and daycare settings for children, adults, and seniors. Although competencies of a B.S.W. have been identified to describe *what* B.S.W.'s do, little has been written to clarify *how* B.S.W.'s do what they do. What procedure or "method" is used by the B.S.W. practitioner?

In order to meet the standards for accreditation by the Council on Social Work Education, an undergraduate social work program must offer students a foundation in social work knowledge, values, and skills with a supervised field experience in general practice. Building on a liberal arts base, content must be provided in the areas of (1) social work practice, (2) social welfare policy and services, (3) human behavior and social environment, and (4) research.[8] In addressing the social work practice area, baccalaureate programs offer a sequence of courses that is usually called "method." According to the Council, the B.S.W. beginning professional is expected to graduate with the identity of a "generalist." The actual method or methods of the generalist have not been clearly described by CSWE.

In 1978 Betty Baer and Ron Federico published their intensive study of curriculum for social workers at the baccalaureate level. Although they did not spell out a method for general practice, they developed a list of ten generic competencies to be expected of B.S.W. graduates. They are:

1. Identify and assess situations where the relationship between people and social institutions needs to be initiated, enhanced, restored, protected, or terminated.
2. Develop and implement a plan for improving the well-being of people based on problem assessment and exploration of obtainable goals and available options.
3. Enhance the problem-solving, coping, and developmental capacities of people.
4. Link people with systems that provide them with resources, services, and opportunities.
5. Intervene effectively on behalf of populations most vulnerable and discriminated against.
6. Promote the effective and humane operation of the systems that provide people with services, resources, and opportunities.
7. Actively participate with others in creating new, modified, or improved service, resource, and opportunity systems that are more equitable, just, and responsive to consumers of services, and work with others to eliminate those systems that are unjust.
8. Evaluate the extent to which the objectives of the intervention plan were achieved.
9. Continually evaluate one's own professional growth and development through assessment of practice behavior and skills.

10. Contribute to the improvement of service delivery by adding to the knowledge base of the profession as appropriate and by supporting and upholding the standards and ethics of the profession.[9]

As mentioned earlier, Baer and Federico, after considering different methods of practice at the baccalaureate level, concluded that the most appropriate approach is that of general practice. They described "the generalist approach" as follows:

> All efforts in the generalist, unitary approach to practice are based on the premise that all of a person's needs involve a variety of systems and that the social worker functions at the interface of people and social systems or societal institutions. Social systems theory is the basis for all efforts to explicate the generalist approach to practice.[10]

Baer and Federico realized the limitations in teaching this approach, because it lacked "guides for actions." They hoped that their identification of basic competencies and of the need for a generalist approach in baccalaureate-level practice would assist others in the development of B.S.W. practice methodology as well as competencies. Apparently, much more work is needed by CSWE and B.S.W. educators in the curriculum area of method.

In addition to clarifying what constitutes the general method that guides the actions of the generalist, there is a need to clarify what actually distinguishes the B.S.W. general practitioner from the M.S.W. practitioner with a "specialized focus" or "concentration" (*Curriculum Policy Statement,* CSWE, 7.23). The concept *specialization* remains quite controversial within the profession.

SPECIALIZATION IN SOCIAL WORK

Throughout the history of the profession of social work, the word *specialization* has been used and recognized, but its meaning is still unclear. By the early 1950s so much splintering or specializing had developed in the profession that social workers recognized a great need to develop a common identity and a clear definition of the base of social work practice. Relinquishing their autonomy according to specialties, workers organized and created the National Association of Social Workers in 1956. After giving much attention to the core of social work, workers and educators began to state the need for specializations as well as for the general base within practice and education. In 1961, Harriet Bartlett wrote:

> We must solve the confusion around "specialization" in Social Work and arrive at an acceptable concept that is workable for both practice and education.[11]

Several attempts were made at formulating universal and acceptable definitions for both *base* and *specialization*. In the Hollis-Taylor Report of the 1950s, a design for graduate social work programs was proposed in which there was a generic focus in the first year, with specialization in the second year. Specializations were understood in this proposal according to the three traditional methods of casework, group work, and community organization.[12]

Bartlett, in her detailed study, proposed "fields of practice" as the most effective way to understand specialization.[13] Henry Maas preferred to consider specializations in terms of specific social problems and the knowledge, programs, and skills required to deal with them.[14] In 1974, 10 councils representing major areas of social work practice submitted reports to the Division of Practice and Knowledge of NASW. This action resulted in an identification of specializations based on "methodological functions." The five essential methodological functions were listed as "clinical social work, social policy and community development, social research, social work administration, and social work education."[15]

Also in 1974, a Task Force of the Council on Social Work Education presented the famous "Bisno Report," in which it was formally recommended that "graduate degree programs in social work shall consist of advanced specialized education."[16] This report strongly endorsed innovation and the development of specializations at the graduate level. As stated in the Report,

> As soon as feasible, efforts should be initiated to identify the core knowledge and skills for one or more specializations as pilot undertakings in connection with the recommendation that graduate professional education be specialized, such undertaking to be coordinated with efforts of NASW along the same lines.[17]

Roland Meinert published a study of 1979, in which he surveyed the concentrations (also referred to as specializations) offered in accredited M.S.W. programs. His review revealed five different concentration patterns currently offered in graduate schools across the country. These were described as (1) traditional (casework, group work, community organization), (2) individualized (diverse courses to meet unique career needs), (3) dual track (micro/macro, direct/indirect), (4) specific (definite field, problem area, or population group), and (5) matrix (combination field and method). Meinert concluded that the results of his study demonstrated the continued need within the profession for further clarification of what constitutes a specialization.[18]

The Council on Social Work Education's Commission on Educational Planning formed two subcommittees to study and further explicate the base and specialization in social work. Both subcommittees presented papers on their respective topics to the Board of Delegates, CSWE, at their Annual Program Meeting in April 1979. Essentially, the definitions and criteria given for specialist or specialization and for generalist or base are as follows:

> Specialist: In order to be considered a specialist in a practice area, a social worker must have a relevant concentration at the graduate level or a demonstrated equivalent via post-graduate continuing education. Concentration should be complex enough to require a minimum of one year of study at the master's level, including field work or practicum, over and above the basic knowledge required to enter the profession. . . .

> Specialization: Within an environment, a population experiencing a common condition to be altered or nurtured, must be identified in some critical number.

> It must be demonstrated that there exists within social work, competence for work with and on behalf of this population and the condition of their situations or environments. It must be shown that the use of this competence could be effective in altering or supporting the condition. The conditions which characterize the population and the competencies required of social work specialists to deal with them must be sufficiently complex to require the guidance of a substantial body of knowledge. Such knowledge must be clearly related to the areas of transaction between people and their environments and must be translatable into effective interventions. . . .

> Generalist: A social work generalist is a human service provider with broad-based skills, generic knowledge of persons and environments, and a commitment to social work values. The generalist is able to demonstrate basic competence in working with a variety of clients and services.[19]

> Base: Base refers to the constellation of knowledge, values, and skills required for beginning professional practice. It is the sine qua non for practice. As such it is a dynamic educational system with knowledge, value, and skill content, which is essentially prerequisite to the practice of social work at an entry level or to advanced education or education for specialization.[20]

The Subcommittee on Specialization proposed that specialization in social work should be in areas such as health, justice, education, economics, and family, child, and adult development.[21]

The question may be asked, Can a student in an accredited B.S.W. program specialize? Although many M.S.W. programs have a "general" or "generic" first year during which students may develop competence for general practice, it is not possible for students in accredited B.S.W. programs to develop the competence to become "specialists."

Many B.S.W. programs offer some elective courses in areas of "specialization," such as child welfare, gerontology, or mental health, but they are not able to provide the "minimum of one year" of intensive graduate study in the specialization. The programs would not meet their primary goal of preparing generalists if their graduates saw themselves as specialists. The elective courses in specialized topics are more appropriately identified as supportive areas of study in undergraduate social work programs.

Much more extensive work is needed on the nature and content of specializations and concentrations in graduate-level practice and education. It is apparent that it is inappropriate to find specializations at the undergraduate level. This distinction alone may at least begin to meet the need for clarification as pointed out by Meyers:

> The attempt to clarify social work as a profession will be a continuous effort but, more importantly, the need to distinguish the educational preparation for professional practice at the baccalaureate and master's degree levels is an effort that requires timely activity.[22]

Some additional considerations of the differences in expectations and methodologies between the beginning generalist and the advanced practitioner will follow. First, it is necessary to clarify the meaning of *method* and of *the General Method* for entry-level practice.

METHOD DEFINED

In the *Working Definition of Social Work Practice,* method is defined as "an orderly systematic mode of procedure."[23] Schwartz describes method as "a systematic process of ordering one's activity in the performance of a function."[24] According to Siporin, method refers to "the 'how' of helping, to purposeful, planned, instrumental activity through which tasks are accomplished and goals are achieved."[25] And, in *Webster's,* method is defined as "a procedure or process for attaining an object" or "a particular approach to problems of truth or knowledge."[26] Basically, *method* means an orderly process of action. The concept connotes thought and purpose in addition to activity.

Morales and Sheafer state: "The social worker's skill is expressed within the framework of one or more social work methods."[27] In addition to skill, a social work method should reflect the knowledge and values of the profession. Method puts the knowledge, values, and skills of a worker into action. As pointed out by Siporin,

> The societal task functions of social work are realized through the "how" of methodic action, in an application of knowledge, attitudes, and skill.[28]

The first methods identified in social work practice focused on the way a social worker proceeded in working with an individual, running a group, or organizing a community. The traditional methods of social casework, social group work, and community organization were seen as separate and distinct methodologies. Each method had its own integral set of theories and skills.

Although some workers and agencies continue to use predominantly one of the traditional methods, there has been a growing recognition of the need for workers to be able to work with systems of different sizes. In some graduate schools, students identify at least two methods for concentration. In many schools, traditional methods have been combined into micro (casework and group work) and macro (community organization, social planning) practice. It has become apparent, as brought out by Carol Meyer, that "the traditional separation of casework, group work, and community organization is no longer tenable."[29]

At the undergraduate level, there is a strong movement toward identifying a procedure that is common to all methods. Schwartz suggests that from experiences with different-size systems "the common methodological components of the helping process in social work" can be extracted.[30] Although Gordon discouraged "the dubious task of trying to extract from each (traditional method) what was common to all,"[31] he recognized "such broad stages as assessment, planning, taking action and evaluating, characteristics of any rationally based problem solving approach."[32] At the base level of practice, Siporin identifies a "common base of method." He does not find "a generic method" in practice, but he uses an emergence of various "modes of social work intervention."[33] In Morales and Sheafer, there is reference to a "generic practice method," but its meaning is not developed.[34]

Many contemporary writers in social work have begun to describe an "orderly systematic mode of procedure" (NASW definition of *method*) but refer to it as something other than a method. There is obvious hesitancy in using the word *method*. The term seems to be reserved for the three methodologic foundations of the profession. Although social workers appreciate the contributions of the original methods that served as pillars for practice, it is time for them to accept and to encourage the emergence of new, relevant methods for contemporary practice at both the B.S.W. and M.S.W. levels.

PROCESSES IN PRACTICE

Several contemporary writings used in social work education and practice describe the "how to" of practice in terms of a basic sequential process. The skills and stages of the processes may be stated in different words, but similarities and overlap among writers are apparent.

Helen Harris Perlman writes that her casework problem-solving process is actually applicable to any problem-solving efforts "in the normal course of living."[35] She identifies several "operations" that are essential to the process. They are seen as not necessarily occurring in order but as possibly taking place simultaneously or even out of sequence. Basically, the components of the process are problem identification; feelings identification (client's); examination of cause and effects of problem; search for means of solution and alternatives; and choices or decision making and action on decisions or alterations of plans and action. In the casework process, Perlman sees the factors of "relationship" and "involvement with significant others" as necessarily present within the process.[36]

In an early analysis of the change process, Kurt Lewin identified the three phases of "unfreezing," "moving," and "freezing."[37] Lippitt, Watson, and Westley expanded the process of planned change to the following seven general phases:

1. The development of a need for change
2. The establishment of a change relationship
3. The clarification or diagnosis of the client system's problem
4. The examination of alternative routes and goals; establishing goals and intentions of action
5. The transformation of intentions into actual change efforts
6. The generalization and stabilization of change
7. Achieving a terminal relationship[38]

The authors state that the process does not necessarily progress in the orderly sequence listed. Often, more than one phase is occurring at the same time. Process is seen as "a kind of cyclic motion starting over and over again as one set of problems is solved and a new set encountered."[39] Lippitt, Watson, and Westley were among the first to identify their process as applicable to work with individuals, groups, organizations, and communities.

Pincus and Minahan describe three "guide posts for the process" in their "Model and Method."[40] They stress that the activities of a worker are cyclical in nature and that at any point there may be overlap in the steps of the process. The major "successive points" in their process are described as "contact," "contract," and "termination." In the contact stage, the worker begins to engage in communications with various systems. In contracting, the worker forms agreements with clients ("primary" contracts) or with other related systems ("secondary" contracts). After contracting, the worker begins to move toward termination.[41]

Compton and Galaway identify three basic phases that are similar to those of Pincus and Minahan, but they develop the phases with additional activities incorporated into the process. The "contact phase" of Compton and Galaway is described as including "problem identification, initial goal setting and data collection." The "contact phase" refers to "joint assessments, goal setting and planning." There is also an entire section in their work on the "implementation of the plan" and on "evaluation." Their "ending phase" includes "referral, transfer and termination."[42]

Max Siporin distinguishes between "the basic helping approach" and "special and eclectic approaches" in practice theory. He presents four "characteristic helping processes" in practice. They are (1) "educational-socializing and structure-building process," (2) "relational process," (3) "rehabilitative-therapeutic process," and (4) "the problem-solving and crisis-resolving process." The stages of the problem-solving process are described as "assessment, planning, interactive action, evaluation monitoring and corrective action."[43] In addition, Siporin develops a "general helping process," also called an "action process," which has the "helping procedures" of "engagement, assessment, planning, intervention, monitoring, and termination."[44]

Gerard Egan presents a three-stage helping model. He describes the three principal stages of his helping process as (1) "responding to the client/client self-exploration," (2) "integrative understanding/dynamic self-understanding," and (3) "facilitating action/action." He calls his model "developmental," with "progressive interdependent stages."[45]

Shulman introduces "A Model of the Helping Process" based on the work phases called "preliminary," "beginning," "work," and "ending." In the preliminary phase, workers are concerned with empathy, communication, responding, and reporting. In the beginning phase, the art of developing a working relationship is central. This includes early contracting and clarification of boundaries. The work phase, according to Shulman, involves a series of skills, including elaboration, containment, and working with silences. The ending phase occurs when the separation process is carried out and skills for transition are utilized.[46]

Within task-centered practice, there is an identifiable "sequence of discrete steps" that may be seen collectively as constituting a process. Although the steps are to be applied systematically, Reid recommends that there be sufficient flexibility to allow for adaptation to the individual circumstances of each case.[47] The sequential steps, called "the task implementation sequence," are stated as follows:

1. Enhancing the commitment of the client to carry out a specific task
2. Planning the specific details of carrying out the task
3. Analyzing obstacles that may be encountered
4. Modeling and rehearsing the behaviors embodied in carrying out the task
5. Summarizing the plan for the implementation of the task and conveying encouragement along with the expectation that the client will carry out the task.[48]

In comparing the different processes, it appears that the authors are in basic agreement in recognizing a general process for practice, and the process consists of progressive stages that lead to goal accomplishment. Several of the writers stress the need for flexibility in applying the process, . .

with the expectation of overlap and occasional inconsistency in the sequencing of phases. In addition to describing foundation values and knowledge, it is apparent that leaders in the profession of social work have worked diligently at finding ways to describe the basic actions or "systematic mode of procedure" used by social workers. Building on these earlier works, this book will describe a method that has characteristics similar to those of the processes identified. As with the cyclical nature of theory building,[49] it is hoped that the General Method that is emerging from these earlier writings will offer greater understanding and utility for practice.

THE GENERAL METHOD

Using the definition of *general* to mean what belongs to the "common nature" of a group and "not confined by specialization or careful limitation"[50] (as stated in Chapter 1), and the definition of *method* to mean "an orderly systematic mode of procedure,"[51] it is possible to identify a General Method of social work practice. This method may be seen as common to all methods and not bound by careful limitation. It is a basic method consisting of a purposeful procedure ordered according to six major stages.

The sequential stages of the General Method are engagement, data collection, assessment, intervention, evaluation, and termination. In the succeeding chapters each stage will be described in greater detail. The stages of the method are not mutually exclusive. They serve as systematic guidelines for organizing the thoughts and actions of workers as they interact with diverse systems. In reality, the stages frequently occur simultaneously or out of order. Within each stage of the process, there may be combinations of such basic components as communication, data collection, contracting, evaluation, and termination. The General Method is a dynamic process composed of clusters of skills according to stages.

The method may be utilized when working with individuals, groups, families, or communities. It is not restricted to any particular system. It is inclusive of work with target and action systems as well as client systems.[52] The General Method is built on the holistic base of knowledge, values, and skills presented in Chapter 1. Its main purpose is to serve as a guide for the actions of entry-level social workers.

The worker who uses primarily the General Method in practice is called a generalist. Brieland, Costin, and Atherton state that the generalist should have a strong foundation in systems theory for problem-solving. They write:

> The generalist is usually well grounded in systems theory which emphasizes the importance of interaction and interdependence. . . . The generalist should understand systems models and use them in problem-solving.[53]

These authors make a distinction between the practice of the bacca-laureate-level generalist (B.S.W.) and the master's level generalist (M.S.W.). The master's level generalist is seen as someone who can demonstrate traditional or specialized methods as well as the General Method. While in graduate school, these workers study both general and specialized methodologies. An example cited is the University of Chicago model of an M.S.W. generalist. Workers from this program begin their helping procedure with a problem-solving approach similar to the General Method of B.S.W. workers. When the time comes for assessment and intervention, however, the graduate workers may utilize specialized methods such as casework or group work if they are needed.

> In this process all social work methods, traditional and innovative, are utilized singly or in combination to meet reality needs and to alleviate stresses in ways that enhance or strengthen the inherent capacities of client systems.[54]

Anne Minahan and Allen Pincus suggest that "all social workers are generalists." They define a generalist as "a person with a broad view who can look at an entire social situation, analyze the interactions between people in all the resource systems connected to that situation, intervene in those interactions, determine which specialists are needed from a variety of disciplines, and coordinate and mobilize the knowledge and skill of many disciplines." Building on a generalist identity, they see students in advanced education (M.S.W. programs) developing a specialization or becoming "a more expert generalist." The advanced generalist acquires "increased competence in assessment, knowledge, and skills related to interactions between resource systems." They emphasize the point that "advanced" practice and "graduate" education are not restricted to specializations or specialists in practice.[55] Whereas B.S.W. programs prepare generalists, M.S.W. programs may, therefore, prepare specialists or advanced generalists.

The generalist, as described in this book, uses the General Method, intended to serve as a guide for beginning social work practitioners at the entry level. In the following sections of this chapter, a comparison will be made of the beginning generalist with the advanced practitioner and of their methodologies. In a later chapter, consideration will be given to the placement of the General Method within the broad sphere of methodologies that exist in human services today.

THE BEGINNING GENERALIST VS.
THE ADVANCED PRACTITIONER

As stated earlier, a social work generalist is a human service provider with broad-based skills, foundation knowledge of persons and environments, and a commitment to social work values. The generalist demonstrates basic competence for working with individuals, groups, families, communities, and other related systems. In this book, a social work generalist is described as an entry-level person who uses the General Method of social work practice. An "advanced" generalist is recognized as a worker with additional knowledge and experience who may use the General Method with additional methodologies.

The advanced practitioner is a person who has the foundation knowledge, values, and skills of the generalist and advanced knowledge and skill for working with a particular population, problem, or area of practice, who may use a traditional or a specialized method or methods. This social worker has an M.S.W. degree in which, or beyond which, there was at least one full year of intensive study and field work in the identified area of concentration.

The holistic conceptualization of foundation identified in Diagram 1-5 of Chapter 1 and the General Method described in this chapter are not exclusive for the B.S.W. generalist. The foundation for social work practice is the same at any level or in any specialized field. In addition to the general base and method, there are specific knowledge and skills taught in graduate schools for advanced practice. In an M.S.W. curriculum and in M.S.W. practice, competence is expected beyond the knowledge, values, skills, and method identified in this book.

CASE EXAMPLE

Mrs. A, a single parent, came to the town social service department on the advice of a friend. She stated that the main reason she was feeling so down was the problems she was having with her son and also with her landlord. Her son, J, was 16 years old and failed to follow Mrs. A's rules and directions. They frequently argued, resulting in J's walking out of the home. In addition, their apartment was in poor condition, with leaking pipes and cockroaches. Mrs. A said she had complained several times to the landlord, but she appears to be ignored by him.

Intervention Plan A (Beginning Generalist)

Worker (B.S.W.) helped Mrs. A clarify her presenting problems and goals. Data collecting included interviews with J and the landlord. An intervention plan was developed and implemented in which: (1) Mrs. A received ongoing support from the worker, which included information and discussion regarding the needs of adolescents. As a result, Mrs. A was able to establish more realistic expectations for her son. (2) J was referred to an adolescent activity group, where he had opportunities for peer support and male identification (male B.S.W. group leader). (3) Worker met with landlord and cited the housing-code regulation that indicated that if he continued to ignore Mrs. A's complaints, he would be in violation of the code. Mrs. A was informed of the rights of tenants and the resources for housing-code enforcement. When the landlord did not make any improvements, Mrs. A contacted the Housing Code Enforcement Bureau, which notified the landlord that it would take court action if he did not follow up on the defects reported by Mrs. A.

Intervention Plan B (Advanced Practitioner)

In gathering information, the B.S.W. worker learned that Mrs. A's feel-ings of inadequacy and discouragement were long-standing and not just re-lated to her son and the landlord. In addition, the worker learned that J had difficulty getting along with his teachers and peers as well as with his mother. Mrs. A had received reports from J's school that he was always trying to be the focus of attention in his classes. With regard to the landlord, Mrs. A in-formed the worker that when she tried notifying the Housing Code Enforce-ment Bureau, the landlord told them that the real problem was Mrs. A's poor housekeeping. Also, Mrs. A had recently found out that the landlord owned several pieces of property in the area, and that many neighbors were having similar problems with him.

Based on these findings, an intervention plan was developed in which: (1) Mrs. A was referred for intensive casework by a clinical social worker who helped Mrs. A gain insight regarding her feelings of inferiority and depression. (2) J was referred to a small therapy group that was led by male and female co-workers, both with M.S.W. degrees, with concentrations in adolescence and psychotherapeutic group work. (3) The housing problem was brought to the attention of a community organizer of the local neighborhood center, a person who had extensive experience in the area of housing.

As stated, graduates of social work programs at the master's level today may concentrate or specialize in a traditional social work method (casework, group work, community organization) or in a problem area (drug abuse, delinquency) or in a particular population (aged, adolescents). As brought out in Meinert's study, a number of graduate programs provide opportuni-ties for a student to select more than one area of specialization to form a "matrix" concentration pattern. In Intervention Plan B, the beginning generalist recognized the need for advanced interventions. Referrals were made to an M.S.W. who had a concentration in casework/mental health; to two group work/adolescence advanced practitioners; and to a community organizer with advanced knowledge and experience in the area of housing.

In Intervention Plan A, beginning generalists used foundation values, knowledge, and skills in a general method to work with individuals, groups, and community resources. The skills utilized included basic relationship, problem-solving, and political skills (as found in Diagram 1-5, Chapter 1). The advanced practitioners of Intervention Plan B would be expected to have more extensive knowledge, skills, and experience. The skills of these workers would include providing insight and dealing with transferences, as well as complex community organizing and case advocacy. Depending on the worker's concentrations, greater knowledge of relevant theory, housing, legislation, group dynamics, depression, and mental illness would be ex-pected. Workers would be using specialized methodologies. Such knowl-edge, skill, and methods would be in addition to what is identified in the holistic foundation for general social work practice.

METHODOLOGIES

Focusing more specifically on methods, it has been stated that the beginning generalist is guided by foundation knowledge, values, and skills while using the General Method in working with a variety of systems. Within an ecological theoretical perspective, the generalist acts according to a basic helping procedure. Realizing human characteristics and, therefore, the uniqueness of each situation, the beginning practitioner is able to move back and forth across lines or stages of the Method, depending on the current reality. The General Method provides the worker with a basic guide for operation.

In contrast, the more advanced methods, traditional or otherwise, may include much that is found in the General Method but may also reflect the usage of advanced knowledge, skills, and procedures for work with particular systems, problems, or populations. Although practitioners and educators at the graduate level of practice have identified knowledge and skills for traditional social work methods, further development is needed in clarifying the content of methods for advanced practice. The worker with a concentration in children, for example, may have a specialized method for working with children through the use of play. The family specialist may have a distinctive method for family therapy. (Currently, the word *model* seems to be a term frequently used to describe advanced methods of intervention at the graduate level.)

How does one decide whether the general or an advanced method of practice is needed in a particular situation? To answer this question, several factors need to be considered. Primarily, it is necessary to collect data on the severity of the problem or need being addressed and on the strength and coping capacities of the persons in need. As depicted in Figure 2-1, when the severity of the problem or need is *great* and when the client has *little* ability and motivation for dealing with the problem, there is a strong indication that an advanced worker is needed (see point 1 in Figure 2-1). To bring about the greatest possible improvement in the client's situation, it is desirable that the M.S.W. practitioner have advanced as well as general expertise. When the problem or need is of little severity and the client system has obvious strengths and coping capacities, the beginning generalist will be able to intervene with high expectancy for goal accomplishment (see point 2 in Figure 2-1).

For example, if Mrs. W has a history of being depressed, with periodic outbursts against her children, and if she is very defensive when approached about her problems, the worker would need to be highly skilled to work with her effectively. If Mrs. W had a history of excellent caretaking of her children, but recently found herself losing control and therefore came to an agency seeking help, there is a strong possibility that a worker could use the General Method to help Mrs. W with her current stressful situation.

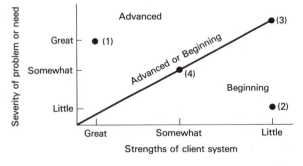

FIGURE 2-1   Beginning and Advanced Methodology

As diagramed in Figure 2-1, some client-problem situations may be serviced by either an advanced or beginning general practitioner. Either the General Method or an advanced method could be used successfully.

Where there is similarity in the assessed severity of the problem with the assessed strengths of the client, a balance may result. In these cases, there is greater question as to whether the advanced or beginning generalist should use their methods for effective goal accomplishment. For example, although Mr. B may have lost his job on the same day his daughter had a serious car accident and he received a doctor's report that he needed major surgery, Mr. B and his family may be strong enough to be able to find ways of coping with their difficulties with the help of a generalist. The advanced practitioner may not be needed, even though there are major (life-and-death) issues, because of the great strength of the client system (see point 3 in Figure 2-1).

In cases where the problem or need falls in the middle of the scale of severity and the client system's strengths are assessed as between the great and little indicators, the selection of method may be arbitrary. For example, the community concerned with an increase in neighborhood crime may have some strengths for mobilizing itself to work on the emerging problem with the help of either a beginning generalist or an advanced practitioner. The general problem-solving method or the specialized community-organization method could be effective (see point 4 in Figure 2-1).

Figure 2-1 may be a helpful tool for case assignment or planning. To use the tool, however, it is important to understand the meaning of the indicators of problem/need severity and of the client system's strengths. A problem or need is assessed at "little" severity when it has recently emerged (time consideration) with limited scope (how many, how deeply involved) and with little life-or-death magnitude. When the client system is assessed as having "little" strength, it means that the persons involved have very limited coping capacities, motivation, and resources. As the assessment moves higher on either scale, it means that there is evidence of a greater degree of client strengths or problem severity. Owing to the human and artful nature of social work practice, it is difficult to identify scientific tools for measurement and prediction. Figure 2-1 is a basic tool for comparing the use of the General Method of beginning workers with the use of more specialized methodologies of advanced workers. It is scientifically limited because it relies heavily on personal judgment and inconclusive data. It does, however, provide a framework for beginning conceptualization of distinctions in the use of the General Method.

SUMMARY

In this chapter, an overview of *method* was presented with focus on the General Method for entry-level practitioners. The meaning, types, and placement of methods in social work were explored. The paramount need for further development of method in the curriculum of generalist social work education programs was stressed. After a brief description of the General Method, some preliminary comparisons were made between the use of the General Method and the use of advanced methods in social work. The beginning generalist and the advanced practitioner were contrasted in definition and in practice.

As beginning social work generalists or advanced workers use their practice methodologies when working with a variety of systems, they need to be sensitive to human diversity. In the next chapter, a range of variables that constitute major human diversities found in social work practice will be presented from a holistic perspective. Chapters 4 through 9 will describe more specific examples to demonstrate sensitivity to human diversity in the General Method.

NOTES

[1]Max Siporin, *Introduction to Social Work Practice* (New York: Macmillan, 1975), p. 43. Copyright 1975 by Macmillan Publishing Company.

[2]*Curriculum Policy for the Master's Degree and Baccalaureate Degree Programs in Social Work Education* found in Appendix I of *Handbook of Accreditation Standards and Procedures 1988* (Washington, D.C.: Council on Social Work Education, 1988), pp. 123–124.

[3]Commission on Social Work Practice, NASW, "Working Definition on Social Work Practice," quoted in Harriet M. Bartlett, "Toward Clarification and Improvement of Social Work Practice," *Social Work* 3, no. 2 (April 1958): 5–8.

[4]Allen Pincus and Anne Minahan, *Social Work Practice: Model and Method* (Itasca, Ill.: Peacock, 1973); Siporin, *Introduction.*

[5]Reprinted with permission from *Educating the Baccalaureate Social Worker*, Volume II: *A Curriculum Development Resource Guide,* Copyright 1979, Ballinger Publishing Company, p. 155.

[6]John P. Meyers, "Undergraduate Education for the Social Work Practitioner," *Choice* 18, no. 6 (February 1981): 759.

[7]Ibid., p. 758.

[8]Council on Social Work Education, "Standards for the Accreditation of Baccalaureate Degree Programs in Social Work," effective July 1, 1974 (New York: Council on Social Work Education, 1974).

[9]Reprinted with permission from *Educating the Baccalaureate Social Worker,* Volume I: *Report of the Undergraduate Social Work Curriculum Development Project,* Copyright 1977, Ballinger Publishing Company, pp. 86–89.

[10]Ibid., Vol. II., p. 155.

[11]Harriett M. Bartlett, *Analyzing Social Work Practice by Fields,* (New York: National Association of Social Workers, 1961), p. 67.

[12]Ernest V. Hollis and Alice Taylor, *Social Work Education in the United States* (New York: Columbia University Press, 1951), pp. 235–36.

[13]Bartlett, *Analyzing Social Work,* pp. 15–17.

[14]Henry S. Maas, "Social Work, Knowledge and Social Responsibility," *Journal of Education for Social Work* 4, no. 1 (Winter 1968): 37–48.

[15]Bo Thiemann and Mark Battle, *Specialization in the Social Work Profession* (Washington, D.C.: National Association of Social Workers, 1974), pp. 19–20.

[16]Herbert Bisno, Chairman, *Report of the Task Force on Structure and Quality in Social Work Education* (New York: Council on Social Work Education, 1974), p. 13.

[17]Ibid., p. 17.

[18]Roland G. Meinert, "Concentrations: Empirical Patterns and Future Prospects," *Journal of Education for Social Work* 15, no. 2 (Spring 1979): 56.

[19]Council on Social Work Education Commission on Educational Planning, Subcommittee on Specialization, "Specialization in the Social Work Profession: (Paper submitted to Board of Delegates, CSWE, 1979 Annual Program Meeting, Boston) p. 4, p. 3.

[20]Council on Social Work Education Commission on Educational Planning, Subcommittee on Base, " A Framework for the Explication of Base in Social Work Education" (Paper submitted to Board of Delegates, CSWE, 1979 Annual Program Meeting, Boston), p. 1.

[21]CSWE Commission on Education Planning, Subcommittee on Specialization, "Specialization," p. 4.

[22]Meyers, "Undergraduate Education," p. 759.

[23]Commission on Social Work Practice, NASW, "Working Definition," p. 7.

[24]William Schwartz, "The Social Worker in the Group," in Beulah Roberts Compton and Burt Galaway, *Social Work Processes,* rev. ed. (Homewood, Ill.: Dorsey, 1979), p. 17.

[25]Siporin, *Introduction,* p. 43.

[26]*Webster's Third New International Dictionary of the English Language,* s.v. "method."

[27]Armado Morales and Bradford W. Sheafer, *Social Work: A Profession of Many Faces* (Boston: Allyn & Bacon, 1977), p. 115.

[28]Siporin, *Introduction,* p. 43.

[29]Carol H. Meyer, "The Changing Concept of Individualized Services," *Social Casework* 47 (May 1966): 284.

[30]Schwartz, "The Social Worker," p. 16.

[31]William E. Gordon, "A Critique of the Working Definition," *Social Work* 7, no. 4 (October 1962): 5.

[32]William E. Gordon, "A Natural Basis for Social Work Specializations," in National Association of Social Workers, "Specialization in the Social Work Profession" (special report of the NASW/CSWE Joint Task Force, December 1980), p. 4.

[33]Siporin, *Introduction,* p. 46.

[34]Morales and Sheafer, *Social Work,* p. 115.

[35]Helen Harris Perlman, "The Problem-Solving Model in Social Casework," in Robert W. Roberts and Robert H. Nee, eds., *Theories of Social Casework* (Chicago: The University of Chicago Press, 1970), p. 137.

[36]Ibid.

[37]Kurt Lewin, "Frontiers in Group Dynamics," *Human Relations* 1, no. 1 (1947): 5–41.

[38]Ronald Lippitt, Jeanne Watson, and Bruce Westley, *The Dynamics of Planned Change* (New York: Harcourt, Brace & World, 1958), pp. 131–42.

[39]Ibid., p. 130.

[40]Pincus and Minahan, *Social Work Practice,* p. 92.

[41]Ibid., pp. 92, 93.

[42]Beulah Roberts Compton and Burt Galaway, *Social Work Processes,* rev. ed. (Homewood, Ill.: Dorsey, 1979), pp. 276–450.

[43]Siporin, *Introduction,* pp. 47–52.

[44]Ibid., pp. 159–61.

[45]From *You and Me,* by Gerard Egan. Copyright © 1977 by Wadsworth Publishing Company, Inc. Reprinted by permission of the publisher, Brooks/Cole Publishing Company, Monterey, California, pp. 29–53.

[46]Lawrence Shullman, *The Skills of Helping Individuals and Groups* (Itasca, Ill.: Peacock, 1979), pp. 14–106.

[47]William J. Reid, "A Test of a Task-Centered Approach," *Social Work* 22, no. 1 (January 1975): 3–9.

[48]Dean H. Hepworth, "Early Removal of Resistance in Task-Centered Casework," *Social Work* 24, no. 4 (July 1979): 318.

[49]Gordon Hearn, *Theory Building in Social Work* (Toronto: University of Toronto Press, 1958).

[50]*Webster's Third New International Dictionary of the English Language,* s.v. "general."

[51]Ibid., s.v. "method."

[52]Pincus and Minahan, *Social Work Practice,* p. 63.

[53]Donald Brieland, Lela B. Costin, and Charles R. Atherton, *Contemporary Social Work: An Introduction to Social Work and Social Welfare,* 2nd ed. (New York: McGraw-Hill, 1981), p. 144.

[54]Ibid., pp. 146, 147.

[55]Anne Minahan and Allen Pincus, "A Conceptual Framework for Social Work Practice," *Social Work* 22, no. 5 (September 1977): 352.

3

Human Diversity in the General Method

A human being is a part of the whole, called by us "universe," a part limited in time and space. He experiences himself, his thoughts and feelings, as something separate from the rest—a kind of optical delusion of his consciousness. This delusion is a kind of prison for us, restricting us to our personal decisions and to affection for a few persons nearest to us. Our task must be to free ourselves from this prison by widening our circle of compassion to embrace all living creatures and the whole nature in its beauty.

—Albert Einstein[1]

A profession has an identifiable value base. At the roots of the social work profession is the belief in the dignity and worth of every human being. Social workers value human beings of any age, limitation, or diversity. The profession of social work has a commitment to the enhancement of human life.

To be human is to have choice. People need to choose their own life styles and behaviors. Social workers respect the need of individuals to choose for themselves. They do not judge the morality of another's behaviors or try to interrupt them, as long as the behaviors of one are not depriving another of life, choice, or expression. When this is the case, social workers act in support of the oppressed to help them to obtain their freedom and growth.

In social work each person is seen as unique, with a right to be treated as an individual. Although there are values and behaviors that commonly characterize a particular group, a worker exercises care to avoid stereotyping a member of any group. To *stereotype* means to attribute uniformly a set of characteristics to a group of people and to deny their individual differences. An understanding of the values and behaviors of diverse cultures, however, is valuable to a worker who is trying to communicate and interact in a meaningful way with different systems. Along with the values of life, choice, and individuality, a knowledge of human diversity is needed to guide a worker's actions.

In this chapter, emphasis will be given to a worker's need for sensitivity to human diversity in general practice. The General Method presented throughout this text is generic for working with diverse peoples or systems. Individuals and groups, nevertheless, do have distinctive characteristics that a worker should consider as the General Method is applied. Among the diversities found within social work practice are ethnic and class diversity, heterosexual-homosexual diversity, male-female diversity, age and stages diversity, and rural-urban diversity. Keeping in mind the values of the profession, a worker demonstrates respect for human life through an informed acceptance of human diversity and a resulting, sensitive application of method.

To promote awareness and skill for working with variations among human beings, the major diversities found in social work practice will be explored in this chapter. There will not be a thorough presentation for any one group. Throughout the following chapters, primary attention will be given to the use of the six-stage General Method when working with human diversity in social work practice.

CULTURAL DIVERSITY

In preparing to communicate with an individual, group, family, or community, a social worker takes time to study the culture of the system to be contacted. *Culture* means the set of values, beliefs, behaviors, language, and thought processes that is learned and exhibited by a group. An *ethnic group* is a subculture within a society, with distinctiveness due to race, national origin, or religion. Some ethnic groups have been identified as *minority* groups. This term is not based on culture or number. *Minority* refers to the extent of a group's power or of its access to the resources and opportunities available in a society. Minority-group members have less control over the circumstances of their lives than do majority members. Minority members experience economic, social, and political inequality, whereas the majority group dominates the society. In the United States, four major ethnic minority cultures have been identified. They are Afro-American, American Indian, Asian-Pacific American, and Hispanic.[2] Although for some people, their ethnic identity gives them access and privilege, for members of minority groups, the social meaning of their ethnicity (race) results in discrimination and prejudice.

Cultural sensitivity can be fostered through a knowledge of different fundamental value orientations of ethnic groups. In addition to knowing about the history of a group, it is important for the social worker to have some understanding of how the group basically perceives and values such life dimensions as time, relationships, activity, human nature, and nature itself. A framework is found in Diagram 3-1, which overviews and compares these value orientations for four ethnic minority groups and the majority (dominant) group in American society (defined as white, Anglo, Caucasian).[3] As suggested in Diagram 3-1, ethnic groups may have differing behavioral expectations based on their fundamental value perspectives. Cultures often interlock as individuals from varied backgrounds come together. An Anglo worker, for example, with a future time perspective, may become very annoyed with a Mexican-American, present-oriented client who does not save her money to last throughout the month. The client, on the other hand, may become irritated by the worker, who is seen as taking too much time to collect data before providing a direct service.

Certain common tension polarities confront all minority groups. Doman Lum identifies these basic problem areas as (1) oppression versus liberation, (2) powerlessness versus empowerment, (3) exploitation versus parity, (4) acculturation versus culture maintenance, and (5) stereotyping versus unique person.[4] To work with minorities, social workers need to understand these existing polarities and to provide the support necessary for minorities to speak and act for themselves as they organize to overcome them. Workers demonstrate an understanding of minorities and an appreciation of cultural diversity by working for cultural maintenance and parity rather than acculturation or conformity to exploitation.

If a worker is to be culturally sensitive, it is not enough to know about general characteristics of ethnic groups. To comprehend the specific culture

DIAGRAM 3-1   Comparison of Value Orientations

GROUP	TIME	RELATIONAL	ACTIVITY	HUMANITY/ NATURE	HUMAN NATURE
Dominant	Future	Individuality	Doing	Human beings over nature	Evil
Asian- Pacific	Past	Lineality/ collaterality	Being to becoming	Human beings in harmony	Good/evil
American Indian	Past/ present	Lineality/ collaterality	Being to becoming	Human beings in harmony	Good/evil
Afro- American	Past/ present	Collaterality/ interdependence	Being to becoming	Human beings in harmony	Good/evil
Hispanic	Present	Lineality	Being	Subjugation to nature	Good/evil

of a person or a group, there has to be further refinement. Car
of the four major minority groups in America has shown that
group, great variation, due to intragroup diversity, has been fou
tine, for example, found 14 distinguishable subcultures within
American minority group.[5] Clustered in the American Indian cat ̖ ̖ ̖ry, 98
subcultures have been found.[6] The Asian-Pacific group has 23 subcultures,[7]
and at least 5 subcultures are contained within the Hispanic minority
group.[8] Each of these subcultures has distinctive customs, attitudes, and life-
styles. Although there may be some similar or common biological characteristics among the members of a minority group, such as the Samoan, Gua-
manian, Chinese, Japanese, and Vietnamese of the Asian-Pacific American
minority, a worker needs to realize that each subgroup has a history and
culture of its own. Each subculture frequently has its own language or dia-
lect. There can thus be variation in meaning of glances, gestures, and body
positionings, as well as verbal statements and expressions.

SELF-ASSESSMENT OF CULTURAL SENSITIVITY

In the use of the General Method of social work practice, a sensitivity to
cultural diversity may be demonstrated within each stage of the process. A
worker's sensitivity to the culture of a system is reflected in the way in which
that worker (1) engages the system in identifying problems and needs, (2)
collects data, (3) makes an assessment and contract, (4) intervenes, (5) evaluates, and (6) terminates. Timing, communications, and actions show the extent to which a worker realizes the value orientations of a culture. The attitude and approach of the worker can also indicate an awareness of the
pressures and problems that persist in the lives of people from ethnic-
minority cultures.

For effective cross-cultural practice (i.e., worker and system from different cultures), a social worker needs to be consciously aware of his or her
own culture, as well as that of the system receiving service. Growing in cultural self-awareness can enable a worker to recognize and to appreciate diversity among cultures. It also may help a worker to begin to see any preju-
dicial or ethnocentric attitudes he or she might have. *Ethnocentrism* is
basically the belief that one's own ethnic group has the only appropriate
and acceptable practices, values, and customary behaviors.

In Exercise 3-1 questions are proposed for reflection and discussion
by workers and students in social work. The purpose of the exercise is to
enhance cultural sensitivity and self-awareness. Through identifying, sharing, and comparing the facts, feelings, and experiences addressed in the
exercise, an empathic understanding of diverse groups may begin to develop.

EXERCISE 3-1   CULTURAL-SENSITIVITY EXERCISE

1. What is your cultural background?
2. Do you identify with a particular ethnic group?
3. Select an ethnic group you come the closest to identifying with, and describe the group's customary behaviors regarding each of the following:
   a. Role of father, mother, children, extended family members
   b. Dating patterns
   c. Eating patterns
   d. Education
   e. Death and dying
4. How do you feel about your ethnic identity? What are the strengths and weaknesses you perceive in your ethnic group?
5. What ethnic groups lived in your home environment when you were growing up? How did your family relate to families of other ethnic groups (consider attitudes, experiences, power relationships, i.e., one dependent on, or subordinate to, another)?
6. What are your earliest memories of meeting people of minority groups (i.e., Afro-American, American Indian, Asian-Pacific American, Hispanic)? How did your family relate to people of minority groups? (Consider attitudes, power relationships, experiences.)
7. Are your feelings about your own ethnic group related to any power relationship you experienced with other ethnic groups?
8. Are your feelings about other ethnic groups related to any power relationships you experienced with other ethnic groups?
9. With someone from a different ethnic background, compare your ethnic groups according to the factors given in Item 3.
10. How do your feelings for your ethnic group compare with this person's feelings for his or her ethnic group?

In the following chapters, a sensitivity to cultural diversity in each of the six stages of the General Method will be more specifically demonstrated. The integration of content on culture and other human diversities within each of the chapters is deliberate, intended to highlight the importance of maintaining this sensitivity throughout any use of the Method.

What is being emphasized at this point is that culture represents a crucial aspect of a person's identity and has a vital impact on that person's social functioning and interactions with human services. Social-class, family, and individual differences are also major influences on the whole person. Adding to a sensitivity to cultural diversity, social workers need to be aware of social classes, sexual variations (homosexuality-heterosexuality), gender (male-female), age and stages of development, geographic location (rural or urban and suburban), and other related variables.

SOCIAL CLASS

As stated, in addition to understanding a system's culture, a worker should be aware of the social class of a system. *Social class* is identified through such variables as income, occupation, education, residence, group identification, and possibly, religious affiliation. When class and ethnicity are seen together, the worker arrives at a clearer picture of a system.

Gordon defines the point where class and ethnicity intersect as "ethclass." He refers to the "ethnic reality" as the dispositions and behaviors that flow from ethclass.[9] Through understanding a system's ethnic reality, a worker may begin to sense more clearly the problems, needs, issues, conflicts, and expectations a system is facing. As ethnicity and class interlock, a system may be experiencing pressures that arise from the incongruence between the two.

For example, although a family may have moved into a higher social class (blue-collar to white-collar occupation, private schools, wealthier neighborhood), family members may not be given full participation in the politics and activities of their new environment because of their ethnicity. In terms of consumption, the class level of the family is high, but in terms of power and participation, the same family is a stratified ethnic minority in its environment. This is frequently the case for members of "new ethnics," as described by Blackwell:

> Social class is only one of the two major systems of stratification in the United States. A second and equally powerful system is ethnic stratification. This system by and large expresses where a particular group falls on a social distance scale, that is, how closely it approximates conventional norms and standards of social acceptability of the white Anglo-Saxon society in the United States. In every social distance scale ethnic groups, particularly the so-called new ethnics—blacks, Chicanos, Puerto Ricans, and Orientals to a lesser degree—are relegated to the bottom position.[10]

People of the new ethnics are often identified as "bicultural," because they live in the two worlds of (1) their ethnic culture and (2) that of wider society. Moreover, a class system (i.e., upper, middle, lower) is also generally found within each cultural group.[11] The ethnic reality for a minority person, therefore, actually includes the interface of his or her biculture with that of his or her social class according to society at large and according to his or her culture's class system.

SEXUAL VARIATIONS

To work with gay or lesbian clients, social workers need to convey an attitude of acceptance of the human person and a basic understanding of sexual variations among human beings. Building on knowledge and values, a worker applies the General Method with skill and sensitivity in response to the problems or needs identified by gay or lesbian persons.

A homosexual person has been defined as "one who is motivated in adult life by a definite preferential erotic attraction to members of the same sex and who usually (but not necessarily) engages in overt sexual relations with them."[12] McNaught describes two primary types of homosexuals: (1) "transitional"—an individual who is basically heterosexual but engages in homosexual behavior when no one of the opposite sex is available (as in prisons or military service), and (2) "constitutional"—an individual whose sexual orientation toward the same sex is set around the ages of 3 to 5 years.[13] Kinsey and his associates formulated a classification system that is a seven-point continuum indicating the extent of overt and covert homosexual experience (see Diagram 3-2).[14]

The scale ranges from exclusive heterosexuality (0) to exclusive homosexuality (6). On the basis of this scale, the term *homosexual* has been used to refer to those individuals who are at levels 5 and 6, and *bisexual* or *ambisexual* for those who are at levels 2, 3, or 4.[15] Today, an extensive list of "homosexualities" has been identified that extends from a brief encounter in a public bath to an exclusive lifelong relationship between two people of the same sex.

Basically, *homosexuality* is a general term used to describe men or women. As many homosexual men prefer to be referred to as *gay* rather than *homosexual,* many women prefer the term *lesbian.* To be gay or lesbian involves psychological and sociological experiences as well as sexual attractions or behaviors. The individual can be better understood if seen in relation to his or her environment and in relation to those who live within that environment. A term frequently used to describe the reactions of heterosexual people toward gay men and lesbians is *homophobia.* As defined by Dulaney and Kelly, "Homophobia refers to an emotional reaction of deep-rooted fear and accompanying hatred of homosexual life-styles and individuals."[16] A prevalence of homophobia has been found to exist in this coun-

DIAGRAM 3-2   Sexual Orientation Scale

0	1	2	3	4	5	6
Exclusively heterosexual	Predominantly heterosexual	Predominantly heterosexual, but more than incidentally homosexual	Equally heterosexual and homosexual	Predominantly homosexual but more than incidentally heterosexual	Predominantly homosexual	Exclusively homosexual

try among helping professionals, particularly social workers.[17] Historically, homosexuality was described in the helping professions as a disturbance or an illness. Today, it is referred to as a sexual orientation or variation.

Numerous studies have been conducted in an attempt to identify physical or environmental factors that are causally related to homosexuality. To date, the etiology of homosexuality has not been clearly determined. Although it has been concluded that gender identity, which leads to erotic arousal patterns, is fundamentally a prepuberty, neurocognitional function, the principles or determinants whereby one's identity is established have not been elucidated.[18]

Studies have been written about the "cure" of homosexuality. The samples for these studies were limited to individuals who sought help because they wanted to become heterosexual. After extensive "treatment," their therapists reported "some increase in heterosexual competence" (rather than a "cure") for only approximately one-fifth of those who sought help.[19] Through additional research, it has been found that the majority of gay men and lesbians do not wish to become heterosexual.[20] They often seek and receive help from professionals, however, to restore or maintain their self-esteem or to be able to cope with the rejections they experience from family, workplace, and society at large. As brought out by Blair, "Those homosexuals who can withstand the destructive forces of an anti-homosexual society emerge usually strong and self-sufficient."[21]

PROBLEMS AND NEEDS RELATED TO SEXUAL VARIATIONS

The problems or needs brought to the attention of social workers by gay or lesbian clients are not necessarily related to their sexual variations in life style. There are, however, a number of tensions, needs, and problems an individual may experience as a result of being gay or lesbian. A knowledgeable and sensitive worker may be of assistance to the individual in these problematic areas.

For example, as a person (at any age) begins to recognize an attraction to members of the same sex or to explore the possibility that he or she may be homosexual, there may be strong feelings of fear, confusion, or guilt. For many, there is no one they can turn to for an open, honest discussion about their questions and concerns. Some, particularly adolescents, find the internal conflict so overwhelming that they turn to drugs or suicide.[22] Social workers can be very helpful as individuals struggle over questions about their sexual identity or decisions to choose or not to choose a gay or lesbian life style, or to "come out" and make their sexual orientation known publicly. Help may be needed in planning when and how they will share their decisions with significant persons in their lives. If a worker is not able to listen to or to support a person who chooses a homosexual life style, it would be better to make a referral to someone who can, rather than to continue to work with the individual. As brought out by McNaught, "coming out" can be extremely traumatic for a person unless there has been careful planning, with supports available. He writes, "Don't jump into the pool unless there is a support system of some sort waiting for you."[23] What is at stake may include the loss of a job, marriage, or self-esteem. Particularly for lesbians, "coming out" may even result in the loss of their children. Repeatedly, in divorce and custody cases, mothers who were known to be lesbians have been pressured to choose between their lovers or their children. There are organizations now available, such as Custody Action for Lesbian Mothers (CALM), to help women in or under the threat of such litigation.[24]

Gay or lesbian persons may seek help from social workers because of problems they may be having with interpersonal relationships. The relationship patterns of homosexual life styles have been described as "committed," "independent," or "ambisexual."[25] *Committed* refers to long-term and same-sex relationships. *Independent relationships* are limited to close friendships and brief, homosexual affairs. The *ambisexual* life style is one in which individuals have relationships with both sexes for long or brief time periods. Help may be sought by individuals or couples to decide about maintaining or terminating a relationship or life style. If two gay or lesbian persons decide to make a lifelong commitment to each other, they may ask a social worker to help them to find a way to legalize their relationship. They may not know about relationship contracts or joint wills. Problems and needs may develop after one of the two dies. The remaining partner may need someone to help him or her to grieve over the loss of the other. Biological family members may have legal access to the remaining assets of the deceased. Even if there has been a joint will, the family may contest it.

As lesbian or gay individuals get older, a number of problems may emerge. These have been classified as institutional, legal, emotional, and medical.[26] Institutional problems may include housing or nursing-home practices in which two nonrelated members may not be allowed to dwell together. If one partner is in a home or hospital, the other may not be allowed to visit or to make medical decisions for the institutionalized person because there is no legal or blood relationship. Legal problems may include restrictive laws regarding property or wills, as cited, or the absence of laws to prevent discriminatory practices by judges, police, or insurance companies. The emotional problems of elderly lesbians and gays may include feelings of rejection by the gay or lesbian community or feelings of abandonment or loss after the death of a partner. In addition, elderly gays who were concerned about concealing their sexual orientation have been found to feel more guilty and fearful of aging and death.[27] The medical problems of homosexuals at any age may include sexually transmitted diseases (pharyngeal or anal gonorrhea, for example, or recently, AIDS, acquired immune deficiency syndrome). Special procedures are needed to diagnose and treat such conditions.

In addition to the help offered directly by a social worker, lesbian or gay persons may need support and services from a variety of professionals and other systems. As they interact with people in diverse settings, they need to be understood and accepted as unique individuals. Social workers can assist by being aware of available, appropriate resources for gay and lesbian clients. The resources needed may include knowledgeable and accepting physicians, lawyers, clergy, and insurance companies. Gay men and lesbians are also enabled to deal with their tensions and problems through active participation in self-help groups, supportive networks, and related political action movements. Social workers may also be of assistance by helping those who are gay or lesbian to locate these resources in their communities and by encouraging them to become involved with them.

Sometimes social workers provide services for members of families of gay or lesbian individuals. For example, groups led by social workers for wives of gay and bisexual men have helped these women to deal with such feelings and issues as anger, betrayal, homophobia, sexuality, care of children, and support.[28] Another growing related area in need of attention is service provision for children found to have AIDS or AIDS Related Complex (ARC). By January 1987, there were 410 pediatric AIDS cases reported to the Centers for Disease Control in Atlanta. It is believed that at least as many as five times this number of children have ARC or test positive for HTLV-III, which is a virus potentially leading to AIDS. The child welfare system in America is finding it difficult to locate homes for these children. Social workers have become involved in developing and maintaining foster care programs specializing in serving children with AIDS.[29]

SELF-ASSESSMENT OF HOMOPHOBIA

There is a growing recognition of the need for human service workers to overcome their stereotypical views and attitudes toward gay or lesbian people.[30] The following questions constitute a brief exercise for self-reflection and discussion regarding homophobia. A fear of or antagonism toward homosexuality may be detected as one answers the questions or dialogues about their content.

EXERCISE 3-2

1. If you learned that a person was gay or lesbian, would it influence your decision about sitting next to him or her?
2. Have you worked with gay or lesbian clients?

3. Do you think gay or lesbian individuals could benefit from being placed in a mixed group (heterosexuals and homosexuals)?
4. Would you protest if an antihomosexual joke was told?
5. Do you think gay or lesbian individuals have had disturbed relationships with one or both parents?
6. Do you have social contacts with gay or lesbian persons?
7. Would you ever discourage gay or lesbian clients from disclosing their sexual orientation to their family, friends or co-workers? Why?
8. Do you think of homosexuality as a sickness or a natural variant in human sexuality?
9. What would be your response if you learned that your sibling or child was gay or a lesbian?
10. Do gay or lesbian persons have a right to be ministers, schoolteachers, social workers, or legislators?

SENSITIVITY TO GENDER: WORKING WITH WOMEN

In addition to diversity in culture, social class, and sexual orientation, a social worker is sensitive to diversity in gender when applying the General Method. More specifically, a worker is expected to communicate with women and with men in a manner that reflects an understanding of and a responsiveness to their distinctive problems and experiences.

The predominant patriarchal ideology found in American society and in other cultures fosters institutional sexism through which women experience inequality and victimization. *Sexism* means the subjugation of one sex to another. When the term is used today, it basically refers to women's being subordinate to men and to the existing attitudes, policies, and practices that demonstrate this discrimination. The unequal treatment of women and the acceptance of male dominance in society is due to differences in gender roles rather than to physiological differences between the sexes. The definitions of masculinity and femininity identified by society dictate the expected behavioral patterns for men and women. These behavioral patterns prescribed by society are called *gender roles*.[31] If social workers are to be helpful to women, it is important that they understand the nature and scope of the female gender role as it has evolved within a sexist society.

The socialization, sex-typed life experiences, and role expectations of women differ from those of men. The traditional gender role imposed on woman as a dependent, long-suffering, conforming, emotionally nurturing, and sweet female has not been a satisfying and health-promoting role for many. Women have often felt constricted and ineffective in this role. They have experienced tensions and conflict that are due to a lack of privilege and power. Some women have internalized society's image of themselves and have accepted a self-concept in which they are helpless, inadequate, and submissive. These women often need help to reject their negative self-attributes and to become resocialized as competent and whole persons.

Problems, such as rape, incest, battering, and harassment of women, have been concealed and even condoned in society. Women have been found to avoid experiencing success in order to prevent the negative consequences they expected as a result of their accomplishments.[32] In addition, the majority of the poor in America are women.[33] There is evidence that employment and promotion opportunities for women are not comparable to those for men. Women earn $6 for every $10 earned by men.[34] Salary ranges descend in the order of (1) white males (highest), (2) black males, (3) white females, (4) black females (lowest).[35] Also, women do not have equal opportunity in the decision-making structures of the job market.[36]

In addition to these problems, some women suffer personally from drinking, drugs, and depression. Although various psychological, physical, economic, and social factors may have an impact on their lives, women with these problems have often expressed strong sentiments of failure as women or helpless feelings of being trapped in a situation where there is no way out.[37] Generally, a relationship can be found between the personal and social problems of women and the negative societal beliefs and practices against women that exist in their environments.

Although in the past, service providers worked to help women to adjust to their feminine role, there is an increasing recognition of the need for workers to help women to become consciously aware of how they have been socialized and to find ways for them to grow in self-actualization. Social workers need to realize that difficulties that in the past may have been identified as individual, personal problems of women are actually a social problem, with a social cause and possibly a political solution, As a woman discusses her problems with a social worker, she may be surprised and supported in learning that other women have similar experiences and that, collectively, they are victims of sexism in society. Through joining together, women have begun to develop a sense of empowerment and to expose the destructive forces they experience. Organized movements, such as the Suffrage Movement, the Women's Trade Union, the National Consumer's League, and the National Organization for Women have greatly contributed to improving the status of women in American society. Social workers can help women to develop skill in assertiveness, self-confidence, self-reliance, expression of anger, confrontation, organization, and leadership. A sense of independence can be enhanced if the worker assumes more the role of a facilitator than an expert. In the General Method, a collaborative approach is used in which a worker and a client system engage in a shared problem-solving process. This method aptly lends itself to working with women in a sensitive, responsive manner.

WORKING WITH MEN: A CALL FOR ANDROGYNY

According to Larry Alsbrook, "The man in our society has been seduced into the oppressor role as surely as woman has inherited the oppressed role."[38] Whether or not men are responsible for the development and maintenance of sexism in society can be debated endlessly. It is more important for women and for men to become involved in searching out the positives and the potential for both as they go through the process of redefining gender roles, which is currently affecting the basic foundation and institutions of American society. Men may struggle with accepting changes in the feminine gender role because it necessitates their letting go of power and privilege. Nevertheless, there are possible advantages for men if the results of women's liberation include a change in the demands and expectations for men in a sexist society.

In essence, men may be seen also as victims of sexism. Having to assume the strong, dominant, breadwinning, protector role has had negative and sometimes fatal effects on men. They have been expected to perform with total success at work and at home. Primarily, a man's occupation has been seen as his status determinant as well as his basic identity. As a result, men have frequently developed into workaholics for whom failure in business is perceived as failure in personhood.[39]

The drive to succeed has even influenced men's suicidal actions. The instruments used by men to commit suicide are more certain to complete the task successfully than those used by women. Over 70 percent of all completed suicides are committed by men.[40]

Being a "strong" male has restricted men from expressing or even having emotions. Supportive relationships have been generally limited to one's wife, with very few sustained peer friendships. Even emotional displays with children have been considered to be out of character for a man. The stress and tensions felt by men and left unexpressed have resulted in stress-related illnesses and an earlier death rate for men than for women. Such problems, directly related to the masculine gender role, can now begin to be identified and, hopefully, resolved if men join in the movement to overcome existing sexism in society. As pointed out by Herb Goldberg:

> The social revolutions of recent years can lessen the male's time-honored burdens, help him reclaim denied emotion, expand his sensual responsiveness, bring new dimensions of honesty and depth of his heterosexual relationships, as well as alert him to the self-destructive compulsions within him.[41]

Rather than respond openly and hopefully to women's liberation, some men are feeling extremely threatened by the changes they are witnessing in their wives, daughters, friends, and associates. They are experiencing shock, hurt, and fear as women change, compete, and achieve in the workplace, the political field, and the family. Instead of fighting the movement, men are often reacting by withdrawal, particularly from encounters with women.[42] Although it may be difficult for a man to seek help with his feelings, a sensitive social worker can help him to understand and to express what he is experiencing. With support, men may begin to see some value in letting go of social norms and moving into a more equal, adult level of sharing with women.

Contemporary social changes have resulted in a variety of significant problems for men. These may include problems in such areas as custody battles, male single-parenting, or fathering after divorce when children remain with their mothers or when parents have joint custody. Social workers are able to help men with these problems through such efforts as establishing support groups for single fathers.[43]

Although sexism has a direct effect on men and women in American society, the problems of racism and poverty overshadow and compound the situation for minority men and women. Nonwhite males have a shorter life expectancy than all females and all other males.[44] Black males, in particular, have the highest risk-status. They constitute the largest group among the American prison population. Black males have the highest rate of being victimized by crime and robbery, of experiencing job injuries, of being in low-status service jobs, and of being unmarried. Black prisoners have stated their desire to be able to care for and to protect their women and children as others do.[45] The lack of opportunities in society have frequently led them to try to improve their economic status by participating in illegal activities. Social workers can demonstrate their sensitivity to the high risk-status of black men through such efforts as promoting community groups to serve as support networks for black males and through advocating social policies that are responsive to their employment and economic needs. Unless efforts to overcome racism and poverty are sustained and achieved, success in gender egalitarianism will be of little significance for poor, minority men and women.

It is possible that the changes that are taking place in gender roles may result in new, ongoing problems for men and women in general. Women may go to such an extreme in their efforts to prove their equality with men that they may become engrossed in competition and political power struggles. They too may develop stress-related illnesses and a lower life expectancy pattern as they suppress affect and stress achievement. With men's changing their masculine role, one development may be a shift to their demonstrating strength through interpersonal and intellectual skills.[46] This may prove to be equally stressful for men as they strive for success and mastery in these skill areas.

Instead of evolving into new problems, the movement for change in gender roles can be a reciprocal process that produces growth and gains for both sexes. Social workers may contribute to making this a reality by helping men and women to clarify who they are, why they are the way they are, and how they are in the process of becoming. The changes and conflicts men and women are experiencing may be better understood through an awareness of the theory of androgyny.[47] According to this theory, every person has actually or potentially both masculine and feminine characteristics. Each individual is both male and female to some degree. To be a whole person, one needs to recognize and to express both dimensions of personhood. Although someone may initially appear to be "totally masculine" or "totally feminine," he or she will naturally move in time to a stage where there is a felt need to develop and to actualize the other side of his or her personhood. To be fully human, therefore, every person is called to be a psychologically androgynous person.

> The psychologically androgynous person is one who freely engages in both "masculine" and "feminine" behaviors, is both instrumental (task oriented) and expressive (socioemotional) and is both assertive and yielding, when the occasion calls for such behavior.[48]

As men and women strive for wholeness, a beneficial goal to work for is the separation of role and status from gender. Emphasis needs to be placed on individuality, with an acceptance of flexible roles as appropriate to each situation. Social workers can help a man or a woman to develop a definition of self and role that is individualized and sensitive to the person's needs and growth. As Frederick Duhl notes, "There is no one way to be a woman or a man in our society except to develop as an individual."[49]

The General Method of social work practice is based on the practice principle of *individuality*. In applying the Method, a worker keeps in mind the unique needs and circumstances of each individual. Ways in which a generalist shows a responsiveness and sensitivity to gender diversity will be explored throughout the presentation of the six stages of the General Method in the following chapters.

SELF-ASSESSMENT OF GENDER SENSITIVITY

As with other types of human diversity, social workers need to be aware of their own personal attitudes and possible stereotypical ideas regarding gender roles. A simple exercise that may assist a student or worker to grow in self-awareness in this area is found in Exercise 3-3. Each individual should ask him- or herself the questions found in the exercise privately at first. An open discussion with one or a group of peers may follow.

EXERCISE 3-3 GENDER-SENSITIVITY QUESTIONS

1. What would be your immediate reaction when hearing about a 30-year-old woman marrying a 20-year-old man?

2. How do you feel about having a woman in charge of
   a. Your bank (president)
   b. Your place of employment
   c. A household
   d. A church
   e. The executive branch of the government (president of the United States)
3. Who did the cooking, cleaning, and shopping in your house when you were growing up?
4. Who does the cooking, cleaning, and shopping in your present home?
5. Who do you think should be responsible for household tasks?
6. What do you think of a man who walks out a door before a woman who is also trying to leave?
7. Do you ever use the expressions
   a. Woman driver
   b. Henpecked husband
   c. Female gossip
   d. Man-sized job
   e. Catty women
   f. The girls

OTHER DIVERSITY VARIABLES: THE PERSON

A social worker who is sensitive to human diversity has an awareness of several diversity variables. In addition to culture, class, sexual orientation, and gender, there are related diversity variables that may be conceptualized in terms of *person* and *environment*. To be sensitive to the person, for example, one should consider the age of the person and the developmental stage or stages the individual is going through at the time. When the system of contact is more than one person, the worker needs to be aware of the age and stage of that system—family, group, or community.

A sensitivity to age and stage can help a worker to find the most appropriate way to communicate with the system and to understand the problems and challenges the system may be facing. There are identifiable communication mediums that are found to be more effective than others when working with particular age groups. For example, small children (approximately up to age 3) have been helped through directly involving the child's parents or significant others in providing the service. The worker directs the parent figure, who works directly with the child. Children around the ages of 4 through 11 often find it difficult, if not impossible, to carry on a verbal conversation with an adult. They are used to having adults teach, direct, or parent them. Social workers are usually more effective with children at this age if they communicate through the use of play (developed further in

Chapter 7). Adolescents (ages 12–17) are often uncomfortable also with lengthy conversations with adults. An advanced type of play, such as sports, chess, or other game activities may help to reduce their apprehensions. The use of peer groups has also been found to be an effective way to reach adolescents. Hearing from peers is generally more acceptable during adolescence than hearing from adults. The adult, on the other hand, functions in a verbal world. Here too, however, the worker needs to be sure that the language and vocabulary used are appropriate for the particular adults receiving service. Those who may be considered "elderly" (over 65) often feel more secure when the social worker comes to them in their own homes; yet here too, depending on need and attitude toward workers who are usually younger, those who are older may be helped through meeting with elderly colleagues with whom they share common concerns and experiences.

Human systems are in process. They naturally go through various stages in their evolution. The human system is a complex whole with diverse functions that may progress independently of one another. The knowledge base of a social worker includes theories about the developmental processes that take place physically, socially, sexually, cognitively, spiritually, and morally in a person. Although an individual may be at one age chronologically, he or she may not be at a matching stage developmentally in one or all functioning dimensions. For example, a 12-year-old youngster may be operating at a 3-year-old level cognitively. Or, a person who is 30 years old may be functioning socially at a young, dependent level.

Using knowledge of human development, the worker considers, from the multidimensional perspective of *person* (i.e., physical, social, sexual, cognitive, moral, and spiritual), the stage at which a person is functioning. In Diagram 3-3, conceptualizations for considering stages of development according to complementary theories are outlined and juxtaposed. When a lag is observed in any dimension of development, the worker may have a beginning idea of the needs, problems, and tasks confronting the person at that time. A worker should keep in mind the fact that each person's development is unique and that a number of interrelated and interacting factors contribute to, and direct, one's development. These factors include endowment (to be explained later), culture, and gender.

Before moving into a consideration of additional diversity variables of *person*, the point should be made here that human systems containing more than one person (e.g., group, family, or community) also go through a developmental process. In general, there are the following six basic stages to the process: (1) testing/tuning in, (2) role clarifying, (3) working, (4) reformulating, (5) accomplishing, and (6) terminating. In the beginning stage, members usually observe and conform. As there is movement for role clarification, power struggles may become apparent. With the acceptance of positioning, purpose, rules, and guidelines, the system moves into a work stage. As tasks and goals begin to be accomplished, members of the system

DIAGRAM 3-3 A Multidimensional Perspective of Human Development[a]

AGE	PHYSICAL	PSYCHOSEXUAL	PSYCHOSOCIAL	COGNITIVE	MORAL	SPIRITUAL
0–3	Marked growth; teething (6–8 months); crawling (9–12 months); self-feeding; walking (1–); bowel and bladder control (2–)	Oral stage (0–1) Anal stage (1–3)	Trust versus mistrust (0–1) Autonomy versus shame and doubt (1–3)	Sensorimotor stage (0–18 months) Object permanence (18 months)	Preconventional level— Stage I: Punishment and obedience	Sensing oneness, being cared for
3–6	First permanent teeth; stronger voice; receptive, alert brain; manual and motor power	Phallic (Oedipal stage)	Initiative versus guilt	Preconceptual stage (2–4)	Stage II: Naive instrumental hedonism—conformity for reward	Beginning sense of separateness, self-will
6–12	Increased muscular ability and co-ordination; girls' growth rate exceeds boys'	Latency stage	Industry versus inferiority	Intuitive stage (4–7) Concrete-operational stage (7–11)	Conventional level Stage III: "Good boy/good girl" conformity to avoid disapproval	Experiencing God's attributes through parents and environment; beginning to hear and use religious words

(continued)

DIAGRAM 3-3 (continued)

AGE	PHYSICAL	PSYCHOSEXUAL	PSYCHOSOCIAL	COGNITIVE	MORAL	SPIRITUAL
6-12 (*cont.*)					Stage IV: Authority, maintaining law and order	Social responses; formal religious education, ritual; loyalty to faith of parents; anthropomorphic religious concepts
13–18	Girls—development of breasts, pubic hair, complexion changes; onset of menstruation Boys—development of pubic and body hair, sperm, voice changes, complexion changes	Adolescence (genital) stage	Identity versus identity diffusion	Formal-operational stage (11–15)	Post conventional level Stage V: Morality of contract; standards of society; individual rights	Religious questioning; religious awakening; varying sense of faith; rebelliousness

Age	Physical	Psychosexual	Psychosocial	Moral	Spiritual
18–35	Leveling off of growth	Maturity—to love and to work	Intimacy versus isolation	Stage VI: Morality of individual principles of conscience; universal ethical principles	Crisis/conversion experience Affiliation with (or withdrawal from) organized religious sect
35–65	Change in weight distribution, metabolism and sensory abilities slow down; menopause—women		Generativity versus stagnation or self-absorption		Search for and deepening of personal religious experience, active church participation
65–	Marked decrease in motor coordination; taste buds decline; organs begin to dysfunction		Ego integrity versus despair		Deepening of personal religion; finding religion to give meaning and support for death

aThe primary theorists who have conceptualized the processes and stages identified above are: physical—Theodore Litz; psychosexual—Sigmund Freud; psychosocial—Erik Erikson; cognitive—Jean Piaget; moral—Lawrence Kohlberg; spiritual—Gordon Allport and Maria Joan O'Neil. Specific references for each would be too numerous to print here.

grow in confidence, and they may venture out into new behaviors and goals. Reformulating roles and responsibilities may cause tensions and conflicts among members. If communication is open and members are able to change, a more mature, equal, or democratic type of functioning may be reached, with a high level of system accomplishment. Eventually, individual members of the system may break away, or the system terminates as a whole. Members often join with other outside individuals or systems to form new functioning units. Just as a worker recognizes diversity in stage development of persons, it is necessary to be able to identify these different growth levels of groups, families, and communities. This knowledge and sensitivity helps a worker in problem assessment, progress evaluation, and ongoing facilitation of growth and development within the systems.

Endowment and *personality* may be seen as additional diversity variables of *person*. The endowment of a person is a major contributor to his or her development of personality. *Endowment* refers to the natural gifts, talents, and abilities that a person has at birth. Genetic traits and characteristics, along with the innate mental, physical, and cognitive abilities of a person, are included. Personality development takes place in human beings as they use endowment and interact with others in their environment. Basically, personality is influenced by (1) the endowment of a person, (2) the inherent qualities and opportunities found within a person's environment, and (3) the transactions that take place between *person* and *environment*. The *personality* of a human being consists of the combination and integration of characteristics and experiences that give a person his or her unique personhood. Social workers realize that a person's behavior and problems may relate to individual endowment and personality as well as to culture, class, gender, sexual orientation, age, and developmental stages.

Other diversity variables that may be found in *person* and *environment* are religion and values. *Religion* may refer to organized institutions or to an individual or group's system of beliefs or practices. Although little is found in social work literature regarding the possible impact of religion on practice, there has become an increasing interest in the topic. Lowenberg, for example, identifies an "urgent need for empirical research to strengthen the social work knowledge base" in the area of religion and social work practice. He writes,

> Practitioners, both those who believe as well as those who do not, must learn to understand religion and its impact on human behavior. Such understanding is a prerequisite for effective practice.[50]

A *value system* is the collection of beliefs and preferences that are esteemed by a system. People, individually or collectively, have different value systems. As stated earlier, the values of a human being are primarily determined by the culture of the person's nurturing system. In addition, the ideas, attitudes, and values of a person are also influenced by the value systems that prevail in the larger societal environment.

SELF-ASSESSMENT OF VALUE ORIENTATION

Social workers and social welfare systems, as well as clients and other work-related systems, may have contrasting values. On this point, Alan Keith-Lucas identified three major types of value systems found in American society. They are (1) capitalist-puritan (CP), (2) humanist-positivist-utopian (HPU), and (3) Judeo-Christian (JC).[51] Basic assumptions for each of these three value systems are given in Exercise 3-4. Capitalistic-puritan value assumptions are described in items 1, 2, 7, 8, and 13 of the exercise. Humanist-positivist-utopian assumptions are given in numbers, 3, 4, 9, 10, and 14. And assumptions of the Judeo-Christian system are indicated in items 5, 6, 11,

EXERCISE 3-4   VALUE-SYSTEM INDEX

ASSUMPTIONS	TOTALLY DISAGREE					TOTALLY AGREE
	0	1	2	3	4	5
1. Human beings are responsible for their own success or failure.						
2. Human nature is basically evil, but it can be overcome by an act of will.						
3. The primary purpose of society is to fulfill human needs, both material and emotional.						
4. If human needs were fulfilled, then we would attain goodness, maturity, adjustment, and productivity, and most of society's problems would be solved.						

(continued)

EXERCISE 3-4   (continued)

ASSUMPTIONS	TOTALLY DISAGREE					TOTALLY AGREE
	0	1	2	3	4	5
5. Human beings are fallible but at the same time are capable of acts of great courage or unselfishness.						
6. People are capable of choice, in the "active and willing" sense, but may need help in making their choices.						
7. The primary purpose of life is the acquisition of material prosperity, which people achieve through hard work.						
8. The primary purpose of society is the maintenance of law and order, which make this acquisition possible.						
9. What hampers people from attaining fulfillment is external circumstance, not in general under their control.						
10. These circumstances are subject to manipulation by those possessed of sufficient technical and scientific knowledge, using the scientific method.						
11. Love is always the ultimate victor over force.						

EXERCISE 3-4 *(continued)*

ASSUMPTIONS	TOTALLY DISAGREE					TOTALLY AGREE
	0	1	2	3	4	5
12. The greatest good lies in terms of people's relationships with their fellows and with their creator.						
13. Unsuccessful or deviant individuals are not deserving of help, although efforts should be made up to a point, to rehabilitate them or to spur them to greater efforts on their own behalf.						
14. Humanity and society are ultimately perfectible.						
15. Human beings are created beings, one of whose major problems is that they act as if they were not and try to be autonomous						
CP 1, 2, 7, 8, 13 HPU 3, 4, 9, 10, 14 JC 5, 6, 11, 12, 15						

12, and 15. The instrument (Exercise 3-4) may be used by students, workers, or teachers for self-assessment of underlying value orientations. After the degree of agreement has been entered for all assumptions, the number entered (0–5) for each item is placed below the questionnaire, in one of three lines labeled CP, HPU, and JC. Each line should have five scores, one for each of the items relating to that line's value system (e.g., items 1, 2, 7, 8, 13 for the CP line). The scores in each line are then added, and the line totals are compared. Usually, a person is not totally identified with any one value perspective. The exercise does highlight predominance. It help workers and students to grow both in awareness of their own values and in sensitivity to the diversity in value systems that often conflict in human welfare services.

THE ENVIRONMENT:
RURAL, URBAN, AND SUBURBAN

In addition to variables of *person,* a social worker needs to be sensitive to diversity in the *environments* of systems receiving service. Geographic environments differ from one another. A knowledge of distinguishing characteristics of environments helps workers to better understand the people of particular localities and the interactions that take place between different people and different environments.

From a holistic perspective, a social worker explores diversity variables individually and in relation to one another. When studying a person or an environment, a worker is mindful of the ongoing interrelationship between the two. As brought out in ecological theory, an environment is affected by the organisms (persons) contained within it. Conversely, organisms are affected by their environments. More specifically, an environment's growth is directly influenced by the endowment, personalities, values, and functioning of its residents. Interdependently, the growth and development of people are directly influenced by the nature, resources, values, and functioning of their environments. An understanding of rural, urban, and suburban localities can help a worker to be aware of diverse ways in which environments and people may affect each other. If an individual, group, family, or community live in a rural environment, its needs, experiences, values, resources, and development may be very different from those of people who live in urban or suburban areas.

Historically, the term *rural* has been used to refer to "the country" or to mean "countrylike." Rural localities are often defined in terms of low population density (2,500–50,000 inhabitants) and relative isolation. *Urban* is a term that pertains to "the city" or things that are "citylike." It is generally used to describe a highly populated area (over 50,000). Other factors that have been used to distinguish rural from urban areas include income sources and occupations (agriculture versus industry), life style (simple versus complex), and structure and number of available human resources (highly structured and numerous versus informal and sparse).[52]

Those outlying regions of cities that often bridge urban and rural areas are called *suburbs.* Legally and demographically, a *suburb* is defined as "an incorporated municipality within a Standard Metropolitan Statistical Area (SMSA) other than a central city."[53] Although apparent changes are taking place in suburbia today, the definition traditionally has included a stereotypical conception of "familism, child-centeredness, single-family dwelling units, sharp segregation of work place from residence, organizational consciousness . . . overlaid by a distinct touch of affluence."[54] Thirty-eight percent of the American population now live in suburbia, as compared with 39 percent in central cities and 22 percent in rural areas.[55]

Within each of the three geographic environments, diversity may exist among populations and practices today. There are, however, general characteristics that make urban, suburban, and rural localities distinguishable from one another. In urban locations, for example, there are generally various organized human services that are highly structured, with clearly stated policies and procedures. Rural areas may be devoid of formal, professional services, but there are usually informal, natural helping networks that provide assistance. Whereas the power structure of an urban area may be described as "pluralistic," with several complex, interacting systems, the power structure of a rural area may be seen as "elitist," with decision makers who may not even hold formal positions of authority (see Figure 3-1).[56] There is a boundary "blurring"[57] of political and sociocultural life in homogeneous rural communities. The laws and procedures of an urban legal control system are more explicitly articulated and executed than those of a rural area, where informal means of regulation are frequently preferred for resolving local problems.[58]

The central and distinguishing problems of rural areas include generational poverty, rigid conservative mores and thinking, and an increasing loss of youth from the area. In addition, 60 percent of the nation's substandard housing is located in rural communities.[59] For those who live in the city, one core problem has been described in terms of depersonalization or loss of individuality. As Carol Meyer writes,

> The fact of urban life that characterizes it and no other living condition is the inevitable claim of the crowded, organized, institutionalized city against the freedom and fulfillment of the individual.[60]

In recent years, urban development has led to the renovation of many old buildings in cities, changing them into upper- or upper-middle-class condominiums or apartments. As a result, the poor and lower-middle-class city residents are often unable to find local housing. The absence of low-income housing in urban and suburban areas and the resistance by suburban residents to building such housing, along with the presence of restric-

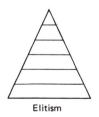

Elitism

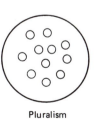

Pluralism

FIGURE 3-1 Power Structures

tive zoning laws, have contributed to the contemporary housing crisis, particularly for the urban poor. Even when low-income people are relocated in a surrounding area, they often have a problem in locating transportation to and from their place of employment and needed human services.

People from urban and suburban areas have been found to discuss their problems and to seek out professional help more readily than those from rural localities.[61] When informal networks are not able to provide the assistance needed, and social workers are not accepted by certain individuals in rural communities, a worker may try to work collaboratively with local leaders or neighbors in order to connect the person in need with a needed resource.

For example, if a family is suffering because of such problems as mental illness, retardation, or alcoholism, and it refuses to discuss its problems with a professional social worker, then the local clergy, doctor, or friend may be willing to speak with the family in behalf of the worker. In rural settings, people are very aware of the problems of their neighbors, and they are generally more willing to get involved and provide assistance.

In urban or suburban areas, a somewhat similar but more formal approach is used when indigenous leaders or "paraprofessionals" are hired to serve as "outreach workers" to link services with people in need. As brought out, the generalist in the metropolis is usually better able to locate specialized services to help with problems such as those described in the above example (i.e., mental illness, retardation, alcoholism). In a rural area, however, the worker may be the only professional resource available. It may be possible to work directly with the family, or it may be necessary to develop a program or write a grant to bring the needed service into the area.

During the 1980s, severe economic losses in rural areas, particularly in farm communities, have led to a decrease in informal social interactions and an increase in family breakdown.[62] Major withdrawals of federal financial supports, soaring interest rates, declining prices, and rising surpluses have led to an increasing number of farm foreclosures and bankruptcies. Rural land values have declined up to 50 percent and more.[63]

The economic crisis of farmers has been little understood; it has resulted in a high incidence of depression, family violence, and suicide. As stated by one farmer, "The loss of the land is not just the loss of one's job, it's the loss of one's life."[64] This is found to be true especially when the land has belonged to a family for several generations. The farmer who experiences property foreclosure by a bank usually sees this as a personal loss and a family disgrace.

Existing services in rural areas, such as Agricultural Extension or Farm Bureaus, are often unable to cope effectively with the financial, psychological, and social crises facing poverty-stricken rural communities. Human service professionals, social service programs, and schools of social work have made some efforts to join with such services in reaching out to farmers in crisis; they have helped farmers organize groups to advocate fairer polici and prices as well as helped locate other sources of income.[65] Although mi-grant workers or farm laborers and farm owners have frequently been seen as adversaries in the past, the threat of losing the land has provided an opportunity to bring the two groups together to work for the common goal of keeping the farm operating.

Although specialists are utilized in urban localities, a generalist prepa-ration has been recognized as the most appropriate to prepare for rural social work practice.[66] In applying the General Method when working in a rural area, however, a worker would find it helpful to have knowledge of rural economics (agriculture, mining, industry), regional planning and de-velopment, labor organizations and employment patterns, and relation-ships between public administration and services and local rural govern-ments and services.[67] In addition, a worker in a rural area needs to be sensitive to local etiquette, folkways, values, the probably strong suspicion of outsiders, and the presence of natural helping networks. The programs introduced by a worker should be geographically appropriate. As Lowell Jenkins and Alicia Cook point out:

> Agents of formal services often try to impose a program designed for an ur-
> ban setting on rural people, ignoring rural values and attitudes. The profes-
> sional worker frequently fails to respect the local residents who serve as natu-
> ral helpers. Conversely, those in the natural helping network tend to reject
> the detached, professional behavior of the formal helper, preferring to "take
> care of their own."[68]

A worker in an urban or suburban area should have some understand-ing of the political struggles that take place in their localities over "the met-ropolitan turf."[69] As the subsystems in an urban or suburban area (whether they are organizations, cultural groups, churches, or geographic communi-ties) compete for space and power in order to live out their values and aspirations, they frequently become involved with the complex political sys-tem. Political power, coalitions, public policy, and legal regulation are among the tools used in urban and suburban areas to secure and maintain land and finite resources.

Cities have been economically drained as people and businesses move out into suburbia. The boundary lines between the suburbs and the central city have been tightened as suburbs have been incorporated with strict zon-ing and land-use restrictions. Efforts made by suburban communities to dic-tate the number and types of people allowed to enter their borders are called "growth controls."[70] A recent decrease in suburban growth may not only reflect a depressed national economy or energy shortage, but also ex-isting discrimination and resistance to growth in suburbia, which is ex-pressed through an increase in the number of growth controls.

Social workers need to be aware of attempts that have been made to

oordinate city and suburban governments. In some in-
on has resulted in a loss of space and resources for par-
rough an understanding of urban politics, workers are
ind to support local groups and individuals in organiz-
̲ ̲ ̲ ̲or preservation or distribution of resources within the locality.

Knowledge, skills, and experience beyond those of a beginning generalist may be needed both by the social worker who becomes involved with
complex urban or suburban politics and by the generalist who works in a
rural area with extensive problems, no formal service-delivery system, and
limited natural helping networks. This rural worker would very likely be
expected to assume roles in administration, teaching, program development, and policy formation, in addition to direct practice. The urban
worker would need to have expertise in the use of the various political tools
cited earlier. Unless a worker is prepared with a realistic understanding of
the specific work environment and job expectations, he or she could easily
"burn out," owing to a disproportionate match between demand and resources. This could be true particularly for the rural worker, because of
the absence of local professional support systems. The social worker with a
sensitivity to diversity in environments comes to a geographic area with
more realistic expectations and preparation. Workers who are realistically
prepared are then better able to help client systems, as well as to help themselves cope with, develop within, and bring about change in the environment.

A HOLISTIC FRAMEWORK FOR SENSITIVITY
TO HUMAN DIVERSITY

As stated, several factors need to be considered if a social worker is to be
sensitive to human diversity in practice. The variables of diversity introduced in this chapter are culture, class, sexual variation, gender, age, developmental stages, endowment, personality, value systems, and environment.
All of the variables described may be organized within a "person-in-environment" framework, as outlined in Diagram 3-4. Using a holistic perspective,

DIAGRAM 3-4 Human Diversity

PERSON	IN	ENVIRONMENT
Gender	Culture	Class
Age and developmental stage(s)	Value system	Geographic location
Endowment and personality	Sexual orientation	

a worker identifies the unique combination of factors that constitute the identity of the system receiving service.

In addition to the factors in the concept of *person,* the *whole* person is not fully understood without also considering his or her functioning *in* his or her *environment.* Besides an awareness and acceptance of an individual's distinguishing age, gender, developmental stages, endowment, and personality, the worker needs to be sensitive to the person's culture, value system, and sexual orientation, and to be able to understand his or her social class and geographic environment.

A profile describing all of these factors about a system can be extremely helpful to a worker who is preparing to contact the system and to actualize the General Method. As information is gathered prior to contact, the framework in Diagram 3-4 may serve as a guide to alert the worker to possible areas of diversity.

A social worker may also benefit by drawing up a self-profile according to the areas found in Diagram 3-4. When, in any of the variables listed, there is a difference between the profile of the worker and that of a system receiving service, the worker should honestly appraise his or her sensitivity toward and ability to work with the identified diversity. Preparation may need to include research and dialogue with one's supervisor or with someone who shares the diversity of the system to be contacted. The system in need of service may find it difficult to work with a social worker who, in one or several of the areas listed, does not share something in common. Whenever possible, the system should be given the opportunity to work with someone who is not different, or at least to request a change in workers when it is believed that their differences are preventing goal accomplishment.

CONCLUSION

A sensitivity to human diversity from a holistic, multivariant perspective is essential for effective social work practice. Although some central concepts and definitions were presented for each of the diversity variables introduced in this chapter, far more extensive reading is necessary for a worker to develop a sound understanding of any one of the variables identified. What has been given is an overview and a framework for conceptualizing the major diversities found by social workers in practice. A social worker must be sensitive to human diversity throughout the entire process of service delivery.

In the following chapters, attention will be given to the need for sensitivity to human diversity during each stage of the General Method. Examples will focus mainly on sensitivity to culture, sexual orientation, and gender diversity.

NOTES

[1]Cited in Elliot M. Goldwag, ed., *Inner Balance: The Power of Holistic Healing* (Englewood Cliffs, N.J.: Prentice-Hall, 1979), p. ii.

[2]Jacquelyn Dupont-Walker, Region IX Child Welfare Training Center, University of California at Los Angeles, School of Social Welfare, *Ethnic Minority Cultures—Shades of Difference?* (Ann Arbor, Mich.: National Child Welfare Center, 1982), p. 2.

[3]Ibid., p. 5.

[4]Doman Lum, "Toward a Framework for Social Work Practice with Minorities," *Social Work* 27, no. 3 (May 1982): 246–48.

[5]Charles Valentine, "Deficit, Difference and Bicultural Models of Afro-American Behavior," *Howard Educational Review* 41, no. 2 (May 1971): 137–57.

[6]Eddie F. Brown and Timothy F. Shaughnessy, eds., *Education for Social Work Practice with American Indian Families,* American Indian Projects for Community Development, Training and Research. (Arizona: School of Social Work, Arizona State University, 1979), cited in Dupont-Walker, *Ethnic Minority Cultures,* p. 16.

[7]Royal F. Morales et al.; *Asian and Pacific American Curriculum on Social Work Education* (Los Angeles: Asian American Community Mental Health Training Center, 1976), p. 2.

[8]Dupont-Walker, *Ethnic Minority Cultures,* p. 2.

[9]Milton M. Gordon, *Assimilation in American Life* (New York: Oxford University Press, 1964), pp. 51–54.

[10]James E. Blackwell, *The Black Community: Diversity and Unity* (New York: Harper & Row, 1975), pp. 67–68.

[11]Ibid., p. 74.

[12]Judd Marmor, ed., *Homosexual Behavior: A Modern Reappraisal* (New York: Basic Books, 1980), p. 5.

[13]Brian McNaught, *a Disturbed Peace* (Washington, D. C.: A Dignity Publication, 1981), p. 4.

[14]Adapted from Alfred C. Kinsey, Wardel B. Pomeroy, and Clyde E. Martin, *Sexual Behavior in the Human Male* (Philadelphia: Saunders, 1948).

[15]Marmor, *Homosexual Behavior,* p. 8.

[16]Diana Dulaney and James Kelly, "Improving Services to Gay and Lesbian Clients," *Social Work* 27, no. 2 (March 1982): 8.

[17]Teresa A. De Crescenzo and Christine McGill, "Homophobia: A Study of the Attitudes of Mental Health Professionals Toward Homosexuality" (M.A. thesis, University of Southern California, School of Social Work, 1978).

[18]J. Money, "Factors in the Genesis of Homosexuality," in George Winokur, ed., *Determinants of Human Sexual Behavior* (Springfield, Ill.: Charles C. Thomas, 1963).

[19]E. Hooker and others, *Final Report of the National Institute of Mental Health Task Force on Homosexuality* (1969), reprinted in the *SIECUS Newsletter* (December 1970): 3–14.

[20]Clifford, Allen, *The Sexual Perversions and Abnormalities* (London: Oxford University Press, 1949).

[21]Ralph Blair, *Etiological and Treatment Literature on Homosexuality* (New York: National Task Force on Student Personnel Services and Homosexuality, 1972), p. 18.

[22]McNaught, *A Disturbed Peace,* p. 9.

[23]Ibid., p. 18.

[24]The Association of Women in Psychology, *Considerations in Therapy with Lesbian Clients* (Philadelphia: Women's Resources, 1979), p. 24.

[25]Adapted from Raymond M. Berger, "The Unseen Minority: Older Gays and Lesbians." Copyright 1982, National Association of Social Workers, Inc. Reprinted with permission, from *Social Work* 27, no. 3 (May 1982): 240.

[26]Ibid., pp. 237–40.

[27]Ibid., p. 237.

[28]Sandra Auerback and Charles Moser, "Groups for the Wives of Gay and Bisexual Men," *Social Work* 32, no. 4 (July–August 1987): 321–25.

[29]Phyllis Gurdin and Gary R. Anderson, "Quality Care for Ill Children: AIDS—Specialized Foster Family Homes," *Child Welfare* 66, no. 4 (July/August 1987): 291–302.

[30]De Crescenzo and McGill, "Homophobia."

[31]Det P. Romero, "Biases in Gender-Role Research," *Social Work* 22, no. 3 (May 1977): 214.

[32]S. V. Levine, L. E. Kamin, and E. L. Levine, "Sexism and Psychiatry: Theory and Review," *American Journal of Orthopsychiatry* 44, no. 3 (April 1974): 327–36.

[33]Maryann Mahaffey, "Sexism and Social Work," *Social Work* 21, no. 6 (November 1976): 419.

[34]Mimi Abramovitz, Thomas J. Hopkins, Victoria Olds, and Mary Waring, "Integrating Content on Women Into the Social Policy Curriculum: A Continuum Model," *Journal on Social Work Education* 18, no. 1 (Winter 1982): 33.

[35]Mahaffey, "Sexism and Social Work," p. 419.

[36]Marita Williams, Liz Ho, and Lucy Fielder, "Career Patterns: More Grist for Women's Liberation," *Social Work* 19, no. 4 (July 1974): 466.

[37]Marcia Guttentag and Susan Salasin, "Women and Mental Health," in Libby Cater, Anne Scott, and Wendy Martyna, eds., *Women and Men: Changing Roles, Relationships, and Perceptions* (Palo Alto, Calif.: Aspen Institute for Humanistic Studies, 1976), p. 2: Sharon C. Welsnack, "The Impact of Sex Roles on Women's Alcohol Use and Abuse," in Milton Greenblatt and Marc Schuckit, eds., *Alcoholism Problems in Women and Children* (New York: Grune & Stratton, 1976), pp. 37–60.

[38]Larry Alsbrook, "Marital Communication and Sexism," *Social Casework* 57, (October 1976): 522.

[39]John F. Longreas and Robert H. Bailey, "Men's Issues and Sexism: A Journal Review," *Social Work* 24, no. 1 (January 1979): 27.

[40]Herb Goldberg, *The New Male* (New York: New American Library, 1978), p. 47.

[41]Ibid., p. 1.

[42]Ibid., p. 220.

[43]Helen A. Mendes, "Single Fatherhood," *Social Work* 21, no. 4 (July 1976): 312.

[44]Lawrence E. Gary and Bogart R. Leashore, "High-Risk Status of Black Men," *Social Work* 27, no. 1 (January 1982): 55–56.

[45]Sister Maria Joan O'Neil, Small-group discussions with inmates at Somers Maximum Security Prison, Somers, Conn., 1980–82.

[46]Joseph H. Pleck, "The Male Sex Role: Definitions, Problems and Sources of Change," *Journal of Social Issues* 32, no. 3 (Summer 1976): 155.

[47]Sandra L. Bem, "The Measurement of Psychological Androgyny," *Journal of Consulting and Clinical Psychology* 42 (April 1974): 155–62; and "Sex Role Adaptability: One Consequence of Psychological Androgyny," *Journal of Personality and Social Psychology* 31, no. 4 (April 1975): 634–43.

[48]Joyce B. Lazar, "Sex Role Adaptability" (Rockville, Md.: Alcohol, Drug Abuse and Mental Health Administration, 1980), p. 3.

[49]Frederick Duhl, "Changing Sex Role-Concepts, Values and Tasks," *Social Casework* 57 (February 1976): 89.

[50]Frank H. Lowenberg, *Religion and Social Work Practice in Contemporary American Society* (New York: Columbia University Press, 1988), p. 149.

[51]Alan Keith-Lucas, *Giving and Taking Help* (Chapel Hill: University of North Carolina Press, 1972), pp. 138–43.

[52]Emilia E. Martinez-Brawley, "Identifying and Describing the Content of Rural in Social Work," *Arete* 5, no. 1 (Fall 1980): 23.

[53]Robert L. Lineberry, "Suburbia and Metropolitan Turf," *The Annals of American Academy of Political and Social Science* 422 (November 1975): 3.

[54]Ibid., p. 2.

[55]Louis H. Masotti, "Preface," *The Annals of American Academy of Political and Social Science* 422 (November 1975): vii.

[56]Emilia E. Martinez-Brawley, personal interview, October 19, 1982, New York.

[57]Marion H. Wijnberg and Louis Colca, "Facing up to the Diversity in Rural Practice: a Curriculum Model," *Journal of Education for Social Work* 17, no. 2 (Spring 1981): 92.

[58]Le Roy G. Schultz, "The Rural Social Worker and Corrections," in Leon H. Ginsberg, ed., *Social Work in Rural Communities* (New York: Council on Social Work Education, 1976), pp. 85–91.

[59]Owen K. Weber, "Preparing Social Workers for Practice in Rural Social Systems," in Wayne Johnson, ed., *Rural Human Services* (Itasca, Ill.: Peacock, 1980), p. 206.

[60]Carol H. Meyer, *Social Work Practice: A Response to the Urban Crisis* (New York: The Free Press, 1970), p. 80.

[61]Arnold J. Auerbach, "The Elderly in Rural Areas: Differences in Urban Areas and Implications for Practice," in Leon H. Ginsberg, ed., *Social Work in Rural Communities* (New York: Council on Social Work Education, 1976), p. 105.

[62]Janet M. Fitchen, *Poverty in Rural America: A Case Study* (Boulder, Col.: Westview, 1981).

[63]Rex R. Campbell, "Crisis on the Farm," *American Demographic* 7, no. 10 (October 1985): 30–34.

[64]Maria J. O'Neil and John R. Ball, "The General Method of Social Work in Rural Environments" (Paper presented at the Council on Social Work Education, Annual Program Meeting, Saint Louis, Mo., March 9, 1987).

[65]Emilia E. Martinez-Brawley, "Social Work and the Rural Crisis: Is Education Responding?" (Paper Presented at an Invitational Session, Council on Social Work Education, Annual Program Meeting, Saint Louis, Mo., March 9, 1987), p. 2.

[66]Leon H. Ginsberg, "An Overview of Social Work Education for Rural Areas," in Leon H. Ginsberg, ed., *Social Work in Rural Communities* (New York: Council on Social Work Education, 1976), p. 9.

[67]Emilia E. Martinez-Brawley, "Historical Perspectives on Rural Social Work: Implications for Curriculum Development," *Journal of Education for Social Work* 16, no. 3 (Fall 1980): 49–52.

[68]Lowell Jenkins and Alicia J. Cook, "The Rural Hospice: Integrating Normal and Informal Helping Systems," *Social Work* 26, no. 5 (September 1961): 415.

[69]Lineberry, "Suburbia," p. 4.

[70]James W. Hughes, "Dilemmas of Suburbanization and Growth Controls," *The Annals of the American Academy of Political and Social Science* 422 (November 1975): 61.

[71]Lineberry, "Suburbia," p. 8.

4

Engagement

Social work is concerned with the interactions between people and their environments which affect their ability to accomplish life tasks, alleviate distress and realize aspirations and values in relation to themselves, the rights of others, the general welfare and social justice.

—CSWE[1]

The first stage of the General Method is called *engagement*. Whether the generalist begins to work with a client, target, or action system, and whether the system is an individual, group, family, community, or institution, the first thing the worker tries to do is to open up the boundary between them (system and worker) for positive interaction. Frequently, there is some resistance by a system to any possible change or intrusion from the outside. From the inception of contact with a system, the generalist needs to use skill and knowledge along with professional values and principles for effective engagement.

In the first stage of the General Method, the worker has three guiding landmarks that help in the initial movement of the procedure. As the generalist begins to interact with a system, the three focal points of *problems, feelings,* and *goals* are kept in mind. All three are often in focus at the same time in the conversation and transactions between worker and system. The generalist makes sure that all three points have been addressed before proceeding to the next stage of the method.

In this chapter, each of the three central elements of the engagement stage will be studied. Techniques will be presented for working with diverse systems on their problems, feelings, and goals. Case vignettes will be given that demonstrate the first stage of the General Method with a variety of systems. Considerations will include the use of the general foundation (Diagram 1-5, Chapter 1) with an ecological perspective during the engagement stage of general practice.

THE PROBLEM

The word *problem* has been used to describe the purpose, definition, focus, and process of the profession of social work. For example, in the "Working Definition of Social Work Practice," the first purpose of the profession is stated as:

> To assist individuals and groups to identify and resolve or minimize problems arising out of disequilibrium between themselves and their environment.[2]

Siporin refers to "social problems" in his definition of practice:

> Social work is defined as a social institutional method of helping people to prevent and resolve their social problems, to restore and enhance their social functioning.[3]

According to Pincus and Minahan, the focus of practice is on "the linkages and interactions between people and resource systems and the problems to be faced in the functioning of both individuals and systems."[4] And Charles Levy writes on the assertion that "social work is a problem-solving process."[5]

The meaning and use of the concept *problem* in social work have been debated and criticized. Some critics see the term as too limiting because it refers to pathological or negative situations and appears to overlook the prevention, maintenance, or enhancement functions of social work. The concept is criticized also because it is seen as too general a term for distinguishing the essence of social work from other professions that describe their work as "problem solving."[6]

One may ask: What is the meaning of *problem* when used in social work? Does it mean "social problem," "dysfunctional behavior," "pathology," or "undesirable conditions"? More specifically, what is the meaning of *problem* in the General Method of social work? After briefly considering how the concept has been defined by different authors, the definition and use of the term *problem* in the General Method will be presented.

The word *problem* goes back to the Greek word *Proballein,* meaning "to throw forward."[7] The word, as found in Webster's, has two central definitions: (1) "a question raised or to be raised for inquiry, consideration, discussion or solution," and (2) "something that is a source of considerable difficulty, perplexity or worry."[8]

In social work research, the word *problem* corresponds to the first of these two definitions. It is the question put forth "that can be studied with hope of adding to relevant knowledge."[9] In describing "an ideal problem," Polansky writes:

> Ideally, it would be cast in theoretical terms (i.e., conceptualized) so that its results might contribute not only to one agency or community but to theory for the field at large, and even beyond social work. At the same time, because this is research for a profession, the hope is to have results that are of immediate, or almost immediate relevance to helping clients.[10]

Perlman seems to lean more toward the second definition in her clarification of the meaning of *problem* within her "problem-solving process."

> "The problem" in the problem-solving model is usually taken to be some difficulty in person-to-person or person-to-task relationships. It is usually focused on as a problem in today's social functioning.[11]

She points out that the problem identified by a client system is not necessarily "the problem" (meaning the basic causative agent in the person's difficulty, the problem of major importance). "It is simply a problem in the help-seeker's current life situation which disturbs or hurts him in some way, and of which he would like to be rid."[12] She also notes that for the majority of people seeking help from social workers, the problem is based on forces outside of themselves and "within their social role transactions."[13]

Merton categorizes social problems as either "deviant behavior" or "social disorganization." He identifies the dual possibility that social problems may originate or result either in the individual or in the society.[14] Siporin builds on Merton's perspectives and describes "problem" as "a reaction pattern to the human-unit environment interaction; it consists of dysfunctional behavior on the part of an individual or social system."[15]

Germain and Gitterman conceptualize "problems" in terms of "disjunction" and "stress" between the person and environment.

> In the Life Model, therefore, human problems and needs are conceptualized as outcomes of transactions between the parts of that whole. Thus they are defined as problems in living which have created stress and taxed coping abilities. Within the interface where person and environment touch, the problem or need reflects a disjunction between coping needs and environmental nutriments.[16]

According to Pincus and Minahan and to Laura Epstein, there must be an evaluator or definer for "a problem" to exist as such. Epstein, for example, writes:

> Problems are not fixed, explicitly bounded things with firm substance. They ordinarily cannot be clearly recognized in a uniform manner by following particular rules of observation. Conditions become defined as problems by a complex and fluid process. Problem definers are those who give voice to an issue.[17]

And Pincus and Minahan state:

> It is useful in this context to define a problem as a social situation or social condition which has been evaluated by someone as undesirable. In this view, no social situation is in itself inherently a problem. When a situation is referred to as a problem, it must be realized that an implied evaluation of it has already been made.[18]

The concept *problem* has been used to describe the central focus of the three traditional methods of casework,[19] group work,[20] and community organization.[21] With the General Method also, "the problem" is the initial focus and pervasive thread throughout the procedure.

Problem in the General Method is defined as the issue, need, question, or difficulty brought forth for study and action by the generalist and the interfacing systems. The definition of *problem* in the General Method relates somewhat to the use of the word in social work research. The question under study is not necessarily labeled as a deviance or a difficulty. Rather, it is seen as an issue of "relevance to helping clients."[22]

The content of a problem in general practice basically deals with the social functioning of human systems within their environments. The generalist may be working for the purpose of enhancement, maintenance, or restoration of human functioning or for the prevention of breakdown in human functioning. Helping clients to fit and function within environmental systems in a mutually productive way is the heart of social work practice. In the General Method, there is a need, issue, question, or difficulty that relates to human functioning and is being brought forth for study and action by the worker and a system. The generalist may be working with an individual, group, family, community, organization, or social institution in order to address the issue, meet the need, or overcome the difficulty.

The identifier of the problem may be the worker, clients, or some other system. For effective work, both the practitioner and the system engaging in the General Method must recognize the problem and agree to work together for resolution. The generalist uses skills to help the system to focus and to partialize, so that one particular issue is receiving the worker's and clients' attention at one time. Problems may be refined and reformulated in the course of the Method. They are not fixed, but evolving.

The problem is the pivot or the focal point of the spiraling process that contains the diverse elements of the General Method (see Figure 4-1).

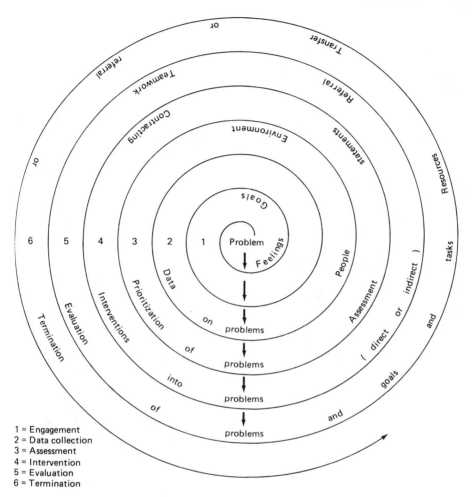

FIGURE 4-1 The Problem as Seen in the General Method of Social Work Practice

It is kept in mind as the worker and the client, action, and target systems move along the various stages toward problem resolution.

The concept of *problem* in the General Method is apparently very broad and inclusive. Although there has been an expressed desire for defining *problem* in social work with more concise terminology,[23] this is not possible in general practice, owing to the nature of the art. The General Method of practice is not bound by "careful limitation."[24] The concepts used to describe general practice are encompassing, adaptive, and general.

Before actually moving on to the problem, it is often helpful to let the person or persons of the system express their feelings and thoughts about the initial contact. If there is any resistance to engaging in dialogue, the feelings should be identified and discussed. For example, the worker might say:

I can see that you are somewhat hesitant in talking, Mrs. B. is it uncomfortable for you to talk about Johnnie with me?

The worker needs to be as explicit as possible in clarifying *who* he or she is, *why* there is contact with the client, and *how* the client feels about it.

With this preliminary work accomplished, the worker continues to use the basic relationship skills of listening, responding, clarifying, paraphrasing, giving information, focusing, partializing, guiding, and supporting. The worker encourages the people who constitute the client system to express their perceptions of the problem or problems under consideration. Primarily using open-ended questions, the worker enables them to share thoughts and feelings.

Many times, the system may identify more than one presenting problem. The worker in the initial stage uses a great deal of echoing or paraphrasing to let the people in the system know that they are being heard. Eventually, the worker will offer some guidance to help them prioritize and partialize the problems. The key point of this initial phase is to have the system's members get a sense of acceptance, with a sincere effort on the worker's part to understand without passing judgment. The worker uses such phrases as, "I hear you saying that . . . ," "Could you explain a little more about . . . ," "I'm wondering if you mean that. . . ."

In addition to listening to the spoken words of system members, the worker observes unspoken movements, gestures, moods, and attitudes. Listening and sensing skills are used to recognize when the tone is of greater intensity or pitch, when feelings are a force behind certain words, or when there is apparent avoidance or blockage on a particular topic.

GETTING TO THE PROBLEM

Before actually discussing the problem with a system in any depth, it is necessary for the worker to prepare for the contact. The social worker tries to learn as much as possible about the culture, needs, and resources of the system. The worker tries not only to understand the system that he or she will interact with, but also to understand his or her own culture, needs, and resources and how the two—worker and system of contact—may form a "fit" for positive interactions. If it appears that there will be stress or difficulty in the match between worker and system, the practitioner seeks help from a supervisor.

At the point of initial contact, after brief introductions, the purpose for coming together needs to be expressed. Within the description of purpose, a problem may be mentioned. The worker keeps this in mind for reference when the time is appropriate.

If the contact is initiated by the worker, he or she states the purpose. If the contact was initiated by a client or some other system, the worker encourages the system to say why the contact was made. For example:

CASE 1: WORKER-INITIATED

Worker: Good morning, Mrs. B. I am Mary Costello, the school social worker. I would like to talk with you about your son Johnnie and how he's doing at school.

CASE 2: CLIENT-INITIATED

Worker: Good morning. I am Mary Costello, the school social worker. I understand you wanted to talk with me.

Client: Yes, I'm Mrs. B, Johnnie's mother. His teacher said that maybe I could talk to you about the problems I've been having with my son lately.

The generalist asks him- or herself: What is the issue, problem, need, or question that appears to be the major concern for this client system? Is there really a problem (or problems) that the system will identify and invest energy in for resolution? The worker begins to clarify what problems he or she and the system are going to work on together.

The General Method is permeated with ecological-systems theory. The generalist knows that when an environment gives an organism the inputs needed to thrive, there are certain outputs that the environment expects from the organism. The environment and the organism have role expectations for each other. Each is expected to behave and produce in a way that is conducive to the well-being of the other. In the General Method, the problem is defined initially in terms of what is taking place at the point of interface and interactions between organism and environment. The problem is seen at the boundary point where a system interlocks with some aspect of its surrounding environment or with some other system in that environment. The expected inputs and outputs for each problem situation are considered.

In time, the plan of intervention that is developed in the procedure may be directed toward a system or its environment rather than toward the boundary where the two come together. As brought out by Hearn: "In short, social work activity is focused inside, outside, and at the boundary between the system and its environment."[25] The initial problem description, however, focuses on the boundary point where there is a need or desire to direct attention to the functioning of system and environment in relation to each other.

For example, in Case 1, the problem as presented by the worker is between Johnnie and the school. He is not behaving or performing academically at the level expected for him to "fit" into the system and be promoted by the school. The problem as introduced by Mrs. B in Case 2 is between Johnnie and his mother at home. He is not acting in the manner his mother expects and thus is not receiving her approval and affection.

Every effort should be made to relate the problem as directly as possible to the system in contact with the worker. The more distant the problem, the more difficult it is to involve the system in a timely change effort. Usually, it is not necessary to identify clearly the causes of the problem in the engagement stage. During data collection, stage 2, there is opportunity to obtain information on causes. Sometimes, however, facts relating to causes may need to be presented to promote greater incentive for cooperation. The worker may need to present data in order to determine the validity of the apparent causes of a problem presented by the system.

For example, if Mrs. B identifies the main problem as Johnnie's not getting along with his teacher, she may think there is little she has to work on to improve the situation. If on the other hand, it is pointed out to Mrs. B that Johnnie's school problems are showing up in classes with different teachers, and if she is helped to see that his problems started around the time her husband was laid off from work and she began working, Mrs. B may begin to get more involved in looking at the problem.

The timing and techniques used in presenting facts to stimulate involvement are dependent on the sensitivity and skills of the worker. Presenting facts too soon or too abruptly may cause the client to become defensive or inhibited. Mrs. B, for example, may find it difficult to talk about her husband or the financial constraints that necessitated her going to work. She may become defensive as she begins to see a correlation between her son's school problems and what is happening with herself and her husband.

In beginning to identify the problem with a system, the skilled generalist is sensitive to delicate, feeling-filled areas. The worker knows that feelings relevant to the problems must be recognized and expressed if there is to be real movement toward problem resolution. As feelings are disclosed, new problems or a clearer understanding of the problem may emerge. As stated, problems are not fixed, but evolving, and feelings are a force that helps to move the problems into clearer focus.

IDENTIFYING FEELINGS

A basic practice principle, as described in Chapter 1, is *purposeful expression of feelings*.[26] The social worker does not encourage indiscriminate ventilation of feelings about any or every issue. The General Method is a purposeful process that calls for the worker to have expertise in the realm of feelings.

The generalist strives to become aware of the feelings of the system in contact as they relate to the problem situation. The worker recognizes when the system is expressing unrelated feelings and uses skill in deciding whether or not these feelings indicate other problem areas in need of attention or whether their expression is an attempt to avoid facing the problem at hand. If the former, the worker and system may need to reconstruct or add to the identified problem; if the latter, the worker may need to discuss the avoidance with the system and redirect the conversation back to the identified problem.

There is also the basic principle called *controlled emotional involvement.*[27] It points to the need for the worker to have self-awareness in terms of his or her own feelings surrounding the problem-system-environment situation. Prior to and throughout the process of working with others, the generalist realizes the fact that he or she has feelings also. At times, they may be very strong and in need of control while working with particular systems or problems. If this is difficult for the worker, help should be sought from a supervisor.

In the General Method, the identification of feelings, as well as problems, is done basically on a rational level. The theoretical foundation of social work practice looks at the whole of human nature and enables the worker to be aware of unconscious as well as conscious factors that may influence human behavior. In general practice, however, the feelings encouraged and expressed are mainly conscious and identifiable. The approach of the worker may be described primarily as rational or "cognitive."

> A cognitive approach holds that the principal determinant of emotions, motives and behavior is an individual's thinking, which is a conscious process. The problems the clients bring to social work are considered to be problems of consciousness.[28]

The generalist does not discard the notion of the unconscious in human behavior, but recognizes that his or her competence is for working on the rational, conscious level. The feelings addressed in practice are conscious or able to be brought into consciousness with a little effort.

Carkhuff points out that each feeling has a rational reason that can be identified. He writes:

> The thing the helper must remember is this: Regardless of the apparent nature of the cause of a particular helpee's feelings, each of those feelings will always turn out to have a sufficient and rational reason! One of the most important goals of all helpee exploration is to identify—to the helper as well as to the helpee—the real reason for each of his or her real feelings.[29]

Even though feelings may be conscious, the worker knows that often they are difficult to share. It may be awkward for a person to engage in a discussion about private feelings with a professional person in the early stages of a working relationship. As stated earlier, in some cultures, words are seldom used to express feelings, particularly with someone outside of the family.[30]

In his book *You and Me,* Gerard Egan lists the following feelings that are commonly "difficult to express": "feelings of being no good," "feelings about not being able to do things," "feelings about not being able to do something about a situation," "not being able to handle affection from others," "feelings of being hurt or rejected," "feelings that come from a need to punish someone else," "feelings coming from a need to be punished," "feelings of guilt," "feelings of shame," "feelings of being dependent on a person," "feelings of being passive," and "feelings of helplessness."[31]

Poor families have been described as unable to express their concerns well enough to talk about them with a social agency, and "so inarticulate that they literally did not have the words for their emotion."[32] Hollis disagrees with this and reports that most social workers do not have difficulty getting clients to express their feelings if the workers themselves use language that is appropriate. She points out that workers should not let "simplicity of language" be understood as "incapacity." Often simple words or expressions are the most valid and meaningful. She writes:

> Exploration may sometimes proceed at a slower pace than with the more verbal, better educated client. But once the low-income client's confidence has been established, he is likely to speak freely, particularly of feelings of anger and frustration, sometimes directed against the worker himself.[33]

To be able to help a system discuss relevant feelings, the generalist needs to have a broad vocabulary to describe feelings. As brought out by Hallowitz:

> The worker also helps the client with feelings that impair his ability to deal with the problems at hand—e.g., anxiety, conflict, resistance. He encourages the client to do the problem-solving work to the fullest possible extent. When the limits of this are reached, he contributes his own thinking and suggestions.[34]

The suggestions offered to help a client with describing feelings have to be carefully and appropriately selected. The word list in Diagram 4-1 may be helpful to workers as they search for ways to most aptly describe particular feelings. Each word may be modified for more accurate indications of degrees of intensity by using such descriptive words as "a little," "somewhat," "rather," or "very."

Feelings are not only described in one or two words. They may be expressed through phrases, behavioral descriptions, and stated desires.[35] For example, to feel "happy" may be described as "I feel great"; "I feel as

DIAGRAM 4-1   Words to Describe Feelings

POSITIVE FEELINGS	NEGATIVE FEELINGS
Relaxed	Up tight, nervous
All together	Spacey, mixed up
Whole	Falling apart
Confident, adequate, potent	Confused, unsure, inept
Graceful	Awkward, clumsy
Well organized	Disorganized
Accepted	Rejected, abandoned
Appreciated	Unappreciated
A part of things	Out of step, left out
Loved	Unloved
Full of life	Burned out, exhausted
Strengthened, firm	Weakened, weak
Witty	Dull
Able to cope	Overwhelmed
Good	Bad
Warm	Cold
Delighted	Unhappy, frustrated
Great	Small
Glad	Sad
Pleased	Displeased, angry, outraged
Loving	Hateful, hostile, furious
Daring	Afraid
in control	Out of control, helpless
Hopeful	Hopeless
Full	Empty
Builtup	Put down, crushed
Serene	Disturbed
Energetic	Exhausted
Healthy	Sick
Powerful	Powerless
Free	Trapped

free as a bird"; "I feel I could jump for joy"; or "I feel I would like to reach out and hug everyone here." The important point in the engagement stage is not so much *how* the feelings are expressed but *that* they are expressed in whatever manner has the most meaning to the system. Central to the art of social work practice is the awareness of feelings in human systems and of the value in their purposeful expression.

As stated earlier, when feelings are expressed, the worker needs to explore with the system of contact "the rational reason" for the feelings.[36] A technique frequently used as the practitioner clarifies the feelings is to say, "I understand that you are feeling ____ because ____ ," or "Is it that you feel ____ because ____ ?" "You seem to be feeling ____ because ____ ."

It is always necessary to receive feedback from the system after a reason for feelings is suggested. This may be accomplished by adding such statements as "Is that correct?" "What do you think?" "Am I right?" or "Is that it?" In this way, the system is encouraged by the worker to participate in the process of finding reasons for feelings, and to accept, modify, or reject the suggestion offered by the worker.

As the worker moves with the system from the identification of feelings to the reasons for the feelings, the worker tries to utilize the ecological perspective. An effort is made to incorporate a view of the system in relation to the environment within the definition of the reason for feelings. The more the members of a system see their roles in the reason for the feelings, the more chance there is that they will begin to use their feelings in dealing with the problem. For example, the worker may say in Case 1,

Mrs. B, I can see that you are troubled because you can't understand why your son is not getting along in school lately. Is that right?

or

Mrs. B, you seem to be very upset right now. Is it because you don't want to hear that Johnnie is having school problems at a time when you and the family are having so many other difficulties?

In the second case, the worker might say:

You are feeling very frustrated because you can't seem to get along with your son lately. Is that it, Mrs. B?

or

You are very angry with your son lately because he is not behaving the way you expect of him. Is that correct?

The reason for the feelings may be closely related to the problem as presented, or after further exploration, the worker may find that the reason for the feelings as clarified becomes a means for uncovering issues that need more immediate attention. In the first case, for example, the worker may begin to see that Mrs. B is currently feeling overwhelmed because of extensive family problems, and Johnnie's behavior at school is but an indicator of a very troubled family situation. In the second case, Mrs. B expressed feelings that relate directly to the presenting problem. The feelings she was expressing were caused by a problem in parent-child interaction.

As the feelings are refined and the problem may be reformulated, it may become apparent through the exploration of feelings and their reasons that there is a problem that needs to be addressed, but that is outside of the scope of the competence of the generalist or the agency's services. A referral to another service may be necessary. A resource may need to be contacted for a collaborative effort, when several problems have emerged and at least one problem continues within the worker's domain. It is important for the worker to keep in mind that every step in the process of the General Method may change the nature of the problem. As pointed out by Spitzer and Welsh:

> Problem focused practice requires an ongoing and continuing process, since problems are rarely totally resolved. As a result of intrapsychic or environmental events, the impact of the social welfare response system, or the responses to the problem by other segments of society, new elements are introduced and the nature of the problem constantly changes.[37]

When needs or expectations are unmet, system members begin to feel unfulfilled. Negative feelings, including anger and rage, may develop. Negative feelings drain energy from a system. When the reason for these feelings is identified and if through some process or intervention the reason may be reversed, there is new energy available for more effective social functioning. Positive feelings generate vitality and energy for growth-promoting transactions. The reasons for positive feelings are seen as something to be maintained or enhanced. As long as the reasons persist, the energy level continues or expands for effective social functioning.

The reasons for feelings may relate closely to the problems and also to the goals. The stating of reasons for negative or positive feelings helps to move the worker and the system into recognizing and discussing goals. Frequently, the initially stated goals either reflect the other side of identified reasons for negative feelings or they reflect an expansion of stated reasons for positive feelings. A technique used to bridge the elements of feelings with goals is to state the reverse side of reasons for negative feelings or to highlight and develop the reasons for positive feelings. For example, the worker would say:

You are angry at yourself because you are not able to give your children the attention and direction they need, and you wish you could give them more attention and direction. Is that so?

or

You are feeling happy because you and your son are getting along better lately, and you would like to see this continue and grow as time goes on. Right?

The introduction of suggestions for preliminary goals should come only after the client has confirmed the stated reasons for feelings. If the suggested goals are unrelated to the feelings of the client, they may be a reflection of the worker's hopes and expectations rather than the client's actual goals.

FEELINGS IN MACROSYSTEMS

The engagement stage initiates the General Method as used with systems of any size or type. Even when working with a target or action system, the generalist tries to discern how the problem is perceived, what feelings there are about the situation, and what goals would be acceptable and feasible for involvement by the system.

As defined earlier, target systems are those that need to change for goal accomplishment. They do not necessarily want to or agree to work with the social worker. Action systems are those that cooperate with the worker to achieve goals or influence target systems. And client systems request or agree to work with the worker to receive benefits from the service.

A target, action, or client system may be an individual, family, group, community, organization, social institution, or society. These are the systems of contact in social work practice. As the generalist works with diverse systems, an important consideration is the distinguishing characteristics that are generally recognized among systems. As depicted in Diagram 4-2, human systems have a basic set of characteristics that vary according to the type of system. The worker prepares for contact with a system by recalling or trying to find out as much as possible about the system. Working from foundation knowledge, the practitioner makes every effort to become aware of the system's characteristics and the degree of intensity of feelings.

For the range of major systems of contact in social work, there are characteristic polarities with intervening degree scales that may be considered (Diagram 4-2). The polarities include facts versus feelings, goal orientation versus process orientation, formality versus informality, explicit nature versus implicit nature, organization versus little organization, structure versus little structure, objectivity versus intimacy, social control versus human concern, law and work versus circumstance and love.

In Diagram 4-2, feelings and goals are found in association with certain types of systems. As indicated in the diagram, there are basically greater expectation and awareness of feelings and process with smaller systems and greater expectation and awareness of facts and goals with larger systems. In beginning to work with a larger system, the generalist sees the need to come prepared to present facts and to work with structure and formality. Generally, feelings are not readily considered or expressed in larger systems.

To work with any system, the worker deals with human beings who naturally have feelings. The worker tries to identify feelings as they relate to the problem and to the worker's efforts. Skill is used to distinguish between those feelings that are the personal feelings of individual representatives and those of the larger system. Whereas the worker may be able to discuss feelings and relationships with individuals, it often takes longer to recognize and discuss them with individuals who are representing a large system. There is a possibility that the expresion of feelings will not be able

DIAGRAM 4-2 Polarities in Systems

```
        Individual . . . Family . . . Group . . . Community . . . Organization
                        . . .Institution . . . Society

Feelings _____ Facts
Process orientation _____ Goal orientation
Informality _____ Formality
Implicit nature _____ Explicit nature
Little organization _____ Much organization
Little structure _____ Much structure
Intimacy _____ Objectivity
Human concern _____ Social control
Circumstance _____ Law
Love· _____ Work
```

to influence or change a situation in a larger system because of policy and structure. Carefully presented facts, however, could be most effective.

In terms of goals, larger systems enter very readily into a dialogue about their goals and expectations. They usually have explicitly stated goals that can be utilized as the worker tries to engage the system in mutual goal setting. The smaller system, however, may take a longer period of time and need more help in understanding and expressing its goals.

As implied in Diagram 4-2, while working with the three major components of the engagement stage (i.e., problem, feelings, and goals), the worker usually finds a natural tendency to get into feelings and relationships with the smaller systems (i.e., individuals, groups, families, and some communities), and to get into facts and goals with larger systems (i.e., some communities, as well as organizations, institutions, and society). As stated, however, all three components—problems, feelings, and goals—must be considered by the worker for successful movement in the engagement stage.

GOAL RECOGNITION

The worker asks the question: What is it that this system really wants? In the first case cited earlier, the worker is hearing that Mrs. B wants Johnnie to remain in school and get promoted, but she also wants some relief from the heavy family burdens she is under. In the second case, Mrs. B is clearly focusing on the goal of improving her relationship with her son. Such clarification of goals is imperative for the worker to determine how to proceed with the system. Goals have to be expressed, understood, and agreed on by both system and worker before moving to the second stage of the method.

What is a goal? Epstein gives a very direct answer when she writes:

The idea of a goal is straightforward. It is the end toward which effort is directed. A goal is a point beyond which something does not or cannot go. . . . Therefore a goal is an attainable wish.[38]

Werner interchanges goal with "objective" and relates the terms to "motive" He writes:

A motive is a goal or objective which we choose on the basis of a personal conception of what is necessary for our welfare, happiness or success.[39]

Epstein points out four main types of goals in social work, "agency, professional, practitioner and client goals." She stresses the need for the client goals to be predominant when working on cases.

Agency, professional, and personal practitioner goals are never out of sight or out of mind. They provide a general climate of opinion and requirements. However, so long as client goals do not seriously contradict vital segments of the broader goal structure, they should determine the individual case goals.[40]

In the General Method, a goal is conceptualized as including objectives, motives, and attainable desires. It is the end toward which the worker and the system or systems direct their efforts. Goals are explicated in the General Method when there is mutual agreement by worker and system. It is possible that the method may be arrested because no goals can be established by mutual agreement. To proceed without this mutuality would be futile.

Although initial goals may be expressed in broad, general terms, the practitioner and the system work toward formulation of concrete goals. General and specific goals of the General Method are of a social-functioning nature, and they are conceptualized from an ecological-systems perspective. General goals relate to social situations in which the exchange at the point of interface between system and environment is central. As the goals are stated, clarified, and refined, the worker keeps in mind the need to have goals be measurable and attainable. They should be practical, limited in number, and obviously related to the identified problems.

As the General Method proceeds into data collection, assessment, and planning, goals may be reformulated and refined for greater specificity. Goal setting leads to the identification of specific tasks that need to be performed for goal accomplishment. The actions needed to obtain the stated goals will be clarified within an identifiable and realistic time span. When completed, the identified problem should have been addressed, alleviated, or resolved.

Moving from preliminary general goals that are stated ecologically and that are related directly to the identified problems, the generalist helps the systems to develop more specific measurable and practical goals and tasks. For example, a general goal stated by Mrs. B may be to improve interactions between herself and her son. As the worker gets more involved with Mrs. B and her son later on in the course of the Method, they would be expected to agree on the general goal and to identify their specific goals and tasks in terms of behaviors and conditions. These might include, for example:

1. To give themselves more time together by spending at least one-half an hour a day listening, talking, and relaxing together (both)
2. To grow in understanding each other by attending biweekly sessions with the social worker until June (both)
3. To develop greater understanding of self and other parents and skills for parenting teenagers by attending the parenting-skills class on Tuesday nights for six weeks (Mrs. B)
4. To grow in understanding self and other teenagers and how to get along with parents by attending the teen meetings until June (Johnnie)
5. To avoid losing temper and striking out at son by talking with him at home and during sessions with the worker about upsetting behavior (Mrs. B)
6. To try to obey mother and avoid getting sarcastic with her by talking with her at home and during sessions with the worker about upsetting behavior (Johnnie)

In item 1, the specific goal is to give themselves more time together, and the measurable task is to spend at least one-half an hour a day listening, talking, and relaxing together.

Goals in the engagement stage of the General Method are beginning goals in a process of goal setting. The main purpose for goal identification in the initial stage is to let the system know that the worker is listening and hears what the system is saying about its wants, needs, or values. The worker skillfully begins to engage the system in thinking about goals, with the hope that this engagement will motivate the system for deeper involvement in a collaborative problem-solving effort. As the Method proceeds, the worker and the system gain a clearer understanding of problems, feelings, and goals.

WORKING WITH DIFFERENT SYSTEMS

To better understand the application of the engagement stage of the General Method to different systems, a complex case situation will be presented. The worker for the family will begin to use the General Method to work with client, target, and action systems. The systems of contact range from an individual to a large business.

CASE SITUATION

Mrs. Armez was sent to the Unity Social Service Department by her pastor. Her husband had to go into the hospital for an operation and, after a few weeks, was told by the doctor he could return to work. When Mr. Armez tried to return, he was told they didn't need him any longer, and he was laid off. While he was in the hospital, Mr. Armez's place of employment had changed hands, and Mr. Armez thinks the new management does not like Hispanic people. Mr. Armez continues to feel weak and doesn't know if he could work the way he used to. Mrs. Armez said that since Mr. Armez's unemployment benefits ran out and the family went on welfare, he hasn't been acting right. He drinks more, and he fought with her when she began to do some part-time work. The children are not doing well in school lately, and the school social worker is afraid that they are being overly disciplined by Mrs. Armez and her husband.

Example 1: Generalist with Mrs. Armez (Client System)

Worker: Good afternoon, Mrs. Armez. My name is Katherine Brown. I understand Rev. Growth suggested that you get in touch with us.

Client: Yes, he thought you might be able to help me.

Worker: I'd be glad to work with you, Mrs. Armez. Where would you like to begin?

Client: I'm not sure. It's just that nothing seems to be working out right now, and I don't know how to explain it.

Worker: I can imagine that it isn't easy for you to begin to talk with me. Was it difficult for you to come in today?

Client: I came right after work. I know my husband would be mad if he knew I stopped off here. I just can't let things go on the way they've been going these last few months.

Worker: It sounds like you are under a lot of pressure right now. Am I right?

Client: I'm so upset with all that's happening at home. It's too much for me to take.

Worker: You're feeling very upset because you just don't know how to handle the many problems at home right now.

Client: Yes, please understand, I love my children and my husband. It's just that everything is going wrong. He's changed since he lost his job. He can't get work, and he's mad that I'm working. I can't let my children starve. I iron for some people in the morning, and that helps a little. The welfare money isn't enough. He just doesn't care—I don't know how to reach him. He's drinking so much lately.

Worker: I can see that you love your children and your husband. You're feeling confused because you can't understand your husband any more, and he doesn't seem to understand what you are trying to do. Is that it?

Client: Yes, but—he's just a man, and in his country, women don't work. He's feeling bad he can't get work. I don't blame him.

Worker: You are trying very hard to understand him. I can see that.

Client: Yes, and it's not just him. The kids are sick a lot lately, and the school is saying they are not behaving themselves. I try to get after them, but they're getting so fresh. And that place where we live—it's getting worse. The landlord doesn't care. I try to clean it, but with my husband home all day—I'm tired of fighting with them.

Worker: Mrs. Armez, I hear you mentioning many problems that you are facing right now—your husband can't find a job and you're worried about his drinking, your children are often sick and having troubles in school lately, you are not pleased with where you are living, and you and your husband and children are not getting along. I can understand that you are feeling overwhelmed because you can't handle all of these problems by yourself.

Client: (Shakes head and begins to sob.) I can't deal with it. It's just too much. I need some help.

Worker: I can see that you are feeling very helpless because you can't change the situation, and you want some help with trying to deal with it all. What is it that you are hoping for, Mrs. Armez?

Client: If only things could be different. I wish Hector could go back to work. He liked where he was, and we were getting along fine. And I wish the kids weren't so sickly and that they would mind in school. I guess I just want things the way they were. Maybe we should move away—but how? It's just so bad right now. If only something could be done.

Worker: I'll be glad to begin to work on it with you, Mrs. Armez. We can't tackle all of these problems at once, but we can take one at a time to see what can be done. But first, would you please talk a little more about the situation with me so that I can understand it better?

In this case vignette, the generalist began with introductions and reviewed the purpose for Mrs. Armez's coming. She gave the client time and encouragement to express her feelings about coming and moved on to clarification of problems, feelings, and goals. With the identification of so many problems, the feelings and goals remain at a very broad level until further information can be obtained and until problems are prioritized.

The worker will need to offer Mrs. Armez much support as the procedure moves into data collection. The worker will need to know information answering such questions as, Why was the husband laid off? How does he perceive the family problems at this time? What are the children's health problems and behavioral problems? How involved is the school or any other agency with the family? When did each problem begin? How motivated are family members to work for change? All of these questions fall within an ecological framework for data collection, which will be presented in the next chapter.

The generalist working with the family would use the General Method for working with several interlocking systems. The target and action systems to be contacted could include employment agencies, hospital and health services, the school, the city's Income Maintenance Department, the landlord, housing authorities, programs for alcoholics, shelters for battered wives, protective services, and other agencies or social institutions.

Example 2: Generalist Talking with the Manager (Bill Jones), the Personnel Director (Tom Wilson), and, later, the Foreman (Joe Casey) of the Factory Where Mr. Armez Had Been Employed (Target System)

(This interview takes place after the worker had met with Mr. Armez in his home and received from him permission to talk with his employer.)

Worker:	Good morning. I'm Katherine Brown, a social worker from Unity Social Service Department. I've asked to meet with you to discuss Mr. Armez, one of your past employees. I understand Mr. Armez was not accepted back to work after he recovered from his hospitalization. Is that correct?
Personnel Director:	Yes, Mr. Armez was only with us about a year before he took off, and we had to hire someone else.
Worker:	I see. Mr. Armez wasn't with you very long before he took a sick leave. Let's see. I believe Mr. Armez said he began to work here in October of last year, making it 14 months of employment before he requested a sick leave. Is that correct?
Manager:	I'll tell you Miss Brown, quite honestly, the company had some concerns about taking him back. We didn't think he was able to work at the level we expect of our employees.
Worker:	I appreciate your honesty, Mr. Jones. You're saying that Mr. Armez wasn't accepted back because the company feared he wouldn't be able to do the work expected. May I ask why you thought that?
Manager:	Well, let's see—do you remember, Tom?
Personnel Director:	Yes, I believe we even had question about his performance before he took off. Let's check with Joe about that. Joe Casey was the foreman over Mr. Armez. Could we get him up here, Bill?
Manager:	(calls on phone)
Worker:	Thank you for trying to trace this back for me.
Manager:	What's the matter, Miss Brown? Hasn't he found work anywhere else?
Worker:	No, he hasn't. I understand he liked his work here and thought he was doing a good job.
Manager:	Here's Joe. Let's find out how he was doing. Joe, this is a local social worker asking about Hector Armez. Do you remember who he is?
Foreman:	Oh yeah, the Spanish guy. He had to leave for some kind of operation, I think.
Worker:	He had trouble with his arm and needed to be hospitalized for an operation.
Personnel Director:	Joe, his performance on the job wasn't that great, was it? We thought it wouldn't be wise to take him back at the time. Do you remember?

Foreman:	I don't know. He was with us about a year or so and was coming along OK. He was still learning. After he left, we needed someone on the machine. We couldn't wait forever. He had been out a lot, and I had given him a warning.
Worker:	I believe I hear three reasons for not taking Mr. Armez back: (1) He was out a lot, (2) you needed a replacement, and (3) there were questions about his performance level. Is that right?
Foreman:	Well, he was doing OK, but we just couldn't wait that long.
Manager:	And, you know, after being in the hospital and all, maybe he wouldn't be able to man that machine. It's heavy work we do here.
Worker:	There was some risk involved in taking him back?
Manager:	Well, we take risks, but not if we can avoid it. We needed to keep the machines going, and we couldn't count on him.
Worker:	I see. You needed to keep the machines going. May I ask how your personnel policy addresses the need for sick leave?
Personnel Director:	Our employees can take a sick leave when they need it, but we get concerned when it's a new man and he's out a lot.
Manager:	We often get new people, like Armez, who just want to take off a few weeks—or even a summer—and we can't be bothered with them.
Worker:	It sounds as if you really doubted that Mr. Armez had to leave for medical reasons because he's a member of a certain group of people.
Manager:	Listen, Miss Brown, I don't have anything against Spanish people or any other group of people. We just didn't want to take him back. You heard the foreman say we gave him a warning for his absenteeism, and he continued to take off.
Worker:	I understand that you didn't want to take him back at the time, and I can see that it's not easy to talk about this. I really don't want to cause any difficulty, but I would like to try and see if there is any way that Mr. Armez could come back to work here. I can understand your limitations in keeping someone who misses a lot of work. Could you tell me how many days did he miss while he was working here?
Personnel Director:	I'll have to review his file to find out the exact number of days he wasn't here.
Manager:	Why are you so concerned about him, anyway? Is he asking for welfare? What do you want from us?

Worker:	I am working with the family while Mr. Armez is trying to find employment. Mr. Casey, the foreman, says that Mr. Armez was doing OK on the job, but he was out a lot. I know Mr. Armez had a health problem that needed medical attention. Apparently, Mr. Armez did not have the opportunity to show that he was better after his hospitalization. I hear that your personnel policy does have sick leave written in it, yet Mr. Armez was not given the chance to come back. What I'm hoping is that there will be some way that we can work together toward giving Mr. Armez the opportunity to return to work here.
Manager:	What is he able to do now? Can he take on a heavy job?
Worker:	The doctor said he could return to work two weeks after the operation.
Manager:	We never saw any doctor's statement. I don't know. We'll have to talk more about it here at our next administrative meeting. I'll meet with you again early next week. No promises.
Worker:	All right. I hope we will be able to work together on this.
Manager:	We'll see what we can do. I'll need that doctor's statement. Why don't you set up another appointment with my secretary for early next week.

In this vignette, it is obvious that the worker needed to have some basic facts (e.g., date employment began, reason for hospitalization, doctor's statement) to break through efforts at avoidance. She was sensitive to feelings and skillfully recognized them. Confrontation, with mention of legal action, was not needed at this time. Initial identification of problems, feelings, and goals took place. The worker would want to move on to clarify why Mr. Armez was absent, what the company expects of its employees, and what the stated benefits are that Mr. Armez could have expected from the company.

It is possible that a worker will not be able to get beyond the engagement stage with a target system. A worker, either alone or with other systems (client or action), may work toward bringing about change in a target system, even if it refuses to engage in the process. Strategies may be implemented outside of the target to cause the change necessary for goal accomplishment. The worker may use the General Method to join with other resources and services to form action system.

Example 3: Generalist and Doctor at Hospital Clinic (Action System)

(This interview takes place after the worker has received and delivered Release-of-Information forms signed by Mr. Armez.)

Worker: Good afternoon, doctor. I'm Kathy Brown from Unity Social Services. Thank you for agreeing to meet with me to discuss Mr. Armez, one of your patients.

Doctor: Yes, Miss Brown, I hope I may be of some help to you.

Worker: Doctor, I am working with Mr. Armez and his family. Mr. Armez has not gone back to work yet. I am wondering about Mr. Armez's condition and his ability to take on a physically taxing job at J. B. Barnes Tractor Factory. I spoke with his employer, and there is hesitancy to take Mr. Armez back. One of the reasons given is their fear he will not be able to do the job because of his operation. Mr. Armez himself says he still feels some weakness in his arm, even though you said he could resume work a few weeks after the operation. I understand that the work Mr. Armez would do calls for heavy lifting and pulling on an assembly line that makes tractors. I am wondering if Mr. Armez is able to take on this kind of work, and I would appreciate your professional assistance.

Doctor: Yes, I'm sorry to hear that Mr. Armez hasn't gone back to work yet. There was a growth on the arm that had to be removed. It was not malignant, and when the wound healed, he was discharged from the clinic. I was not aware that Mr. Armez was continuing to feel weakness in the arm. It could be simply because it hasn't been used for a while and it needs exercise.

Worker: I see. The employer has requested a written medical statement about Mr. Armez's ability to work.

Doctor: I am concerned that Mr. Armez continues to feel weakness in his arm. I would be glad to take another look at it, Miss Brown, and let you know what I find.

Worker: I can see that you are concerned about the situation, doctor, and I am glad you are interested in working with me to help Mr. Armez get back to work.

Doctor: Yes. If I find that he should be able to do the work, I'll be happy to write up a statement to that effect.

Worker: I'll suggest to Mr. Armez that he contact you for an appointment and I'll call you after you have seen him. Is that all right with you, doctor?

Here too, the worker tries to engage a system in joint action as they work on the identification of problem, feelings, and goals. The worker senses the concern and willingness of the doctor to get involved in the situation. He doesn't get defensive, but agrees to reconsider his assessment. The worker recognizes this openness and moves quickly to initial goal setting. The doctor agrees to become engaged in the process and will proceed with Miss Brown in collecting data. This stage of the method would not have proceeded so smoothly if the doctor had to bring up policy constraints or rules and regulations of the clinic about taking back discharged patients. In this case example, the doctor as a staff member of the clinic apparently did not find any conflict in being able to cooperate with the worker for goal accomplishment.

As the worker continued to work with the Armez family and their multiple problems, additional client systems might emerge. It is possible she would begin to work with a community or a group that would include members of the Armez family. For example, it could become apparent that poor housing conditions are felt by many people in the apartment complex of the Armez family. A community effort by all of the tenants might be the most effective means to improve the situation.

It could be that the company would not take Mr. Armez back, and that Mr. Armez would tell the worker he knew of six other Hispanic men who were laid off since the company went under new management. The worker could meet with all six as a group, who might collectively agree to involve the Human Rights Commission.

With all of these examples, the generalist begins by engaging the system in the identification and expression of presenting problems, purposeful feelings, and desirable goals. As stated, the General Method is applicable to systems of any size.

USING THE HOLISTIC FOUNDATION IN ENGAGEMENT

As the generalist begins to have contact with a system, and throughout the process of the General Method, the foundation knowledge, values, and skills (Diagram 1-5, Chapter 1) are called into action. The perspective of the worker is pervasively ecological as he or she observes the matching and interacting of systems and carefully applies theories and skills to practice.

As pointed out in the examples in this chapter, the generalist demonstrates in words and actions an unfolding of the principles of acceptance, individualization, nonjudgmental attitude, purposeful expression of feelings, controlled emotional involvement, self-determination, and confidentiality.[41] In the engagement stage, relationship and problem-solving skills are readily applied. The worker uses skills in listening, responding, guiding, paraphrasing, and clarifying, along with skills for identifying problems, feelings, and goals. It is also possible, as in the target-system example, that some political skills may be needed. In trying to engage a target system in the initial stage of the General Method, the generalist may need to provide evidence, enter into bargaining, or propose legal action.

Knowledge about people, families, organizations, physical conditions, role theory, and stress theory is very helpful to a worker during engagement. In the case vignettes just presented, the worker used knowledge of people, their environments, and the interdependence of both as she formulated descriptions of the problems, feelings, and goals of the situation. Problems were seen as taking place at the interface between a system and other systems in the environment. Feelings and their reasons were related to a need or failure in matching expectations between client systems and environmental systems. Goals were generally described in terms of developing or enhancing the fit and transactions among systems.

The use of foundation knowledge, values, and skills from an ecological perspective continues as a generalist moves into the second stage of the General Method. As data are collected, the worker knows that in the evolving procedure of the Method, a refinement takes place in identifying and expressing problems, feelings, and goals—the three guiding landmarks of the engagement stage. Although each of the six stages of the General Method has its own particular landmarks to guide the worker and system, the elements of foundation and the landmarks of earlier stages remain present and are called upon throughout the procedure (see Figure 4-1).

HUMAN DIVERSITY IN ENGAGEMENT

Culture

As stated earlier, a sensitivity to human diversity may be demonstrated within each stage of the General Method of social work practice. During engagement, for example, as a worker and a client system begin to identify purpose, problems, feelings, and goals, an awareness of the culture of the system can help the worker to create an atmosphere of understanding and responsiveness. Care can be demonstrated even in the selection of place for the initial contact. To foster a sense of security and trust, it may be more appropriate for the worker to meet with members of a particular cultural system outside of the office or agency. For example, outreach in the neighborhood and home visits have proven to be effective, especially within the Hispanic community.[42]

Members of ethnic groups incorporate knowledge of their ethnic history and personal experiences with people of diverse cultures as they relate cross-culturally. (*Cross-culturally* refers to systems of different cultures.) Consumers of services may view service providers and agencies from different perspectives, particularly if there are no apparent members of the consumer's culture in the service-providing system. Guardedness, hostility, fear, and defensiveness are often present when a system begins to have contact with a social worker from a different culture. Defenses vary according to ethnic backgrounds. Chinese culturally derived defenses, for example, include politeness, quietness, and friendliness when confronted with potentially threatening situations.[43]

In approaching a system and beginning to identify the purpose of contact, a worker needs to be sensitive to basic communication patterns, according to the culture of the system. To give and to expect eye-to-eye contact with American Indians or Asians, for example, would be insensitive, because eye contact is seen generally as a lack of respect in these cultures.[44] Although a worker may feel more comfortable with informality toward clients (i.e., using first names, casual dress, attitude of friendliness), members of certain cultures, such as Asian-American and Afro-American, may need and expect a formal approach from a professional worker, at least initially. Asian-Americans are particularly uncomfortable with functioning in ambiguity. During first contacts, there is a need to have the purpose and function of a service clearly stated.[45]

In proceeding, the worker keeps in mind the time orientation of a culture. Whereas for urban blacks and Japanese, time may be needed to build up a sense of trust and openness, Mexican-Americans move quickly into relationships and decision-making, relying heavily on inferential abilities. Repetition and calculations are often unwelcomed by Mexican-Americans as they proceed with problem solving.[46]

In identifying and expressing feelings, diversity is also found among cultures. People from Eastern European ethnic groups, such as Poles, Hungarians, and Czechoslovakians, indicate strong feelings of shame over having to seek professional help.[47] Members of some ethnic groups are very reluctant to talk about personal feelings and problems with outsiders. This is particularly true with Asians and American Indians. On the other hand, members of Jewish and Italian cultures are often found to be openly expressive of their feelings, needs, and problems.[48]

Problems or needs may be perceived and described from various perspectives, according to culture. For example, Chinese and Mexican-Americans basically see problems collectively rathern than individually. The deviant behavior of one is seen as a direct assault on the pride of the community. Also, problems may need to be described in material rather than emotional terms. Pei-Ngor Chen found, for example, that many Chinese clients would only work on emotional problems if they were receiving concrete assistance at the time.[49]

Although a problem may come to the attention of a worker as a personal problem of an individual or group, a culturally sensitive social worker is cognizant of the fact that environments themselves, with their institutional pressures and prejudices, may really be the problem that needs to be addressed. In the engagement stage, a worker fosters a sense of openness when the person or people that make up a system can begin to see that the worker understands both the real problem and how they perceive and experience it.

Goals may be more clearly understood and articulated if a worker is aware of the value orientation of a culture. The aspirations and goals of individuals, groups, families, and communities are usually reflective of the values that have been transmitted through their culture.

The values of *person, family, tribe,* and *community* are commonly upheld by several cultures. There may be, however, discrete meaning for such values in particular groups. For example, although *individualism* is valued by both Puerto Ricans and the American majority, there is a distinction that should be realized by social workers as they begin to work with Puerto Ricans. Joseph Fitzpatrick offers the following clarification:

The basic value of Puerto Rican culture, as of Latin cultures in general, is a form of individualism which focuses on the inner importance of the person. In contrast to the individualism of the United States, which values the individual in terms of his ability to compete for higher social and economic status, the culture of Puerto Rico centers attention on those inner qualities which constitute the uniqueness of the person, and his goodness or worth in himself.[50]

An astute understanding of the values of a system helps a worker to locate what motivates members of the system and give direction for how to express relevant goals. Members of the Puerto Rican culture, for example, would be motivated to work on goals that appeal to personal responsibility and leadership, rather than those that appeal to platforms or programs.

Sexual Variation

Throughout each stage of the General Method, a social worker may demonstrate sensitivity to sexual variations. During engagement, for example, as purpose and problems are identified, the worker shows respect and acceptance by beginning where the client system is. Focus is given to only those problems and needs that the client system wishes to address. When a worker knows that an individual is gay or lesbian, there must not be a hidden agenda on the worker's part, in which he or she expects to discuss (or to change) the life style of the individual. If the client system is having difficulties that relate to sexual orientation, a worker may begin to be helpful by making known that he or she is aware of the pressures and problems gay and lesbian persons often have to face in American society. As generally found in helping relationships, a client is usually more comfortable by beginning with external problems (related to societal institutions, policies, and practices). Eventually, problems that are more personal (primary relationships, for example) and then intrapersonal (dual identities, self-esteem, fears) may be shared.

During engagement a worker encourages and accepts a client's expression of feelings. For gay or lesbian clients, these feelings may include loneliness, alienation, isolation, hurt, and anger and outrage toward a rejecting, condemning family or society. A worker who becomes defensive or judgmental will be indicating a lack of self-awareness and sensitivity to the needs of the client system. Through supervision, the worker may begin to see that he or she has homophobic tendencies and to discuss the possible need to refer the client to someone else.

As initial goals are stated during engagement, the worker carefully listens and articulates the aspirations and expectations of a client system. If the worker cannot support the goals of a client in any way, this should be recognized and resolved before proceeding into the second stage of the General Method. As with members of other minority groups, the problems faced by those who are gay or lesbian are frequently caused by discriminatory practices of large institutions. Goals, therefore, are often long-range, social-change goals as well as personal, immediate-need goals. The worker takes time throughout the Method to engage the system in the process of realistically stating, understanding, and refining long- and short-range goals, which may be personal, interpersonal, institutional, or societal in nature.

Gender Sensitivity

With each stage of the General Method, a social worker may also indicate sensitivity to gender diversity. In engaging a system in the first stage of the Method, a worker begins with an awareness of the sex of those in the system as well as of his or her own sex. If there is a gender difference, the sensitive worker is attuned to the way in which he or she is being perceived by the system.

If, for example, the system of contact is a man or a group of men who are strongly identified with the masculine, "macho" role, and if the worker is a woman, it may be difficult initially for the man or men to see the social worker as a unique individual with expertise in problem solving. In engagement, as the worker proceeds with the process of identifying problems, feelings, and goals, she may find it equally difficult for men to express or to admit that they have problems and feelings. There may also be hesitancy in articulating goals to be worked on collaboratively with a female.

If the system of contact is a woman or a group of women who are strongly identified with the female, dependent role, it may be difficult for the worker to engage the woman or women in a shared, problem-solving process, particularly if the worker is male. Time and skill will be needed in either case for the worker to create an open, trusting atmosphere of mutual respect and interdependence.

During engagement, a worker would also be mindful of the other diversity variables identified in Chapter 3 under the headings of "person," "in," and "environment." These include the age and stages, endowment and personality, value system, class, and geographic location of the system receiving service.

ENGAGEMENT IN DIVERSE FIELD AREAS

In each chapter of this text that describes one of the six stages of the General Method (Chapters 4 through 9), a section that contains case examples from diverse areas of the field of social work is given. Examples are selected from the areas of child welfare, gerontology, public social welfare, community services, education, and corrections. The examples demonstrate the apparent applicability of the General Method, with its six stages and major focal points for each stage, in all areas of the field of practice. Although the persons, problems, and needs addressed in each example relate directly to a specific field area, the General Method is used by all of the workers. The examples given are based on actual situations assigned to entry-level generalist practitioners or students in field placements. Names and other identifiable information have been disguised to preserve confidentiality.

In the following section, the application of konwledge and skills during the *engagement stage* of the General Method will be demonstrated by entry-level generalists in six diverse field areas.

I. FIELD AREA: CHILD WELFARE

A. Agency: State Department of Children's Services

B. Client System

K is a 15-year-old female of French-American ethnicity. The police referred her to Children's Services two and a half years ago because she was physically abused by her mother. K had also been sexually abused by her stepfather on two occasions. She was committed to the state and placed in a group home, where she lived for over two years. She then requested and was placed in foster care. After two months in a foster home, K ran away. The police picked her up and placed her in an emergency shelter. She was at the shelter when the case was assigned to a new worker from the State Department of Children's Services.

C. Engagement

Problem: During engagement, K said she knew she had two problems: (1) She had no place to go to live, and (2) she was missing school. She said she did not want to return to her foster home, but would not say why she ran away. She shared that she had run away with a boyfriend, who left her after a few days. K spoke about hating herself and knowing that no place or school would want her. She described herself as "dumb" and "ugly." During engagement, the worker identified additional problems. These included the personal problems of (1) poor self-esteem, (2) identity confusion, (3) problems concerning her sexuality and how to relate to males, and (4) depression.

Feelings: K expressed feelings of nervousness and loneliness. She said she knew she was "jittery" and just couldn't settle down to anything. She also said that she "hated" her mother and stepfather and never wanted to see them again. She wished she could live with her "real father."

At one point, K began to cry and left the room. When she returned the worker identified feelings of pain and depression. K admitted that she was "really down" and believed that no one really cared if she lived or died. She said that her "rotten boyfriend" got tired of her, even though she gave him "everything," and she knew her parents couldn't stand her either.

Goals: K's stated goals were (1) to obtain and maintain a permanent placement (*permanent placement* means a place to live until adulthood), and

(2) to get back into school as soon as possible. K said she wanted to leave the shelter but didn't know where to go. She thought she would like to go back to the group home where she had lived before she was placed in the foster home. The worker hoped that K would eventually see the need for help with her more personal problems, although K was not ready to discuss this need at the time of engagement.

D. Charted Progress

By the end of the engagement period, the worker recorded the items in Diagram 4-3 to begin to chart a formal plan of action (explained in detail in this chapter). The date of contact, the problems identified at the time by the worker or the client, and the goals mutually agreed on by both K and the worker were listed as seen in Diagram 4-3.

II. FIELD AREA: GERONTOLOGY

A. Agency: Seaside Nursing Home

B. Client System

Mrs. J is an 80-year-old Portuguese woman who was admitted to the skilled-nursing facility at Seaside Nursing Home two weeks ago. She was released from the hospital with a diagnosis of "organic brain syndrome." The summary from the hospital social worker indicated that Mrs. J was a housewife with no formal education. Her family refused to be involved with her and left no name or address for contact. Mrs. J can't remember where members of her family live. At the nursing home, she remained seclusive and appeared to be afraid to leave her room. An entry-level generalist was assigned to work with Mrs. J to help her adjust to the nursing home.

C. Engagement

Problem: During the first interview, Mrs. J expressed displeasure with her placement in the institution. She said she did not like it at the nursing

DIAGRAM 4-3   Initial Recording

DATE IDENTIFIED	PROBLEM/NEED	GOAL
1/12	No permanent home	a. To obtain a permanent placement b. To maintain a permanent placement
1/12	Out of school	a. To reenter school
1/12	Personal problems a. Poor self-esteem b. Identity confusion c. Sexuality (relationships, behavior) d. Depression	

home and wished she could go somewhere else. She did not respond when asked where she would like to go. Mrs. J could not speak English fluently, and wished there was someone who could speak Portuguese with her. She said she was afraid that if she left her room, her things would be stolen. She would only leave her room if someone came to take her to the dining room for meals.

Feelings: Mrs. J began to express feelings of distrust, anger, and abandonment. She didn't feel comfortable in a cross-cultural environment. Whenever the worker began to talk about where Mrs. J came from or where she would like to go, Mrs. J became quiet and looked very sad and hurt. She would shake her head and look out the window. During the second interview, she said she had three children but they all went away and left her. She would not talk about her husband.

Goals: Mrs. J said that she wished she were able to go out on her own. She realized that she had to first be able to leave her room before she could go anywhere else. She didn't think she liked the people at the nursing home, but was willing to meet twice a week with the worker to talk about how she was getting along. She said she hoped that someone who spoke Portuguese would come to see her.

The goals for Mrs. J that were agreed on by herself and the worker during engagement were the following:

1. To be able to leave her room on her own
2. To have someone who speaks Portuguese visit with her
3. To get to know the staff and resources of the nursing home

D. Charted Progress

As the worker charted progress at the end of the engagement stage, dates, problems, and goals identified were recorded as shown in Diagram 4-4. At this time, it was also possible to record the initial contract for biweekly meetings of the worker and Mrs. J.

III. FIELD AREA: PUBLIC SOCIAL WELFARE

A. Agency: State Social Services

B. Client System

Mr. and Mrs. P and their two children, ages 2 and 4, arrived at the agency with their suitcase. Mrs. P's father had called the agency a week earlier, saying that his daughter and her two children had come to live with him, but he didn't have any room. He wanted "the state" to find housing for his daughter and grandchildren. He also said that his daughter and her husband were separated, but that her husband was waiting at their old apartment to take their AFDC check (Aid to Families with Dependent Children). Mrs. P's father wanted the check held for his daughter, who would come in to pick it up. When the P family arrived at the Social Services unit, the case was assigned to an entry-level generalist.

DIAGRAM 4-4   Initial Recording

DATE IDENTIFIED	PROBLEM/ NEED	GOAL	TASK	CONTRACT	DATE ANTICIPATED
9/25	Poor adjustment: seclusiveness— not leaving room alone	To be able to leave room alone			
9/25	Cultural isolation: need to communicate in native language	To be visited by someone who speaks Portuguese			
9/27	Unfamiliar with staff and resources of the nursing home	To get to know the staff and resources of the nursing home	To meet twice a week	Worker and Mrs. J	10/4 and every Tuesday and Thursday thereafter

C. Engagement

During the initial interview, because of the urgent nature of the situation, the problem, feelings, and goals of engagement were explored and specific data were collected. Preliminary assessment, planning, and intervention also took place during the first day of contact with the family.

Problem: In this situation, housing was the obvious immediate problem. Because of repeated tardiness in paying their rent, the P family were evicted from their apartment. Mrs. P thought that she and her children could find temporary shelter with her father. After two weeks, however, he said they would have to leave. Mr. P expected to take the money from their welfare check and return to Maine, where his mother lived. He said he had planned to send for his family once he got settled. At this time, however, Mr. and Mrs. P said that they decided they would prefer to find another apartment locally.

Feelings: Mrs. P was feeling rejected by her father and blamed him for their current problem. Mr. P was angry at the state for not sending their check and food stamps. (After the initial call from Mrs. P's father, the check and food stamps had been held by the post office and were later returned to the central welfare office.) Both felt that no one really wanted them or cared. They appeared to be confused and said that they were feeling helpless and didn't know what to do.

Goals: When asked what they hoped the worker could do for them, the P's said that they wanted him to find them a place to stay. The worker clarified his own role and said that he could assist them by locating temporary shelter, but that they would have to become active in searching for and in documenting their search for more permanent housing. The immediate goals agreed on by the worker and Mr. and Mrs. P were (1) to find emergency shelter for the family (short-range goal) and (2) to locate an apartment in the local or neighboring geographic area for extended residency by the family (long-range goal).

D. Charted Progress

As the worker began recording for a formal plan of action, the basic information obtained through engagement was charted as in Diagram 4-5.

IV. FIELD AREA: COMMUNITY SERVICES

A. Agency: Clayton Neighborhood House

B. Client System

Mrs. T lives with her husband and three children in a one-room apartment at 33 L Street. She came to Clayton House to request clothing for her children and to complain about the lack of heating in their room. She informed the worker that there were three other Hispanic families in their building who also were without heat. None of the adults in the four families spoke English. A Spanish-speaking entry-level generalist went out and visited all four families. They met to organize and work together to obtain heating in their homes.

C. Engagement

Mrs. T was encouraged to express her problems, feelings, and goals when she met with the worker. Her initial request for clothing was granted on the same day at the first interview. She was directed to the clothing room at Clayton House and told to take whatever she needed.

After the worker and Mrs. T talked together about the heating problem, the client system in this case expanded to include members from the other three families who shared the problem. Before trying to resolve the issue with Mrs. T, the worker wanted to meet with the others who were experiencing the problem and to find out more about the situation. After visiting each family individually in their apartments, the worker met with members of all four families in Mr. and Mrs. T's room. Together, they began to identify problems, feelings, and goals.

Problem: The basic problem identified during the engagement period was the lack of heat on the second floor of the L Street apartment building. All of the residents who met with the worker lived on the second floor. They said that they had had very little, if any, heat over the past month. There were some nights when the temperature dropped below freezing, and the only means of keeping warm was to turn on all of the burners and the ovens of their stoves.

When the worker inquired about the residents on the first floor, she was told that they do not have a heating problem. They were described as "English

DIAGRAM 4-5   Initial Recording

DATE IDENTIFIED	PROBLEM/ NEED	GOAL
9/28	Housing for P family	a. To find emergency shelter for the P family
		b. To locate an apartment for long-term residence by the family

speaking," and it was felt that they received better treatment from the land-lord.

Feelings: The community of residents who met with the worker shared feelings of frustration and victimization. They felt helpless and angry. They did not think that their landlord listened to them or cared about what happened to them. They were afraid that if they put pressure on the landlord, he would evict them and they would not be able to find another place to live.

Goal: All present agreed that something had to be done. They asked the worker to help them. A mutually agreed-on goal was to get their apartments heated. They wanted assurance that heating would be provided consistently throughout the winter.

D. Charted Progress

The worker recorded the basic information obtained during engagement as outlined in Diagram 4-6. She saw a possible problem of discrimination by the landlord, but decided to wait until further data were collected before recording the problem in the record.

V. FIELD AREA: EDUCATION

A. Agency: Keeney Elementary School

B. Client System

Jim G is an 8-year-old black child in third grade. His teacher referred him to school social services because he began to miss school or to come late each morning. His behavior was becoming increasingly inappropriate. He often kept his head down on his desk and remained silent when his teacher called on him. He no longer raised his hand in class or showed any interest in learning. His grades were beginning to drop, and his teacher feared he would get so far behind in his work that he might have to be moved to a different classroom. The teacher also noted that Jim was not eating his lunch. These behaviors were not apparent until the second month of the school year. An entry-level generalist was assigned to talk with Jim and to make a home visit.

C. Engagement

Problem: When Jim entered the worker's office, he sat at the table and kept his head down. The worker asked if he knew why she wanted to see him, and he shook his head negatively. She reviewed his teacher's concerns and

DIAGRAM 4-6 Initial Recording

DATE IDENTIFIED	PROBLEM/ NEED	GOAL
12/3	Lack of heat on second floor	To obtain consistent, adequate heating for second-floor residents of L Street apartment house

assured Jim that the people at school wanted to try to help him so that he wouldn't get behind in his schoolwork. The worker wondered if Jim could talk about what was bothering him lately. Jim didn't answer, but got up and walked over to the bookcase containing toys and games. He asked who the toys were for, and the worker explained that any of the children who came to the office could use them. Jim took out the game Chutes and Ladders and asked if the worker wanted to play it with him. As they were setting up the game, the worker said that she could see that it wasn't easy for Jim to talk about what was troubling him, but she hoped that he would eventually. With his mother's permission, the worker began to see Jim twice a week in her office.

After the first meeting with Jim, the worker visited his mother at home. Jim lived with his mother and father in a middle-class neighborhood. Mrs. G expressed concern over her son's regressive school behavior and said that she noticed that he was acting somewhat strange at home also lately. He wouldn't go to sleep at night unless his mother stayed in his room and kept a light on. She could not identify anything different or painful that Jim might have experienced since school began. She said that her son did excellent school work when he was in first and second grade, and she couldn't understand what was happening to him to bring about the changes he was going through. She offered to work with the school in whatever way possible. She said that she would see that Jim got to school on time each day even if she or her husband had to drive him. Mrs. G agreed to come to school to talk with the worker again in two weeks.

The problems identified during the initial interviews with Jim and his mother were (1) school tardiness and absenteeism, (2) declining academic functioning (interest, participation, grades), and (3) refusal to sleep without his mother and a light in his room.

Feelings: In early sessions with Jim and with his mother, very little feeling was expressed by either of them. Jim avoided talking about anything personal. Mrs. G only expressed concern over her son's school performance.

Goal: Mrs. G and the worker agreed to work together to help Jim to improve his attendance at school and his academic performance. Both agreed to talk with Jim to try to motivate him to want the same goals.

D. Charted Progress

As the worker extended the engagement period with Jim and his mother, she recorded the initially identified problems as found in Diagram 4-7. She also recorded the goals and tasks that she and Mrs. G developed.

VI. FIELD AREA: CORRECTIONS

A. Agency: Juvenile Court

B. Client System

A group was formed for seven male adolescents, all age 14, who were on probation for burglary, theft of automobiles, or minor larceny (shoplifting). The usual probationary period was six months. If a youth attended and participated regularly in group meetings and met all of the other requirements of

DIAGRAM 4-7   Initial Recording

DATE IDENTIFIED	PROBLEM/ NEED	GOAL	TASK	CONTRACT	DATE ANTICIPATED
11/1	Jim's school tardiness and absenteeism	Jim's regular school attendance (on time every day)	1. See that Jim gets to school on time each day	1. Mrs. G	11/5–each day thereafter
11/1	Jim's declining academic performance	Improved academic functioning (interest, participation, grades)	1. Talk with Jim about school problems	1a. Worker and Jim b. Mrs G and Jim	11/6 and twice a week thereafter
			2. Follow-up	2. Worker and Mrs. G	11/15
11/2	Jim's getting to sleep at night				

probation, the time of probation could be reduced to four months. All of the group participants knew that they were expected to attend weekly group meetings from four to six months, depending on when their probationary period would be over. A new B.S.W. female social worker was assigned to co-lead the group with an M.S.W. male worker who had worked in corrections for six years and who had specialized in social group work while in graduate school.

C. Engagement

Problem: The presenting problem shared by all of the youths was being on probation for illegal actions. Discussion centered on clarifying the problem. Was it being on probation or was it committing illegal acts? At this time, most of the group members saw the problem more in terms of having gotten caught rather than having broken the law. One member said that their basic problem was "law-breaking leading to probation." All agreed that this was a good way to describe it.

As group participants began to talk more about themselves, several other common problems began to surface. The youths were surprised to learn that all of them were in special classes in school because of learning disabilities. They all said that they had "bad tempers" and made some reference to problems at home. Two of the youths mentioned their drug habits.

Feelings: In early group sessions, members expressed strong feelings of mistrust, particularly toward the group leaders. Some members complained about having to come to the group but eventually admitted that they were angry really because they had gotten caught by the police and put on probation. They said that it was "dumb" of them to get caught. Members repeatedly indicated a sense of little self-worth.

Goals: The goal most clearly expressed by all of the participants was to get off probation as soon as possible. They also admitted that they wished they could stay out of trouble, but that it wasn't easy. They said, too, that they would like to be able to handle their tempers better. They expressed interest also in being able to understand more about "the changes" they were going through.

Although reference had been made to problems they were having with parents, there was not a general agreement that group members wanted to work on getting along better with their parents. They also didn't like to talk about the fact that they didn't think they were worth very much.

D. Charted Progress

The worker recorded the problems and goals that were identified by the group during the engagement period, as found in Diagram 4-8. She did not list the problems of learning disabilities and drug habits, because the youths were receiving help with these problems from other services. The preliminary agreement of group attendance and participation in order to get off probation was recorded in the columns called "task," "contract," and "date anticipated."

DIAGRAM 4-8   Initial Recording

DATE IDENTIFIED	PROBLEM/ NEED	GOAL	TASK	CONTRACT	DATE ANTICIPATED
10/1	Law-breaking leading to probation	To get off probation in four months	1. To attend weekly group meetings	Seven members, two workers	10/1 and each Monday at 4:00 P.M. for at least four months
10/1	Bad tempers	To learn to control tempers in school, home, neighborhood			
10/1	Need to understand "changes" of teenagers	To learn about "changes" youth go through			
10/1	Parent-son conflicts				
10/1	Low self-worth				

CONCLUSION

In this chapter, focus was on the engagement stage of the General Method. The three focal points of problem, feeling, and goal were highlighted. Skills for working in these three major areas were pointed out. The use of ecological-systems theory throughout the stage was emphasized. The traditional purpose of social work, to enhance social functioning, was evident as the engagement process was described within an ecological perspective.

Case vignettes offered a demonstration of the use of skills, the ecological perspective, and the three guiding landmarks of the engagement stage. Examples described the work of a generalist as she began to engage a family, a business employer, and a health service in the General Method. The use of foundation knowledge, values, and skills during engagement was discussed. Additional examples included cases from diverse field areas. Several ways in which a worker demonstrates sensitivity to human diversity during engagement were also described.

The expected timing of the engagement stage was not stated in this chapter because actual timing of any stage in the General Method is not clearly predictable. Sometimes a worker and system may move through engagement or any other stage in one interview. Sometimes it takes months, or as discussed, it may never be completed. The Method and each of its stages have an evolving, dynamic, and relative nature.

In the next chapter, the generalist will be seen in movement to the second stage of the Method, data collection. The overlap and natural flow from the first to the second stage will be shown. In the second stage of the systematic procedure, worker and system of contact take a deeper and sharper look at the issue, need, question, or difficulty brought forth for study and action.

NOTES

[1]CSWE Commission on Educational Planning, *CSWE Curriculum Policy Statement* (New York: Council on Social Work Education, March 1981), p. 3.

[2]Commission on Social Work Practice, NASW, "Working Definition on Social Work Practice," in Harriett M. Bartlett, "Toward Clarification and Improvement of Social Work Practice," *Social Work* 3, no. 2 (April 1958): 6.

[3]Max Siporin, *Introduction to Social Work Practice* (New York: Macmillan, 1975), p. 3. Copyright 1975 by Macmillan Publishing Company.

[4]Allen Pincus and Anne Minahan, *Social Work Practice: Model and Method* (Itasca, Ill.: Peacock, 1973), p. 9.

[5]Charles S. Levy, "The Problem in the Social Work Problem-Solving Process," *Journal of Jewish Communal Service* 43 (Summer 1967): 311.

[6]Ibid., pp. 305–306.

[7]*Webster's Third New International Dictionary of the English Language,* s.v. "problem."

[8]Ibid.

[9]Norman A. Polansky, ed., *Social Work Research: Methods for the Helping Professions,* rev. ed. (Chicago: University of Chicago Press, 1975), p. 30.

[10]Ibid.

[11]Helen Harris Perlman, "The Problem-Solving Model in Social Casework," in Robert W. Roberts and Robert H. Nees, eds., *Theories of Social Casework* (Chicago: University of Chicago Press, 1970), p. 147.

[12]Ibid., p. 146.

[13]Ibid., p. 148.

[14]Robert K. Merton and Robert A. Nisbet, eds., *Contemporary Social Problems,* 3rd ed. (New York: Harcourt, Brace & World, 1971), p. viii.

[15]Siporin, *Introduction,* p. 22.

[16]Carel Germain and Alex Gitterman, "The Life Model of Social Work Practice" in Francis J. Turner, ed., *Social Work Treatment: Interlocking Theoretical Approaches,* 2nd ed. (New York: The Free Press, 1979), p. 371. Copyright 1979 by The Free Press.

[17]Laura Epstein, *Helping People: The Task-Centered Approach* (St. Louis: The C. V. Mosby Company, 1980), p. 55.

[18]Pincus and Minahan, *Social Work Practice,* p. 104.

[19]Helen Harris Perlman, *Social Casework: A Problem-Solving Process* (Chicago: University of Chicago Press, 1957), pp. 4–5.

[20]Gisela Konopka, "The Methods of Social Group Work," in Walter A. Friedlander, ed., *Concepts and Methods of Social Work* (Englewood Cliffs, N.J.: Prentice-Hall, 1955), pp. 117–18.

[21]Murray Ross, *Case Histories in Community Organization* (New York: Harper and Brothers, 1958), p. 13.

[22]Polansky, *Social Work Research.*

[23]Levy, "The Problem," pp. 305–10.

[24]*Webster's Third New International Dictionary of the English Language,* s.v. "general."

[25]Gordon Hearn, *The General Systems Approach: Contributions Toward an Holistic Conception of Social Work* (New York: Council on Social Work Education, 1969), p. 69.

[26]Felix P. Biestek, S. J., *The Casework Relationship* (Chicago: Loyola University Press, 1957), p. 33.

[27]Ibid., p. 48.

[28]Harold D. Werner, "Cognitive Theory," in Francis J. Turner, ed., *Social Work Treatment: Interlocking Theoretical Approaches,* 2nd ed. (New York: The Free Press, 1979), p. 243.

[29]Robert R. Carkhuff and William A. Anthony, *The Skills of Helping: An Introduction to Counseling Skills* (Amherst, Mass.: Human Resource Development Press, 1979), p. 79.

[30]Bok-Lim C. Kim, "Casework with Japanese and Korean Wives of Americans," *Social Casework* 53, no. 5 (May 1972): 273–79.

[31]From *You and Me,* by Gerard Egan. Copyright © 1977 by Wadsworth Publishing Company, Inc. Reprinted by permission of the publisher, Brooks/Cole Publishing Company, Monterey, California, pp. 80–83.

[32]Florence Hollis, "Casework and Social Class," *Social Casework* 46, no. 10 (October 1965): 466.

[33]Ibid., p. 469.

[34]David Hallowitz, "Problem-Solving Theory," in Francis J. Turner, ed., *Social Work Treatment: Interlocking Theoretical Approaches,* 2nd ed. (New York: The Free Press, 1979), p. 111.

[35]Egan, *You and Me,* pp. 87–88.

[36]Carkhuff and Anthony, *The Skills of Helping,* p. 79.

[37]Kurt Spitzer and Betty Welsh, "A Problem-Focused Model of Practice," in Beulah Compton and Burt Galaway, eds., *Social Work Processes,* rev. ed. (Homewood, Ill.: Dorsey, 1979), p. 259.

[38]Epstein, *Helping People,* p. 125.

[39]Werner, "Cognitive Theory," p. 244.

[40]Epstein, *Helping People,* p. 133.

[41]Biestek, *The Casework Relationship.*

[42]Ted R. Watkins and Richard Gonzales, "Outreach to Mexican Americans," *Social Work* 27, no. 3 (May 1982): 246.

[43]Doman Lum, "Toward a Framework for Social Work Practice with Minorities," *Social Work* 27, no. 3 (May 1982): 246.

[44]Wynetta Devore and Elfriede G. Schlesinger, *Ethnic-Sensitive Social Work Practice* (St. Louis: Mosby, 1981), p. 173.

[45]Ibid., p. 194.

[46]Jerome B. Kernan and Lawrence L. Schkade, "A Cross-Cultural Analysis of Stimulus Sampling," *Administrative Science Quarterly* 17 (September 1972): 351–58.

[47]Joseph Giordano and Grace P. Giordano, *The Ethno-Cultural Factor in Mental Health—A Literature Review and Bibliography* (New York: American Jewish Community, 1977).

[48]Mark Zborowski, "Cultural Components in Response to Pain," *Journal of Social Issues* 8, no. 4 (1952): 16–30.

[49]Pei-Ngor Chen, "The Chinese Community in Los Angeles," *Social Casework* 51 (December 1970): 591–98.

[50]Joseph P. Fitzpatrick, *Puerto Rican Americans* (Englewood Cliffs, N.J.: Prentice-Hall, 1971), p. 90.

5

Data Collection

The social worker should respect the privacy of clients and hold in confidence all information obtained in the course of professional service.

—NASW Code of Ethics[1]

In the second stage of the General Method, information is gathered systematically for understanding and planning. When the information that the worker collects can be verified as fact, it becomes data. Demonstrating the scientific aspect of professional social work, the generalist uses research skills to distinguish fact from impression or assumption. Inasmuch as possible, the worker strives to acquire information that is factual in the data-collection stage of the General Method.

The worker organizes the collected data under the three categorical headings of (1) problem, (2) person, and (3) environment. Using an ecological framework, the generalist directs inquiry to find out about the problems presented, the persons involved in the problems, and the potential or actual resources and restraints in the environment that may affect the person-problem-environment situation.

GATHERING DATA

After an initial engagement period with a system, the generalist begins to collect specific information according to the three general categories cited. Workers may obtain information in a variety of ways. The most direct means of gathering data is through question and answer in a personal interview. Kerlinger describes the interview as "a psychological and sociological measuring instrument." He points out that a respondent's answers to carefully planned questions may be translated into measures and used as data.[2] Having begun to identify what information is needed for an accurate assessment, the worker also begins to plan how to formulate questions to be used in interviewing for gathering the needed data. Thought is also given to finding other possible ways for obtaining relevant information.

In addition to the direct approach of questioning in interviews with primary sources of information, workers may find answers through listening and observing. Whereas direct questioning may cause fear or defensiveness, skilled listening and observing may disclose the information needed without provoking anxiety or discomfort. A worker may find out if a mother has grown in patience with her child by observing their interaction at home. A group's interest in a particular problem may be identified by noting their reaction when it is mentioned in a general discussion. If a worker has any doubt about how he or she is interpreting what is seen or observed, further validation is to be solicited. Sometimes, formal testing is requested for precise information.

Data may be collected through secondary sources such as reading records, documents, and written materials, and also through verbal or written communication with outside systems. All data about clients should be collected only with the client's knowledge and permission. Before any information is obtained, written release-of-information forms must be signed by the client and sent to the sources from which information is being sought. An example of a release-of-information form may be found in Diagram 5-1. What type of information is being requested and why the information is needed should be clearly explained to clients before a worker asks for information or a signature on a release form. If data are being obtained through a study of public documents (i.e., state records of births, marriages, deaths, etc.), no permission is needed. Only information that is relevant and necessary for an accurate assessment should be sought by the worker. It is possible that the system of contact will not allow the worker to collect information on some problems, and that the worker will, therefore, have to limit the focus of attention to those problem areas accepted by the client for study and intervention. If a client will not give permission to release information that must be obtained in order to proceed with a case, the worker may have to point out to the client that services will be terminated unless the information is made available.

DIAGRAM 5-1   Release-of-Information Consent Form

I _____ give permission
      (person giving consent)
for _____ to release to
      (system with information)
_____ the following
      (system to receive information)
information:

_____
_____
_____
_____
_____
_____

I understand that _____
                        (system receiving information)

will use this information for the following purpose:

_____
_____
_____
_____
_____

This consent is to expire on   _____
                                              (date)
Signed _____   _____
                                              (date)
Witness _____   _____
                                              (date)
Agency representative_____   _____
                                              (date)

FACT VERSUS ASSUMPTION

As a worker collects data, skill is needed to distinguish between fact and
assumption. Interpretation of what is heard or seen may be influenced by
the worker's frame of reference, past experiences, values, needs, and impressions. Through unconscious association, a worker may quickly assume
that one word, description, or event is similar to another, and a label may
be given that is actually incorrect. When a worker believes data have been
found, he or she should ask: How is this documented? Did I really see this—
hear this—find this?

Facts answer the question: Is this true or false? Assumptions, because
they are not based on facts, may be either true or false. With assumptions,

missing information is taken for granted. An activity to help refine one's skills for data collection is given in Exercise 5-1.

EXERCISE 5-1   INFORMATION

STORY

A woman was leaving the office when a man appeared at the door and demanded money. The secretary opened a drawer. The contents of the drawer were scooped up, and the man sped away.

If the following statement is true, circle *T.* If it is false, circle *F.* If the statement is an assumption, circle *?*

1. A man appeared as a client was leaving the office.	T F ?
2. The intruder was a man.	T F ?
3. No one demanded money.	T F ?
4. The secretary was the woman who opened the drawer.	T F ?
5. The man took the contents of the drawer.	T F ?
6. Someone opened a drawer.	T F ?
7. Money was in the drawer.	T F ?
8. The man ran away.	T F ?
9. The man demanded money from the woman.	T F ?
10. There are three people in this story.	T F ?

In this exercise, all statements contain assumptions except for number 3, which is false, and number 6, which is true. The assumptions that cannot be substantiated by the words of the story are the following:

1. It is assumed that the woman is a client.
2. It is assumed that the man is an intruder.
3. (False)
4. It is assumed that the secretary is a woman.
5. It is assumed that the contents were taken (not just "scooped up") and that this was done by the man.
6. (True)
7. It is assumed that the contents were money.
8. It is assumed that "sped away" means "ran away."
9. It is assumed that the money was demanded from the woman and not from the secretary.
10. It is assumed that the woman was not the secretary.

These assumptions could be correct, but they could be incorrect also. In this exercise, the question mark should have been circled for 8 out of 10 answers.

A worker tries to tap all possible resources for reliable data before beginning to make an assessment. The validity of each piece of information is considered before an effort is made to categorize and to integrate information. If the worker recognizes that he or she is drawn toward making an assumption, the question "Why am I assuming this?" should be asked. It is possible that the assumption comes from one's "sixth sense," which may be a useful guide to tracking down the facts for a valid assessment.

THE PROBLEMS

As stated earlier, when data are gathered, they are clustered under the three headings of "problem," "person," and "environment." The "problem" is the need, concern, issue, or difficulty that has been identified for study and action by both the worker and the system of contact. Before deciding what needs to be done, or even which problem should be considered first, the worker and the system need to have a clear understanding of the scope, duration, and severity of each problem.

What is the scope of the problem? How many people are involved in the cause or the effect of the problem? What other systems are feeling this problem? Where can the boundary be drawn between those who have the problem and those who are outside of the problem?

The worker also studies the duration of the problem. When did it begin? How long has it been going on? Has it been continuous or intermittent? The longer a problem exists, very likely, the longer it will take to break the pattern and bring about whatever change is needed. The shorter the duration, the greater the chance of quick and effective intervention.

And finally, the worker asks: How serious is this problem? A guide for understanding the severity of a problem is to consider it in terms of a life-or-death scale. If, for example, the problem is physical, the worker asks: Is the illness terminal? What is the potential for cure? If the problem is more interpersonal or social, the worker considers the possibility of its leading to the breakdown or destruction of the family, the person, the group, the community, or the relationship.

THE PERSONS

Another major category for data collection is the person or persons who are experiencing the problem. A central concern is the coping capacity of the persons who have the problem. To what extent are the persons experiencing this problem capable of maintaining or improving their level of functioning? How have the persons been able to cope with this or similar problems before? Do the persons have physical, psychological, intellectual, economic, spiritual strengths for dealing with the problem?

In addition to coping capacity, the worker seeks indicators of the extent of motivation the persons have to work on the problem. Do they express a desire to change the situation or to overcome the problem? Do they have hope that things can change? Is any person feeling anxiety, enthusiasm, fear, or pressure that is directly related to the problem, and can this serve as impetus for change? Where do the persons want to begin? Why there? If any person does not seem to have hope that a particular situation can change, why not? What could be a source for motivating this person? What does this person value or want?

THE ENVIRONMENT

The third basic category for data collection is that of the environment that surrounds the persons and problems under study. What is there in the environment that could be relating to this person-problem-environment situation? An ecological foundation emphasizes the need and potential for transactions between organisms and their environments. Environmental factors, qualities, or systems may be present that could serve as resources. Currently, the persons may not be utilizing these resources, owing either to a lack of awareness or understanding or to a fear of rejection. To identify formal and informal resources, the worker gathers information from systems in the environment as well as from client systems. The person is asked, What have you tried before? Did you go anywhere or to anyone to receive help with this problem before? Explorations move from a consideration of the person's immediate environment, with informal resources of family, friends, and local community services, to a study of more formal resources, public or private, in the extended societal environment. The worker asks, What resources are available and appropriate to meet this need with these persons at this time?

In addition to gathering data on environmental resources, the worker looks for information about systems or circumstances in the environment that may have a negative influence on the persons or that may be a contributing factor to the problem. These too may be informal sources—family, friends, community—or formal systems, such as schools, hospitals, and organizations. Is the problem caused or compounded by the person's interaction or interdependence with the environment? More specifically, what systems of the environment relate to the person-problem-environment situation, and how do they promote or prevent the growth or functioning of the persons involved?

In summary, the worker asks, What is the scope, duration, and severity of the problem? Do the persons have the capacity and motivation to work on the problem? What resources or influences are there in the environment that could or do have an impact on the problem? After data are gathered in all three categories for each identified problem, the worker proceeds in the General Method to a collective, comprehensive study for preliminary assessments and problem prioritization.

Throughout all of the stages of the General Method, the skilled worker is recognizing and processing data. As with the identified problem and goals of other stages, the information collected is dynamic and changing. Newly acquired data may lead to a reformulation of the problem, goals, assessment, or planned intervention. It is in the second stage of the General Method that particular emphasis is given to procuring and documenting any information that is missing and believed essential for effective assessment and planning.

MAINTAINING CONFIDENTIALITY

As stated earlier, throughout the process of collecting data, the worker demonstrates belief in the dignity of persons by respecting a client's right to privacy. The worker understands and upholds the principle of confidentiality when information about a system is requested, released, and utilized. Prior to receiving any information about a client, the worker must be sure of having the informed consent of the client. When requesting information, the worker has the responsibility to clarify why the information is needed, how it will be used, and who will have access to the data collected.

In interacting with client systems, the worker helps the client to understand the implications of sharing information. A client who comes to an agency for help is asking for service from the agency. Occasionally, a client may ask a worker not to tell "anyone," including other agency employees, what is being disclosed. In this case, the worker will need to point out to the client that information is shared with those in the agency whose roles relate directly to service delivery, such as supervisors, secretaries, or other service providers who are working on the case. This type of sharing is not a breach of confidentiality. It is in accordance with the Federal Privacy Act of 1974, which recognizes the need for information exchange among those employees of an agency "who have a need for the record in the performance of their duties."[3]

The client should be assured that information shared with a worker will not go outside of the agency without the client's permission. Exceptions to this (e.g., if the person threatens to harm another person or the worker, or if the record is subpoenaed by the court) should be stated also. Unless a state has privileged-communication statutes for social workers, a worker will be expected to comply if issued a subpoena requesting disclosure of information about a client to the court. A worker who receives a subpoena should consult with an attorney to discuss how information is to be disclosed or retained.

As stated, before requesting or releasing information about a client from or to a third party, a worker needs to have the expressed consent of a client. According to Suanna Wilson, ten conditions must be met if a client is to give his or her informed consent:

1. The consumer must be told that there is a desire or a request to release certain data.
2. The consumer must understand exactly what information is to be disclosed. He cannot intelligently decide if he wants it revealed unless he knows exactly what material is in question.
3. In order for the consumer to know what is to be released, he should actually see the material and/or have it read to him and explained in terms he can understand.
4. The consumer must be told exactly to whom the information is being released—name, position, and affiliation.
5. The client must be told why the information is being requested and exactly how it will be used by the receiving party.
6. There must be a way for the consumer to correct or amend the information to ensure its accuracy and completeness before it is released.
7. The consumer must understand whether or not the receiving party has the right to pass the information on to a third party. The consumer must have the right to specify that this not be done without his knowledge and consent.
8. The consumer should be fully informed of any repercussions that might occur should he (a) grant permission for the disclosure or (b) not give permission.
9. The consumer should be advised that his consent for release of information is time-limited and revocable. He should be advised how he can withdraw his consent and be given periodic opportunities for doing so.
10. The consumer's consent for release of information must be in writing on a "Release-of-Information Consent Form."

Generally, workers are cautious in disseminating confidential information to outside agencies. There are times, however, when workers are somewhat careless in discussing the lives and problems of their clients. Occasionally, workers feel a need to let go of the heavy input received during interviews, and to find outlets during informal situations with family, friends, or colleagues. This is not only a serious failure in confidentiality, but also a failure to use supervision or other appropriate channels for ventilation and support.

As data are received, skill is needed in selecting and documenting information for the record. Clients have the right to verify personally the accuracy of information recorded in the permanent files of the agency. When a worker explains what will be done with the information collected, the client should be told about the kind of record kept by the agency and the policy regarding access to records. Discussion about records and confidentiality does not have to be prolonged enough to cause alarm or suspicion. A worker uses skill in determining when and how to talk about different aspects of confidentiality with a client system.

CASE EXAMPLES

Example 1: Agency Boundary

Client: Miss Brown, there's a problem I'm having right now at home that I'd like to talk with you about, but I don't want Mr. Johnson, my husband's worker, to know about it. He would tell my husband, and there would be trouble.

Worker: I'd be happy to talk with you about any problem you may be having, Mrs. Armez, but I'm afraid I can't agree to withholding information from Mr. Johnson. Mr. Johnson and I are working as a team with your family, and we do share information. Is it that you are afraid that Mr. Johnson will discuss the problem with your husband?

Client: Yes, I don't trust Mr. Johnson. He sees my husband every week, and I know they talk about me. He would end up telling my husband what I said.

Worker: You are afraid of what would happen if your husband found out about the problem, is that it?

Client: Yes, I couldn't deal with it if he found out. It would be awful. Do you think Mr. Johnson would tell my husband?

Worker: Mr. Johnson and I talk together to help each other gain a more total understanding of the family situation. We respect what each of you shares with us, and we do not report back on what was said by one to the other.

Client: I don't think I could risk it.

Worker: I can see that you are troubled, Mrs. Armez, and I hope that you will grow in trusting us here at the clinic. I would like to see you get help with whatever is bothering you.

Example 2: Release of Information

Worker: Mr. Armez, when I spoke with your employer, he said he needed a doctor's statement indicating that you are ready to go back to work. I understand that you had a doctor's examination last week. Is that right?

Client: Yes, I saw Dr. Gross last Tuesday. He said I could go back to work by Thursday.

Worker: Fine. In order for me to get a statement from the doctor for your employer, I need to have your consent in writing. I will indicate on this release-of-information form that the doctor's statement will be sent to your employer with a copy to be kept in our file. Is this agreeable with you, Mr. Armez?

Client: Yes, sure. That's OK.

Worker: All right. Let's go over what is stated here on this consent form before you sign it.

In the first example, the worker encourages the client to speak about her problems but makes it clear that what she says will be shared with the co-worker for the case. It is better to have the client hold back from sharing at this time than to have co-workers holding back information from each other. The honesty and concern expressed by the worker in this case help to strengthen the client's trust in the workers and in the agency. In the second case, the worker points out what information is needed, from whom, and for what purpose. The content of the consent form is carefully described and reviewed before the form is signed.

RECORDING DATA

Because of the possibility of a client's misunderstanding or misusing information found in his or her record, one might ask why we bother to keep records. A worker needs to record data for several reasons, including:

1. To enhance service delivery through monitoring progress or regression
2. To account for services and to document need
3. To allow for easy transferability if a worker leaves an agency
4. To contribute to research leading to improved services

Each service agency has its own identified methods for keeping records. Three commonly known ways of recording in social work are (1) process recording, (2) summary recording, and (3) problem-oriented recordings.

Process Recording

Most agencies do not use process recording for their permanent records. This type of recording is a lengthy narrative that describes in detail the interactions and communications that took place during a single interview. This recording may be subdivided into four basic parts (1) presenting situation, (2) narrative, (3) worker's impressions, and (4) future plans. An example of a process recording may be found in Diagram 5-2. After stating the basic information of who, when, where, and why in the section called "presenting situation," the worker narrates what actually took place in the interview. This narrative should include not only what the client said but also what exactly was said by the worker in the sequence as it happened.

The third section of a process recording is for the worker's initial impressions of the person-problem-environment situation and of the worker-system relationship, based on what was said and felt during the interview. This is not a formal assessment of the case but, rather, a current indication of the worker's thoughts about the case and the interview. The worker tries to clarify what he or she thinks now about the persons, problems, and envi-

DIAGRAM 5-2   Process Recording

CASE OF MR. D

I. Presenting Situation

Mr. D is a 40-year-old black male who was seen by social services on 10/7 at his own request. He was presently hospitalized for surgery on his ankle, which did not heal properly. The initial injury occurred about a year ago, at which time, according to the patient, he fell off a ladder.

II. Interview

Mr. D was dozing when I entered the room but stirred and said he was willing to talk for a few minutes. I asked him how he was feeling following his surgery ten days ago. He stated that his ankle was better but his hip was sore from being in bed so much. It is still painful if he moves too much.

He then asked me what I had been able to find out about financial help, since he no longer had any health insurance, and the money he received for Social Security Disability could not possibly take care of the hospital bills. I said that I had been in contact with our business office, which informed me that the necessary forms had been sent to the Department of Social Services informing them of Mr. D's need for assistance. I explained that DSS would contact him following his release to try to reach an agreement regarding his bills.

At this, Mr. D expressed his impatience over his hospitalization. He said he was anxious to be released from the hospital, feeling that he can sit in bed at home as well as he could here. When I suggested that perhaps he was still in need of special services that could best be delivered in the hospital, he replied that he was not receiving any special services that would keep him from going home. Mr. D stated further that he "doesn't trust" the staff. I asked him why he felt this way. He said the doctors did not tell him the truth when he was seen in the clinic prior to his hospital admission. He said he was left with the impression that they were going to break and reset his ankle. He felt that they knew at the time that more extensive surgery was possible, and that he should have been told about this. He was not informed of their decision to do a bone graft until the day he was admitted to the hospital before his surgery. I suggested that perhaps they had not made a definite decision until they had made more careful examination of his X-rays following his visit to the outpatient clinic. I agreed that they could have informed him that this type of surgery was a possibility. Mr. D seemed to accept what I said and made no further comments on the subject.

I then asked Mr. D how things were going at home. He said that his mother, who lived in the apartment below, continued to take care of his two boys and that the boys came to see him almost every afternoon. Mr. D seemed a bit reluctant at this point to discuss his home situation in much depth. When asked about his divorce, he said that this did not become final until last April. Neither he nor the boys ever see his ex-wife. He stated that he had to fight to get custody of the boys but felt his wife didn't want them very much, since she makes no attempt to see them. Mr. D mentioned that during his past hospitalization his sister, rather than his ex-wife, had taken care of his daughter. I asked where his daughter was now, and he said that she had fallen through the ice at Carney Park and drowned last winter while he was recuperating at Rocky Neck Veterans' Home. I asked him how he felt about this incident. He said, while looking out the window towards the park, that his feelings did not matter. His concern was for his sons at present, particularly the older boy, age 11, who was with her at the time. When asked how he felt the boys were doing, he said he thought they had recovered all right, and

DIAGRAM 5-2   (continued)

things were pretty much back to normal. Mr. D. seemed particularly uneasy during this part of our conversation, during which time he began fidgeting with his covers and gazing out the window. Since I did not feel that he trusted me enough at this point to explore his feelings any further, I closed this part of the discussion by saying that perhaps in time it would be easier for him to talk about it. He agreed by saying "yes."

I asked Mr. D if he would like me to come back again next week, if I could stop in for a few minutes to see how he was doing. I mentioned that perhaps by then he would be allowed to get up and around a bit. He added that he had hoped he would be home by next week but if he was still here, he wouldn't mind if I came to see him.

III. Worker's Impressions

My impressions of this client, and this interview in particular, were that there was a great deal to be discussed here, but that at the present time, Mr. D was reluctant to discuss many of his feelings with me. He was satisfied insofar as Social Services had met his financial needs. He did not seem to want the help that could be provided in a social work relationship, helping him to work at his feelings in many areas, including his hospitalization, his divorce, and his daughter's death.

IV. Future Plans

While the patient refuses to discuss his feelings and concerns regarding areas such as his daughter's death and his divorce at this time, he may open up after a few more interviews. I plan to see him again next week.

ronment and the worker-system interaction that just took place. Impressions may include a consideration of how the worker thinks he or she conducted the interview.

In the fourth section of a process recording, the worker describes future plans for the case. He or she asks the question, What next? This section includes what the worker and the system have agreed on as the next step in the process, and any other actions the worker expects to take concerning the case.

Process recording is primarily a tool for supervision. It is submitted to a supervisor for review prior to a supervisory session. The supervisor reviews the record with the worker and indicates strengths and weaknesses in interviewing skills. The worker is helped to consider possible options or directions for proceeding with the case. Usually, process recordings are kept in a separate folder for the worker and do not become a part of the permanent record.

Summary Recording

Many agencies use a type of summary recording for their permanent records. Here, contacts for a period of time, generally not longer than three months, are summarized. In a summary recording, a worker follows a four-part outline similar to that of process recording. The topical headings used are (1) basic information, (2) content summary, (3) worker's impressions, and (4) future plans. The basic information given in a summary recording states the dates and places of contact, the persons interviewed, and the purpose for coming together. The content section highlights the topics and themes addressed during sessions, along with any major decisions reached during the period of time covered in the summary. The last two sections give the worker's impressions of what has happened over the period of time covered and the future plans for continued work by worker and system.

Problem-Oriented Recording

Problem-oriented recording (POR) is a clearly identified system of recording that originated with Dr. Lawrence Weed in health-care systems.[5] Several modified versions of this method are presently in use by many human service agencies.[6] Using a problem focus, recording usually begins with a list of all the problems identified to date, with an indication of when the problem was first recognized. For each problem listed, a brief assessment is given according to a "SOAP" format. The *S*ubjective data (according to client's perception of the problem), the *O*bjective data (as documented by testing, observation, and written and oral verification), the *A*ssessment (worker's judgment), and the *P*lan (immediate) for each problem on the list are stated in a concise manner.

For example, a problem listed for Jerry (15 years old, oldest of five children, both parents at home) was "below-average school performance— potential school dropout." The SOAP assessment for this problem was recorded as follows:

S— 7/10: Jerry says he finds school boring, and he plans to quit when he is 16. 7/12 and 7/14: His teachers say he doesn't seem to be able to grasp the material, although he tries very hard.

O— Jerry's full-scale IQ is 80 (Performance 90, Verbal 70, WISC-R, 5/21/83). He repeated eighth grade. With current grades, he may have to repeat ninth grade. There is only one ninth grade at Brown Junior High, and it is geared toward students of average or above-average intelligence.

A— Jerry is finding school work difficult, owing to his limited intellectual abilities and his being placed in a class for students with average or above-average intelligence. He has a growing sense of inferiority and will probably drop out if he does not receive help.

P— 1. Discuss Jerry's learning needs with Jerry, his parents, the school principal, and Jerry's teachers.
2. Explore resources for tutoring and supportive services for Jerry.
3. Explore other schools for Jerry.
4. Work with all people in item 1 to provide Jerry with the learning opportunities he needs.

Prior to closing a case with POR, a "closing summary" for each problem is stated that includes (1) the status of the problem, (2) the prognosis, and (3) recommendations.

The problem-oriented recording method emphasizes the importance of organization and preciseness in recording. Information is recorded in a manner that is very available for research, documentation, and evaluation. The method offers a framework for immediate recall and immediate information provision. The worker is challenged to clarify problems and to progress in a skillful, accountable way. This recording method is particularly appropriate for general practice in which a problem-solving approach is used throughout the process of service.

Other Record Forms

In addition to the three types of recording cited, information collected on a case may also be recorded on fact sheets and in social histories or referral summaries. In most agency files, a basic fact sheet is found inside the cover of each record (see the example in Diagram 5-3). Names of the family members and related resources, dates, addresses, and other factual information are often listed on fact sheets.

In social histories, a brief narrative is given for a variety of general headings. These include family composition, family background, developmental history, education, work, health, religion, economic history, other agencies involved, problem assessment, goals, and future plans. In a referral summary, the worker may add or delete any of these headings, depending on the nature and needs of the setting receiving the referral.

In any recording for permanent records or referrals, the information presented should be as factual as possible. Workers need to be able to document their statements and to substantiate their conclusions. If a worker is making a statement that is an assumption or an opinion, it should begin with such phrases as "It appears to me at this time that . . . because . . ." or "Based on . . . , my impressions at this time are. . . . " Accurate, effective recording calls for skill and sensitivity. As a worker collects data in the second stage of the General Method, it is essential that he or she have skill in recognizing and recording relevant, accurate data in a systematic and professional manner.

WORKING WITH DIFFERENT SYSTEMS

Is there a difference in data collection when it is done with systems of different sizes? Are there variations in the techniques or processes used when a worker is gathering information about a group or community rather than an individual? How is information about a group or community kept confidential when it is frequently disclosed in the presence of several people

DIAGRAM 5-3   Identification and Summary Sheet

```
ADMISSION  NO. _____ DATE  OF  ADMISSION _____ ROOM  NO. _____

PATIENT'S  NAME _____ SEX ____ PHONE _____

HOME ADDRESS _____
                  street              town            state              zip

ADMISSION DATE _____ DISCHARGE DATE _____

PRIOR  ADMISSION _____ ADMISSION  DATE _____ DISCHARGE  DATE _____

ADMITTING DIAGNOSIS _____

_____

FINANCIALLY RESPONSIBLE PARTY _____ RELATIONSHIP _____

ADDRESS _____ PHONE _____
                                                            home      work

POWER OF ATTORNEY     YES _____ NO _____

NOTIFY IN CASE OF EMERGENCY _____ RELATIONSHIP _____

ADDRESS _____ PHONE _____
                                                            home      work

DATE OF  BIRTH _____ AGE ____ PLACE OF  BIRTH _____

U.S.  CITIZEN _____ RELIGION _____ CHURCH _____

MARITAL  STATUS: S  M  W  D _____ MEDICARE  NO. _____

SOCIAL SECURITY NO. _____ BLUE CROSS NO. _____

WELFARE: TITLE XIX NO. _____ OTHERS _____

ATTENDING  PHYSICIAN: NAME _____ PHONE _____

ADDRESS _____

PREVIOUS PHYSICIAN: NAME _____ PHONE _____

ADDRESS _____

PHARMACIST: _____ PHONE _____

DENTIST: _____ PHONE _____

PODIATRIST: NAME _____ PHONE _____

FUNERAL  DIRECTOR _____ PHONE _____

HOSPITAL  PREFERENCE _____ PHONE _____

DISCHARGED DIAGNOSIS _____

_____

DISCHARGE DATE _____ TO _____
```

who are not agency personnel? Is there a different method for recording information when working with a family, group, or community?

The size of a system does not alter the framework for organizing data under the three basic headings of "problem," "person," and "environment." The process and techniques used in collecting data, however, may differ when one is working with a larger system, such as a group or a community. Keeping in mind that the system of contact is made up of distinctive parts, the worker is sensitive to the needs and perceptions of individual members. Focus, however, is directed toward identifying the felt needs of the system as a whole. The worker tries to relate to the system in its entirety and to help its members to grow in an awareness of their common identity and concerns.

Techniques are needed to locate information of a common nature and to sift out uncommon information of a personal nature. To determine the problems, motivation, and capacity of a larger system, and not just of a few outspoken members of the larger system, is a major challenge for a worker. In the data-collection stage of the General Method, the worker tries to become aware of the problems, persons, and environmental resources and influences of the entire system. An effort is made to collaborate with the members of the system in collecting information. They are encouraged to distinguish fact from assumption, to be open to diverse perceptions and feelings, and to focus on common problems and needs.

Even prior to bringing the members of a system together to engage in a working relationship, workers frequently begin the process with a preliminary period of data collection by individual contact. Before convening the entire system, the worker needs to find out what constitutes the boundary of the system and to develop an initial awareness of its members and their felt needs. A worker will often speak with individual members of a family, group, or community to give them the opportunity to share freely and in confidence their perceptions of the system and its problems. This enables the worker to locate motivating issues and potential leaders for the system. Once the system and the worker start to work together for identified goals, they jointly collect data on particular problems, related influences, and resources.

Although the categories for data collection within the ecological framework of problems, persons, and environment are basically the same for all systems, the nature of the content addressed may differ. When working with a larger system such as a community, for example, the resources for and influences on the environment are generally of a formal nature. These may include foundations, federal and local policy makers, and organizations or their representatives. Information collected to be presented to these resources or influences usually has to be clearly factual with documentation. Although skill for recognizing feelings is strongly needed when collecting information with smaller systems, skill in acquiring and presenting facts is paramount in working with larger systems. Workers need to be aware of the general feeling tones of larger systems and their individual members, but change in larger systems is strongly dependent on documented facts. Members of an organization may be very sympathetic toward a cause, but they may not be able to change their larger structure unless there is documented evidence of the need for and value in changing the policies or procedures of the organization. With larger complex systems, the information collected is mainly of a formal, factual nature.

As mentioned, a person may be hesitant to speak out about issues or concerns in a large system. This hesitance may be due to a fear of reprisal later by other members of the system or by outsiders who have been informed of what the person said. Before they can develop confidence in sharing openly, members of a large system need clarification of what will happen when information is disclosed within the system. Although a worker may state how he or she and the agency will handle information obtained, the worker is not able to guarantee that other members of the system will keep in confidence what will be shared. Prior to encouraging the disclosure of information within a system, a worker makes an effort to get the members of the system to mutually agree on a code for themselves regarding how they will treat what is said at their meetings. This code should be restated or reconsidered whenever new members are added or there is some question whether it will continue being enacted.

CASE EXAMPLE

Group Worker: Before we go on, I would like to talk with all of you about the confidential nature of what goes on in this group. As far as the agency is concerned, anything shared within the group is kept within the agency unless we all give our consent to have certain information shared outside. A summary of each meeting is recorded in the agency record, and any group member may request to review these recordings. The only exception for allowing information to go outside the agency would be if you revealed that you planned to injure someone or if I or our records were subpoenaed to court. Any questions about this?

Mary (group member): Yeah, but what about everyone else here? How do I know that what I say won't be talked about out on the street by someone here?

Worker: Well, let's talk about that. What do we think about a group member sharing what is said here with someone outside of the group? How do you want to handle what is said during our meetings?

John (group member): I don't think it's right to go and tell other people. We came here because we wanted help, but I don't want everyone in the world to know my business.

Worker: I hear you saying that you don't think members should talk about what we share here with others. I wonder what the rest of the members think about this.

Others: (Five others speak in support of John's position.)

Worker: Are we saying as a group that we will keep in confidence whatever is said within this group? Are there any exceptions to this?

In terms of record keeping, all of the three methods described earlier for recording data collected during an interview (process, summary, problem-oriented) may be used to record contacts with systems of any size.

Whether working with an individual, group, family, or community, the worker records fundamental facts about the presenting situation (who, when, where, why), the essential content addressed during the contact (problems, needs, feelings, decisions), and the goals and plans that were established. In recording each contact or contacts over a period of time, a worker may also include his or her impressions of the person-problem-environment situation.

When recording about a large system, a worker needs to distinguish between what is recognized as a problem or need of one or some members of the system and what is seen as a common problem or need of the entire system. For example, when compiling the problem list for problem-oriented recording for a family system, the worker indicates when a problem belongs to one or some members rather than to the whole family.

CASE EXAMPLE

PROBLEM LIST

ACTIVE	DATE
Father's unemployment	10/2
Inadequate housing	10/2
Father's drinking	11/3
Mother-father communication	11/3
Jimmy's sore throat	11/3

In this example, whereas the housing need is common to all, it is apparent that there are individuals within the family who have particular problems that influence the functioning of the entire family: The unemployment and drinking problems are the father's; mother and father have a problem with communication; and Jimmy has the sore throat.

In using summary recording to record an activity group session, a format may be followed such as that illustrated in Diagram 5-4. Here again, the worker basically indicates the presenting situation, central content (activity, process, problem), the leader's impressions, and future plans. The recording format provides opportunity for the worker not only to describe the problems and behaviors of the group, but also to identify the problems and behaviors of individuals that influence the functioning of the group.

Making a process record of a community meeting may be extremely lengthy and time-consuming. The framework found in Diagram 5-5 provides guidance for highlighting important aspects of a meeting. Basically, the content addressed includes facts about the presenting situation, content discussed, and future plans and goals. The topics that are covered include how the worker perceived his or her role, before, during, and after the meeting, as well as the worker's impressions. This recording, as with all process

DIAGRAM 5-4   Weekly Group Record

DATE _____

GROUP _____ LEADER _____

ATTENDANCE: TOTAL MEMBERS PRESENT—MALE _____ FEMALE _____

       VISITORS _____

BRIEF DESCRIPTION OF MEETING: Please record briefly important discussions, decisions, and problems. *Give your own evaluation of the meeting.*

WHAT WAS THE MAIN ACTIVITY OF THE GROUP AT THIS MEETING? Who initiated the main activity, and how did the group as a whole respond to the suggested activities? What program suggestions did you mention or bring up in the meeting?

SITUATIONS REQUIRING INDIVIDUAL ATTENTION: Please record problems, group or individual conflicts, and other incidents that you may want some help with from your supervisor.

LEADER'S INTERPRETATION REGARDING BEHAVIOR OF INDIVIDUALS: If there was any unusual behavior, why do you think the individuals and the group as a whole behaved as they did?

PLANS FOR THE NEXT MEETING:

---

recordings, may be used in supervision as a teaching tool. It lends itself to pointing out a worker's skill and sensitivity for working with communities.

USING THE HOLISTIC FOUNDATION IN DATA COLLECTION

In the second stage of the General Method, the social worker uses values, knowledge, and skills from the holistic foundation of practice identified in Diagram 1-5, Chapter 1. The practice principles of confidentiality, self-determination, and nonjudgmental attitude are strongly apparent in the actions and transactions of the worker during data collection. As pointed

DIAGRAM 5-5   Process Recording for a Community Meeting

I. Presenting Situation
   Worker's name
   Name of community
   Place of meeting
   Date of meeting
   Who called the meeting?
   For what purpose?
   Number of people attending
   Who were the people at the meeting? (Whom did they represent?)

II. Meeting
   What took place? Topics, decisions, actions (including worker's), in sequence.

III. Worker's Impressions
   How do the community members see themselves? See you?
   Do they see themselves as a community?
   What are your impressions of the roles and behaviors of participants?
   What do they want to accomplish individually? As a community?
   What do they want from you?
   Did they and you come away with something as a result of the meeting?
   How did you use yourself during the meeting?
   How did you feel about the meeting—before, during, and after?

IV. Future Plans
   What do they do now?
   What do you do now?

out, the client has the right to choose what personal information will be disclosed, as well as to choose how this information will be used. The worker strives to gather factual information for a documented assessment that is free from assumption or personal value judgments.

In proceeding in the helping process with collecting data about persons and environments, the worker uses various theories to comprehend the nature and functioning of client, target, and resource systems. Through observing and inquiring directly or indirectly, the worker obtains information in a manner that reflects the use of theories from the holistic foundation. Seeing the data collected in the light of basic theory, the worker is able to identify such characteristics as coping capacities, developmental levels, communication patterns, and role expectations. Theory also helps the worker to recognize whether certain factors are the cause or the effect of problem situations. For example, in inquiring about the time when 8-year-old Jim started to insist that the light be kept on in his room at night, the worker learned that it was around this same time that Jim started to have learning problems at school, to become increasingly possessive of his mother, and to act fearful toward his father. Knowledge of such theories as psychosexual and psychosocial development, as well as role and stress theory, helped the worker to pursue inquiry for understanding the regressive behavior.

The skills of the holistic foundation that are used in the data-collection stage of the General Method include relationship skills, problem-solving skills, and professional skills. In sifting out facts of importance for understanding and planning, the worker listens, questions, and clarifies. He or she may work with various systems to identify problems and needs or to collaborate in exchanging information for effective teamwork. Recording and research skills are used to test out and to register the findings collected.

HUMAN DIVERSITY IN DATA COLLECTION

Culture

From an identification of problems, feelings, and goals in the engagement stage, the worker and system move on to gathering information for problem assessment. As a worker begins to collect information about problem, person, and environment, some cultural systems may be hesitant to give information about personal or family problems, particularly to someone from a different ethnic group. The worker, therefore, needs to be explicit in making known what information is needed and how it will be used. Whereas some systems may wish to move quickly through this stage, with reliance on intuition (Mexican-American, for example), others may need to move cautiously, with reliance on fact and reason (Japanese, for example).

To collect data on the actual participants in a problem-person-environment situation, it is important for a worker to understand the roles and structures in the culture of the system. For example, there is a "four-fold structural typology" found among Puerto Rican families. As described by Fitzpatrick, there are (1) extended family systems—a wide range of natural or ritual kin, (2) the nuclear family—father, mother, and children, (3) father, mother, their children, and children of other unions of the husband or wife, and (4) the mother-based family with children of one or more men, but no permanent male figure in the home.[7]

In locating resources or influences in the environment, a worker needs to know who or what resource would be appropriate to contact for certain problems. In the Puerto Rican culture, for example, there may be ready acceptance to have *compadres* and *comadres* (godparents) become foster parents if a child needs to be placed. To mediate in matters such as property disputes, however, it may be more appropriate in this culture to use distant relatives, in order to avoid the risk of losing friendships with closer relatives if they became involved.[8]

Sexual Variation

During data collection in the General Method, as the three focal points of problem, person, and environment are explored, the problems of gay and lesbian clients may be seen more clearly by a worker when the "dual perspective" is applied.[9] In gathering information about person and environment, a worker looks to see if an individual has a "nurturing system" as well as a "sustaining system" in his or her environment. The worker also considers the values and expectations of all three (individual, nurturing system, and sustaining system), realizing that the more they share in common, the greater their congruence, "goodness of fit,"[10] and mutual health and growth. Even if an individual is found to be different or nonacceptable by a sustaining system, he or she can grow and thrive, provided there is a strong, supportive nurturing system. Unfortunately, many gay or lesbian individuals have no nurturing system where they are understood and supported, and they live in a very rejecting, condemning sustaining system. Even if there is a family or cultural community, a gay or lesbian person may not be accepted by them because they reject his or her sexual life style.

In collecting data, a worker inquires about a system's current and potential environment. When working on problems related to sexual variation with gay or lesbian clients, a worker gathers information not only about existing resources in the client system's life space, but also about possible formal and informal resources that could offer support for gay and lesbian persons in their environments.

Gender Sensitivity

In collecting data during the second stage of the General Method, a worker needs to have a sensitivity to gender when information about problem, person, and environment is gathered. Again, a man who believes he should be strong and successful may resist exposure of his personal, family, or social problems. He may withdraw from talking about himself at any length. His environment may be limited in nurturing networks. He may feel comfortable only when talking objectively about his work or society at large with its organizations and institutions.

Women may be in a protective, unknowing position in which they actually or apparently know little about the facts of and influences on their problem-person-environment situation. They may express feelings of helplessness and even fear of succeeding in resolving their problems. They may be struggling over a sense of being disloyal or ungrateful if they criticize or talk about their husbands or family problems. Guilt feelings may emerge if a woman begins to explore and reach out to her extended environment for support and strength.

In collecting data, a worker is also sensitive to the other diversity variables of age and stages, endowment and personality, value systems, class, and geographic location. The worker's skill in inquiry, use of informative resources, and in recognizing facts, custom, and feelings will reflect the extent of sensitivity the worker has to various dimensions of human diversity.

DATA COLLECTION IN DIVERSE FIELD AREAS

1. FIELD AREA: CHILD WELFARE

A. Agency: State Department of Children's Services

B. Client System

K, a 15-year-old female in an emergency shelter. (For more background information, see Chapter 4, Engagement in Diverse Field Areas, I. Child Welfare.)

C. Engagement Summary

The feelings expressed during engagement included loneliness, restlessness, hatred of self and others, and depression. The problems and goals identified during this stage are listed in Diagram 4-3, Chapter 4.

D. Data Collection

Problem: During data collection, the worker learned that K was well-liked by those who lived in the group home where she was first placed. The group parents described K as quiet and fearful. She seemed to get lost in the group, and therefore, they thought a foster home was a good plan for her at the time. The foster home parents described K as stubborn and pouty. She never seemed to get enough attention and didn't want to do her share of the work. They said they tried to tell K to stay away from the boy she ran away with, but she would not listen to them.

In school, K had been performing at an average level while she lived in the group home. During her stay in the foster home, she remained in the same school she had attended while in the group home. Her grades started to drop before she ran away. Her teachers said that K daydreamed a lot, but they thought she did have the potential for at least average achievement. As her marks started to drop, the school personnel had a pupil-appraisal team meeting. The Children's Services worker who had the case prior to the current worker attended the meeting. It was agreed at this meeting that K would be referred to the local mental health center for counseling. K refused to go to the center, saying she was not "crazy."

Person: During data collection, the worker discovered that K was extremely motivated to work on her two stated goals. She said she missed school and even missed her teachers. She wished she could go back to the group home, where they were "nice" to her. K began to say that she knew that she was "messed up," and that she probably needed to go for counseling. She hoped someone could help her so she wouldn't feel "so awful inside."

She thought that a boy at the shelter was starting to like her, but she was "afraid of getting too close." The worker at the shelter described K as "shy" and "noninvolved with the activities or residents of the shelter."

Environment: The emergency shelter had a residence time limit of four weeks. In exploring possible resources for K, the worker learned that K's biological father had moved out of state and left no forwarding address. K's stepfather had been taken to court for child sexual assault, and her mother blamed K for reporting it. K's mother did not want K to be returned home, "ever." There were no relatives interested in caring for K. K's foster parents did not want her to return either. Although there was no opening in K's previous group-home placement, the worker located another group home with an opening in a neighboring city. Services available for residents in this home included ongoing casework by an M.S.W. and weekly peer-group meetings, where discussions focused on such topics as "sex," "parents," and "growing up confused."

E. Charted Progress

During the process of data collection, goals were expanded to include K's expressed desire to get help with her personal feelings and problems. These new, mutually agreed upon goals were added to the two goals identified during engagement and were recorded as shown in Diagram 5-6. Since the date when these goals were agreed on was different from the date of problem identification, the later date was recorded in the "goal" column.

Note: The paperwork required throughout the process of working with K included the following:

> Summary recordings of all contacts with K and related resources
>
> Referral summary for the group home
>
> Case summary for the court in preparation for a petition to seek continuance of commitment
>
> Transfer summary at termination

DIAGRAM 5-6   Ongoing Recording

DATE IDENTIFIED	PROBLEM/ NEED	GOAL
1/12	No permanent home	a. To obtain a permanent placement b. To maintain a permanent placement
1/12	Out of school	To reeneter school
1/12	Personal problems a. Poor self-esteem b. Identity confusion c. Sexuality (relation- ships, behavior) d. Depression	Personal goals (1/19) a. To feel better about self b. To clarify identity c. To be able to have good friendships with males d. To stop "feeling down"

II. FIELD AREA: GERONTOLOGY

A. Agency: Seaside Nursing Home

B. Client System

Mrs. J, an 80-year-old Portuguese woman in a skilled nursing facility. (For additional background information, see Chapter 4, Engagement in Diverse Field Areas, II. Gerontology.)

C. Engagement Summary

The feelings expressed during engagement included distrust, fear, anger, and abandonment. The problems and goals identified during this stage are listed in Diagram 4-4, Chapter 4.

D. Data Collection

Problem: The worker attended a patient-care conference on Mrs. J with the staff of the nursing home. She learned at this time that Mrs. J was causing a disruption on her floor. She was fighting with the nurses when they came to give her a bath. She sometimes stood at the door of her room and called the other residents names. On occasion, she would refuse to go to meals or to leave her room. She was often found talking to herself in Portuguese. Also reported were minor incidents of confusion and irrational mood swings.

Person: As data were being collected, Mrs. J began to talk more freely with the worker about herself and her background. She said she came to America when she was 20 years old. She married shortly after arriving and had three children by the time she was 25. Her husband left the family when the youngest child was 13 years old. Mrs. J used to clean houses and take in washing to earn money. All of her children had to leave school and get jobs. She said she was "hard" on her children and wished she had been nicer to them. Mrs. J said she wished she could go back to Portugal, where she believes her husband is living. She could not recall the marriage names of her children or the name of her husband's village.

Mrs. J began to express an interest in knowing more about the other residents. She said she yelled at them because they would not look at her. She was angry at the nurses because they tried to undress her for a bath late in the morning after she was up and dressed. She wished the nurses and the people would like her and agreed that she was willing to try to get along better with them.

Environment: During data collection, the worker learned from the hospital social worker who made the referral to the nursing home that one of Mrs. J's daughters had admitted her to the hospital. During admission, the daughter stated that her father left the family several years ago and could not be located, and that Mrs. J had been living alone until she no longer could go out by herself. The daughter said that she was moving out of state and would send a forwarding address (which never arrived). She said that her sister and brother also lived out of state.

The worker also learned that there was no one in the nursing facility who spoke Portuguese. The director of volunteers offered to try to locate someone who spoke the language and who would be willing to visit with Mrs. J. The worker learned from Mrs. J that she used to attend a church where the pastor and several members of the congregation were Portuguese. The worker located the church, and the pastor said he would go to see Mrs. J. Other resources available to Mrs. J in the nursing home included program planning, recreational therapy, choir, and church services. There were also weekly resident meetings that Mrs. J could attend.

E. Charted Progress

During the data-collection stage, the problem list was extended to include Mrs. J's disruptive behavior on her floor. The additional problems were recorded as indicated in Diagram 5-7. Mrs. J's organic brain syndrome was not listed as a problem in the social service record because she was receiving treatment for this from the medical staff.

Note: The recording required throughout the process of working with Mrs. J included the following:

Intake summary

Weekly summaries of contacts with Mrs. J

Patient-care conference reports

Social service tasks, entered in the problem-oriented recordings of the nursing home

Record of outside contacts made and information obtained as data were collected

On-going contracted plan

Termination summary

III. FIELD AREA: PUBLIC SOCIAL WELFARE

A. Agency: State Social Services

B. Client System

Mr. and Mrs. P and their two children, ages 2 and 4, in need of emergency shelter and more permanent housing. (For more background information, see Chapter 4, Engagement in Diverse Field Areas, III. Public Social Welfare.)

C. Engagement Summary

The feelings expressed during engagement included helplessness, anger, rejection, and confusion. The problems and goals identified during engagement are listed in Diagram 4-5, Chapter 4.

D. Data Collection

Problem: Shelter is a basic human need. There is a lack of available housing for low-income families in the local city and surrounding areas. Housing is a crucial need for the P family at this time. The P's have had several

DIAGRAM 5-7   Ongoing Recording

DATE IDENTIFIED	PROBLEM/ NEED	GOAL	TASKS	CONTRACT	DATE ANTICI-PATED	DATE ACCOMP-LISHED
9/25	Poor adjustment: seclusiveness—not leaving room alone	To be able to leave room alone				
9/25	Cultural isolation: need to communicate in native language	To be visited by someone who speaks Portuguese				
9/27	Unfamiliar with staff and resources of nursing home	To get to know staff and resources of the nursing home	To meet twice a week with worker	Worker and Mrs. J	10/4 and every Tuesday and Thursday thereafter	10/4 10/9 10/11 10/16
10/2	Fighting with nurses over bath	To work out bath schedule with nurses				
10/2	Calling residents names	To stop calling residents names				

moves since their marriage five years ago. They have been evicted from apartments at least three times in the past because they failed to keep up with rent payments. The P's said that they had to use the money they received from AFDC to buy food. The worker also learned that they currently had no money left for food. The family receive AFDC because Mr. P's psychological problems prevent him from maintaining employment (confirmed by Income Maintenance Department's eligibility technician, who has letters from psychiatrists on file). The AFDC check and food stamps for the month are being held at central office until the status and address of the family are clarified.

Persons: Although Mr. P said he bought a newspaper to see if there are any available apartments in the area, he and his wife do not appear to be motivated to get involved in apartment hunting. They are anxious to be relocated, but they expect that others (the state or Mrs. P's father) will find a place for them. They are blaming others (the state, Mrs. P's father, landlords, friends) for their problem of being homeless. They express a strong dependency on others to meet their needs. They do not seem to have the ability or the desire to become actively involved in problem-solving or in changing their perspective or behavior. With Mr. P's written permission, the worker contacted his psychiatrist at the mental health center, Saint John's Hospital (where he had been treated), and also got in touch with the Vocational Rehabilitation Department (where he had been tested). Mr. P's mental illness and continued inability to work were verified. The psychiatrist said that Mr. P is faithful in keeping his weekly appointments at the center. The children appear to be in good health. Mrs. P said that it was about time for the children to go for a checkup at the health clinic, but that she had lost their medical card. She said the income-maintenance worker was sending her another one.

Environment: Mr. and Mrs. P said that they have no family or friends who are willing to take them in, even for the night. Mrs. P said she knew that her father was trying to find a place where she and the children could live.

Three possible temporary shelters were located: (1) Salvation Army, (2) City Hotel, and (3) Center City Motor Inn. For more permanent housing, the worker contacted five social service agencies in the surrounding area. None of them were able to provide any information on possible housing. The process of making a Section-8 (rent subsidy) application to the Housing Department was reviewed.

During the initial period of data collection, the worker also explored possible resources for emergency food donations. The following sources were identified: (1) Community Renewal Center, (2) Salvation Army, (3) Saint Michael's Church, (4) Center City Churches Food Bank, and (5) Good News Soup Kitchen.

Throughout the entire process of working with the P family, information continued to be collected as additional needs and possible resources emerged. Data collection extended to information about the following (including referral procedures):

Protective services (possible placement of children)

Social Security

Appeal process when placement extension was refused (fair hearing)

Housing resources

Emergency fuel banks

Moving coverage

Medical transportation service

Appliance repair

Resources for Thanksgiving basket and children's Christmas presents

Community health services

E. Charted Progress

Adding to the recorded problem and goals, the worker listed the immediate need for food and the identified problem of poor money management (Diagram 5-8). The family agreed with the goal of securing food, but they were resistant to admitting that help was needed with managing their money (no goal recorded). Although the worker became aware of the additional problems of Mr. P's unemployment and mental incapacity, these problems were not added to the problem list for service from the worker, because they were already being addressed by the Income Maintenance Department and the mental health center.

Note: Information about Mr. P's unemployment and mental illness was recorded as part of data collection in the record. Additional paperwork during the total time the generalist worked with the P family included the completion of the following:

Authorization forms for placement of family

Section-8 housing application

Emergency food applications

Documentation that the P's were searching for housing

Letter to authorize medical care

Request for medical transportation

Release-of-information forms

Request for extension of emergency placement

Request for fair hearing

Application for Social Security benefits

Application for energy assistance

IV. FIELD AREA: COMMUNITY SERVICE

A. Agency: Clayton Neighborhood House

B. Client System

Four Hispanic families without heating in their apartments on the second floor of 33 L Street. (For more background information, see Chapter 4, Engagement in Diverse Field Areas, IV. Community Services.)

DIAGRAM 5-8   Ongoing Recording

DATE IDENTIFIED	PROBLEM/ NEED	GOALS
9/28	Housing for P family	a. To find emergency shelter for the P family b. To locate an apartment for long-term residence by the family
9/28	Emergency food	a. To obtain emergency food supply b. To find resource to supply food until AFDC check is received
9/28	Poor money management	

C. Engagement Summary

As the worker engaged the families in the problem-solving process, they expressed feelings of frustration and helplessness. There were also feelings of fear and anger expressed toward the landlord. The problem of inadequate heating was identified, and all agreed on the recorded goal, "To obtain consistent and adequate heating for second-floor residences of the L Street apartment house."

D. Data Collection

Problem: As the worker explored the problem further, she learned that residents were paying a monthly rent of $250 for a one-room apartment. The families were told that heating was included in the rent. Although one person in each of the families was employed, they said that they could not afford any increase in rent or to pay for heating themselves.

The worker had brought a thermometer with her on the visit. She checked the temperature in each of the apartments, and all of them registered about 50°F.

Since none of the residents at the meeting had lived in the building the previous winter, they did not know if a similar problem had existed last year. They shared how difficult it was for them to find a place to live. No one was requesting help with relocation at this time.

Persons: The worker learned that there were fifteen children (ages 6 months to 16 years) and seven adults (no one over 50) living in the four apartments. Although the residents were motivated to come together to discuss their heating problem, everyone was afraid to have a direct confrontation with the landlord. Mrs. T said that she and her husband had tried to call the landlord, but he was not available and never returned their call. Some members said he is hard to talk with, because he doesn't understand Spanish and they don't speak English. The residents were motivated to work on the heating problem with the worker, but they asked her to contact the landlord in their behalf.

Environment: The worker learned from those attending the meeting that an individual who lived downstairs worked as a janitor in the building. They said that they had complained to him about a lack of heat upstairs, but he told them that they would have to tell the landlord. The worker stopped at the janitor's apartment on the way out, but he was not home. The name and phone number of the landlord were obtained from the residents.

With further inquiry, the worker learned that the landlord lived in a neighboring town, and that he had owned two other buildings in the same area where the L Street apartment was located. The two buildings were recently sold to the city.

When the worker called Mr. X, the landlord, he said that he was not aware of a problem with heating for the second floor. The worker informed him that each of the apartments on the floor was registering a temperature of 50° or below. Mr. X said that he had asked the janitor of the building to help to keep heating costs to a minimum, but he didn't realize this was being done through an uneven distribution of heat in the building. He said he would contact the janitor and have the problem taken care of right away.

The worker inquired if Mr. X knew that his residents had tried to reach him to tell him about the heating problem. Mr. X said he was very busy and often found it hard to find time to return all of his calls. He said also that his secretary finds it difficult to understand what the Spanish-speaking tenants are trying to say over the phone.

E. Charted Progress

The worker entered a summary report of her visit to L Street in the record. She recorded pertinent information collected from speaking with the landlord and the residents. Paperwork completed while working with the community of residents included a planned contract that was developed with the residents (see Chapter 6).

V. FIELD AREA: EDUCATION

A. Agency: Keeney Elementary School

B. Client System

Jim G, an 8-year-old black third grader with regressive behavior in school and at home. (For more background information, see Chapter 4, Engagement in Diverse Field Areas, V. Education.)

C. Engagement Summary

Although presenting problems and goals were discussed with Jim and his mother (as outlined in Diagram 4-7, Chapter 4), feelings were not expressed, and there was not a clear understanding of the cause of Jim's problems throughout the first three weeks of contact. The worker proceeded with data collection, realizing that the engagement period needed to be extended.

D. Data Collection

Problem: The worker reviewed Jim's school record and the nurse's report. Jim was in good health and he had performed at an above average academic level during his first two years of school. His teacher said that in September, when school first started, Jim seemed happy and interested in school. She wondered if he should be placed in a learning-disability classroom because he was getting so far behind in his work. Jim's previous testing and academic performance showed that he did not have a learning disability.

Persons: Although Jim seemed to like meeting with the social worker, he did not care if he did not do well in school. He hoped he wouldn't have to repeat a grade. He said his father had told him that school wasn't really that important and that Jim could come to work with him in the car lot when he got older. Whenever Jim or the worker began to talk about home or his parents, Jim became restless and looked a little frightened.

In one session, after meeting for three weeks, Jim began to play with the black man and woman puppets. He had them begin to dance together and then they started to hit each other. He took the frog puppet and had him yell out, "Hey, stop that!" The worker commented, "It sounds like froggie wants them to stop." Jim continued with the frog shouting, "Stop that fighting, do you hear?" The worker said it looked like froggie was getting upset, and she wondered what froggie was feeling. Jim said, "He's scared. He hates it." The worker said, "I wonder what froggie's afraid of." Jim took the woman doll and put her back on the shelf. He then became quiet and sat down. The worker asked if that was it. "Was froggie afraid that she would go away?" Jim didn't answer. The worker softly said that she knew that sometimes children are afraid that their parents will go away if they fight with each other. Jim looked away. The worker asked if Jim was ever afraid that his mother might go away. Jim whispered, "Sometimes." The worker then asked if Jim ever told his mother what he was afraid of, and Jim shook his head negatively. The worker wondered if Jim would mind if she told his mother what he was afraid of, and as he got up to leave the room he said, "I don't care."

Environment: The worker learned from the school record that Jim's mother was a nurse and that his father managed a car lot. During the second interview with Mrs. G, the worker asked if she could meet with Jim's father, but Mrs. G said that he was always very busy and worked long hours running the car lot. At the third meeting with Mrs. G, the worker shared with her what had happened in play with Jim. Mrs. G's eyes filled with tears. She then told the worker that in October, she learned that her husband had gone out with another woman. She said that she didn't think Jim noticed that she and her husband were quarreling. She recalled that at one point she did tell her husband that she might take off and leave him and the children. She said she wouldn't really do it but just wanted to scare him. She said her husband assures her that he will never see the woman again, but she finds it hard to trust him and to forgive him.

The worker encouraged Mrs. G to talk with Jim about his fear and to assure him that she doesn't plan to leave home. The worker also asked if Mrs. G couldn't talk with her husband about what was happening with Jim. Mrs. G said that she would try to get her husband to take time off to come in to see the worker with her next week.

E. Charted Progress

During the process of data collection and the extended engagement period, the worker added the newly identified problem of Mr. and Mrs. G's strained relationship to the problem list, as shown in Diagram 5-9. The plan to have Mrs. G talk with Jim and to have Mr. G come in to meet the worker with Mrs. G was also recorded.

Note: The recording of the worker included an ongoing contracted plan developed by the worker, Mr. and Mrs. G, and Jim (presented throughout Chapters 4-9), which was kept in the social service file. The worker also recorded basic factual information in Jim's school record. In addition, a summary of

DIAGRAM 5-9 Ongoing Recording

DATE IDENTIFIED	PROBLEM/ NEED	GOAL	TASKS	CONTRACT	DATE ANTICIPATED	DATE ACCOMPLISHED
11/1	Jim's school tardiness and absenteeism	Jim's regular school attendance (on time every day)	1. See that Jim gets to school on time every day	1. Mrs G	11/5–each school day thereafter	11/5–ongoing
11/1	Jim's declining academic performance	Improved academic functioning (interest, participation, grades)	1. Talk with Jim about school problems	1a. Worker and Jim	11/6 and twice a week thereafter	11/6, 11/8, 11/13, 11/15, 11/20, 11/27
				b. Mrs. G and Jim	11/2	11/2
			2. Follow-up	2. Worker and Jim	11/5	11/15, 11/21
			3. Talk with Jim about home tensions and assure him she will not leave	3. Mrs. G and Jim	11/21	
			4. Meet to discuss Jim's problems in relation to parents' problems	4. Worker, Mr. and Mrs. G	11/27	
11/2	Jim's getting to sleep at night					
11/21	Strain in Mr. and Mrs. G's marital relationship					

each contact was included in the social service file, and a closing summary was added at the time of termination.

VI. FIELD AREA: CORRECTIONS

A. Agency: Juvenile Court

B. Client System

A group of seven male adolescents (all 14 years old) on probation. (For additional background information, see Chapter 4, Engagement in Diverse Field Areas, VI. Corrections.)

C. Engagement Summary

During engagement, the primary goal of getting off probation as soon as possible was clearly stated by all members of the group. The youths also wanted help both with controlling their tempers and with understanding better the "changes" they were all going through (as outlined in Diagram 4-8, Chapter 4). Although they recognized problems they were having in communicating with their parents, they did not want to work on trying to improve their relationships with them. They did not want to talk about their low self-esteem. They expressed anger at having been picked up by the police and put on probation.

D. Data Collection

After an initial period of testing and attempted manipulation of the leaders, group members began to talk more openly about their family backgrounds and life experiences. In addition to collecting data from the youths themselves, the two workers visited the homes of each group member and talked with parents. The workers also talked with the youths' teachers and social workers at the schools they attended. The files of the court for each of the youths were also reveiwed carefully.

Problem: The workers learned that each member of the group had committed more than once the offense that led to his being put on probation. All seven of the youths were seen in their schools as "problem students" who had difficulties in learning and in getting along with teachers and classmates. They were described by teachers as "troublemakers" or "attention seekers." Two of the youths were believed to be junior members of the Savage Nomads or the Ghetto Brothers street gangs.

The group members said that they got into trouble usually when they were mad about something or dared to do it by friends. In one case, breaking and entering was required for initiation into a gang.

Persons: Three of the group members were highly motivated to get the most out of the group and to get off probation (MK, ML, and B). Two others laughed a lot and seemed to take the group "as a joke" (J and T). The remaining two were quiet and less easy to understand (A and C). C appeared very upset over being on probation.

The school reported that test scores indicated that two of the boys had borderline intelligence (A and MK). The others had average or above-average intelligence, even though they had problems with learning.

The racial-ethnic backgrounds of the group participants were as follows: one Italian-American; one Irish-American; two white with mixed ethnic backgrounds; two Afro-American, and one Hispanic.

Environment: All of the youths came from single-parent families. Five lived with their mothers, one lived with his father, and one lived with his grandmother. All came from lower-class or lower-middle-class neighborhoods. The youths had not been active in local recreational centers or programs. Three said they used to attend some church activities for teenagers, but they only went to church when their parents made them go.

The parents and grandmother of the youths expressed interest and concern for their children. Three mothers and T's grandmother said they were afraid that they had no control over their sons (grandson). They all hoped the youths had learned their lesson and would now stay out of trouble. C's father only spoke Spanish. He appeared to be totally overwhelmed, and said he might have to send C back home to Puerto Rico. J's mother had an apparent drinking problem. She said she was thinking seriously of "putting J away" because he was getting too hard to manage. She did not say where she thought she might put him. She had heard that J's father was in jail. Three other group members had older brothers who were in jail or correctional centers (A, T, and ML).

E. Charted Progress

Summary recordings were written that briefly described contacts with the group members' parents, teachers, and school social workers. Brief entries were made each week in the records to indicate attendance and participation in the group. Later, detailed studies of each youth were written when he became eligible to be removed from probation.

CONCLUSION

A frequent mistake of untrained workers is to overlook the need for data collection before intervening with services. Unplanned interventions are often costly, time-consuming, and unsuccessful. Although the process of data collection, which includes recording and documenting facts, may be seen as somewhat arduous and unsatisfying, it is an essential component of professional practice.

In this chapter, central focus was given to identifying and organizing relevant data, distinguishing fact from assumption, understanding the meaning of informed consent, and using appropriate recording formats to document information in writing. These dimensions of data collection are basic to the process, and they prepare the worker to move on to the next stage, assessment. As with all of the stages of helping, circumstances change in human situations, and the art of identifying facts about current realities goes on throughout the dynamic process. A worker must remain open to reformulating or supplementing the information collected, even after it has been organized and used in developing an assessment and planned intervention.

NOTES

[1]*Code of Ethics of the National Association of Social Workers.* NASW Policy Statements 1. (Washington, D.C.: NASW, 1980), p. 5.

[2]Fred N. Kerlinger, *Foundations of Behavioral Research,* 2nd ed. (New York: Holt, Rinehart & Winston, 1973), p. 480.

[3]Federal Privacy Act of 1974. Public Law 93-579, December 31, 1974 (effective September 27, 1975), section 552a (b) (1).

[4]Suanna J. Wilson, *Confidentiality in Social Work: Issues and Principles* (New York: The Free Press, 1978), p. 57. Copyright 1978 by The Free Press.

[5]Lawrence L. Weed, *Medical Records, Medical Education and Patient Care* (Cleveland: Case Western Reserve University Press, 1971).

[6]Wilma Martens and Elizabeth Holmstrum, "Problem-Oriented Recording," *Social Casework* 55 (November 1974): 554–61.

[7]Joseph P. Fitzpatrick, *Puerto Rican Americans* (Englewood Cliffs, N.J.: Prentice-Hall, 1971), p. 83.

[8]Sonia Badillo Ghali, "Culture Sensitivity and the Puerto Rican Client," *Social Casework* 58 (October 1977): 459–68.

[9]Dolores J. Norton, *The Dual Perspective* (New York: Council on Social Work Education, 1978).

[10]Carel B. Germain and Alex Gitterman, "The Life Model of Social Work Practice," in Francis J. Turner, ed., *Social Work Treatment: Interlocking Theoretical Approaches,* 2nd ed. (New York: The Free Press, 1979), p. 362. Copyright 1979 by The Free Press.

6

Assessment

> *The client's meaningful participation in making decisions and formulating the contract is based on the recognition that people are spontaneously active, seeking, and striving beings.*
> —Anthony Maluccio and Wilma Marlow[1]

Throughout the helping process, a worker is listening, evaluating, and acting. There is, however, a certain period of time in the process that is specifically designated as the assessment stage. Assessment is a time for appraising the problem-person-environment triplex and for planning interventions. Collaborative judgment and collaborative decision making are central characteristics of this stage of the General Method. Worker and system of contact move into formal planning based on the information collected in earlier stages. After a clear assessment of the nature of the problems as conceived within the context of *persons in environment,* decisions are made concerning where to begin and how to proceed.

The three major components of the assessment stage are (1) an assessment statement, (2) problem prioritization, and (3) the contracted plan. All three dimensions need to be addressed prior to intervening. The worker who moves directly into implementing change, without taking time for assessment and planning, frequently has to undo or add to the actions taken as he or she comes to realize that such interventions were precipitous or inappropriate.

It is possible that in certain situations a worker will have to act before a full assessment has been completed. A client system may have immediate, urgent needs that must be met before the necessary data can be collected for a formal assessment. There may not be time to plan and contract with a system before intervening in a crisis situation. Action may have to be taken immediately in order to stabilize a life-at-risk situation. Once this is accomplished, however, every effort is made by the worker to involve the system in a mutual process of assessment.

ASSESSMENT STATEMENT

After much listening and gathering of information, the worker is expected to write an *assessment statement* for each problem identified. In the past, an assessment statement was referred to as a *diagnosis* in social work. In 1917, Mary Richmond modified the concept for greater relevance to the profession by calling it a "social diagnosis."[2] Problems that are frequently brought to the attention of social workers are of a material, interpersonal, institutional, or interdependent nature. Using the term *assessment* rather than *diagnosis* helps to avoid the possible inference that an identified problem is seen as a client's illness.

In the assessment statement, the worker begins by clearly indicating who has the problem, what the problem is, and why the problem exists at this time. By the third stage of the General Method, the worker should have sufficient data to describe the actual scope and cause of each problem. A simple formula to keep in mind for initiating an assessment statement is:

_____ has _____ because _____
  (who)   (what problem)   (why)

The "why," or cause of the problem, may be seen in many layers. Often, an immediate causal factor has touched off the problematic situation. In addition, several sequential factors may have led to the immediate cause. For example, Mr. R may be unemployed because he does not have marketable skills in this state, but he lacks such skills because he came from a country where he was socialized into a work world of a very different nature. Or, a client may be unemployed because he was laid off from his job, and maybe this was the result of fiscal cutbacks by the national administration.

In looking for the cause of a problem, the worker realizes that there is a wide range of possible causes, from personal to interpersonal to structural or societal. The cause cited in an assessment statement should be the one most directly related to the problem. If in the worker's judgment, it is necessary to go back further to preceding causes in order to understand the problem for planning and intervention, these causes should also be cited, with a clear explanation of how they are connected to the problem.

In addition to the opening causal statement, an appraisal of the change potential of the problem should be presented in a full assessment statement. A problem's change potential is dependent on the three variables of problem, person, and environment. All three factors are interdependent, with direct impact on the maintenance or resolution of the problem.

First, the worker and the system of contact consider the nature of the problem itself, asking how serious the problem is and what its change potential is. Is this a problem that can be resolved? Is the problem of such a nature that it is irreversible (e.g., suicide, terminal illness, bankruptcy)? More specifically, how wide or deep is the problem? Are many people involved, and to what extent? How long has it been going on? Although the potential for employment of someone who has been unemployed for years may be assessed as low, the potential for employment of someone with a strong work history who was recently laid off may be considered high.

Secondly, the strengths and weaknesses of the person or persons having the problem need to be assessed. What is his or her or their motivation and capacity to make whatever changes may be necessary? Are they able to cope with it alone or to accept help from others? What is their change potential? In order to document a clinical assessment of the strengths or weaknesses of a person or a relationship, *rapid-assessment instruments* are available for use during interviews. A worker's appraisal of clients in such areas as anxiety level, social interaction, marital adjustment, assertiveness, and alcohol or drug use may be supported by scores obtained on the assessment instruments.[3] Of course, there are limitations in the use of scores from questionnaires. A worker would want to cite additional evidence, such as documentation from other professionals or direct observation, to support the assessment.

The third area to be partialized before an integrated assessment of the problem's change potential can be made involves the environment in which the problem is located. What is available in the environment in terms of formal or informal resources to promote the necessary changes? Are there restraining forces in the environment that are stronger than supportive resources? With optimum use of available resources, what is the expected outcome? What is the change potential of the environment for dealing with the problem?

After the three variables of problem, person, and environment are assessed individually, a cumulative assessment of the potential for change may be made for the particular problem within its person-environment context. Basically, the worker's statement may be framed as follows:

The change potential for _____ problem/need of _____
                       (whose)   (what problem)

is assessed as _____ because _____
              (high, somewhat   (reasons: nature of problem,
              high, medium,   person's motivation or capac-
              somewhat low, or   ity, resources and restraints in
              low)   the environment)

In addition to a causal statement and a change-potential statement, the assessment statement should include a judgment about the seriousness or urgency of the problem. The question to be asked here is, To what extent is this a life-or-death matter for these people (or this person) at this time? Even if the change potential for a problem is judged to be very low, immediate attention has to be given to a life-endangering situation. Action must be taken in whatever way possible to protect the lives of those involved. In critical situations, the worker may have to make an immediate referral or serve as an advocate, even though there is little support from the persons or environment involved with the problem. Further considerations of types of interventions will be presented in the next chapter. The point being highlighted here is that an assessment statement should include a professional judgment on the urgency and seriousness of the problem, with supportive data.

EXAMPLE 1: Mr. L, 37 years old, French-Canadian, unmarried, no family
            Problem—unemployment

Assessment Statement

     Mr. L has the problem of unemployment because he is unskilled and unmotivated to seek employment. The nature of the problem is such that the potential for change is very low. Mr. L has been out of work since he moved to this state three years ago. His capacity for work is limited because he does not have the skills sought by employers in this area. He has low motivation to seek work because he experienced a series of rejections in his early efforts to find employment. He is feeling hopeless and depressed. Resources for training or hiring unskilled laborers are extremely difficult to locate in this state. For these reasons, the overall change potential for Mr. L's problem of unemployment is assessed as very low. This is a very serious problem for Mr. L, because he does not qualify for public assistance in this state, and the savings he brought with him are depleted.

EXAMPLE 2: North Central City Community (approximately 600 families, 6-block area, low-income housing)
Problem—no public transportation

Assessment Statement

The North Central City Community has a need for public transportation because the local bus company recently cut off its route into the neighborhood. The problem is somewhat serious, because most people in the neighborhood do not have cars, and they now have to walk eight blocks to get a bus. The people of the community are highly motivated for active involvement in resolving the problem, and they have an organized leadership. The bus company has expressed an openness to reconsider its action and to meet with community representatives. In this situation, the change potential is assessed as high, since resources are available inside and outside of the community.

In assessing data according to the triplex of problem, person, and environment, a worker needs to maintain a holistic perspective of the dynamic interrelationships of social, cultural, and psychological factors. Tools and instruments have been developed to help the professional to see the relationship of a client's psychological and social needs with institutional and environmental resources.[4] In juxtaposing one's professional assessment of the problem, person, and environment triplex, a worker may see more clearly how to partialize and prioritize multiple problems in complex situations.

PROBLEM PRIORITIZATION

Before entering into the goal setting and contracting of this stage of the method, the worker and the system of contact need to prioritize the problems identified and assessed. The questions asked are: What problem do we work on first? Where do we begin? On what basis should a problem be selected as the primary focus for intervention?

As the worker compiles, categorizes, and reviews data, it often becomes apparent that several problems are in need of attention. In response to the question of where to begin, the worker and the system of contact enter into a process for prioritizing the problems identified. To select the most appropriate starting point, the worker must reconsider the initial assessment of the information that was gathered according to the problem-person-environment triplex for each identified problem.

In studying each problem or triplex, the worker keeps in mind the fact that a client needs to build up a sense of trust in the worker's and agency's ability to be helpful. To foster client involvement in a growing, working relationship with the worker, there has to be an experience of success or satisfaction of need as soon as possible. The worker, therefore, tries to select *first* a problem that has a high change potential for resolution or need satisfaction.

As stated earlier, in writing an assessment statement for a problem, the worker asks: What is the change potential of the problem itself, of the persons involved, and of the related environment? Only after assessing all three dimensions for a problem will the worker be able to arrive at a comprehensive and accurate prognosis that can be used for problem prioritization. For some problems, the persons may have high motivation and capabilities, but the environment may provide little opportunity to actualize the persons' potential. An unemployed person, for example, may have skills and high motivation to find a job, but there may be no job openings in the environment. A person may have a problem or need that does not appear to be serious in nature, such as an absence of a support system. If, however, the person has little motivation, or if there are no available support groups or resources in the environment, the prognosis for change in this problem area is low. After considering the total change potential for problems such as those just cited, the worker would continue to try to find a problem with high potential for change in all three areas before beginning to intervene with the system.

At times, it may be impossible to find a starting problem with high change potential in all three areas. From a list of problems, it may be very difficult to distinguish and select the one that should be given priority. A tool has been developed to assist a worker in conceptualizing and analyzing a number of problems. It serves as a framework to compare change expectations for different problems and, through juxtaposition, to visualize which problems have the greatest change potential.

According to the tool depicted in Diagram 6-1, each problem is studied and scaled according to an assessment of the change potential of the problem-person-environment triplex. On the basis of data collected previously, the worker estimates the potential for change, using a scale of 0–10. Scoring criteria are as follows: 0 = no potential, 1 = very low, 2 = low, 3 = somewhat low, 4 = medium—leaning toward low, 5 = medium, 6 = medium—leaning toward high, 7 = somewhat high, 8 = high, 9 = very high, and 10 = maximum potential for change. For example, in looking at the problem identified as "child's illness" in Diagram 6-1, the worker first asks about the nature and duration of the illness. If information has been gathered that indicates the child has just developed a strep throat, and the worker knows that there is a high incidence of cure for this illness, the change potential for "problem" may be scored as high (8). If there are accessible health care resources and the parents and child will take or administer the prescribed medication, the change potential in "person" and "environment" is also high (scored 8 and 9). Because the total change-potential score for the problem of "child's illness" is very high (25), this problem may be seen as the highest priority on the list of problems for initial intervention.

DIAGRAM 6-1   Problem Prioritization

	CHANGE-POTENTIAL SCORES (0–10)			TOTAL CHANGE POTEN-TIAL	PROBLEM PRIORITI-ZATION	SEVERITY
PROBLEM LIST	PROBLEM	PERSON(S)	ENVIRON-MENT			
Child's illness	8	8	9	25	1	
Father's drinking	2	1	4	7	8	*
Father's unemployment	5	8	5	18	3	
Mother's depression	6	4	6	16	5	
Wife abuse	3	2	4	9	7	*
Housing conditions	6	5	3	14	6	
School truancy	8	7	8	23	2	
Husband-wife communication	6	5	6	17	4	

*Life-at-risk situation.

The change potential scores for the problem identified as "father's drinking" are not as hopeful. On the basis of data observed and obtained, the worker has assessed all three categories with extremely low scores. In looking at the nature and duration of the problem itself, the worker knows that the problem has gone on for years and that alcoholism is a serious physical and socially pathological illness (scored 2). In terms of the father's motivation and capacity to change at this time, the worker assesses the "person" category also as very low (1), because the father denies he has a drinking problem and refuses to go for help. The worker studied the formal and informal resources of the father's environment and averaged out a score of 4. Although formal resources are available in the environment to help the father with his drinking problem (AA and local hospital and clinic), his wife and family deny that the father has a drinking problem, saying that he and most of his buddies are just heavy drinkers. Apparently, the total change potential for the "father's drinking" is very low (7). The worker recognizes that it is a very serious problem, but one that will not be resolved in the near future.

In selecting the problem with the highest change potential for beginning intervention, the worker is aware of the fact that there are problems of greater severity in need of ongoing attention. It is expected that these problems will probably take a long time before any marked change will occur. Because of the serious nature of these problems, the worker continues to direct efforts toward overcoming them while at the same time working on those problems or needs for which progress and success may be expected.

For example, in Diagram 6-1, there are two problems with low change-potential scores (father's drinking; wife abuse). These problems are asterisked in the "severity" column because they are assessed as life-at-risk situations. The worker will continue ongoing efforts to study and intervene in these areas while working with the family on problems that have high potential for change.

CONTRACTING

After a problem has been selected for action, the worker and the system of contact begin to plan what needs to be done, by whom, and when. It is possible that they will choose to work on more than one problem at a time. It is important that they clearly understand, however, which problems are being addressed and which ones are not, and the reasons for the selection.

As pointed out earlier, in the problem-solving approach of the General Method, every effort is made to conceptualize and to verbalize the identified problems and corresponding goals. During the third stage of the Method, worker and system also conceptualize and verbalize the specific tasks that need to be performed in order to accomplish the goals. Not only are the tasks identified, but they are also placed in sequence. Dialogue between worker and system includes a consideration of which tasks need to precede others. The discussion about each task extends to a consideration of possible consequences that may result from its enactment.

Careful planning is needed in determining who should be expected to perform what task. A basic guiding principle is "Inasmuch as possible, a person should do for him- or herself." A worker would agree to carry out a task for a client only when it is apparent that the person or system is unable to perform the needed task and that no other resources are available to call on.

Social workers do not foster dependency. Nevertheless, they do recognize that there are certain actions that some individuals are unable to perform, owing to internal or external circumstances. When such actions are necessary for goal accomplishment, a worker using the General Method would try first to mobilize other resources of the system, such as family, friends, church, or community support systems. If no internal or informal resources are available, the worker may initiate or execute a needed task. As quickly as possible, however, the worker would try to enable the person to perform such tasks for him- or herself.

EXAMPLE 1

A client may have been trying to contact his landlord for days to register a complaint. Although the landlord has been avoiding contact with the client, he may be more readily available when an agency worker contacts him. The worker would try to arrange for the landlord to meet with the client to discuss the complaint. If necessary, the worker may have to go with the client. If neither of these two options is feasible, the worker may have to go in behalf of the client.

EXAMPLE 2

A woman recuperating from an operation may be unable to drive her son to the clinic. The worker would try to see if another family member or neighbor could bring him. There may be a volunteer service within or outside of the clinic that could be tapped to provide the needed transportation. Only after options such as these were explored would the worker offer to go out and pick up the child.

During the contracting period, when worker and system of contact clarify who will do what, it is important for both to identify also the date when each task is expected to be carried out. Little progress can be made and time may be wasted unless timing is discussed and there is a sense of expectation for task and goal accomplishment.

As each task is considered and contracted through mutual agreement on task assignments, an anticipated date is stated for the performance of each task, even though the date may have to be altered due to unexpected circumstances. The projection of dates for task execution serves as a guide for general planning and review. If a task is not completed on the expected date, worker and system can grow in understanding the dynamics of problem, person, and environment by asking why it was not accomplished as anticipated. More realistic comprehension and planning could result from this inquiry.

A tool for use in general practice has been developed that integrates the essential components of a contracted plan (see Diagram 6-2). As a worker proceeds in the process of problem solving with a system of contact, this tool may be used to state in writing what is agreed on as (1) the prob-

DIAGRAM 6-2 Contracted Plan

DATE IDENTIFIED	PROBLEM/ NEED	GOAL	TASK	CONTRACT	DATE ANTICI- PATED	DATE ACCOM- PLISHED

lems or needs to be addressed, (2) the goals to be accomplished, (3) the tasks to be performed, (4) the persons to execute each task, (5) the dates anticipated to enact each task, and (6) the actual dates of task accomplishment. Once the tool is filled out by worker and system, they may refer to it each time they need to assess progress or impediments to progress. Skill is needed for precise identification of the problems and needs and the goals and tasks. The goals and tasks should focus on behaviors that can be measured or observed.

As each problem or need is selected for action, the name of the problem is entered on the instrument, along with the date when the worker and the system of contact agree that it is a problem for intervention. The list of problems and needs should be prioritized according to the criteria and process stated earlier. The goals for each problem may be stated as long-range goals, short-range goals, or both. The tasks to accomplish the goals for each problem need to be stated in sequence. The person or system indicated as contracting to perform each task should be identified in accordance with the principle of "doing for self as much as possible." The dates anticipated are written down after realistic consideration of what is feasible. As each task is accomplished, the final column should be filled in with the accurate date of completion.

The instrument, as shown in Diagram 6-2, can be placed in the front of any record for immediate identification of plan and progress. It becomes obvious, on first glance at the "date accomplished" column, whether there are tasks that were contracted but not completed. Rather than having to review all of the recordings of various contacts contained within a record to find out what has been happening with a case, the worker (or supervisor), by reviewing the instrument, can receive a synthesis of the essence of the work being done to date.

The instrument in Diagram 6-2 fits well with problem-oriented recording (described in Chapter 5). The contracted plan (Diagram 6-2) may be seen as a direct follow-up and complement to the steps taken for POR. The problems and dates identified on the problem list of POR are readily available for problem prioritization and listing in the first and second column of the contracted plan. Also the "assessment" and "plan" stated in the "SOAP" for each problem with POR will help in the identification of goals, tasks, contracts, and dates anticipated to be listed on the contracted plan. As each task of the contract is performed, its date of accomplishment is indicated on the contracted plan. This information will facilitate the writing of summary statements, as expected for each problem in a POR.

The contracted plan (Diagram 6-2) is a tool for ongoing use. Problems and needs, goals, tasks, and contracted enactor may change in the course of service. Once begun, there is a need for continued updating and review of the plan. As brought out in a later chapter, this tool may also serve as a major instrument for evaluation through goal analysis.

EXAMPLE

An example of a contracted plan for the problems prioritized in Diagram 6-1 may be found in Diagram 6-3. For the first problem, child's illness, it is clear in the "contract" column that the worker planned to take Mrs. C and her child to the clinic. She (worker) did this because Mrs. C had a history of missing clinic appointments. Also, Mrs. C had no way of getting to the clinic except by bus. The worker was unable to locate any available informal resources to provide transportation.

As the worker proceeded in problem solving with the family, she found that some of the problems identified during the first interview had decreased, owing to relief in other problem areas. For example, once Mr. C returned to work, Mrs. C was not so depressed and there was less physical abuse by her husband. Both Mr. and Mrs. C recognized their need to better understand and communicate with each other, and they agreed to go for marital counseling. They were also ready to begin to work on finding better housing. Mr. C was not ready, however, to talk about his heavy drinking. He and his wife denied that this was a problem, especially now that Mr. C was back at work. The worker planned to continue to be involved with the family as they worked on finding better housing, but she was not able to go any further with Mr. C's drinking problem at this time.

WORKING WITH DIFFERENT SYSTEMS

As stated earlier, the General Method of social work practice is applicable to working with a variety of systems. A worker may be working with a family, an individual, a group, or a community, but in any case, worker and system go through an assessment stage. A question to be considered is, Are there any differences in writing an assessment statement, prioritizing problems or drawing up a contracted plan when working with different-size systems? Various writers in the field of social work have focused on the art of assessment with particular systems, such as group[5] or family.[6] The approach and tools presented in this chapter, however, are used in working with any type of system.

In applying and adopting assessment tools to particular systems, a worker is sensitive to the knowledge that exists about each system. In working with a community, for example, the worker knows that a community consists of a complex body of persons with a common characteristic of place, problem, heritage, values, or commitment. There are often very distinctive subsystems within a community that may contract, contest, and conflict with one another. The worker calls on the knowledge and skills identified in the profession by those who have expertise in community work and supplements their work with the newly developed tools for general practice.

DIAGRAM 6-3   Contracted Plan—The C Family

DATE IDENTIFIED	PROBLEM/ NEED	GOAL	TASK	CONTRACT	DATE ANTICIPATED	DATE ACCOMPLISHED
2/8	1. Child's illness	2. Child's health— no strep throat	1. Call health clinic for appointment	1. Mrs. C	2/9	2/9
			2. Take child to clinic	2. Mrs. C and worker	2/12	2/15
2/8	2. School truancy	2. School attend- ance daily	1. Speak with mother	1. Worker	2/9	2/9
			2. Speak with child	2. Mrs. C and worker	2/9	2/12
			3. Speak with teacher	3. Mrs. C and worker	2/12	2/12
			4. Wake child on time	4. Mrs. C	3/1	3/1
			5. Put child on bus	5. Mrs. C	3/1	3/1
2/8	3. Father's unemployment	3. Employment of father (steady)	1. Discuss with Mr. C	1. Worker	2/15	2/18
			2. Contact employ- ment agencies	2. Mr. C	2/16	2/19
			3. Check out training programs	3. Worker	2/16	2/17
			4. Locate job or train- ing (J/T) for Mr. C	4. Mr. C, employment agencies, or worker	2/25	3/15
			5. Apply for J/T	5. Mr. C	3/16	3/16

Date	Problem	Goal	Plan	Responsibility	Date	Date
2/8	4. Lack of communication between husband and wife	4. Improved husband-wife communication. Talking out instead of fighting out	1. Speak with Mr. C	1. Worker	3/22	3/22
			2. Speak with Mr. and Mrs. C	2. Worker	3/25	3/25
			3. Refer Mr. and Mrs. C to marital counseling center	3. Worker	3/25	3/25
			4. Contact marital counseling center	4. Mrs. C	3/26	3/29
			5. Attend sessions at marital counseling center	5. Mr. and Mrs. C	4/5	4/5
			6. Support their attendance	6. Worker	4/7	4/7
2/8	5. Overcrowded housing	5. Larger living quarters	1. Discuss with Mr. and Mrs. C	1. Worker	4/7	4/7
			2. Explore housing options and contact possible resources	2. Mr. and Mrs. C and worker	4/8	4/8
			3. Apply for housing	3. Mr. and Mrs. C	5/10	
			4. Move family	4. The C family and movers		

In 1955, Murray Ross identified the process of organizing a community according to the following six stages: The community

1. identifies its needs and objectives
2. orders or ranks needs or objectives
3. develops the confidence and will to work at needs and objectives
4. finds resources (internal and/or external) to deal with needs or objectives
5. takes action in respect to them
6. extends and develops co-operative and collaborative attitudes and practices in the community.[7]

The stages for community organization as described by Ross are basically consistent with the stages of the General Method. Each method has a six-stage process. In both processes, worker and community go through phases where problems and objectives are identified, data are collected, and action is taken. Although Ross does not state the specific need for an assessment stage, it is implicit that prior to taking action, problems are prioritized with an appraisal of resources and that actions are planned. Before moving into the action stage (item 5 of Ross), the worker and community now have tools available to help them with prioritizing problems and planning interventions.

For example, in the South End Community, the stated problems and needs were listed as follows:

High prices at local grocery stores
Rat- and roach-infested housing
No local control or input in neighborhood schools
Gang wars among community youths
No traffic light at the corner of Fifth Street and Silver Street

After drawing on assessment statements for each of these problems, the tool for prioritization of problems was completed, as found in Diagram 6-4.

Apparently, the community was motivated to begin to work on the need for a traffic light and the problem of high prices in local stores. In addition to motivation, the worker assessed the nature and scope of each problem, as well as the extent of related resources. After all factors were considered, it became clear that the problem with the highest change potential was the need for a traffic light. This was a serious (life-at-risk) problem with a good chance of resolution. The problem of gang wars was seen as serious (a youth having been stabbed last month), but community members did not indicate high motivation to work on this. They said gang wars were going on for years because people from certain blocks just didn't get along. Also, few resources were available for youth in the area. The worker, while not losing sight of this problem, would begin with an issue with high success potential in order to build up a sense of trust and accomplishment within the community.

DIAGRAM 6-4   The South End Community—Problem Prioritization

| PROBLEM LIST | CHANGE-POTENTIAL SCORES (0–10) | | | TOTAL CHANGE POTEN-TIAL | PROBLEM PRIORITI-ZATION | SEVERITY |
	PROBLEM	PERSON(S)	ENVIRON-MENT			
High prices	3	8	3	14	2	
Infested housing	3	5	3	11	3	
No school control	2	3	2	7	5	
Youth fights	3	4	2	9	4	*
Traffic light	8	7	8	23	1	*

*Life-at-risk situation.

After prioritizing problems and needs, the worker and community would move to planning specific tasks and responsibilities for goal accomplishment. The tool for contracted planning could aptly be used at this point. An example of how a contract could be developed with this community is found in Diagram 6-5. In this case, as community members begin to witness success from their efforts, a sense of pride and power develops. They begin to hope for greater accomplishments and to demonstrate motivation to work on complex tasks, such as finding funding sources and writing grant proposals. In time, the community begins to focus on what could be as well as what was, on prevention as well as problem resolution. Residents begin to talk about the need for them to overcome their interpersonal conflicts because they could gain so much more by working together. Some people identify past feelings of helplessness or isolation. According to Diagram 6-5, once the community finds out that there is funding for building a youth recreational center, they begin to think about other projects for enriching the community. The social worker's role as leader and activator decreases as members feel more confident and assume more leadership themselves.

Although the complexity of community work may be somewhat frightening to entry-level social workers, the general tools for assessment, as demonstrated, enable a worker to partialize and to coordinate the complex dimensions of needs and actions within community practice. As stated earlier, these assessment tools may be applied similarly when working with groups, families, or individuals.

There may be a major shift in the size of the system of contact during the helping process, as tasks become identified and implemented. Client systems may expand or decrease in number. Although a worker may begin contact with an individual, in the course of planning it may become apparent that the worker will need to intervene with the family or a larger system to achieve goals. Fortunately, a worker using the General Method employs knowledge and skills that are applicable to systems of any size. General

DIAGRAM 6-5 South End Community—Contracted Plan

DATE IDENTIFIED	PROBLEM/ NEED	GOAL	TASK	CONTRACT	DATE ANTICIPATED	DATE ACCOMPLISHED
3/15	1. Need for traffic light	1. Traffic light at Fifth and Silver Streets	1. Inquire about meeting with traffic commissioner (in three weeks)	1. Mr. G and worker	3/19	3/24
			2. Draw up a petition	2. Petition committee (Mr. and Mrs. K, Mr. F, Ms. Q, Mrs. R) and worker	3/20	3/26
			3. Get 500 signatures	3. Petition committe and six others (Rev. J, Mrs. B, Capt. P, Mr. S, Mr. and Mrs. B)	4/3	4/5
			4. Collect information on accidents at Fifth and Silver Streets	4. Mrs. A	3/20	3/22
			5. Draw up a traffic-flow chart	5. Traffic committee (Mr. and Mrs. M, Mr. McN, Ms. W, Mr. T) and worker	4/3	3/31
			6. Meeting of community	6. Whole community	4/4	4/4
			7. See commissioner with petition and information	7. Petition committee, Mr. G, and worker	4/9	

			Task	Responsibility		
			8. Committee meeting to discuss cancellation by commissioner	8. Community and worker	4/13	4/13
			9. Arrange to meet with mayor	9. Mr. G	4/15	
			10. Meet with mayor	10. Same as for contract 7	4/30	4/20
			11. If task 9 is not possible, meet to plan a demonstration	11. Community and worker	4/20	4/20
			12. Make signs	12. Traffic committee	4/22	4/22
			13. Notify communications media	13. Mr. G and Mrs. P	4/26	4/26
			14. Demonstration at Fifth and Silver Streets	14. Community and worker	4/27	4/27
			15. Get traffic light	15. Town officials	5/3	5/4
			16. Community meeting	16. Community and worker	5/7	5/7
3/15	2. High prices	2. Lower prices in local grocery stores	1. Compare prices and prepare report	1. Comparative price committee (Mrs. B, Mr. G, Mr. and Mrs. N, Ms. W, Mr. T)	5/12	5/12
			2. Meet with store owners and present data	2. Teams a. Mr. B, Mrs. Q, Mrs. J b. Mr. and Mrs. K, Mr. F	5/20	5/27
			3. Community meeting	3. Community and worker	5/27	5/27

(continued)

DIAGRAM 6-5 (continued)

DATE IDENTIFIED	PROBLEM/ NEED	GOAL	TASK	CONTRACT	DATE ANTICIPATED	DATE ACCOMPLISHED
			4. Meet with consumer-protection worker	4. Mr. G, Mr. F, Mrs. J	6/3	6/3
			5. Meet with store owners and consumer-protection worker	5. Comparative price committee, Mr. F, Mrs. J, and worker, store owners, and consumer-protection worker	6/20	6/22
			6. Monitor prices	6. Teams as in contract 2	6/30 and ongoing	
3/15	3. Infested housing	3. Extermination of rats and roaches in community housing	1. Community meeting	1. Community and worker	6/24	6/24
			2. Identify locations and extent of infestation—bring in housing inspector	2. Data collection committee (Mr. and Mrs. M, Mrs. B, Mr. F, Ms. R, Mr. McW.	7/9	7/8
			3. Draw up petition and get signatures	3. Petition committee	7/17	7/17
			4. See landlords with data and petition	4. Teams a. Mr. F, Mrs. Q, Mr. and Mrs. M b. Mr. B, Ms. J, Mrs. R	7/30	7/31
			5. Speak with Housing Authority and Housing Court	5. Mr. G, Mr. F, Mrs. J	8/6	8/10

		Task	Responsible		
		6. Community meeting	6. Community and worker	8/10	8/12
		7. Withhold rents	7. Tenants of infested housing	8/31	8/31
		8. Get publicity	8. Mrs. P and Mrs. Q	8/30	8/29
		9. Hire sanitation specialist	9. Landlords	9/2	9/10
3/15	4. Gang wars	4. End of gang wars	1. Community meeting	1. Community and worker	9/7	9/7
			2. Identify scope and causes—talk with youth and with police	2. Data collection committee (Mr. F, Mrs. Q, Ms. R, Rev. J, Mr. McN)	9/20	9/22
			3. Locate funding to build recreation hall for community youth—talk with local officials	3. Mr. G, Mrs. R, and worker	9/20	9/24
			4. Draw up funding proposal	4. Funding committee (Mr. and Mrs. S, Ms. W, Mr. T)	9/30	10/8
			5. Build recreational center (on church grounds)	5. Contractors and community	8/30	11/30
			6. Hire recreation director	6. Recreation center committe (Rev. J, Mrs. R, Mr. and Mrs. M, Ms. Q, Mr. G)	10/30	11/20
			7. Monitor center	7. Recreation center committee	11/1	

(continued)

DIAGRAM 6-5 (continued)

DATE IDENTIFIED	PROBLEM/ NEED	GOAL	TASK	CONTRACT	DATE ANTICIPATED	DATE ACCOMPLISHED
6/15	5. No school input or control	5. Direct input into local school	1. Community meeting	1. Community and worker	8/24	8/24
			2. Study structure of school and compare with other schools	2. School committee (Mr. and Mrs. K, Mr. F, Mrs. W)	8/30	9/4
			3. Meet with principal	3. Mr. G, Mr. and Mrs. M	8/26	8/29
			4. Meet with Board of Education	4. Mr. G, Mrs. Q, Rev. J, Mr. W	9/14	9/15
			5. Locate funding sources	5. Mrs. R, Mrs. P, Mr. F	9/11	9/20
			6. Get other community people involved—elderly, singles, etc.	6. Rev. J, Capt. P, Mrs. R, worker		
			7. Draw up proposal for community programs of school	7. Mrs. R, Mr. W	9/30	

practice does not have the limitation of size as found in the traditional methods of casework, group work, or community organization.

USING THE HOLISTIC FOUNDATION
IN ASSESSMENT

The skills and approach a worker uses in the assessment stage should reflect the foundation value of *belief in the dignity and worth of every person* (see Diagram 1-5, Chapter 1). As the worker and system of contact collaborate in assessing and planning, the basic practice principles, particularly individualization, self-determination, and acceptance, are demonstrated.

A system needs to have an individualized assessment. No two people or systems are exactly alike. Each one has a unique combination of problems, needs, resources, and circumstances. Thus, the principle of *individualization* is highlighted in the assessment stage of the General Method.

In prioritizing problems, the worker knows that an essential factor to consider prior to problem selection is the extent of motivation in a system to work on a particular problem or need. Unless there is client *self-determination* in problem prioritization, a worker will undoubtedly meet with resistance and failure. The worker who forges ahead for problem resolution will be unsuccessful without the agreement and support of the client system.

Although it is easy to wish that a system have greater strengths or motivation, the worker must convey an attitude of acceptance toward the system as it is. If several problems are assessed as having low potential for change, the worker may feel a sense of frustration or helplessness. The worker must begin with accepting the system "as a given." Through discussion, support, and assessment, within an atmosphere of acceptance, the worker enables the system to view itself more realistically and to consider possible and desirable goals.

In addition to foundation values and principles, a worker in the assessment stage uses knowledge and skills from the holistic foundation for general social work practice (Diagram 1-5, Chapter 1). When writing a statement of cause for a problem, the worker may be using such theories as ecology, role, or socialization to explain how a system has been influenced by others. Knowledge of cultures, policies, and formal and informal resources is used in developing priorities for planning and intervention. The worker utilizes various theories to understand persons, problems, and environments and their interactions as an appraisal of their change potential is being made.

The foundation skills that are used during assessment include goal setting, planning, contracting, and recording. As the worker involves the system in contracting, some degree of clarifying, bargaining, and confronting may be needed. The supportive skills of listening, guiding, and feeling and sensing are prevalent throughout the assessment process. With the individualization of each person-problem-environment triplex during assessment, the worker applies foundation skills and theories as deemed appropriate to the situation.

HUMAN DIVERSITY FOR ASSESSMENT

Culture

During the assessment stage, as problems and needs are prioritized and contracts are formulated, a worker and system may find it difficult to determine where to begin, particularly when the work is with minorities. Often, the problems identified are both personal and societal in nature. Although it may be necessary to invest major energy first in providing for immediate material needs, a worker should also plan to deal with the larger social-change issues that need to be addressed. A worker's involvement in the larger issues helps to demonstrate to the client the worker's understanding and acceptance. As interventions are contracted, the worker strives to promote empowerment by strongly encouraging and supporting minority members to speak and act for themselves to meet immediate needs and to bring about institutional change.

In working out a contract with a system, the worker may find different degrees of participation and active involvement by systems, depending on cultural orientations. When a worker is seen as an authority person in a lineal relationship (as with Asian-Americans), members of the system may show passivity and dependence. The speed with which a contract is drawn up may also be influenced by the culture of a system.

The planning and selection of tasks on a contract should reflect a sensitivity to cultural values and beliefs. For example, to suggest institutional care of the elderly as an acceptable plan for many blacks, Puerto Ricans, or Asians would be inappropriate. Placing a child with a relative in the tribe would be a much more acceptable plan for an American Indian family than a foster-home placement would be.

Sexual Variation

As pointed out in Chapter 3, the problems listed when working with gay or lesbian clients may also range from personal to broad societal problems. Many personal problems may be assessed as stemming from tensions and rejections the individual has experienced when trying to participate in societal systems. The worker and the system study all of the identified problems, but priority is given to those with high potential for change. The broad, general goals that were stated during engagement are refined during assessment into more specific, attainable, measurable goals for contract formulation. In every possible way, the worker tries to empower the gay or lesbian client system to implement independently the tasks identified in the contract or to implement them with a community of others who face similar pressures or injustices.

Information gathered about potential supportive resources is discussed during assessment, and the plan drawn up by worker and system may include initial contact with outside resources. If no local resources are available, the plan may be developed to organize a support group for gay or lesbian persons in or outside of the worker's agency.

When it becomes apparent that a problem raised by a gay or lesbian client is interpersonal in nature, the worker knows that the most effective and often the only way to help with an interpersonal problem is to involve the other partner in sessions with the worker and the client. The plan and contract, therefore, may need to include a process for bringing into the service a third party who may be hesitant to talk with a professional about his or her gay or lesbian relationship. If it is not possible to include this person, the worker is expected to state clearly to the client the limitations to achieving interpersonal goals.

Gender Sensitivity

During assessment, as the causes of problems are stated, men and women who adhere to narrowly defined gender roles may avoid considering the possibility that their problems may be related to social injustices in a sexist society. In prioritizing problems, they may be closed to the idea of giving priority to a need for change in how they define their gender-role identity. The plan articulated in a contract may reflect a woman's continued dependence, for example, if a worker or others are expected to carry out a major portion of the identified tasks. A man's inability to accept interdependence may be seen in his refusing to allow a worker or other resources to accomplish tasks in behalf of his family or himself.

Using an ecological perspective in planning, a social worker realizes that an individual with a goal to change his or her behavior and image may experience pressure and negative reactions from the environment. In any work on redefining gender roles, whether with men or women, individually or in groups, attention needs to be given to the possible consequences that may result from any change. The reality is that change is usually a painful process for both the individual and the environment. Although a person may become self-sufficient and independent, it is true that no man or woman can be an island, totally independent from others, for very long. Human beings by nature are interdependent. To move into a truly collaborative, balanced interdependence, however, may be impossible for some individuals in their existing environments. Women who have been greatly dependent, for example, may have to go to the other polarity of total inde-pendence before they and others can see them as equal, complementary counterparts. The implications of these actions need to be given serious consideration before choices and changes are made. Various support sys-tems and reinforcements need to be located and ensured if change is to be positive and stabilized.

It may be equally difficult for a man who is in a position of power and decision making to move into a more democratic, egalitarian way of functioning within a system, even when he wants to do so. Those who are dependent on him may resist having to assume more responsibility and independence. It may be necessary, therefore, to plan to involve significant others in the helping process.

Thus in writing assessment statements, prioritizing problems, and con-tracting with different systems, social workers use their knowledge of, and sensitivity to, culture, sexual variation, and gender-role diversity. They also make reference to the additional diversity variables of age and stages, en-dowment and personality, value systems, class, and geographic location (de-scribed in Chapter 3).

ASSESSMENT IN DIVERSE FIELD AREAS

I. FIELD AREA: CHILD WELFARE

A. Agency: State Department of Children's Services

B. Client System

K, a 15-year-old female in an emergency shelter. (For more background information see Chapter 4, Engagement in Diverse Field Areas, I. Child Wel-fare.)

C. Summary of Preceding Stages

The problem and goals identified during engagement and data collec-tion are listed in Diagram 6-6. During engagement, K expressed feelings of loneliness, hatred, nervousness, and depression. In collecting data, the worker learned that K had experienced some difficulty adjusting in both the group home and the foster home placements that she had before she ran away, particularly in the foster home. Her schoolwork had also deteriorated prior to her running away and being placed in the emergency shelter. After exploring informal and formal resources in the environment, the worker lo-cated a group home for young women (ages 14–19) in Jewett City that had an opening. K expressed a strong desire to move into a group home, to return to school, and to get help with her personal problems.

D. Assessment

Assessment statement: K has no permanent residence because she cannot live at home with her abusive parents (mother and stepfather), and she ran away from her foster home. She has personal needs (problem 3 in Diagram 6-6) that interfere with her functioning. The etiology of K's personal problems go back to her traumatic home environment, where she was physically and sexually abused. K is out of school because she is living in a temporary shelter awaiting placement. Her school performance had dropped to below average while she was living in the foster home because she became involved with a boyfriend and was having an increasing number of arguments with her foster parents.

The change potential for K's problem of homelessness is assessed as somewhat high because K is motivated to accept a group-home placement and a resource is available. The change potential for K's need to reenter school is assessed as somewhat high because there is a school near the group home. The change potential for K's problems with adjustment to placement and school is assessed as somewhat high because K is now motivated to accept ongoing help with her personal problems and because there will be opportunity for K to receive help individually and in group while living in the group home.

Problem prioritization: The problem-prioritization tool was used by the worker, as recorded in Diagram 6-7.

The need for a placement is given top priority because it has the highest change potential (24) and also because of the urgency (severity) of the situation (living in temporary shelter). Finding a school placement is not a difficult problem to resolve. It received the second-highest score and became second in priority.

The personal problems have lower change scores because it is expected that these problems will take more time for resolution. K is particularly motivated to try to get over "feeling down." She is ready to talk about how hurt and angry she is. She also wants to feel better about herself and to understand what has happened to her. She hesitates to talk about her sexuality, even though problems related to her sexual identity, behavior, and relationships, are assessed as serious (severity). K ran away from home when she became involved with a boyfriend, and she fears new heterosexual friendships. Since the worker has been able to locate environmental resources for all the problems listed, the change potential scores in the "environment" column are high (9's). Even though the problem relating to K's sexuality is prioritized last, the worker sees the seriousness of this problem and will bring it to the attention of the person who will be working with K individually in the group home.

Contracting: Building on the list of problems and goals identified during engagement and data collection, the worker and K then began to plan the tasks that needed to be performed to achieve the stated goals. They also identified who would be responsible for carrying out each task, and they set the dates when task completion could be anticipated. Their contracted plan is given in Diagram 6-6.

DIAGRAM 6-6 Contracted Plan

DATE IDENTIFIED	PROBLEM/ NEED	GOAL	TASK	CONTRACT	DATE ANTICIPATED	DATE ACCOMPLISHED
1/12	1. No permanent home	1a. To obtain a permanent placement	1. Make referral	1. Worker	1/19	
		b. To maintain a permanent placement	2. Visit group home	2. K and worker	1/22	
			3. Move to group home	3. K, with worker's help	1/24	
			4. Follow-up	4. Worker, K, and group home staff	1/30 and every second week	
1/12	2. Out of school	2. To reenter school	1. To enroll in local school	1. K and group home staff worker	1/28	
			2. Follow-up	2. Worker, school personnel, group home staff	1/30 and other school conferences on K	

| 1/12 | 3. Personal problems
a. Depression
b. Poor self-esteem
c. Identity confusion
d. Sexuality | 3. Personal goals (1/19)
a. To stop "feeling down" so much
b. To feel better about self
c. To clarify identity
d. To be able to have good friendships with males | 1. To have weekly individual sessions with social worker at the group home
2. To participate in weekly peer-group meetings
3. Follow-up | 1. K and group home social worker

2. K

3. Worker, K, and social worker at group home | 1/25 and once a week thereafter
1/25 and once a week thereafter
1/30 and every second week |

DIAGRAM 6-7   Problem Prioritization

PROBLEM LIST	CHANGE-POTENTIAL SCORES (0–10)			TOTAL CHANGE POTEN-TIAL	PROBLEM PRIORITI-ZATION	SEVERITY
	PROBLEM	PERSON(S)	ENVIRON-MENT			
No permanent home	7	8	9	24	1	*
Out of school	7	7	9	23	2	
Personal problems						
Poor self-esteem	5	6	9	20	4	
Identity confusion	5	6	9	20	4	
Sexuality	5	5	9	19	5	*
Depression	5	7	9	21	3	

*Life-at-risk situation.

FIELD AREA: GERONTOLOGY

A. Agency: Seaside Nursing Home

B. Client System

Mrs. J, an 80-year-old Portuguese woman in a skilled-nursing facility. (For more background information, see Chapter 4, Engagement in Diverse Field Areas, II. Gerontology.)

C. Summary of Preceding Stages

The problems and goals identified during engagement and data collection may be found in Diagram 6-8. During engagement, Mrs. J expressed feelings of distrust, fear, anger, and abandonment. In collecting data, the worker learned that Mrs. J's failure to adjust included disruptive behavior in the unit. She was agitating the nurses and the residents. More information was obtained about Mrs. J's history and her family, who could not be located. Portuguese-speaking resource people in the nursing home (a new volunteer) and in the community (the church pastor) were being located to visit with Mrs. J. The client herself was becoming more open and motivated to adjust to the nursing home.

D. Assessment

Assessment statement: Mrs. J is seclusive, uncooperative, and agitating because she is culturally isolated in the nursing home and because she has been abandoned by her family. She will not leave her room alone because she is afraid that the little she has left will be stolen. She finds it difficult to go out and meet with others because she can't speak English fluently, and she feels uncomfortable with people of a different culture. Mrs. J fights with the nurses when they come to give her a bath because it distresses her to have to get undressed at 10 o'clock in the morning. Mrs. J has been yelling at the residents and calling them names because she wants to get their attention and to make them communicate with her. She displays anger and confusion at times, as a result of her organic brain syndrome.

The change potential for Mrs. J to overcome her seclusiveness is assessed as medium high because Mrs. J is somewhat motivated to be able to leave her room on her own and because she is physically able to do so at this time. The potential to overcome her cultural isolation is assessed as medium because she can speak some English, a volunteer has been located who is Portuguese, and the pastor of Mrs. J's former church will also come to see her. The change potential for Mrs. J to get to know the staff and the resources of the nursing home is assessed as high, because Mrs. J has agreed to meet twice a week with the social worker, and she has expressed interest in meeting other staff members and hearing about available resources. Her involvement in activities at the nursing home will depend on how comfortable she feels with the activities and with those who participate in them.

The change potential for overcoming the bath-scheduling problem is assessed as high because the nurses are open to reconsidering the time Mrs. J is scheduled for her bath. Mrs. J and the head nurse are willing to meet to discuss the problem. The change potential for overcoming Mrs. J's yelling at the residents is also assessed as high, because Mrs. J is motivated to work for better communication with others. She says she will stop the name-calling.

Mrs. J's overall functioning and adjustment are dependent also on the rate of deterioration due to organic brain syndrome.

Problem prioritization: The worker prioritized the identified problems, using the prioritization tool as shown in Diagram 6-9.

The problem of seclusiveness has a high change-potential score (9), because in considering the nature of the problem itself, residents who are physically able to leave their rooms may do so. The change potential for "person" is assessed as somewhat high (7). Although Mrs. J has the physical capacity to leave her room and expresses a desire to get out more, she still feels afraid and strange in the nursing home. "Environment" is also assessed at a 7 for this problem. Resources (persons and programs) in the nursing-home environment are available to help Mrs. J leave her room. They do not, however, reflect her culture, except for one possible volunteer. Mrs. J's problem of seclusiveness is asterisked in the "severity" column, because it can be seen as potentially a life-or-death issue. If Mrs. J regresses to the point of refusing to leave her room even for meals, she could become seriously ill and have to be moved into the chronic-care unit.

In assessing the problem of cultural isolation, the change potential is seen as medium, and "problem" is given a 6. People of different cultures do not have to feel or be isolated. Even though Mrs. J does not speak English fluently, she can carry on a conversation in English ("person" score of 8). She could help others in the environment to understand and respond to her cultural needs. Although there are no Portuguese residents or staff members in the nursing home at the time, this may change, because the number of Portuguese moving into the local geographic area is increasing. Mrs. J has also expressed some desire to get to understand others at the nursing home,

DIAGRAM 6-8 Contracted Plan

DATE IDENTIFIED	PROBLEM/ NEED	GOAL	TASK	CONTRACT	DATE ANTICIPATED	DATE ACCOMPLISHED
9/27	1. Unfamiliarity with staff and resources of nursing home	1. To get to know the staff and resources of the nursing home	1. To meet twice a week with worker	1. Worker and Mrs. J	10/4 and every Tuesday and Thursday thereafter	10/4, 9, 11
			2. To meet with program planner	2. Worker, Mrs. J, and program planner	10/16	
			3. To meet with a person from recreation staff	3. Worker, Mrs. J, and recreation staff person	10/23	
10/2	2. Fighting with nurses over bath	2. To work out bath schedule with nurses	1. To meet with head nurse to discuss bath schedule	1. Mrs. J and head nurse	10/16	
9/25	3. Seclusiveness: not leaving room alone	3a. to leave room alone (at least once a day)	1. To walk down to nursing station alone at least once a day	1. Mrs. J	10/25 and each day thereafter	

182

Date				
	b. To attend a house activity, program, or meeting (at least once a week)	1. To go to a house activity, program, or meeting (at least once a week)	1. Worker or staff member and Mrs. J first two times	Starting week of 10/22
			2. Mrs. J with residents each week thereafter	Starting week of 11/5
10/2	4. Calling residents names	4. To stop calling residents names	1. To stop name-calling — 1. Mrs. J	10/16 and thereafter
			2. To say "hello" to residents — 2. Mrs. J	10/16 and thereafter
9/25	5. Cultural isolation	5. To share culture with others	1. To meet director of volunteers — 1. Mrs. J, worker, and director of volunteers	10/25
			2. To visit with Portuguese volunteer — 2. Mrs. J and volunteer	?
			3. To visit with pastor of church — 3. Mrs. J and pastor	?

DIAGRAM 6-9   Problem Prioritization

PROBLEM LIST	CHANGE-POTENTIAL SCORES (0–10)			TOTAL CHANGE POTEN-TIAL	PROBLEM PRIORITI-ZATION	SEVERITY
	PROBLEM	PERSON(S)	ENVIRON-MENT			
Seclusiveness: not leaving room	9	7	7	23	3	*
Cultural isolation	6	8	7	21	5	
Unfamiliarity with staff and re-sources	9	8	9	26	1	
Fighting with nurses over bath	7	8	9	24	2	
Calling residents names	7	9	6	22	4	

*Life-at-risk situation.

and the staff of the home, particularly those who are Spanish-speaking, have indicated an interest in helping Mrs. J feel welcome. They talked about serving Portuguese food and playing music from Portugal at the next resident-and-staff party. The "environment" assessment at this time is scored a 7. If a Portuguese volunteer or Mrs. J's pastor becomes actively involved with her, the environment score may be raised.

The lack of familiarity with the staff and resources of the home was seen as a problem easily remedied (9). Mrs. J is capable of understanding the staff and resources, and she is somewhat motivated to learn about them (8). The program planner, recreational director, head nurse, chaplain, and others on the staff of the nursing home are very willing to talk with Mrs. J and to develop an individualized program for her. The planned program for Mrs. J could include recreational, social, and spiritual activities. "Environment," therefore, is given a high change-potential score (9) for the problem of "unfamiliarity with staff and resources of the nursing home."

The potential for changing the problem of fighting with the nurses over the bath is assessed at 7. Even though the problem is not a life-or-death issue, changing the schedule for Mrs. J's bath time would affect the schedule for many others. It is possible, however, for the schedule to be changed and thus prevent further fighting by Mrs. J over the bath. The change potential for "person" is 8 because Mrs. J is capable of being cooperative and has said she would like to get along better with the nurses. The nurses are open to rescheduling Mrs. J's bath time, and the head nurse has agreed to meet with Mrs. J about it ("environment" score of 9).

In considering the problem of calling other residents names, the worker assessed the change potential for the problem itself as 7. The act of holding back from name-calling is possible for Mrs. J. She realizes that it isn't right and wants to stop this behavior (9). The residents ("environment") are not interested in going near Mrs. J at this time (change potential of 6), but some will probably respond if they are encouraged by the staff to try and reach out to her.

In totaling the change potential scores, the problems become prioritized as follows: (1) unfamiliarity with staff and resources at the home, (2) fighting with nurses over bath, (3) seclusiveness: not leaving room alone, (4) calling residents names, and (5) cultural isolation.

Contracting: Building on the prioritized problem list, the worker and Mrs. J began to plan and to contract for what needed to be accomplished in order to achieve their mutually agreed on goals. The contracted plan they developed is shown in Diagram 6-8.

III. FIELD AREA: PUBLIC SOCIAL WELFARE

A. Agency: State Social Service

B. Client System

Mr. and Mrs. P and their two children, ages 2 and 4, in need of emergency and permanent housing. (For additional background information, see Chapter 4, Engagement in Diverse Field Areas, III. Public Social Welfare.)

C. Summary of Preceding Stages

The problems and goals identified during engagement and data collection are listed in Diagram 6-10. During engagement, Mr. and Mrs. P expressed feelings of helplessness, anger, confusion, and rejection. As data were collected, the worker learned that the P's had a history of frequent moves, often caused by evictions due to their failure to pay the rent. The P's were receiving AFDC but had difficulty in planning and budgeting their money. Mr. P was unable to maintain employment because of his psychological incapacity. He was receiving weekly outpatient treatment at the local mental health center. At the time of initial assessment, the P's were asking for help only in locating housing and food.

D. Assessment

Assessment statement: The P family do not have a place to stay because they were evicted from their apartment two weeks ago. They were evicted because they did not pay their rent on time. They do not plan and budget the money they receive from AFDC to last throughout the month. The P's are in need of emergency food because they do not have any money left from last month, and the check and food stamps for this month are being held at central office until the family is relocated.

The change potential for the P's housing problem is assessed as low because of the P's limited motivation to become actively involved in searching for an apartment. Although there are possible resources for emergency shelter, the authorized payment for temporary placement is only for a maximum of 14 days.

The potential for meeting the need for food is assessed as high because

DIAGRAM 6-10 Contracted Plan

DATE IDENTIFIED	PROBLEM/ NEED	GOAL	TASK	CONTRACT	DATE ANTICIPATED	DATE ACCOMPLISHED
9/28	1. Food—emergency food	1. To obtain emergency food supply	1. Discuss resources	1. Worker and P's	9/28	
			2. Contact resource	2. Worker and P's	9/28	
			3. Obtain food	3. The P's	9/28	
9/28	2. Housing—emergency shelter	2. To move into emergency shelter	1. To locate resource	1. Worker	9/28	
			2. Discuss resources	2. Worker and P's	9/28	
			3. Contact resource	3. Worker and P's	9/28	
			4. To move to resource	4. P's with worker's help	9/28	
9/28	3. Food until AFDC check and food stamps arrive	3. To recieve a food supply until AFDC check and food stamps arrive	1. Locate resource	1. Worker	9/29	
			2. Discuss	2. Worker and P's	9/29	
			3. Contact resource	3. Worker and P's	9/29	
			4. Receive food	4. P's and resource	9/29 until check and food stamps arrive	
9/28	4. Housing—long-term	4. To move into an apartment for long-term residence	1. Explore resources	1. Mr. and Mrs. P and worker	9/29	
			2. Contact resources	2. Mr. and Mrs. P	9/29	
			3. Move	3. The P's	10/12	
			4. Update	4. Worker, Mr. P's doctor, income-maintenance technician	9/29 and weekly	

several resources are available. Finding a way to transport a food supply to the P's should not be a problem unless the worker is unable to get an agency car.

Problem prioritization: During initial assessment, the worker used the problem prioritization tool for conceptualization. It was clear and urgent that the first two areas in need of immediate attention were food and temporary shelter for the family. In prioritizing, the housing problem was divided into the two parts of (1) emergency shelter and (2) long-term residence. The food need was also subdivided. Considering these two housing needs along with the two food-supply needs, the worker drew up the prioritization shown in Diagram 6-11.

The problem/need with the highest change potential is obviously finding immediate food for the family. The second-prioritized area is emergency shelter. The worker and the family will then need to plan for receiving a food supply to last until the P's receive AFDC income and food stamps. The fourth problem area, the last prioritized because of its low change potential, is the need for a long-term residence for the family. There is a pressing need to work on this fourth problem, because the temporary shelter can only be for two weeks. The worker knows also that the only way the temporary placement will be supported financially by the agency is if the P's make ongoing efforts to secure more permanent housing. An extension in temporary placement is granted only if there is evidence that every effort is being made by the family to locate a residence. Through problem assessment and prioritization, it became clear to the worker that pressure needed to be exerted on Mr. and Mrs. P to have them become more actively involved in the search for housing.

Contracting: The worker and the P's developed the contract identified in Diagram 6-10. Permission was given by Mr. and Mrs. P to have the worker discuss their plan and progress with Mr. P's doctor and the income-maintenance technician. The worker asked Mr. P's doctor and the family's income-

DIAGRAM 6-11   Problem Prioritization

PROBLEM LIST	CHANGE-POTENTIAL SCORES (0–10)			TOTAL CHANGE POTEN- TIAL	PROBLEM PRIORITI- ZATION	SEVERITY
	PROBLEM	PERSON(S)	ENVIRON- MENT			
1. Housing						
a. Emergency shelter	8	8	8	24	2	*
b. Long-term	2	1	2	5	4	*
2. Food						
a. Emergency food	9	9	8	26	1	*
b. Until check and food stamps come	8	8	7	23	3	*

*Life-at-risk situation.

maintenance technician to help with motivating the P's to become more involved.

IV. FIELD AREA: COMMUNITY SERVICES

A. Agency: Clayton Neighborhood House

B. Client System

Four Hispanic families without heating in their apartments on the second floor of the 33 L Street apartment building. (For more background information, see Chapter 4, Engagement in Diverse Field Areas, IV. Community Services.)

C. Summary of Preceding Stages

The problem and goal identified during engagement and data collection are stated in Diagram 6-12. During engagement, residents from four apartments met with the worker and expressed feelings of anger, frustration, fear, helplessness, and victimization. In gathering information, the worker learned that residents were paying $250 for a one-room apartment, heat included. The name and address of the landlord was obtained and he was contacted. Because of the urgent nature of the problem, the worker and the residents moved quickly through engagement, data collection, and assessment.

D. Assessment

Assessment Statement: The four families who live on the second floor of the 33 L Street apartment building do not have adequate heating because the heating for the building has not been regulated for adequate, even distribution. There also is a problem with direct communication between residents and the landlord. The residents and the landlord do not speak the same language, and Mr. X does not return calls made to him by tenants. (The worker added the communication problem to the problem list in the record; see Diagram 6-12.)

The change potential for the problem of inadequate heating is assessed as somewhat high at this time because Mr. X, the landlord, is now aware of the problem and has stated that he will see that it gets resolved. As long as the problem of poor communication between residents and landlord remains, however, there is a possibility that a heating loss could recur and that the families would continue to have difficulty notifying Mr. X.

The problem of poor communication has a low potential for change at this time, because neither the families nor the landlord appear motivated to work on improving their communication. The families are afraid that if they meet with Mr. X, he may think that they are complaining too much and raise their rent. Mr. X indicated that he is very busy, with no time to contact residents.

Problem prioritization: Because there was only one problem that the client system was presenting at this time, the worker did not use the problem prioritization tool. The need for heating was primary and urgent.

DIAGRAM 6-12 Contracted Plan

DATE IDENTIFIED	PROBLEM/ NEED	GOAL	TASK	CONTRACT	DATE ANTICIPATED	DATE ACCOMPLISHED
12/3	1. Lack of heat on second floor	1. To obtain consistent, adequate heating for second floor residents of L street apartment house	1. Contact janitor	1. Worker	12/3	
			2. Contact landlord	2. Worker	12/4	12/4
			3. Meet for follow-up	3. Residents and worker	12/5	12/5
12/5	2. Communication problem with landlord					

Contracting: The worker and the residents developed the contracted plan shown in Diagram 6-12 during their first meeting. The communication problem was added after the worker had contacted the landlord.

V. FIELD AREA: EDUCATION

A. Agency: Keeney Elementary School

B. Client System

Jim G, an 8-year-old black child, a third-grader with regressive behavior in school and at home. (For additional background information, see Chapter 4, Engagement in Diverse Field Areas, V. Education.)

C. Summary of Preceding Stages

The problems, goals, and tasks identified prior to a formal assessment are indicated in Diagram 6-13. Through play, Jim began to express his fear that his mother might leave him. Mrs. G shared feelings of anger and hurt regarding her husband and their relationship. She was finding it difficult to forgive him and to trust him. A meeting was arranged for the worker to meet with Mr. and Mrs. G to discuss Jim's problems and how they were being affected by the problem between Mr. and Mrs. G.

D. Assessment

When the worker met with Mr. and Mrs. G, they moved into the assessment stage of the General Method. Problems and goals were clarified, and a contracted plan was articulated by the worker, Jim, and both of his parents.

Assessment statement: Jim has a problem being present at school physically, emotionally, and cognitively, owing to his upset feelings and his fears, which are caused by tension and quarreling at home between his parents. Jim has refused to fall asleep at night unless his mother is with him and a light is on in the room because he is afraid that she will leave him, as he overheard her saying to his father. He was overly tired in school because he was trying to keep awake during the night. He did not want to go to school because he feared his mother would leave for good while he was gone. Mr. and Mrs. G have been quarreling because Mrs. G recently learned that her husband had gone out with another woman.

The change potential for Jim's school and home problems is assessed as high. The problems have had a short duration. Jim is reacting to external circumstances, and Mr. and Mrs. G are eager to improve the situation. Mrs. G is reassuring Jim that she will not leave him, and she and her husband are willing to go for professional help with their relationship.

Problem prioritization: The worker used the problem prioritization tool as shown in Diagram 6-14.

The change potential for the school tardiness and absenteeism problem was assessed as very high (9), because Jim did not have a history of missing school and the problem merely involved physical presence. The "person" change-potential score was assessed as medium (5). Even though Jim has the

DIAGRAM 6-13 Contracted Plan

DATE IDENTIFIED	PROBLEM/ NEED	GOAL	TASK	CONTRACT	DATE ANTICIPATED	DATE ACCOMPLISHED
11/1	1. Jim's school tardiness and absenteeism	1. Jim's regular school attendance (on time every day)	1. Get J to school on time each day	1. Mr. and Mrs. G	11/5-each school day thereafter	11/5-ongoing
11/21	2. Strain in Mr. and Mrs. G's marital relationship	2. Improved marital relationship (less quarreling, growing trust)	1. Explore counseling resources 2. Select resource 3. Contact resource for appointment 4. Attend counseling sessions	1. Worker and Mr. and Mrs. G 2. Mr. and Mrs. G 3. Mr. G 4. Mr. and Mrs. G	11/27 11/27 11/28 Beginning week of 12/3	11/27 11/27
11/1	3. Jim's declining school performance	3. Improved school performance (interest, participation, grades)	1. Talk with Jim about school problems in relation to home problem 2. Check on Jim's performance 3. Update Mr. and Mrs. G on Jim's school performance 4. Continue to meet with Jim 5. Home meeting to evaluate progress	1. Mr. and Mr. G, Jim, and worker 2. Worker with Jim's teacher 3. Worker 4. Worker 5. Worker, Mr. and Mrs. G, and Jim	11/27 11/28 and weekly 12/4 and 12/11 telephone contacts 11/29 12/17	11/27
11/2	4. Jim's problem getting to sleep at night	4. Jim's going to sleep at night without mother in room	1. Continue to assure Jim that Mrs. G was not going to leave him	1. Mrs. G	11/27 and each night thereafter	

DIAGRAM 6-14   Problem Prioritization

PROBLEM LIST	CHANGE-POTENTIAL SCORES (0–10)			TOTAL CHANGE POTEN- TIAL	PROBLEM PRIORITI- ZATION	SEVERITY
	PROBLEM	PERSON(S)	ENVIRON- MENT			
School tardiness and absen- teeism	9	5	9	23	1	
Declining aca- demic per- formance	6	5	9	20	2	*
Sleeping problem	5	3	5	13	3	
Strain in marital relationship	6	8	9	23	1	

*Life-at-risk situation.

capacity to go to school, he did not appear to have the necessary motivation. The potential of the "environment" to change for problem resolution was assessed at a 9, very high, because Mr. and Mrs. G were being very cooperative and gave assurance that they would see that Jim came to school on time each day.

The change potential for the problem of declining academic performance was assessed as a 6 (medium—leaning toward high) because the nature of the problem was reactive (related directly to external circumstances) rather than internalized (present regardless of external circumstances), and because the problems had only become observable over the past month. It could become a serious problem if it persisted and Jim had to be removed from his classroom (asterisk in "severity" column).

The change-potential score for "person" as related to the school-performance problem was assessed as 5 (medium), because here too, although Jim has the capacity to do the work, he is not motivated for school achievement at this time. The "environment" score was appraised as a 9 (high), because Jim was beginning to be helped by his parents and the school. His parents were committed to try to reduce the causes for Jim's decline in his school work.

The change potential for Jim's problem with falling asleep was given a 5 (medium), because of the somewhat serious nature of the problem, even though it had only recently developed. If Jim continued to get little sleep, he could become physically ill. The "person" potential was assessed as a 3 (somewhat low) because Jim was too upset to sleep and he continued to want a night light even after his mother assured him she would not leave. The "environment" score was a 5 for this problem, because J's parents were unable to make Jim fall asleep and they did not want to give him sleeping pills.

The change potential for the problem of a strained marital relationship was assessed as high (8) because Mr. and Mrs. G said that this was the first time they had had such a problem. Mr. G said that it was the first time he had gone out with someone else and that it would not happen again. The "person" potential was seen as high (8) because both Mr. and Mrs. G were motivated to work on their problem and to seek outside help. The "environment" potential was seen as very high (9) because several resources for marital counseling were available in the area.

Through problem prioritization, it became clear that the first two areas to be addressed were (1) Jim's school attendance and (2) Mr. and Mrs. G's marital relationship. With improvement in these two areas, it was hoped that Jim's school performance and sleeping at night would improve. Efforts for problem resolution would be primarily directed, therefore, according to the following sequence: (1) Jim's school tardiness and absenteeism, (2) the strain in Mr. and Mrs. G's relationship, (3) Jim's declining school performance, and (4) Jim's sleeping problem.

Contracting: When the worker met with Mr. and Mrs. G, they reviewed the problems, goals, and tasks that were identified earlier, and they agreed on the contracted plan outlined in Diagram 6-13. As highlighted in the "contract" column, Mr. and Mrs. G planned to become actively involved in going for help with their marital relationship and in working with Jim and the school on Jim's school problems.

VI. FIELD AREA: CORRECTIONS

A. Agency: Juvenile Court

B. Client System

Seven male youths, age 14, on probation, attending weekly group meetings led by co-workers at Juvenile Court. (For further background information, see Chapter 4, Engagement in Diverse Field Areas, VI. Corrections.)

C. Summary of Preceding Stages

The problems and goals identified by the group during engagement and data collection are outlined in Diagram 6-15. The youths in the group had low self-esteem and frequently referred to themselves as "stupid." All of the youths were in special classes at school for learning-disabled students. The workers also learned that all of the group participants were from single-parent homes and had trouble communicating with their parents. In visiting the homes and schools, the co-leaders learned that all seven youths were seen as "problems" by parents and teachers. The group members agreed to come to weekly group meetings in order to get off probation sooner (possibly a two-month reduction from a six-month probationary period).

D. Assessment

Assessment statement: The youths in the group are on probation because they committed the following crimes: three members—breaking, entering, and stealing from homes; two members—theft of automobiles; two members—shoplifting. The problem of law-breaking is assessed as very serious for at least five of the youths (J, T, ML, B, and A). There is a history of law-breaking in their families (by fathers or brothers), and little discipline or sup-

DIAGRAM 6-15 Contracted Plan

DATE IDENTIFIED	PROBLEM/ NEED	GOAL	TASK	CONTRACT	DATE ANTICIPATED	DATE ACCOMPLISHED
10/1	1. Law-breaking leading to probation	1. To get off probation in four months	1. To attend and participate in weekly group meetings	1. Seven members, two workers	10/1 and each Monday at 4:00 P.M. for at least four months	10/1–8/15
			2. To participate in group meetings	2. Seven members	10/1 and each Monday at 4:00 P.M. for at least four months	
			3. To obey rules of school, home, community	3. Seven members	10/1	
			4. To receive weekly reports on behavior from home and school	4. Social workers, parents, school social workers	Week of 10/1 and once a week for four months	

		5. To chart progress at meetings	5. Workers and members	10/22 and at each meeting thereafter
10/1	2. Bad tempers	2. To control tempers in school, home, neighborhood		
		1. Discuss the problem dealing with anger	1. Workers and members	10/22
10/1	3. Need to understand "changes" of teenagers	3. To learn more about "changes" (including becoming independent, sex and family planning, and job training)		
		1. Select first topic	1. Workers and members	10/22
10/1	4. Parent-son conflicts			
10/1	5. Low self-worth			

port is offered in their homes. All of these five express a desire to get off probation and to make sure they "don't get caught again." They do not have a strong motivation to keep within the law. Although C appears to be sincerely sorry that he got into trouble and upset his father, the problem could become serious if he continues with the street gang he has joined. MK's offense was shoplifting for the third time. His mother said she never has enough money to provide for the children, and she thinks M was trying to bring home things for her and his sisters and brother. Although Mrs. K was finding it difficult to discipline M, she said she had started attending a "parenting" class at church that was helping her to work better with him. She was trying to get M to promise that he would not steal any more.

The youths in the group are having a problem generally with their development and their feelings, because they are entering adolescence with low self-concepts and limited support systems at home and in school. Low self-esteem is reinforced by placement in special classes at school. All of the members have said that they don't like being told what to do, and that they get angry when someone puts pressure on them. They wish they could be independent, but they are afraid to try to make it on their own. They don't understand "the changes," physical and emotional, that they are going through, and they said there isn't someone they can talk to about them.

The lack of understanding about their "changes" has a high change potential because issues and topics related to the boys' development can be addressed and discussed in group meetings. Efforts can also be made through the group to help them with gaining temper control. The youths' motivation to work on both of these problem areas ("changes" and "temper") also contributes to an affirmative assessment of change potential.

Problem prioritization: In prioritizing problems, the workers considered mainly those problems that the group members said they wanted to work on. Although parent-son conflicts and low self-worth were seen by the workers as two problem areas, the group proceeded with identifying goals and tasks only for the following: (1) law-breaking leading to probation, (2) bad tempers, and (3) lack of understanding of the changes they were experiencing.

All of the youths knew that probation requirements included abiding by the rules of society and school, attending school, and obeying at home. They were also expected to attend weekly group meetings and to actively participate in them. If the youths had not agreed to the group, they would have been required to have weekly contact individually with a probation officer.

In discussing the prioritization of problems and goals with the group, everyone said top priority was to be given to getting off probation in four months (shortest possible time period). They knew that to achieve this goal, they had to meet all of the requirements of probation. In order to get along and abide by the rules at school and at home, the youths knew that they needed to work on controlling their tempers. They listed this as the second most important problem to be addressed. Finally, they agreed that basically they really didn't understand themselves and what was happening to them. They wanted to talk about the changes they had to learn to deal with.

Without having to use the prioritization tool, therefore, the group prioritized and clarified their goals as follows:

1. To get off probation in four months
2. To control their tempers at home and at school
3. To learn more about some of the changes they were facing (including becoming independent, understanding sex and family planning, and getting training and jobs)

There was a lengthy discussion over goal 1. Some wanted to add "and to stay off." What it would take "to stay off" was debated. Some said it meant they couldn't break the law any more. Others said they would just have to be more careful. The workers said that, hopefully, as participants grew in understanding and respecting themselves and others, they wouldn't need to be involved in law-breaking, and this would ensure their not getting caught again.

Contracting: Using the prioritized problems and goals, a contracted plan was initiated with the group, as shown in Diagram 6-15. As indicated in the diagram, no goals or tasks were specifically planned at this time for problems 4 and 5, because the group didn't want to work on these problems. Since the group gave first priority to the goal of getting off probation, the planned contract centered on this problem. Later, additional tasks were added to the contract for accomplishment of goals 2 and 3 (described in Chapter 7).

E. Ongoing Evaluation

During the assessment period, as the plan was made to chart progress weekly in the areas required for probation, evaluation graphs (explained in detail in Chapter 8) were designed to show the following: (1) group attendance, (2) group participation, (3) behavior in school (i.e., compliance with rules and expectations) and (4) behavior at home (i.e., compliance with rules and expectations). (See Figures 6-1, 6-2, 6-3, and 6-4.) Assessments of group attendance and participation were first scored by the co-leaders, and eventually by the youths themselves. The home assessments were made by the parents and given weekly over the phone to the workers. The school evaluation was made weekly by the youths' teachers and given to the school social worker, who had weekly contact with the court workers.

In addition to these weekly assessments, the workers checked each week to see if any of the group members had been reported to or picked up by police. Any incident was recorded in the youth's record and discussed with the youth individually.

FIGURE 6-1 Group Attendance

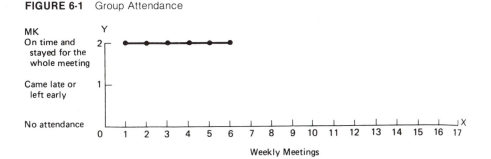

Weekly Meetings

MK

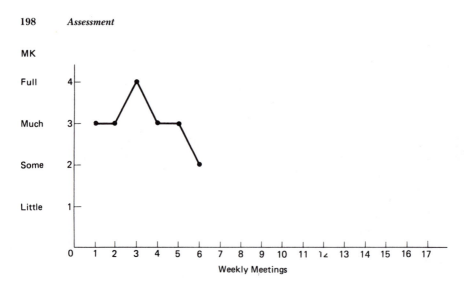

FIGURE 6-2   Group Participation

As indicated in Figure 6-1, group attendance was charted by a graph point that indicated the number of the meeting (1, 2, 3, etc.) and an attendance score of 0, 1, or 2. A score of 0 meant "no attendance." A score of 1 was used if a youth came late or left early. A score of 2 meant he was on time and stayed for the full meeting. The youths knew that to get a two-month reduction in probation, they needed to maintain a score of 2 every week unless they were excused by a worker.

In Figure 6-2, group participation was assessed on a 0–4 vertical scale in terms of 0 = none, 1 = little, 2 = some, 3 = much, and 4 = full. The points were plotted to indicate (*X*) the number of the weekly meeting and (*Y*) the

FIGURE 6-3   School Behavior (Compliance with Rules and Expectations at School)

MK

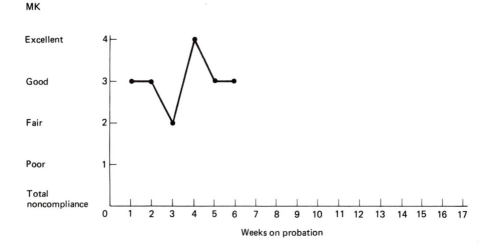

MK

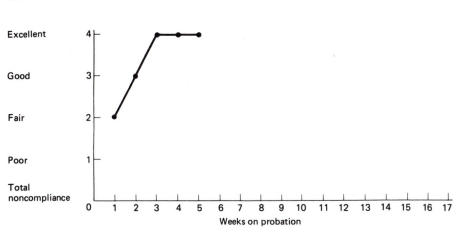

FIGURE 6-4   Home Behavior (Compliance with Rules and Expectations at Home)

score for participation. An attempt was made to give more specific criteria for participation scores by the leaders. If a youth came and did not seem interested and never said anything at the meetings, he was given a 0. If he spoke at least once or twice at the meeting, he was given a 1. Speaking up about three or four times and being somewhat interested earned a 2. Sharing or responding five or six times and showing much effort at a meeting to participate was a 3, and being fully involved and fully sharing at a meeting was a 4. Group members were informed that they would need to average 3 points in group participation if they were to have a reduced probationary period.

The graphs for charting home and school reports on behavior had scale points ranging from 0 to 4 (0 = total noncompliance, 1 = poor, 2 = fair, 3 = good, 4 = excellent). The workers requested descriptions of behaviors and incidents if a youth was assessed by his parent or teacher as showing "poor" or "fair" behavior (Figures 6-3 and 6-4).

CONCLUSION

In this chapter, the assessment stage of the General Method was described as consisting of the three major dimensions of (1) assessment statement, (2) problem prioritization, and (3) contracted plan. Tools were presented to assist the general practitioner in this stage of the Method.

Untrained workers have been found to move quickly into intervention after a problem is stated, without taking the time to assess the situation carefully.[8] A point emphasized in this chapter is the need for documented assessments and plans for each case before a worker takes action. Even when working with a crisis, the worker needs to demonstrate skill in planning where, when, and how to intervene. Through practice and supervised experience, the generalist learns to apply the tools in the process of assessment very quickly and accurately.

The General Method and each of its stages is a dynamic process. As circumstances change, the worker needs to be open to the possibility of having to reassess a situation or to reformulate a contract. There has been evidence that some workers resist finding out new information that would necessitate a reformulation of goals and plans.[9] A major challenge of general practice is to be able to stand on a diversified but solid foundation where one is expected to demonstrate flexibility and adaptation to emerging tensions, growth, and change.

Although the range of tasks and interventions by a generalist appears to be limitless, some parameters and guidelines need to be identified. An entry-level worker does have limitations in knowledge and skills. A skillful assessment may lead to a plan for referral to a specialized service. In the next chapter, an effort will be made to clarify and to categorize the interventions of a general practitioner during the fourth stage of the General Method. In the intervention stage, the worker collaborates with other systems in carrying out the plan that was contracted during assessment.

NOTES

[1]Anthony N. Maluccio and Wilma D. Marlow, "The Case for the Contract," in Beulah Roberts Compton and Burt Galaway, *Social Work Processes,* rev. ed. (Homewood, Ill.: Dorsey, 1979), p. 332.

[2]Mary E. Richmond, *Social Diagnosis* (New York: Russell Sage Foundation, 1917).

[3]John L. Levitt and William J. Reid, "Rapid-assessment Instruments for Practice," *Social Work Research and Abstracts* 17, no. 1 (Spring 1981): 13–19.

[4]See, for example, Florence Wexler Vigilante and Mildred D. Mailick, "Needs—Resource Evaluation in the Assessment Process," *Social Work* 33, no. 2 (March-April 1988): 101–104.

[5]Rosemary Sarri, "Diagnosis in Group Work," in Robert Vinter, ed., *Readings in Group Work Practice* (Ann Arbor, Mich.: Campus Publishers, 1967), pp. 37–71.

[6]Ann Hartman, "Diagnostic Assessment of Family Relationships," *Social Casework* 59 (October 1978): 465–76.

[7]Murray G. Ross, *Community Organization: Theory and Principles* (New York: Harper & Brothers, 1955), p. 39.

[8]Sister Maria Joan O'Neil, "Study of Direct Service Workers of the Department of Human Resources" (Unpublished report, Hartford, Conn., April 1980).

[9]Henry Miller and Toni Tripodi, "Information Accrual and Clinical Judgment," *Social Work* 12, no. 4 (July 1967): 63–69.

7

Intervention

A professional practice that is defined by its knowledge of theories, its methods, processes, modalities, and techniques, is meaningless to all but its own practitioners if it is not delivered appropriately to those who need its services.

—Carol H. Meyer[1]

The role of the worker during the intervention stage of the General Method evolves according to the tasks identified in the contracted plan described in the preceding chapter. Several roles have been identified as appropriate for an entry-level generalist. These include broker, advocate, reformer, educator, counselor, and mediator.[2] Before assuming any particular role, however, the generalist needs to clarify the nature of the problem to be addressed, the goals to be accomplished, the resources to be utilized, and the plan to be followed. Only after a period of engagement, data collection, and assessment will the worker be ready to assume the role necessary for appropriate intervention at any particular time. A generalist may move from one role to another or may assume multiple roles while using interventions during the process of helping. Often a worker may move from working with one to working with many, from the individual to the large bureaucracy. In general, the various activities of the entry-level generalist may be classified under the four major headings of (1) direct intervention, (2) information and referral, (3) case management and teamwork, and (4) indirect intervention. With each of these four major interventions, particular techniques and skills are used to work with different problems, age groups, or types of systems. In this chapter, the four general types of intervention will be presented as they are found in general practice.

As stated earlier, the generalist stands at the interface of persons and environment and carefully tries to collaborate with both systems in a planned intervention process to enhance their fit and interactions with each other. The selection of the type of intervention to be used is based on a skillful assessment.

DIRECT INTERVENTION

When a worker, in agreement with a system, intervenes directly with the system, that worker is engaging in *direct intervention*. The goals of direct intervention are primarily seen as (1) to give ongoing support to a system as it carries out contracted tasks, and (2) to help a system to bring about change in itself. Either or both of these goals may describe the purpose for direct intervention.

Planned intervention that directly involves a client system and a social work generalist may be brief or extended, depending on the identified need or problem and the capacities of the client and the worker. The extent of direction or leadership offered by the worker in direct intervention is influenced also by the seriousness or crisis level of the situation and by the strengths and coping capacities of the client. The nature of the interaction is usually supportive and growth-promoting.

The generalist uses a broad range of relationship and problem-solving skills in the course of intervening with members of a client system. The relationship itself is central to the entire process. Particularly in the intervention stage, a strong working relationship is necessary. During the course of direct intervention, the worker may use the relationship skills of listening, responding, guiding, paraphrasing, clarifying feeling, sensing, and, possibly, confronting. In addition, the problem-solving skills of problem and need identification, data collection, assessment, problem prioritization, goal-setting, planning, contracting, and evaluating may be repeated as problems are added or changed.

A client may begin with identifying immediate material needs or problems with institutions. As a working relationship develops and the worker is able to help with the presenting problems, clients frequently begin to discuss more interpersonal or personal problems. Information is gathered and assessments are made regarding each of these problems. Worker and client may agree to tasks on the contracted plan that entail direct, ongoing contact between worker and client system. This contact may be seen as a means for the client to achieve greater understanding of self and others or to bring about a change in self. If the goal identified is to bring about a change in someone outside of the client system, the intervention will need to include the outsider directly (becoming a part of the client system) or indirectly (becoming a target system). For example, if Mrs. N wants her husband to overcome his drinking problem, there is little chance of accomplishing this goal just by direct intervention with Mrs. N.

In addition to the foundation skills identified in Diagram 1-4, Chapter 1, contemporary techniques are being used, primarily by advanced workers, in direct practice with particular systems. Beginning generalists are not expected to use these techniques unless they have studied and practiced them under supervision. For example, eco-maps,[3] sculpting,[4] and genograms[5] are valuable tools to use when working with a family. They provide a technical and vivid means for helping clients to understand diverse perceptions of the family. (These techniques may also be adapted for use in working with individuals, groups, and communities.)

For working with groups, techniques and concepts have been identified to enable a worker to handle disruptive behavior[6] and scapegoating.[7] The use of force-field analysis[8] helps a worker to pinpoint the supportive and the constraining forces that have impact on the life and growth of an organization. The technique of force-field analysis and techniques to handle disruptive behavior and prevent scapegoating may also be adapted for use with individuals and families as well as groups and communities.

For working with adolescents, an effective technique to promote greater self-awareness is the use of the "adolescent grid."[9] By engaging youth in recalling major events within a visible framework, the adolescent can avoid the discomfort often felt in face-to-face interviewing. The grid identifies crisis points chronologically, according to place, family, school, health, activities, and other areas. Adults or children, individuals, groups, or families may also find that this structured instrument is a helpful device to overcome their fears of interacting with a worker.

The use of play is a valuable technique for working with children. Basically, a child is limited in communicating with words. Play is a natural means for children to express fears, wishes, hurtful experiences, and unmet needs. Repetitious play helps a child to master unpleasant experiences. To expect a child to be able to talk with a strange adult about his or her problems or painful experiences is unrealistic and insensitive. Children usually expect adults to speak to them in order to teach, direct, or correct them. A child may feel great fear and discomfort on being led into a room where there is nothing to indicate that it is a place for children. Social workers can learn how to select appropriate toys and to engage in play that is supportive and helpful to children. This technique is useful during every stage of the General Method when working with children. If it becomes apparent that the child's behavior patterns are inappropriate for the current reality, and that the supportive intervention of the generalist is insufficient to bring about the necessary change, a referral should be made to a child specialist. Through play therapy, a child may be helped to grow in insight and to be free to find appropriate responses to life situations.

As a worker intervenes directly with any person, family, group, or community, it may become clear that giving support or understanding is insufficient to achieve certain goals. If it is necessary for a change to take place in a system, the worker may use some techniques from behavioral modification, as well as problem-solving skills. In addition to helping a client system to develop a rational, systematic way to solve problems, a worker may use specific behavioral techniques for more immediate control of undesirable behaviors, thoughts, or feelings. Although behavior modification in its entirety is a specialized treatment approach, individual techniques such as behavior reinforcement, cognitive restructuring, relaxation exercises, and thought stopping can be selected for use in general practice.[10]

As stated, all of the contemporary techniques that have been cited are supplementary to the basic skills found in the foundation of general practice (Diagram 1-5, Chapter 1). Eco-maps, sculpting, genograms, techniques for handling disruptive behavior and scapegoating, force-field analysis, the adolescent grid, communicating through play, behavior reinforcement, cognitive restructuring, relaxation exercises, and thought stopping are tools that enable a client to grow in understanding. Also, they may facilitate change in a client by helping to clarify, objectify, and promote greater control of self or a situation.

There are times when it becomes clear that a client needs to change through gaining insight. If a pattern of behavior emerges that continues to cause problems, the generalist will try to confront the client about it in a cognitive, supportive, and problem-solving type of intervention. Some of the techniques identified above may be utilized. If this is insufficient to bring about the change necessary for goal achievement, the generalist has to be able to realize that a client system may need more intensive help to gain insight and overcome its problematic behavior. For the individual, family, group, or community, this could involve delving into buried feelings or past experiences over a prolonged period of time through an uncovering, sequential process. In time, the client system can be helped to connect current behaviors with feelings that are triggered by certain situations that relate to past experiences. Barriers and dynamics that cause conflict and broken relationships can be exposed. Through this intensive work, the system may be freed to choose more acceptable behaviors in the future.

This intensive direct work is not within the parameters of entry-level general practice. Occasionally, a system may come with enough strengths or past experiences to be able to grow in such insight with support from the generalist. Usually, however, the generalist brings the client system with this type of need to the point of realizing that more specialized help is needed, and they enter into the process of referral. Whether the client system is an individual, family, group, or community, there are times when the generalist is unable to help the system bring about the change needed through direct intervention, and a referral is made. A community worker, for example, may find that major factions within a community are preventing goal accomplishment. The power and political struggles may be so intense that the generalist is unable to break through these dynamics. A referral would be made to a community organizer with advanced skills and experience.

INFORMATION AND REFERRAL

There are times when it becomes apparent that a client system does not have the information needed for problem resolution. Often, clients have received misinformation or they have misconceptions about environmental resources. They may contact a worker to receive assistance which the worker or agency may not be able to provide. In these cases, the worker's intervention is primarily that of information and referral.

The process in which a worker directs a system to another resource for help with an identified problem or need is called *referral*. Often workers are surprised to learn that a resource has not picked up on a case as expected. Several factors can lead to an unsuccessful referral. There is, in fact, an art to knowing where, when, and how to make a referral. Time, planning, and processing are needed for an appropriate match between system in need and available resource. The act of referral may be described as a six-stage process. If any one of the stages is overlooked, the referral may fail. The experience of an unsuccessful referral may build up in the client system feelings of negativism and fear, as well as resistance to reaching out and trying again with another resource.

The referral process consists of the following essential stages to be enacted by worker and system in need.

1. Clarification and statement of the problem or need for which help is sought and of the goals to be accomplished
2. Researching appropriate and available resources and informing client about them
3. Discussion of options and selection of resource with the system in need
4. Planning and contracting the means of contact with the selected resource (initial contact, sending information, providing transportation, client-resource meeting)
5. Meeting of system in need with resource
6. Follow-up by worker to see if goal is being or has been accomplished

The basic principle of having the client do for him- or herself is paramount throughout the referral process. Only when it is clear that the client does not have the knowledge or ability to carry out a task in the process should the worker intervene and take action.

In stage 1, the generalist helps the client system to clarify what the problem or need is that cannot be taken care of by the generalist. The feelings and goals that relate directly with the identified problem or need are also explored. The feelings both client and worker may have about sending the client to a different resource need to be expressed. Either one might see a referral as a personal failure and feel somewhat guilty. The limitations of the worker and/or the agency should be presented as factually as possible. The client may need to be reassured that the referral is not a rejection by the worker. The worker needs to convey to the client system a sincere desire to see the client system achieve its goals and a strong belief in the ability of a resource to make this possible.

In stage 2 of the process, worker and, if possible, client system work on locating resources to meet the identified needs. Both formal and informal resources are explored. If a need or problem can be resolved through utilizing informal resources (family, friends, community), this may be more desirable to the client. Some clients may prefer not to have these local networks know about their problem, and formal resources (agencies, programs, institutions) will need to be considered.

It is imperative to find resources that are appropriate and available. A resource is appropriate not only because it provides services that address the identified problem or need, but also because it suits the persons and environment of the particular system in need. For example, a person who speaks only Spanish would need to receive help from an agency that understands and works with Hispanic people. Further, if the resource is not accessible to people from the neighborhood or environment of the client system, it is usually not an appropriate resource. If contact with the resource is expected to be brief and transportation can be assured, it is possible to use a resource that is not located near the environment of the client system. Sometimes, workers incorrectly assume that client systems are able to find bus fare or transportation on their own.

Agency resources may not be available for certain clients, owing to the hours when services are provided. Although a resource may be appropriate, it may have a long waiting list because of an insufficient number of staff members available to deliver the services. Moreover, the cost for the service may be outside the price range of some clients and, therefore, the resource is not available to them.

In stage 3 of the referral process, the worker and system share their findings about possible resources, and the client system is the one to choose the resource to be contacted. The worker helps the system to consider alternatives, with probable outcomes or consequences for each option. If there is some question or doubt about a resource, this should be explored. No false hope or reassurance should be given. Even when it appears that an appropriate and available resource has been located and selected, it may prove beneficial to help the client system at this time to identify a second choice in case the first does not work out.

In stage 4 of the referral process, time is given for planning and contracting to decide who will (1) make the initial contact with the resource (usually by phone), (2) give whatever information is necessary for the referral to be accepted, (3) arrange for transportation or provide it, (4) meet with the resource to initiate the services. There is a whole range of possible ways to achieve each of these four tasks. The two extremes on a scale to indicate the range of options would be (1) the client carrying out the task, and (2) the worker carrying it out. In between are different worker-client combinations for which the task may be subdivided. For example, in the first task of initial contact, the worker could (1) dial the number and have the client speak, (2) dial and speak first and then put the client on the phone, (3) have the client dial, but the worker speaks, (4) have a three-way conference call in which worker, client, and resource person all speak together. The initial contact might also involve writing a letter or going to the agency to set up an appointment. These tasks also could be done by the worker, by the client, or by some combination. The same range of options exists for deciding about giving information, arranging transportation, and having the first client-resource meeting. The guiding principle of having the members of the system do for themselves whenever possible should be used as the contract is formulated and tasks are planned.

In stage 5, the new helping process begins as the client system meets directly with the resource. Here, too, the art of referral operates, in the worker's careful assessment of whether or not the client system can or should have the first session alone with the resource. The worker not only considers the motivation and capacity of the client system to have this be a fruitful encounter, but also the motivation and capacity of the resource itself to truly be of help to the system in need. In some individual situations, it may be better to have the worker present in the first contact to offer support, information, or advocacy if needed. As soon as possible, however, the worker should back out and let the system become involved with the resource on its own.

Every referral should have some type of follow-up by the worker. When a person, family, group, or community come to a professional person or agency for help, they share—sometimes painfully—their problems, needs, and aspirations. The professional person and human-service agency show a sense of respect and commitment to people in need by working diligently at getting the necessary help for them. People asking for help are often vulnerable and dependent on the expertise and sensitivity of those sanctioned to give service. Social workers are expected to know what resources are available and how to help people utilize them. It is true that many times circumstances outside of the control of a worker or agency prevent the carrying through of a service. However, the social worker must find out if the person who asked for help did receive it. If the person did not receive help, the worker needs to find out why help was not given and to consider whether anything else could be done.

The worker finds out if help was provided by checking directly with the resource, with the client, or with both. It is important that both resource and client know that the worker will be calling back, and when to expect the follow-up. This should be clarified prior to the worker's last contact with each. In planning, the worker will skillfully discern what a follow-up contact with the client might do to the beginning working relationship of the client and the new resource. The worker will also need to consider what effect it might have on the client system to hear that the worker called the resource to see how things were going. As long as all three parties (worker, client, and resource system) know in advance that the worker will be doing a follow-up and it is clear who will be contacted and when, negative repercussions are avoided.

When it appears that the goals for the referral are being accomplished, the worker is able to close the case. If there are other problems or needs that are not being addressed by the resource, and the client system continues to ask for the services of the worker, a collaborative arrangement must be worked out between the resource and the worker. Using a holistic perspective, the generalist knows that problems and needs of a system are interdependent, and that when service provision is carried out by more than one resource, collaboration and teamwork among the resources are needed. A third type of intervention frequently found in general practice, therefore, may be identified as teamwork.

CASE MANAGEMENT AND TEAMWORK

Because of the nature of the work of the generalist, an entry-level social worker frequently needs to call on other resources for collaboration in providing service. On a contracted plan (Chapter 6), the identification of who will complete the task often includes a worker with one or more other helping persons. The individuals, groups, families, or communities that seek help from a generalist usually have many problems and, therefore, need assistance from several service providers. The generalist has skills to form action systems with these other resource persons in a cooperative effort to achieve their common purpose of providing human services.

Case management is a contemporary term that is used to refer to the actions taken by a worker to mobilize and to bring together the various services needed in a case for efficient, effective service delivery. A case manager tries to coordinate, monitor, and evaluate the services provided.[11] If identified as the case manager, the generalist must use skill to work with the various resources for a case to develop an atmosphere of shared leadership and openness. When diverse resources work together in common planning, decision making, and consolidated action, the efforts of this organized group may be called *teamwork*. Unless the service providers who are working with one system move to become a team, the generalist may carry the heavy burden not only of managing the case, but also of being seen as primarily responsible for its outcome. When resources truly become a team, there is a strong sense of sharing and commitment and of a group responsibility for final outcome.

To begin to grow in the art of teamwork, it is important to realize that there is no *one* model of teamwork that should be used at all times. Some teams have a designated leader, and some have a rotating leadership. A leader needs to have an understanding of group process, as well as goal-directed abilities and skill in bringing forth contributions and leadership from other members of the group.

There are six basic principles for effective teamwork. When a team is not achieving its goals, a review of the principles could reveal possible causes for difficulties incurred. The principles are summarized as follows:

1. *Obtain sanction:* Team members must be free to communicate openly in collaborative service planning and provision. The system in need must sanction the team with the understanding that there will be open communication among members.
2. *Know yourself:* All members of the team must clearly know their own professional identities and the distinctive contribution they and their agencies can make to the team.
3. *Respect one another:* Members of the team must respect each discipline, recognizing similarities and differences without being threatened or "turf protective."
4. *Meet regularly:* The team must meet on a regular basis for shared communication, planning, and evaluation.
5. *Define task assignments:* The team must define clearly each person's tasks and role in providing service.
6. *Share responsibility:* The team must assume collective responsibility for service outcome.

A team proceeds through stages that are similar to the six stages of the General Method. Collectively, members of the team clarify the problem and purpose for organizing, share data, agree on goals and a plan for intervention, assign tasks, evaluate, and terminate contact. The struggle for power or status, the emergence of conflict, and the development of group norms and expectations are important dimensions of a growing team, as they are for any human system.

Although teamwork may be emotionally draining and time-consuming, it can help to avoid duplication and excessive demands on limited, declining resources. Working together as a team can prevent fragmentation or overlap in service delivery. Through a team approach, client systems are not left with the burden of trying to integrate services on their own. A sense of unity and community is fostered.[12]

INDIRECT INTERVENTION

Currently, the concept "indirect practice" is defined in different ways within the profession of social work. On the one hand, it refers to practice in such areas as administration, supervision, management, or class advocacy. From this perspective, the practitioner is not having client contact. On the other hand, the term "indirect practice" is used to refer to work with target systems or outside agencies in order to achieve goals for a worker's client or clients. Because of possible confusion in the use of the concept, a distinction is made in this edition between "indirect practice" and "indirect intervention." The term "indirect practice" means advanced professional activities, such as administration and management. "Indirect intervention" refers to interactions with systems that affect clients during the intervention stage of the General Method. The worker intervenes with these systems in order to bring about changes needed for clients to achieve their identified goals.

Getting a system involved and responsive frequently uses a worker's political skills. The generalist may find a potential resource that is resistant to the requests of a client or the worker. Such skills as providing evidence, publicizing, bargaining, organizing, demonstrating, taking legal action, and influencing policy development may have to be utilized. For example, a hospital worker with refugee patients has been unsuccessful in obtaining services from a refugee program. The worker knows that the program is being funded to offer the services requested. The generalist may need to present to her supervisor and to the administrator of the refugee program evidence that several requests were made without results. If this intervention is unsuccessful and efforts at bargaining are also unproductive, a form of publicizing may need to take place.

Often a worker will need to use a combination of political skills to bring about change in a target system. For example, legislators may have to be contacted for funding to be allocated to expand needed programs. Evidence of need will have to be presented, and bargaining or demonstration may take place. The generalist may have to give testimony or to speak at open hearings. Interested groups may have to be organized for their participation in the change process. As indirect interventions are planned, the worker keeps in mind the need to involve the clients—those that are suffering from the problems—as much as possible in all of the planned activities.

Indirect interventions may be enacted with any size or type of system.

A worker and client system may be unable to achieve identified goals because of a refusal or resistance on the part of an individual, family, group, community, organization, or institution. Frequently, a worker serves a client through indirect interventions with target systems that are represented by members of various professions. Although every effort is made to develop a cooperative working relationship with these representatives, the generalist may have to move into an adversary process in behalf of the client system.

As a client advocate in an adversary process, a social worker tries to persuade a system to decide in favor of the client. The role of adversary is often difficult for a social worker with a basic practice principle of self-determination. The competition or drive for victory in an adversary process can become very strong. It may not be easy for a worker to remain calm and emotionally controlled if the opponent is presenting half-truths or attacking what the worker has presented as valid.

To interact effectively with members of different professions or within their work environments, a social worker needs to understand each profession and environmental system. For example, if social workers are to form alliances or adversary systems with lawyers, they need to have a working knowledge of the vocabulary, methods, and motivations of lawyers, of the requirements of law, and of the functioning of the legal system. Unfortunately, research shows that there is often a tense, untrusting relationship between social workers and lawyers.[13] The frustration that exists as these two professions interface may be due to a basic lack of understanding of each other. The use of words and the approach to problem-solving found in each discipline are different. The professionals may use the same words, but not mean the same thing. For example, the use of the words *contract* and *fact* may cause confusion in communication between lawyers and social workers. A contract used in the process of assessment by a social worker is not the same as the legal contract used in a legal process. Social workers collect data on feelings and attitudes as well as such facts as names, dates, and circumstances. They are concerned with "why" something happened in order to arrive at a plan for problem resolution. A lawyer is concerned with evidence and "what" happened to see if legal action can be taken. Although a social worker may know that something is true, it is not useful information in the court unless it can be documented and admitted into evidence. Whereas the law of the lawyer is technical and specific, the theory of the social worker is dynamic and evolving.[14]

Prior to any indirect intervention, the generalist needs to prepare for interaction with a system by studying the system and its representatives. It may be helpful to consult with someone from a similar system or discipline to identify the most effective way to contact, communicate, and intervene with the system.

Indirect interventions are usually the most challenging and difficult type of interventions for beginning generalists. Social work education pro-grams seldom provide students with a working knowledge of other profes-sional disciplines. Beginning generalists are primarily prepared for direct work with client systems.[15] The entry-level worker, therefore, needs strong educational and emotional support through supervision and consultation to persevere and accomplish indirect interventions.

DESIGNS FOR GENERAL INTERVENTIONS

The four major types of intervention by a generalist may be depicted in designs composed of circle clusters. In Figure 7-1, the worker (W) is seen in interaction with a client system (C) through overlapping circles. This simple design is used to demonstrate *direct intervention.*

A case example for Figure 7-1 is a generalist working with a family (father, mother, and son) as they grow in understanding the changing behav-iors of their adolescent son (age 15).

In Figure 7-2, a *referral* is pictured by a worker (W) interacting with a client system (C) as the client begins to interact with a resource (R). If con-tact with a particular resource system has not yet been actualized, but is the intent of the intervention, the resource system (R) may be depicted by a broken line. If both a worker and a client have direct contact with a re-source, the W circle would extend to the right and intersect the R circle also (Figure 7-3).

An example for Figures 7-2 and 7-3 would be a worker whose client is a depressed woman who is talking about suicide. As indicated in the design, the worker is trying to help the client to face the seriousness of her problem and to admit herself to the local mental health center.

In the design found in Figure 7-4, the worker (W) and other resources (A, B) join together in a team effort. Collectively, the worker (W) and other resources (A, B) interact with a client system (C). The overlapping circles reflect the *teamwork* in human service provision. For example, in working with a community that has experienced a number of unexplained fires lately, a generalist may be working with representatives from the fire depart-ment and the local police force to help the community members express

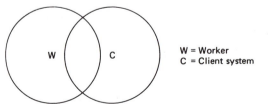

FIGURE 7-1   Direct Intervention

W = Worker
C = Client system

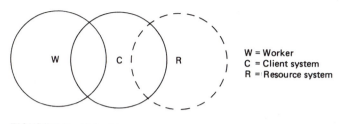

FIGURE 7-2 Referral

their concerns and to find ways to combat fires and to report suspected arsonists. In Figure 7-4, all three resources (worker, fire department, and police) are shown as coming together to form a team for ongoing service to the community. In Figure 7-5, the worker remains in the role of case manager because teamwork has not been established with all three resources to work together. The local police and the fire department are called upon by the worker to meet separately with the community on different occasions. The absence of an ongoing team effort is depicted in Figure 7-5 by boundaries that do not overlap (A and B), except with the worker (W) who contacts and coordinates the services for the community.

Figure 7-6 is a diagram of *indirect intervention.* In this design, the generalist (W) is interacting with a target system (T) to mobilize it to meet the needs of a client system (C).

A case example of indirect intervention as shown in Figure 7-6 could involve a group of youngsters who need tutoring. The generalist (W) can be seen as putting pressure on the school system (T) to provide the services needed for the group (C).

Additional designs in intervention may be drawn up to reflect combined intervention types. Sometimes, as shown in Figure 7-7, a generalist (W) may be involved with a number of community resources (A, B) in a team effort to influence a target system (T) for client service (C).

For example, a generalist (W) working in behalf of an elderly community (C) plagued by vandalism may join with town officials (A) and the local newspaper (B) to advocate better police protection (T) of the elderly community.

FIGURE 7-3 Referral—Worker and Client Contact

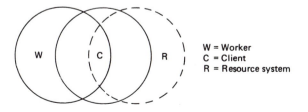

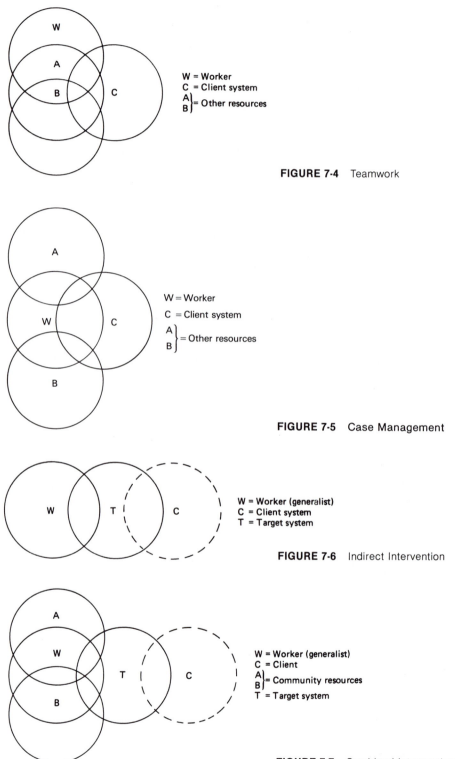

FIGURE 7-4 Teamwork

W = Worker
C = Client system
$\left.{A \atop B}\right\}$ = Other resources

FIGURE 7-5 Case Management

W = Worker
C = Client system
$\left.{A \atop B}\right\}$ = Other resources

FIGURE 7-6 Indirect Intervention

W = Worker (generalist)
C = Client system
T = Target system

FIGURE 7-7 Combined Interventions

W = Worker (generalist)
C = Client
$\left.{A \atop B}\right\}$ = Community resources
T = Target system

In the course of working with a system, a generalist may change the design of intervention as problems or needs emerge or are resolved. At any given time, a worker should be able to identify the design (or designs) currently being used.

WORKING WITH DIFFERENT SYSTEMS

As stated in the section on direct interventions, a generalist has skills and techniques for work with systems of any size. In addition to the relationship skills, problem-solving skills, and political skills, as categorized in the foundation framework (Diagram 1-5, Chapter 1), there is a range of techniques that can be called on as needed with particular systems. Techniques may be appropriately identified as general-practice techniques if they can be used with more than one type of system or problem. Specialized techniques are specifically designed for and used in a particular area of specialization, according to problem, population, institution, traditional or specialized method, or theoretical approach. Some techniques that originate in a specialized area may later be extended for use with a variety of systems by the generalist with additional knowledge, skills, and experience under supervision.

For example, although the technique known as "sculpting" has been used primarily in family work, as stated earlier, it could be used with a group or community. Basically, sculpting is a technique in which a person creates a live "sculpture" to portray the way he or she views the members of a system in relation to one another. The worker asks a volunteer to create a space and action configuration: to bodily place all members of the system as he or she sees them—according to distance and body position in relation to one another and to the volunteer. When placed in the position, each person stays as still as a sculpture. The sculptor is encouraged to discuss how and why each person has his or her position, and every member of the configuration is asked to describe what it feels like to be in that position. Each individual in the system is given the opportunity to sculpt out his or her perception of the system. The technique enables all present to grow in understanding the perceptions and feelings of one another. It helps to break down any personal barriers against verbalization and to lessen anxieties. Through this type of play activity, the less powerful or less verbal individuals in the system are freed to express their views and to receive the attention of everyone present.[16]

Often, there is a need within a group or a community, as well as within a family, for greater understanding and sharing among members. Individual members of a group can be encouraged by a worker to sculpt out how they see the interactions and relationships among group members through a sculpted tableau of the group.

In a meeting of a community, a generalist can ask for representatives of the subsystems that constitute the community to portray through space and action positioning how they perceive the relationships among subsystems of the community. Other members of the subsystem may be allowed to help their representative find the best way to depict relationships within the community from the collective eyes of the subsystem. Again, the technique of sculpting can expand the sensitivity of the parts to the perceptions of the whole. Communications within a community can be enriched as fears and feelings of insignificance are exposed.

The sculpting technique may be used also by a group of professionals for team building. If the process of teamwork is not moving along, the technique may be introduced to help members of the team become more aware of how each of them sees the emerging relationships and lines of communication within the team.

Actually, the sculpting technique may be used with different systems during any of the stages of the General Method. In addition to intervention, sculpting may facilitate progress during engagement, data collection, assessment, evaluation, and termination. The technique may be helpful in identifying goals as well as problems and feelings. Not only could the generalist ask the volunteer to sculpt out how he or she perceives the system at present (identifying problems and feelings), but also how he or she would hope to see the system in the future (goals). Through a discussion about each member's views for the future, a consensus may be reached on goals for the system.

Another example of the generic nature of techniques used by a generalist can be found in the behavioral technique of relaxation. The technique of relaxation exercises is done usually on a one-to-one basis. However, just as the individual becomes tense during times of stress, there are obvious periods in the meetings of groups, families, and communities when tensions rise and stress is heightened. As stress builds up within any one of these systems, energy to think and act rationally can become blocked. The generalist can help to reduce the mounting anxiety through a relaxation exercise.

Members of the system are first encouraged to become aware of the reality that tension is building, and they are asked to stop the process and the conversation for a few minutes to relax. One relaxation technique is to have members alternate in tensing and relaxing various muscles and to focus on the different feelings that result. They begin to sense the power within themselves to control the mounting or releasing of tension within their bodies. In addition, members are asked to take deep breaths and to be sensitive to the way deep breathing helps to relax muscles. As the system becomes peaceful and progressively relaxed, some cue words, such as "calm," "still," or "serene," may be said. Later, if tension begins to build again, these words may be used to help the system to recall the relaxed state. With anxiety reduced, the system may be helped to talk about what was triggering the mounting stress. Usually, something has been said that caused members of the system to feel threatened, angered, or afraid.[17]

Force-field analysis is a third example of a technique that may be used by a generalist during intervention with systems of different sizes. This technique, based on Kurt Lewin's "field theory"[18] has been developed primarily as a tool to assist in data collection and assessment of organizations.[19] With a little creative thinking and modification, the technique can readily be used in general practice with individuals, groups, families, and communities. Whenever any system is not able to change or to accomplish tasks that were identified in a contracted plan (Chapter 6), there are usually restraining forces operating that are stronger than the driving forces. The generalist may try to offer the system support and understanding of the situation by using a force-field analysis.

Basically, the technique is a procedure that uses a framework to organize information as it relates to the accomplishment of a goal. The forces that influence those individuals responsible for enacting tasks necessary for goal accomplishment are organized and classified as either "driving" or "restraining" forces. The process begins with a clarification of a specific goal. Then, those who are the primary actors or persons needed to achieve the goal are identified. Next, each of the forces impinging on these persons is categorized as either driving or restraining. The forces are then evaluated in terms of their openness to and potential for change. The consistency and stability of each force during a period of change is also questioned. Finally, a judgment is made regarding the strengths of the driving forces as compared with restraining forces in the light of the desirable goal. If there is no imbalance in which the change-producing forces have greater weight, the failure in goal accomplishment can be understood and predicted. The technique could help any individual, group, family, community, or organization to see more clearly why certain tasks are not being performed and goals are not being accomplished. It also provides direction for planned intervention to counteract the restraining forces and to build up those that are change-producing.

The technique of force-field analysis has characteristics similar to those of the tool used for problem prioritization as found in Chapter 6, and also of the procedure used for evaluation through goal analysis to be presented in the next chapter (Chapter 8). In addition to using the technique during direct intervention, the generalist and other resources of a team may find it helpful as they collectively plan strategies for intervention with target systems.

There are several other techniques that a generalist may use in the General Method when working with more than one type of system or problem. The four basic interventions (direct; information and referral; case management and teamwork; and indirect) are selectively applied with a range of techniques as the generalist interacts with different systems.

USING THE HOLISTIC FOUNDATION
IN INTERVENTION

Basic values, theories, and skills used by the generalist during the intervention stage of the General Method are identified in the holistic conceptualization of the foundation for general social work practice (Chapter 1). The practice principles that reflect the basic values of social work are very evident in the judgments and actions of the worker as interventions are planned and implemented. Interventions by a social worker are dependent on the willingness of a system to accept and cooperate with the worker. Inasmuch as possible, the system of contact is given the opportunity to determine for itself the types of involvement the worker will provide. Each problem-person-environment situation is individualized as the worker accepts or suggests certain rules or task responsibilities.

Throughout the four major types of interventions, different practice principles are highlighted. For example, *controlled emotional involvement* is a principle that is strongly needed during indirect intervention, especially when the worker is in an adversary process. *Individualization* and *purposeful expression of feelings* are central to direct intervention. *Acceptance* is crucial for effective teamwork. And *confidentiality* and *self-determination* are highlighted during referral.[20]

Knowledge used during intervention varies according to the task at hand. During direct intervention, theories about the type of system (individual, group, family, community, organization) the worker is interacting with are used. With indirect intervention, knowledge of policies, procedures, institutions, and social-change theory is particularly relevant. In referral, the worker needs to know resources. For teamwork to be successful, individual members need to know about their own profession and other professions, as well as group dynamics and processes.

In addition to the various techniques used by the generalist as described earlier in this chapter, the skills listed in the holistic foundation (Chapter 1) are demonstrated during the intervention stage. Relationship skills and problem-solving skills are pervasive during direct intervention. Political skills are used primarily with indirect interventions. In the referral process and during teamwork, a worker may find it necessary to use all three major types of skills: relationship, problem-solving, and political.

The heart of the General Method may be seen as intervention; the appropriate use of skills and techniques at this time is crucial to the fulfillment of the process. As emphasized, the selection of skills and techniques is guided by a worker's application of basic values and knowledge. The holistic conceptualization of the foundation for practice is a helpful reference for the generalist who must artfully apply foundation knowledge, values, and skills when intervening in each unique situation.

HUMAN DIVERSITY IN INTERVENTION

Culture

As brought out in this chapter, the interventions of the generalist may be identified as direct service, indirect service, referral, and teamwork. When a worker is intervening directly with a system of another culture, an interpreter may be needed to overcome language differences. In one sense, direct intervention becomes a type of teamwork when an interpreter is used. Although interpreters repeat what has been said verbatim as they translate, they also need the ability and sensitivity to convey the feelings and attitudes that are being communicated. Interpreters for social workers need to have some understanding of the basic principles and practices of the worker. They need to realize the difference between relating to a friend and to a client, and to be able to convey the personal style of the social worker. Open communication with a strong sense of trust and mutual commitment should exist between the worker and the interpreter. The worker needs to make every effort to communicate directly and respectfully with a client system, even when an interpreter is being used. At no time should any member of the client system be made to feel like an object to supply information or to be talked about. Children should not be used as interpreters for their parents because it puts them in a position that generally contradicts their role and place in their culture. It may also prevent a parent from dealing with content he or she does not wish to discuss in front of the children.

In working with minorities, the interventions of a worker may be more often indirect than they are in work with people of the majority. In addition to direct provision of services, a worker may serve minorities through various types of indirect involvements with target systems. The nature of such involvements may be primarily educational, with presentations of research findings to document need. A worker may be intervening through applying political pressures on institutions, legislators, or agencies. For example, a worker may become actively involved in promoting legislation to insure an adequate income for all children and families, or in changing policies or structures of traditional agencies that have to be changed if members of minority groups are to receive adequate services. Agencies may need to be encouraged to join up with representatives of minority groups to organize for more sensitive and relevant service provision. As brought out by Leon Chestang, the three essential criteria for programs serving minorities are proximity, relevance, and community participation.[21]

When an agency cannot supply the needed type of intervention, a referral must be made. The worker looks for resources that appear to be sensitive to the culture of the client. This may become apparent by considering

(1) the cultural background and languages of those administering and providing the service, (2) the location of the service, (3) the involvement or input by the particular cultural group in the resource, and (4) the extent to which members of the cultural community have received satisfactory services from the resource in the past. Before contacting a formal resource, a worker and system should explore thoroughly the possibility of locating available informal resources. In meeting emotional, social, and personal needs, particularly for minority members, familial and community resources are often far more effective than formal agencies or programs. Also, informal resources usually provide greater stability through ongoing availability. It is in the black community, for example, that members of the Afro-American culture receive their emotional support and positive identity. As Chestang writes:

> The black person finds emotional solace within the black community. Here are the comforts of family, the protections of supportive institutions such as churches, fraternal organizations and civil rights groups. Here the black person has an opportunity to build self-esteem through the exercise of talents and skills, to develop a sense of personal identity through enduring relationships with family, friends and significant others, and to struggle in the company of others who face common barriers to the pursuit of a better life.[22]

When a worker intervenes through teamwork with other professionals, it is important to see that team members are sensitive to the culture of the system receiving service. Ideally, there would be at least one member of the team who shares the culture of the consumer. If this is not possible, the team should seek periodic consultation from someone with a cultural background similar to that of the consumer receiving service or at least from someone with knowledge, experience, and demonstrated sensitivity for working with people of the particular culture.

Sexual Variation

The use of groups has been emphasized in the literature as a very effective intervention when working with lesbian and gay persons.[23] Especially for those individuals who do not have a nurturing, accepting family or community network, a group of people who share common values, problems, pressures, concerns, and life style can be very supportive and strengthening. With regard to confidentiality, particular caution may need to be taken by a gay or lesbian group. Some members may not want to have their sexual orientation known outside of the group for various reasons, including the risk of losing job or children. In working with gay or lesbian groups or individuals, a generalist will be promoting self-esteem and self-sufficiency by using the General Method because it is a collaborative,

problem-solving approach that encourages assertiveness and empowerment. As presented throughout this text, a guiding principle is to have members of a system do whatever there is to be done by themselves whenever
possible.

Gender Sensitivity

The interventions for working with men and women on gender-role
problems may include working with groups as well as with individuals.
Women may need to be helped, individually or collectively, to speak with
self-respect and to find ways to influence their current life situations for
greater personal fulfillment. Men may need to be encouraged to form bud-
dyships or to join groups for men and to realize that their emotions are
healthy, helpful guides to reality. Workers may join with men and/or women
in advocating for changes in policies and practices of sexist institutions. As
men and women are enabled to communicate honestly about themselves
and their needs and to take action in their own behalf, they begin to experience a sense of freedom and wholeness. As stated, they may need ongoing
support from the worker and others as this personal growth is taking place.

In addition to culture, sexual variation, and gender, the interventions
of a worker during this stage should also reflect a sensitivity to such other
diversity variables as age and stages, endowment and personality, value systems, class, and geographic location.

INTERVENTION IN DIVERSE FIELD AREAS

I. FIELD AREA: CHILD WELFARE

A. Agency: State Department of Children's Services

B. Client System

K, 15 years old, female, moving from emergency shelter into group
home. (For more background information, see Chapter 4, Engagement in Diverse Field Areas, I. Child Welfare.)

C. Summary of Preceding Stages

The problems, goals, and contracted tasks identified during engagement, data collection, and assessment are listed in Diagram 6-6 of Chapter 6.
The three major problems were assessed in terms of change-potential scores
and prioritized as follows: (1) permanent placement, 24; (2) school placement,
23; (3) personal problems—(a) depression, 21; (b) poor self-esteem, 20; (c) identity confusion, 20; and (d) sexuality, 19.

D. Intervention

The types of interventions by the worker were (1) direct work, (2) referral, and (3) teamwork. In addition to working directly with K and to making a referral to the group home, the child-welfare worker continued as K's state worker (the state maintained custody) and formed an action system (teamwork) with the administrator and other members of the staff of the group home. The worker also participated in school conferences on K, thus forming an alliance with the teacher and social worker of the school. Prior to K's placement in her present group home, the worker had also worked collaboratively with the staff at the shelter. The design that primarily depicts the interventions of the child-welfare worker is found in Figure 7-8.

The direct work with K was primarily to give her support as she carried out the tasks identified in the contracted plan (Diagram 6-6, Chapter 6) and to discuss her adjustment in the group home and in school. Contacts with personnel from the group home and school were mainly for the purpose of monitoring K's adjustment and personal growth and to see if any additional services were needed.

A month after K's placement in the group home, K and the worker reviewed the reasons for K's commitment to the state. K understood the need for the worker to petition the court for a continuance of her commitment. This need and its related goals and tasks were added to the planned contract, as recorded in Diagram 7-1. After K was in the group home for three months, the worker and K evaluated the progress that had been made.

II. FIELD AREA: GERONTOLOGY

A. Agency: Seaside Nursing Home

B. Client System

Mrs. J, an 80-year-old Portuguese woman in a skilled-nursing facility. (For additional background information, see Chapter 4, Engagement in Diverse Field Areas, II. Gerontology.)

C. Summary of Preceding Stages

The problems, goals, and tasks identified during engagement, data collection, and assessment are indicated in the contracted plan found in Diagram 6-8, Chapter 6. During assessment, problems were prioritized as follows: (1) unfamiliarity with staff and resources of the home, (2) fighting with nurses over bath, (3) seclusiveness (not leaving room), (4) calling residents names, and (5) cultural isolation.

D. Intervention

Interventions by the worker in this case were (1) direct work with the client through twice a week sessions, and (2) teamwork with the nursing-home

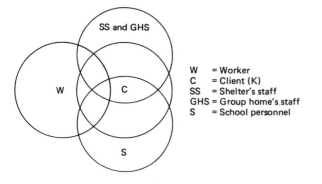

W   = Worker
C   = Client (K)
SS = Shelter's staff
GHS = Group home's staff
S   = School personnel

FIGURE 7-8   Worker's Combined Interventions: Field Area I

staff (nurses, program planner, recreational staff, volunteer director, and a volunteer) and also with the pastor of the church Mrs. J attended before hospitalization. The designs that demonstrate these primary interventions of the worker are found in Figures 7-9 and 7-10.

Through working with the church pastor, members of his congregation who knew Mrs. J began to visit her and to take her out to special church celebrations (a concert and the Christmas prayer service). Mrs. J was extremely happy to have them visit her and take her out to church activities. She also began to attend Bible services held in the nursing home. At first she went with the worker; later, she would go with other residents. Mrs. J began to carry on a conversation with other residents at her dining-room table and on her corridor. She became friendly with her roommate, and they would go together to entertainments put on by the recreation department at the home.

Eventually, a Portuguese-speaking volunteer began to visit Mrs. J. This young woman came only three times before she dropped out of the volunteer program. The worker continued to try to locate Mrs. J's family members but was unsuccessful. If family members had been reached, they would probably have been target systems, and the worker's indirect intervention would be depicted as shown in Figure 7-11. If Mrs. J's children had been responsive to the worker's efforts and asked for the worker's help, they would have become an extended part of the client system (Figure 7-9). If they joined with the worker and the home in providing support for their mother, they would be seen as constituent members of the action system and perceived by the worker and the staff as team members in collaborative effort for goal attainment (Figure 7-9).

E. Charted Progress

As the tasks of the contract were executed, the worker recorded their completion by indicating the dates of accomplishment on the contracted plan. Visits by members of her former church were also recorded in the task column (see Diagram 7-2).

DIAGRAM 7-1 Contracted Plan Continued

DATE IDENTIFIED	PROBLEM/ NEED	GOAL	TASK	CONTRACT	DATE ANTICIPATED	DATE ACCOMPLISHED
2/24	4. Need to remain in custody of state (abusive parents)	4. To obtain continuance of custody	1. Discuss	1. Worker and K	2/24	
			2. Prepare case summary	2. Worker	2/24	
			3. Petition court for continuance	3. Worker	3/1	
			4. Attend court hearing	4. Worker	3/30	

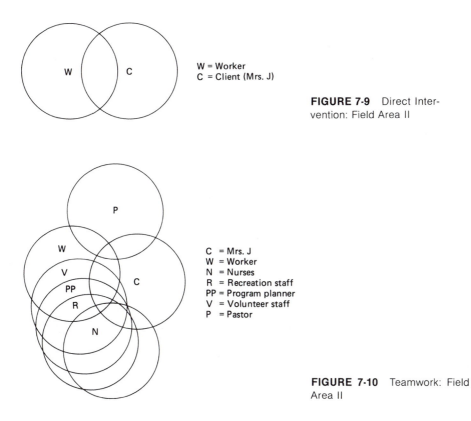

W = Worker
C = Client (Mrs. J)

FIGURE 7-9 Direct Intervention: Field Area II

C = Mrs. J
W = Worker
N = Nurses
R = Recreation staff
PP = Program planner
V = Volunteer staff
P = Pastor

FIGURE 7-10 Teamwork: Field Area II

FIGURE 7-11 Indirect Intervention: Field Area II

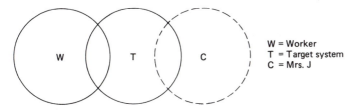

W = Worker
T = Target system
C = Mrs. J

III. FIELD AREA: PUBLIC SOCIAL WELFARE

A. Agency: State Social Service

B. Client System

Mr. and Mrs. P and their two children (2 and 4 years old) in need of housing (emergency and long-term) and food (emergency and supply until AFDC payment). (For additional background information, see Chapter 4, Engagement in Diverse Field Areas, III. Public Social Welfare.)

DIAGRAM 7-2 Contracted Plan

DATE IDENTIFIED	PROBLEM/ NEED	GOAL	TASK	CONTRACT	DATE ANTICIPATED	DATE ACCOMPLISHED
9/27	1. Unfamiliarity with staff and resources of nursing home	1. To get to know staff and the resources of the nursing home	1. To meet twice a week with worker	1. Worker and Mrs. J	10/4 and every Tuesday and Thursday	10/4, 10/9, 10/11, 10/16, 10/18, 10/23, 10/25, 10/30
			2. To meet with program planner	2. Worker, Mrs. J, and program planner	10/16	11/1, 11/6, 11/8, 11/13, 11/15, 11/20, 11/22, 11/27; 12/6, 12/11, 12/13
			3. To meet with a person from recreational staff	3. Worker, Mrs. J, and recreation-staff person	10/23	10/23
10/2	2. Fighting with nurses over bath	2. To work out bath schedule with nurses	1. To meet with head nurse to discuss bath schedule	1. Mrs. J and head nurse	10/16	10/16
9/25	3. Seclusiveness: not leaving room alone	3a. To leave room alone (at least once a day)	1. To walk down to nursing station alone (at least once a day)	1. Mrs. J	10/25 and each day thereafter	10/26; 11/6, 11/14, 11/20; 12/3, 12/5, 12/12, 12/15

	b. To attend a house activity (at least once a week)	1. To go to house activity, program, or meeting (at least once a week)	1. Worker or staff member and Mrs. J first two times	Starting week of 10/22	10/24, 12/30
			2. Mrs. J with residents each week thereafter	Starting week of 11/5	11/5, 11/12, 11/21 11/28; 12/3, 12/7, 12/12, 12/17
10/2	4. Calling residents names	4. To stop calling residents names	1. Mrs. J	10/16 and thereafter	10/16 until 10/20 (argument 10/21) and thereafter
		1. To stop name-calling			
		2. To say "hello" to residents	2. Mrs. J	10/16 and thereafter	
9/25	5. Cultural isolation	5. To share culture with others	1. Mrs. J, worker, director of volunteers	10/25	10/25
		1. To meet director of volunteers			
		2. To visit with Portuguese volunteer	2. Mrs. J and volunteer	?	11/13, 11/20, 11/30
		3. To visit with pastor of church	3. Mrs. J and pastor	?	11/14, 11/20, 11/30
		4. To visit with member of church	4. Mrs. J, pastor and congregation	11/20	11/30
		5. To go off grounds to attend church activity	4. Mrs. J and congregation (Mr. and Mrs. T)	12/4, 12/17	12/4, 12/17

C. Summary of Preceding Stages:

The problems, goals, and tasks contracted as the worker and the P's moved quickly (crisis situation) through the stages of engagement, data collection, and assessment are indicated in Diagram 6-10, Chapter 6. The problems and needs of the family were prioritized as follows: (1) food—emergency food, (2) housing—temporary shelter, (3) food supply until AFDC payment, and (4) long-term housing.

D. Intervention

The types of interventions by the worker were (1) referral, (2) direct interventions, and (3) teamwork. The worker placed the family at Center City Motor Inn on the same day that they arrived at the agency. The family rejected the options of Salvation Army (mother and father would be placed in separate facilities) and the City Hotel (disliked the location). Before going to the Motor Inn, the worker took the family to the Good News Soup Kitchen for a meal and picked up a bag of groceries at the Center Churches Food Bank.

While at the motel, Mrs. P asked the worker to try to get a medical card for her to take the children to the health center for a checkup. The worker learned that the medical card was being processed at central office and it would take another eight days. The worker wrote a letter to the health center verifying the status of the P family. The letter was cosigned by the family's income-maintenance technician. Medical transportation was requested and provided for Mr. and Mrs. P and the children to go to the health center.

Mr. and Mrs. P did not actively search for permanent living quarters. They said that they didn't think they liked the locations of the apartments listed in the paper. The worker offered to drive them to look at places, but they only went to two places with him. By the end of ten days, the worker stressed that their time was running out, and the P's requested an extension of time. The application for an extension was denied, and the P's asked for a fair hearing. They were again denied at the hearing and told that they would have to leave the motel by the following Monday. When Monday came, the P's informed the worker that they had located an apartment and requested help with moving their furniture from Mrs. P's father's house to the new apartment. After the family got the three required moving estimates, their moving expenses were covered through the Income Maintenance Department.

In their new apartment, the family requested help with obtaining fuel assistance. The worker informed them that they needed to keep their fuel bills and showed them how to apply for assistance. Their AFDC check was detained because of the address change, and the worker hand-delivered the check and food stamps.

The family had a problem with the refrigerator and asked the worker to help them to obtain funding to have it repaired. The worker suggested that they try the Salvation Army, which might pay for new parts. The worker learned later that the P's received a new refrigerator and that this was handled through the income-maintenance technician. Mr. P asked if the worker thought he should reapply to Social Security for Supplemental Security Income benefits. The worker inquired about the procedure for reapplication and encouraged Mr. P to begin the process.

Mrs. P asked if the worker knew of any place where the family could go to receive a Thanksgiving basket. Mr. P also wondered if there was any place where he could get Christmas presents for the children. The worker inquired and informed Mr. P that baskets were being given by several local churches and that the Salvation Army had children's gifts.

At one point earlier, when it seemed that the P's were not going to find housing, the worker had explored the process for referring the family to the Protective Services Department. It appeared that placement of the children might be needed until housing for the family was located. Fortunately, this was not necessary.

In the case of the P family, a number of resources were mobilized by the B.S.W. worker. The worker went with the P's to obtain food and shelter. Initial contacts were made by the worker for the P's with the fuel-assistance program, Social Security office, medical transportation services, and Salvation Army (Figure 7-12).

In addition to referral, the worker maintained ongoing direct intervention with the family for three months. (Figure 7-13). Throughout this period the worker engaged in teamwork with the income-maintenance technician and with Mr. P's psychiatrist. Contact with the income-maintenance technician averaged once a week. The worker spoke with the psychiatrist on five different occasions. These team efforts (Figure 7-14) provided the family with coordinated services and offered the service providers an opportunity for shared service delivery.

E. Charted Progress

As various interventions were identified and enacted, the worker recorded them, along with the dates of task accomplishment, on the contracted plan. After the P's were placed in temporary shelter, the goal of locating a long-term residence took longer to accomplish than anticipated. The efforts to obtain a time extension for temporary placement were also recorded, as were additional problems and needs that surfaced. Goals and contracts for

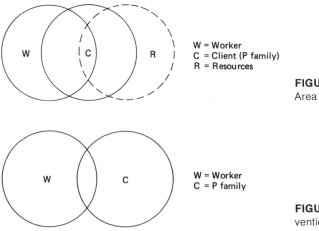

W = Worker
C = Client (P family)
R = Resources

FIGURE 7-12 Referral: Field Area III

W = Worker
C = P family

FIGURE 7-13 Direct Intervention: Field Area III

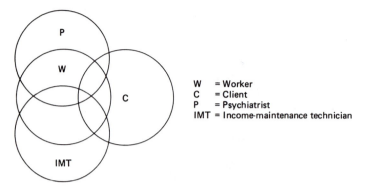

W   = Worker
C   = Client
P   = Psychiatrist
IMT = Income-maintenance technician

FIGURE 7-14   Teamwork: Field Area III

each new problem were developed with the P's and charted on the contracted plan. (See Diagram 7-3.)

As indicated in the diagram, task 3 (move to new apartment) for problem 4 (housing—long-term) was not accomplished until 11/7, even though the anticipated date was "not later than 10/12." The additional needs of a medical exam for the children (including transportation), fuel assistance, AFDC check delivery, refrigerator repair, Thanksgiving baskets, and Christmas presents for the children were also listed and contracted.

IV. FIELD AREA: COMMUNITY SERVICES

A. Agency: Clayton Neighborhood House

B. Client System

Four Hispanic families without heating in their apartments on the second floor of 33 L Street. (For more background information, see Chapter 4, Engagement in Diverse Field Areas, IV. Community Services.)

C. Summary of Preceding Stages

The problem, goal, and contracted tasks developed by the worker and the community of residents in earlier stages are outlined in Diagram 6-12 of Chapter 6. In addition to the need for heating in their apartments, the families recognized that they had a communication problem with their landlord. They were not, however, interested in trying to find ways to improve communication with him at this time.

D. Intervention

The interventions of the worker were both direct and indirect. The worker met with the residents directly to plan and monitor change. She also served as their advocate through indirect work with Mr. X, the landlord. Designs depicting the worker's intervention are found in Figures 7-15 and 7-16.

DIAGRAM 7-3 Contracted Plan Continued

DATE IDENTIFIED	PROBLEM/ NEED	GOAL	TASK	CONTRACT	DATE ANTICIPATED	DATE ACCOMPLISHED
9/28	4. Housing— long-term	4. To move into an apartment for long-term residence	1. Explore resources	1. Mr. and Mrs. P and worker	9/29	9/30
			2. Contact resources	2. Mr. and Mrs. P	9/29	9/30, 10/10
			3. Move	3. The P's	10/12	11/7
			4. Update	4. Worker, Mr. P's doctor, income-maintenance technician	9/29 and weekly	9/29; 10/6, 13, 20, 27; 11/3, 10, 17
			5. Request extension for temporary placement	5. Worker	10/11	10/11
			6. Fair hearing	6. Mr. and Mrs. P, worker, and de-partment board	10/31	10/31
			7. Request moving assistance	7. Worker	11/5	11/5
9/28	5. Poor money management					
10/1	6. Medical exam for children	6. To have chil-dren exam-ined at health center	1. Find out about medical cared	1. Worker	10/2	10/2

(continued)

DIAGRAM 7-3 (continued)

DATE IDENTIFIED	PROBLEM/ NEED	GOAL	TASK	CONTRACT	DATE ANTICIPATED	DATE ACCOMPLISHED
10/1 (cont.)			2. See if health center will accept letter of authorization	2. Worker	10/2	10/2
			3. Write letter	3. Worker and income-maintenance technician	10/5	10/5
			4. Make appointment	4. Mrs. P	10/5	10/8
			5. Make arrangements for medical transport	5. Worker and income-maintenance technician	10/8	10/8
			6. Take children to health center	6. Mr. and Mrs. P and medical transport service	10/12	10/12
11/14	7. Need for fuel assistance	7. To obtain fuel assistance	1. Explore resources	1. Worker	11/15	11/15
			2. Discuss	2. Worker and P's	11/16	11/16
			3. Fill out application	3. P's with worker's help	11/20	11/20
			4. Follow up if necessary	4. Mr. P	11/26	
11/14	8. Check and food stamps	8. To receive AFDC check and food stamps	1. To find out about delay in delivery	1. Worker	11/14	11/14
			2. To get check at central office	2. Worker	11/15	11/15
			3. To deliver check to P's	3. Worker	11/16	11/16

Date	Problem	Goal	Task	Responsible	Date	Date
11/20	9. Malfunctioning refrigerator	9. To fix refrigerator	1. Get estimates on repairs needed	1. Mr. P	11/20	
			2. Explore funding resources	2. Worker	11/20	11/20
			3. Contact Salvation Army	3. Mr. P	11/22	
			4. Have refrigerator repaired	4. Mr. P	11/23	(Problem withdrawn 12/4—new refrigerator)
			5. Send bill to Salvation Army	5. Mr. P	11/26	
11/20	10. Supplemental Security Income	10. To receive Supplemental Security Income	1. Contact Social Security office	1. Worker	11/21	11/21
			2. Discuss	2. Worker and P's	11/22	11/22
			3. Complete application	3. Mr. P	11/22	
			4. Follow-up call	4. Mr. P	11/26	
			5. Go for interview	5. Mr. P	11/27	
11/20	11. Thanksgiving food basket	11. To receive a food basket	1. Explore resources	1. Worker	11/21	11/21
			2. Contact churches	2. Mr. P	11/22	
			3. Go for basket	3. Mr. P	11/24	
11/27	12. Gifts for children	12. To obtain Christmas gifts for children	1. Explore resources	1. Worker	11/28	11/28
			2. Contact resources	2. Mr. P	11/29	
			3. Pick up gifts	3. Mr. P	12/5	

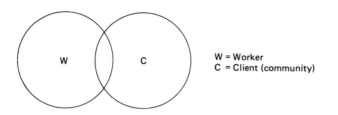

FIGURE 7-15   Direct Intervention: Field Area IV

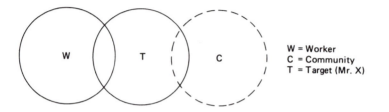

FIGURE 7-16   Indirect Intervention: Field Area IV

When the worker returned to meet with the residents on the day after she contacted the landlord, she found that their apartments were heated. She had brought thermometers with her for each apartment. They registered 68°. The residents expressed gratitude and hoped that the heating would continue throughout the winter. The worker told the group about her conversation with the landlord. They admitted that they didn't really know the man but continued to be afraid to have contact with him. They agreed to monitor the heating in their apartments by checking their thermometers each day. They would meet with the worker in one week to report on their findings.

E. Charted Progress

As the worker and the residents planned additional tasks, the worker recorded the extended plan by adding items to the "task," "contract," and "date anticipated" columns of the contracted plan (Diagram 7-4).

V. FIELD AREA: EDUCATION

A. Agency: Keeney Elementary School

B. Client System

Mr. and Mrs. G and their son Jim, 8 years old, in third grade, with problems at school and at home directly related to his parents' problem with their marital relationship. (For further background information, see Chapter 4, Engagement in Diverse Field Areas, V. Education.)

DIAGRAM 7-4 Contracted Plan Continued

DATE IDENTIFIED	PROBLEM/ NEED	GOAL	TASK	CONTRACT	DATE ANTICIPATED	DATE ACCOMPLISHED
			4. Monitor heat daily in each apartment	4. One person from each family (Mr. T, Mrs. V, Mr. A, and CR)	12/5 to 12/12	
			5. Meet to review findings	5. Worker and residents	12/12	

C. Summary of Preceding Stages

The problems, goals, and contracted tasks identified during preceding stages are outlined in Diagram 6-14, Chapter 6. The two primary tasks prioritized and contracted for Mr. and Mrs. G were (1) getting Jim to school on time each day and (2) going together for marital counseling. Jim's poor school performance and his sleeping problem were seen as reactions to Mr. and Mrs. G's quarreling and, especially, to Mrs. G's threat that she was going to leave her husband and children. The social worker's primary contracted tasks included meeting with Jim, his teacher, and his parents regarding Jim's school performance and general progress.

D. Intervention

The interventions of the worker may be identified as (1) direct (Jim; Mr. and Mrs. G; Jim and his parents) (see Figure 7-17); (2) referral (marital counseling for Mr. and Mrs. G) (see Figure 7-18); and (3) teamwork (worker and Jim's teacher, working with Mr. and Mrs. G to help Jim) (see Figure 7-19). The worker also attended a student study team conference on Jim with several members of the school faculty (principal, nurse, classroom teacher, learning-disabilities teacher, social service supervisor, worker). Jim's parents had been invited to this conference but they said that they couldn't attend because they were working.

During their meeting with the worker at school, Mr. and Mrs. G invited Jim to join them before the end of the meeting. At this time, Mr. and Mrs. G informed Jim that they knew that he had been worried about them because he had heard them arguing. They admitted to Jim that they had been having some problems but assured him that they were going to work out their difficulties. They told Jim they were going to get help themselves so they could learn to get along better with each other. They stressed that it was not Jim's problem and that he really didn't have to worry about them. They also assured Jim that neither one of them was thinking of giving up or leaving home. Jim was encouraged to try to do better in school. They said they knew it must have been hard for Jim. Mr. G said he knew it was hard enough for Jim to be "a little man in a big world," and that Jim didn't have to take onto his shoulders the problem of his mother and father. As he hugged his parents, Jim said he would try to work harder in school.

Before leaving this interview, it was agreed by all that the worker would continue to see Jim twice a week and that the follow-up contacts between

FIGURE 7-17   Direct Intervention: Field Area V

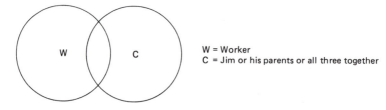

W = Worker
C = Jim or his parents or all three together

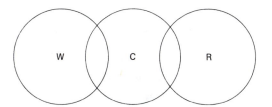

W = Worker
C = Mr. and Mrs. G
R = Resource (family
      counseling center)

FIGURE 7-18   Referral: Field Area V

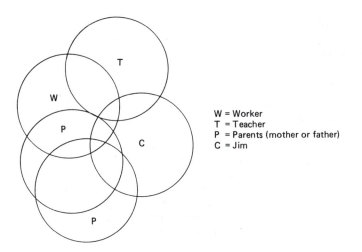

W = Worker
T = Teacher
P = Parents (mother or father)
C = Jim

FIGURE 7-19   Teamwork: Field Area V

the worker and Mr. and Mrs. G would be by telephone for 2 weeks. These would be followed by a home visit by the worker, at which time they all would consider termination of planned contacts if progress was apparent.

In talking with Mrs. G on the telephone the following week, the worker learned that Mr. G had made the appointment and that Mr. and Mrs. G had begun counseling sessions at the family counseling center. Mrs. G said that Jim still wanted a light left in his room at night but he didn't need to have his mother with him. He settled for a small night light.

Jim's teacher reported that Jim was beginning to look happier and to show more interest in his schoolwork. The worker continued to meet with Jim in her office twice a week, and Jim was interested in playing age-appropriate games. They drew up ongoing evaluation graphs to chart Jim's progress in school (to be presented in the next chapter).

E. Charted Progress

As tasks contracted in the plan developed by Mr. and Mrs. G, Jim, and the worker (Diagram 6-13, Chapter 6) were carried out, the worker recorded the date they were completed in the "date accomplished" column of the contracted plan. At the last meeting of the worker with Mr. and Mrs. G in their home, the worker shared the updated plan with them as they reviewed and evaluated progress.

VI. FIELD AREA: CORRECTIONS

A. Agency: Juvenile Court

B. Client System

Seven male adolescents, age 14, on probation for burglary, theft of automobiles, or minor larceny (shoplifting), attending weekly group sessions led by co-workers from the Juvenile Court. (For further background information, see Chapter 4, Engagement in Diverse Field Areas, VI. Corrections.)

C. Summary of Preceding Stages

The problems, goals, and contracted tasks identified in earlier stages are outlined in Diagram 6-15, Chapter 6. The youths prioritized their problems as (1) lawbreaking leading to probation, (2) bad tempers, and (3) lack of understanding of the changes they were experiencing. Group members admitted that they didn't think much of themselves (low self-worth) and that they had problems with their parents (parent-son conflicts), but they didn't appear interested in working directly on these problems. In developing the contracted plan in the group, the need for ongoing evaluation instruments was recognized, and graphs were developed to monitor group attendance, group participation by members, and members' behavior at school and at home.

D. Intervention

The interventions of the B.S.W. worker were mainly varied types of teamwork. The worker and her co-leader met with the seven youths in weekly group meetings, and the workers engaged in ongoing communication with each other as team members. They met at least twice a week to discuss the process, problems, and progress of the group and any developments that were taking place with individual members. The workers went together to visit every home of the group participants. They divided the task of visiting the schools (the B.S.W. went to four schools, the M.S.W. to three) and the tasks of receiving weekly reports from parents and school social workers. The approach used with teachers and parents also highlighted a team effort as they worked together to help the youths accomplish their goals.

The primary teamwork designs to depict the interventions of the B.S.W. worker are found in Figures 7-20 and 7-21.

After charting progress in group attendance, group participation, and school and home behavior, the group began to focus on their problem with their tempers. All saw a relationship between this problem and the problems they were having at home and at school. They agreed to take home an index card each week, and every time they lost their tempers, they would put a check on it. If they forgot during the day to check the card, they would try to remember the incidents and to mark the card each night before going to bed.

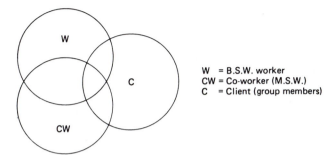

FIGURE 7-20 Worker and Co-worker Teamwork: Field Area VI

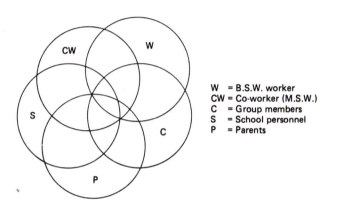

FIGURE 7-21 Extended Teamwork: Field Area VI

They would bring the card back each week and report the total number of checks they had for the week to the group. At the meeting, members entered their total number of checks for the week on a weekly chart (Diagram 7-5). The group members said that they also wanted to check on the other side of the card every time they felt like losing their tempers but didn't. The cards were labeled on each side "temper loss" or "temper control." A matching weekly chart was designed to indicate temper control (Diagram 7-6). During meetings, the group also discussed ways to let out anger that are acceptable and not seen as a loss of temper. For example, some said they find it helpful when they start to feel angry if they can get out and play ball. Others suggested turning on the radio and singing, going for walks, or finding a friend to talk with. One youth said he learned taking deep breaths and thinking about something that makes him happy help. They joked about what he might be thinking.

After six group meetings, A was picked up by the police and charged with breaking into a store (fifth time). He was found guilty and sent to a correctional institution for six months. J and T often came late to the meetings and continued to say they only came because they had to.

DIAGRAM 7-5   Temper Loss

NAMES	1	2	3	4	5	6	7	8	9	10	11	12	13	14	15	16
							WEEKS									
J																
MK																
T																
ML																
B																
A																
C																

As the group began to work on goal 3 (to learn about "changes"), a topic or issue of interest was selected each week by the members, and a plan was developed to study the issue the following week. Topics studied included living in prison, human sexuality and birth control, vocational training and jobs, managing money, and cooking. Films and guest speakers were used to provide information for discussion. The group also went on a trip to visit a vocational-training school.

E. Charted Progress

Each week, as additional tasks were planned by the group, the worker would record them on the contracted plan. For example, the additional tasks that were developed for goal 2 (to control tempers) and for goal 3 (to learn about "changes") were added as outlined in Diagram 7-7.

DIAGRAM 7-6   Temper Control

NAMES	1	2	3	4	5	6	7	8	9	10	11	12	13	14	15	16
							WEEKS									
J																
MK																
T																
ML																
B																
A																
C																

DIAGRAM 7-7 Contracted Plan Continued

DATE IDENTIFIED	PROBLEM/ NEED	GOAL	TASK	CONTRACT	DATE ANTICIPATED	DATE ACCOMPLISHED
10/1	2. Bad tempers	2. To control tempers in school, home, and neighborhood	1. Discuss the problem dealing with anger	1. Workers and members	10/22	10/22
			2. Notice when angry	2. Individual members	10/22 and each day	10/22–ongoing
			3. Find acceptable outlet	3. Individaul members	10/22 and each day	
			4. Keep track of successes and slip-ups on card	4. Individual members	10/22 and each day	
			5. Report to group and chart number	5. Individual members	10/29 and each Monday at group	
10/1	3. Need to understand "changes" of teenagers	3. To learn about some of the "changes" (including becoming independent, sex and birth control, and job training)	1. Select first topic—life in prison	1. Group and members	10/22	10/22
			2. Plan program	2. Group members	10/23	
			3. Call Prison Association for speaker	3. Worker	10/23	
			4. Have a talk and discussion	4. Guest and group	10/29	

SUMMARY

In this chapter, the four major types of general interventions were presented. Designs to depict each type of intervention, along with case examples, were given. A number of techniques were identified, and their application to systems of different sizes was demonstrated. The use of these techniques throughout the General Method was also considered.

As the generalist interacts with a system for goal accomplishment, tasks are identified and implemented. The tasks of the worker may be categorized individually or collectively as direct interventions; indirect interventions, information and referral; and case management and teamwork. While working in a helping capacity with one system over a period of time, a worker may use more than one intervention. In addition to direct work, for example, the generalist may need to refer a system to an outside resource and collaborate with the resource in a team effort for integrated service delivery. An individual task may in itself reflect a combination of interventions. For example, a worker may meet with collaborating resources (teamwork), a client system (direct intervention), and a target system (indirect intervention) at the same time.

In each intervention, a worker utilizes knowledge, values, and skills from the foundation for general practice. The art of general practice is highlighted in the careful selection and application of interventions and techniques at the appropriate time and in a manner that is sensitive to human diversity.

Throughout the General Method, worker and system of contact are charting progress and monitoring change. As each task is carried out during intervention, an appraisal is made of its effectiveness. When all the contracted tasks have been accomplished, a formal period of evaluation takes place. In the next chapter, focus will be on the fifth stage of the General Method, called *evaluation*.

NOTES

[1]Carol H. Meyer, "Direct Services in New and Old Contexts," in Alfred J. Kahn, ed., *Shaping the New Social Work* (New York: Columbia University Press, 1973), p. 40.

[2]See Frank R. Baskind, *Defining Generalist Social Work Practice* (Lanham, Md.: University Press of America, 1984); Ronda S. Connaway and Martha E. Gentry, *Social Work Practice* (Englewood Cliffs, N.J.: Prentice-Hall, 1988).

[3]Ann Hartman, "Diagrammatic Assessment of Family Relationships," *Social Casework* 59, no. 10 (October 1978): 465–76.

[4]Frederick J. Duhl, David Kantor, and Bunny S. Duhl, "Learning, Space and Action in Family Therapy: A Primer of Sculpture," in Donald A. Bloch, ed., *Techniques of Family Psychotherapy: A Primer* (New York: Grune & Stratton, 1973), p. 60.

[5]Philip J. Guerin and Eileen J. Pendagast, "Evaluation of Family System and Genogram," in Philip T. Guerin, ed., *Family Therapy: Theory and Practice* (New York: Gardner Press, 1976), pp. 450–64.

[6]Fritz Redl and David Wineman, *Controls from Within* (New York: The Free Press, 1965), pp. 153–244.

[7]James A. Garland and Ralph L. Kolodny, "Characteristics and Resolution of Scapegoating," in Saul Bernstein, ed., *Further Explorations in Group Work* (Boston: Milford House, Inc., 1973), pp. 55–74.

[8]George Broger and Stephen Holloway, *Changing Human Service Organizations: Politics and Practice* (New York: The Free Press, 1978), pp. 107–28.

[9]James E. Anderson and Ralph A. Brown, "Life History Grid for Adolescents," *Social Work* 25, no. 4 (July 1980): 321–23.

[10]William L. Mikulas, *Behavior Modification* (New York: Harper & Row, 1978).

[11]Theodore J. Stein, "Child Welfare: New Directions in the Field and Their Implications for Education," *Journal of Education for Social Work* 18, no. 1 (Winter 1982): 107–108.

[12]Donald Brieland, Thomas Briggs, and Paul Luenberger, *The Team Model in Social Work Practice* (New York: Syracuse University School of Social Work, 1973); Naomi Brill, *Teamwork: Working Together in Human Services* (Philadelphia: Lippincott, 1976); Rosalee Kane, *Interprofessional Teamwork* (New York: Syracuse University School of Social Work, 1975).

[13]Edward E. Mueller and Philip J. Murphy, "Communication Problems: Social Workers and Lawyers," *Social Work* 10, no. 2 (April 1965): 97–103.

[14]Patricia Wilson-Coker, "Working Effectively with Attorneys in the Adversary System: Observations and Suggestions for Protective Service Social Workers" (unpublished paper, Saint Joseph College, West Hartford, Conn., 1982).

[15]Council on Social Work Education, "Curriculum Policy Statement for the Master's Degree and Baccalaureate Degree Programs in Social Work Education" (New York: Council on Social Work Education, 1982), p. 7.

[16]Joseph F. Perez, *Family Counseling: Theory and Practice* (New York: Van Nostrand, 1979), pp. 102–104.

[17]Mikulas, *Behavior Modification*, pp. 35–36.

[18]Kurt Lewin, *Field Theory in Social Science* (New York: Harper & Row, 1951).

[19]Broger and Holloway, *Changing Human Service Organizations*, pp. 107–108.

[20]Felix P. Biestek, S. J., *The Casework Relationship* (Chicago: Loyola University Press, 1957), p. 17.

[21]Leon W. Chestang, "The Delivery of Child Welfare Services to Minority Group Children and Their Families," in *Working with Black Families and Children* (Richmond, Va.: Region III Child Welfare Training Center, 1982), p. 30.

[22]Ibid., p. 19.

[23]Association for Women in Psychology, *Considerations in Therapy with Lesbian Clients* (Philadelphia: Women's Resources, 1979), p. 33.

8

Evaluation

> *Professional accountability demands systematic evaluation. We should not have to rely on infrequent reports of field experiments to learn of intervention effectiveness.*
>
> *—Edward Mullen and James Dumpson[1]*

Evaluation is a time to study and measure the results of the actions taken during intervention. Although a worker and system of contact may frequently stop to consider progress and future plans, a formal evaluative process takes place in the General Method just prior to a worker's termination with a system.

Central to the process of evaluation is an analysis of the level of goal attainment, for which a scale may be used. The contracted plan (Chapter 6) may serve also as a tool to guide the generalist and the system as they go through the process of goal analysis. In this chapter, a model is suggested in which tools and procedures are used by the generalist during the evaluation stage of the General Method. In addition, a tool for ongoing evaluation throughout the Method will be presented.

A balance between art and science, fact and feeling, subjective and objective data is particularly needed during evaluation. The demand for accountability in an age of declining resources strongly supports efforts to develop valid instruments to document the effectiveness of social work intervention. As a worker and system interact during evaluation, the generalist tries to objectify information and procedures and to avoid the biases of client and worker that could lead to an uncritical service appraisal. The worker knows that an evaluation containing documented, unbiased information is less deniable as a reality and that it provides data for research and funding requests. Nevertheless, the worker knows that the primary purpose of evaluation during practice is to enhance the progress of the services being offered to a system. The content addressed and the process used in evaluation, therefore, should remain individualized and sensitive to personal attitudes and feelings in order to have impact on the unique system receiving service.

During the evaluation process, the generalist uses such research skills as data collection, measurement, and analysis. The skills and procedures of the generalist are not, however, strictly based on scientifically sound research methodology. Instead of the hypothesis testing, standardized tests, generalized results, and purely factual data found in scientific research, the generalist uses individualized criteria, personal opinion, and professional judgment. As stated, the worker does try to use measurable goals and systematic procedures in an objective manner, but he or she knows that if the process becomes too technical or impersonal, the system of contact may lose interest and disengage from the process.

Realizing the need to be scientific and at the same time to individualize during evaluation in practice, contemporary researchers in the profession have begun to introduce tools and scientific procedures for individualized case evaluations. For example, "single-system designs,"[2] "practice-outcome inventories,"[3] and "goal-attainment scales"[4] are now being used to evaluate progress and change with a system in practice. A range of scientific, research-oriented techniques, including graphs, scales, and statistical analyses, may be found within these approaches. In this chapter, the model for evaluation that will be presented has some similarity to these contemporary approaches. For example, concepts of a baseline starting point, measured goal accomplishment, and a study of practice outcomes will be contained within the general evaluation process. The model to be suggested is a guiding framework that reflects a balance between research and counseling techniques for evaluation in general practice.

GOAL ANALYSIS

The fifth stage of the General Method begins with the question: Has the goal been accomplished? For every task or set of tasks, a goal was stated on the contracted plan. That goal related directly to the problem listed in the column that preceded it. If the goal has been accomplished, the problem should now be resolved or modified, depending on how the goal was originally stated.

To answer the basic question cited, an intensive consideration is made of the change or progress that has taken place since the beginning of the worker-and-system interaction. First, the starting point is recalled; the worker and system of contact ask, What was the problem when we first met? The description that follows of the starting point (which may be referred to as the baseline) should be as precise and factual as possible. For example, if the presenting problem was Mr. and Mrs. S's constant quarreling, the worker will try to be more specific by recalling that Mrs. S said every time she and her husband spoke to each other, they quarreled and that this was at least six times a week. On the contract that was agreed to by both Mr. and Mrs. S, the stated goal read, "To be able to talk and to listen to each other without quarreling." The worker and system would ask, therefore: Has the communication between Mr. and Mrs. S improved? Are they speaking together without quarreling? Can they go a whole week without quarreling?

Answers to such questions may be received from different sources. The primary respondents are the system receiving service and the worker. In addition, information for goal analysis may be requested from other knowledgeable resources, such as family members, teachers, employers, and others. If a worker does not think that the perception of a system of contact joined with the observations of the worker is sufficient, reliable, or accurate, then outsiders may be brought into the evaluation process. As with data collection in the second stage of the General Method, the use of outside resources during evaluation with client systems should be discussed with, and sanctioned, by the clients prior to contacting the resources.

If the answer to the basic question of goal accomplishment is not a clear 100 percent yes, a study is made to determine to what extent the goal has been accomplished. Beginning at the baseline starting point, the question is asked: From where you started when we first had contact, how much closer to or further from the goal have you moved? A scale may be used to help the worker and the system become more specific in answering this question (see Diagram 8-1). It is a nine-point bipolar scale with an equal number of categories for progression and for regression. The midpoint on the scale (0) indicates the starting point. Descriptive criteria for this point should indicate the problem that led to the stated goal under study. The extreme right of the scale is numbered + 4, and the anchoring description for this point is 100 percent goal accomplishment. More specifically, this score indicates that the problem at the starting point has been eliminated or reduced, according to the way it is spelled out in the stated goal. Conversely, the opposite end of the scale is numbered − 4, and the descriptive criterion is "goal given up," with no attainment. The intermediate points

DIAGRAM 8-1   Goal-Accomplishment Scale

−4	−3	−2	−1	0	+1	+2	+3	+4
Goal given up	Large extent worse	Somewhat worse	Little worse than starting point	Starting point	Little better than starting point	Somewhat better	Large extent better	Goal accomplished

on either side of the 0 are balanced to reflect movement to a little, some, or a large extent better or worse than the starting point.

The number of scale points to be used depends on the individual goal in each situation. Sometimes the goal may be a single activity that cannot be broken down into a measurable sequence. For example, a goal may be to get food stamps for a family or tutoring for a child. It may be sufficient here to have a simple 3-point scale (-1 = goal given up, 0 = starting point, $+1$ = goal accomplished). If any movement, even slight, can be detected, it is important to have a scale that can show this. Too few scale points may prevent the recognition of some progress, which could increase hope and motivation. Even the identification of going backwards and a consideration of how the situation may end if regression continues may cause sufficient anxiety to promote greater effort and involvement.

With each individual situation, an attempt is made to use objective descriptors, including numbers or times and events. For example, in the situation presented earlier, the problem at the starting point was Mr. and Mrs. S's repeated quarreling whenever they tried to communicate (at least six times a week). The long-range goal was to have the couple speak and listen to each other without quarreling. During intervention, techniques were used to help them to listen to each other and to try to understand each other's viewpoints. A sensitivity to nonverbal communication was encouraged, and words were suggested to help them express their feelings. After the worker and Mr. and Mrs. S worked together for the period of time indicated in the contracted plan, they began to evaluate goal accomplishment. The scale in Diagram 8-2 was developed under the guidance of the worker.

In finding regressive descriptors, the worker and the system discern what have been or could be ways in which the situation would grow worse than when the problem was first identified. In the case of Mr. and Mrs. S, they said that at one time they had started to physically fight, and they feared this might happen again. The negative indicators, therefore, reflect the typical pattern of regression for this system. If they had feared an increasing withdrawal from any interaction with each other, then withdrawal would be indicated in the negative descriptors.

What needs to be emphasized is that during the evaluation stage of the General Method, there must be an opportunity to identify possible deterioration as well as growth in a situation. Even with general intervention, the communication between Mr. and Mrs. S, for example, could have become worse than when they first set the goal. The cause of this deterioration would need to be considered as the evaluation progresses. It could be that the intervention was inappropriate because the relationship was too pathological or because Mr. and Mrs. S lacked sufficient motivation or capacity to work on it. The regression in the relationship could be caused by other factors, including those outside of the worker's control, such as influences

DIAGRAM 8-2 Case Example: Mr. and Mrs. S

−4	−3	−2	−1	0	+1	+2	+3	+4
Goal given up; injury and separation	Large extent worse; no communication without fighting	Somewhat worse; quarrels moving into physical fights half the time they talk	Little worse; quarrels moving into physical fights once or twice a week	Start; no communication without quarreling (at least six times a week)	Little better; communicating without quarreling once or twice a week	Somewhat better; communicating without quarreling half the time they talk	Large extent better; communicating without quarreling most of the time (may be one quarrel a week)	Goal accomplished; open communication without quarreling

from individuals or systems unknown to the worker. Before asking why the goal has or has not been attained, however, worker and system need to take time to judge what movement, forward or backward, has taken place on the goal-accomplishment scale. After this appraisal, they proceed to an analysis of why they have arrived at the particular point on the scale. Here again, the contracted plan is a helpful guide to worker and system of contact as they analyze causation.

CONTRACT REVIEW

An evaluation does not stop at this point, even when the first question in the process is answered with a 100 percent yes. Although a goal has been attained, it is important to find out why this has happened. The question to be asked is, Has the goal been accomplished through the planned interventions identified by worker and system in the contracted plan? An honest appraisal of causality can build a stronger working relationship, and it can give direction for further interactions between worker and system. It is possible that a goal's accomplishment is due to negative circumstances that may have to be addressed with a reformulation of goals. For example, a goal of getting someone off welfare may have been accomplished because the person was imprisoned rather than because of the interventions of the worker. More immediate goals may emerge, such as providing care for the children of the person incarcerated. If it appears that the goal has been accomplished as a result of the tasks identified in the contracted plan, then worker and system may move on to other problems and goals, or they may move into the process of termination (to be developed in the next chapter).

If a goal has not been accomplished by the date anticipated for the completion of tasks in a plan, the question must be asked, "Why not?" Again, the response may point to some unexpected circumstances; for example, a death or sudden tragedy may have caused the failure in goal accomplishment. If such circumstances are not readily identifiable, the worker and system begin a systematic review of the planned contract, starting with the last column on the right, to find out why the goal has not been attained. The question is not only, "Why has the goal not been accomplished?" but also, "Why has movement toward goal accomplishment reached the point identified on the goal-attainment scale?"

The last column on a contracted plan indicates the dates when planned tasks have or have not been accomplished to date. After recognizing which tasks have not been completed, focus should move over to the next column to find out when it was expected that these tasks would be accomplished. Questions to be asked at this point are, "Was there an error in date anticipation?" "Is more time needed?" "Why was our timing off?" If it appears that what is needed is an adjustment in the date anticipated, this can readily take place, and intervention will be continued. For example, a worker may have worked out a contracted plan with a group of citizens in which it was anticipated that they would meet with a member of congress by a certain date. It was found out later that the politician's schedule was fully booked until two weeks after the anticipated date on the plan. If the reason for a failure to accomplish a goal on the date expected is something other than insufficient time for task completion, evaluation continues by moving over to the "contract" column (the third column from the right) of the plan.

In analyzing the "contract" column, a review is made of the people or system responsible for carrying out the identified tasks. Questions include, "Did the persons or system designated to carry out a task in the plan complete that task? If not, why not?" There are several possible reasons for a failure in task execution. Basically, a review of motivation, capacity, opportunity, and understanding of expectations should be made. The failure could be due to work overload, insufficient resources, or environmental pressures greater than anticipated. A change or redistribution in task responsibilities may be all that is needed to move forward toward goal accomplishment. Perhaps a worker or resource will have to withdraw from carrying out tasks in order to have a client system become more directly involved in problem resolution. Perhaps the worker or a new resource will have to become directly involved in collaborating with a client system to accomplish certain tasks. For example, a worker and Mr. M may have planned that Mr. M would go to the Vocational Rehabilitation Office to complete a set of tests. He was then expected to call the worker to let her know how he made out. What actually happened was that Mr. M changed his mind as the date for the testing drew closer, because he was afraid to hear the results of his testing. When he called the worker, he told her he didn't keep the appointment because he didn't feel well. The worker asked Mr. M to come in to talk with her, and as they evaluated the plan they had made, Mr. M shared the fact that he couldn't face going for the tests and hearing the results by himself. The contract had to be changed so that the worker would go with Mr. M to the Vocational Rehabilitation Office.

Through analysis of the contract column, it may become apparent that, even when everyone carries out the tasks as agreed to in the plan, goals may still not be accomplished. The next area to be considered then would be the "tasks" column, to see if there could be an error in identifying what tasks had to be performed to fulfill the stated goals. When the tasks outlined in the contracted plan are studied, the question to be asked should call for an evaluation not only of the identified task, but also of the sequencing of the tasks as listed in the plan. The worker asks: "Were the tasks appropriately selected, clearly described, and properly sequenced in order to achieve the goal?" Perhaps some steps were omitted in the process. There may have been resources or influences in the environment that needed to be contacted but were overlooked in the planning. The nature of the task itself may have been inappropriate for a particular system. For example, Mrs. L did not follow through with a plan to take her mother to visit a nursing home. Although Mrs. L passively agreed with the worker that a nursing home would be good for her mother, and Mrs. L said that she would take her on a certain date, she never completed the task. Placing an elderly parent in a nursing home might in some cases be a successful plan to achieve the goal of providing needed care for a parent or of getting relief for a family strained by caring for an elderly person. In this situation, however, sending an elderly parent to a nursing home was not an acceptable or possible option for the family, because it was contrary to their basic cultural beliefs and customs.

Occasionally, tasks are identified, sequenced, and implemented and the stated goals are accomplished, but the problem may continue to be present. At this time, the worker and system would have to review carefully the "goal" column to see whether the stated goal actually related to or reflected the opposite of the identified problem or need. The worker asks: "Did the accomplishment of this goal resolve, reduce, or prevent further growth of, the problem? If not, why not?" It could be that the goal indicated the outcome desired by the worker but not by the client system. The needs of the client may continue to be unmet until the worker clearly understands and expresses the goal of the client. For example, Mrs. F may have expressed strong dissatisfaction with her apartment, complaining about rats and cockroaches, and the worker may have thought that Mrs. F was identifying the goal of extermination of rats and cockroaches from the apartment. When the problem of rats and cockroaches decreased after much activity involving the landlord and the Housing Code, Mrs. F was still dissatisfied with her apartment. Her true goal was to be relocated with the worker's help.

If there is not an overall improvement in a situation even after a contracted plan has been fully implemented, another reason could be an inappropriate identification of the problem or need in the first place. In the case just cited, for example, the worker thought that the client was presenting the problem of infested housing when, in fact, she was trying to give reasons for the worker to help her move. She felt isolated and did not get along with her neighbors. She hoped the worker would be able to arrange for her to move to the south end of town, where some of her relatives lived. As the generalist reviewed the case during evaluation, the question would be asked: "What in fact was the problem?" With hindsight, the worker would be able to see that the real problem with Mrs. F was a lack of social adjustment. The goal she really wanted to accomplish was relocation.

It is apparent, therefore, that a worker may use the contracted plan for evaluation in the General Method. There are six areas or columns that can be analyzed to locate possible causes for failure in problem resolution. At any step in the evaluated process, an understanding may take place that highlights the error in planning and pinpoints where reformulation must take place in the contracted plan.

CONTRACT REFORMULATION

The General Method is a cyclical, ongoing process. It is more common than exceptional to have the helping process in social work move three steps forward and two steps backward all along the way. By the time the worker and system of contact move into evaluation, however, they are often sensitive to the possibility that the next phase in their working together may be termination. If the evaluation leads to an awareness that little or no progress has been made and that the contracted plan has to be reformulated, there may be resistance or expressed frustration on the part of both worker and system. This is particularly true when it becomes apparent that there is regression in a situation after much time and energy has been invested by both worker and system. A worker may need special support from his or her supervisor and a system of contact may need to receive special support from the worker, if they are to find the energy necessary to persevere in the process of plan reformulation. A worker needs to maintain a flexible, realistic attitude throughout the General Method, and this attitude must be conveyed to the systems he or she is working with.

As problems, goals, tasks, contract, or dates are reformulated during the evaluation period, it is imperative that the system of contact play a major role in the revision. Learning to recognize and accept setbacks, to try again without giving up, to change expectations and plans when necessary, and, finally, to see results from planned and persistent action can be extremely valuable to the growth of any human being.

When the evaluation has taken place that leads to a reformulation of some aspect of the contracted plan, the worker records the dates of the evaluation and the planned revisions on the contracted plan. As shown in Diagram 8-3, in the "date identified" and "problem/need" columns, the worker indicates the dates when the evaluation took place and the problems that were being evaluated. In the "problem/need" column, the worker also states what reformulations are necessary. In the columns where reformulations are to be made, the worker describes the changes or additions and then proceeds to fill in the other columns of the plan to reflect the revisions.

As shown in Diagram 8-3, the worker had originally set the goal of having Mr. M grow in awareness of his intellectual potential and marketable skills. He was to complete a battery of tests and learn the results at the Vocational Rehabilitation Office. After he completed the tests and learned their results, he was to call the worker. Mr. M failed to keep the appointment because he was afraid to hear the results. When Mr. M called to say he didn't go for the testing, the worker arranged to meet with him. During

DIAGRAM 8-3 Contracted Plan Continued

DATE IDENTIFIED	PROBLEM/ NEED	GOAL	TASK	CONTRACT	DATE ANTICIPATED	DATE ACCOMPLISHED
2/6	1. Lack of self-awareness of potential— Mr. M	1. To grow in awareness of potential (intelligence skills)	1. Talk with Mr. M	1. Worker and Mr. M	2/13	2/13
			2. Talk with Mrs. M	2. Worker and Mrs. M	2/15	2/15
			3. Talk with Mr. and Mrs. M	3. Worker and Mr. and Mrs. M	2/22	2/22
			4. Call Vocational Rehabilitation	4. Worker	2/23	2/23
			5. Discuss Vocational Rehabilitation with Mr. M	5. Worker and Mr. M	2/28	2/28
			6. Call Vocational Rehabilitation for appointment	6. Mr. M	3/1	3/1
			7. Go to Vocational Rehabilitation	7. Mr. M	3/14	
			8. Call worker	8. Mr. M	3/15	3/15
3/17 Evaluation	Evaluation of problem 1 (as cited above)	Goal 1 (as cited above)	1. Recall goal 1; evaluate why not accomplished; reformulate contract	1. Worker and Mr. M	3/17	3/17
3/17 Contract reformulation	Change in contract 7 and in task 8 and contract 8		7. Go to Vocational Rehabilitation	7. Worker and Mr. M	3/25	
			8. Meet to review contract 7	8. Worker and Mr. M	3/27	

this meeting, they evaluated how far they had come and identified where the plan was incomplete. The difficulty was in Mr. M's not being able to carry out task 7 on his own. After much discussion, the worker offered to go with Mr. M for the testing. He agreed, and they also planned to meet again for a follow-up session. The evaluation, with reformulations of tasks and contract, is shown in Diagram 8-3.

EVALUATION QUESTIONS

In essence, evaluation may be described as a ten-question process. In addition to those questions already identified that relate to the different areas of the contracted plan, the worker raises questions about external and internal circumstances that may have affected goal accomplishment. As stated earlier, the worker first considers the possibility that planning did not anticipate outside factors that may have caused failure or success in goal attainment. After considering outside factors and after reviewing the contracted plan, the worker and system of contact should also ask if any internal factors or dynamics within their relationship have prevented progress. This would include an assessment of the level of trust, openness, and honesty within the relationship. If it is agreed that there has been some resistance or holding back in their interactions, this should be explored. A direct discussion about the worker-system relationship, its progress, and its setbacks can be a powerful source for movement during evaluation.

Basically, therefore, the essential questions to be asked during evaluation may be summarized as follows:

1. Has the goal been accomplished? (yes or no)
2. If yes, has the goal been accomplished as a result of circumstances outside of the contracted plan? (external causes)

If the goal has not been accomplished as expected at this time, the following questions are asked:

3. From when the problem was first identified, how much closer to or further from the goal have you moved? (goal-accomplishment scale)
4. Has the goal not been accomplished as expected because of circumstances outside of the contracted plan? (external causes)
5. Was there an error in date anticipation? (timing)
6. Did a person or system designated to complete a task fail to accomplish it? (contract)
7. Were the tasks inappropriately selected, sequenced, or described? (tasks)
8. If the goal has been accomplished, but the problem continues, was the goal inaccurately identified? (goal)

9. If the goal has been accomplished, but the problem continues, was the problem inaccurately identified? (problem)
10. Was there anything in the worker-system relationship that inhibited goal accomplishment? (internal causes)

As these questions are answered, the causes for failure in goal attainment become increasingly evident. The reason a goal has not been accomplished to the extent anticipated may be pinpointed to some area on the contracted plan or to external or internal circumstances. When there has been clarification of what prevented goal accomplishment, the worker and system then begin to ask: "Why did this happen?" and "What can be done to remedy the situation and make goal accomplishment feasible?" A reformulation of the plan takes place.

Not all of the evaluation questions have to be asked if it becomes clear that a goal has not been attained for a reason suggested in earlier questions. Instead of proceeding with further questioning, the worker and system move into an analysis of why the particular drawback existed and a consideration of what modifications or additions need to be made in the contracted plan. With a reformulation of identified problems, goals, tasks, contract, or dates, the worker and system return to the intervention stage for further action. After the newly developed plan has been enacted, another evaluation takes place. If goals have been attained at this time, the worker and system are then ready either to work on other problems and needs or to move into the final stage of the General Method, called *termination*.

ONGOING EVALUATION

As stated, the formal stage of evaluation begins with the question, "Has the goal been accomplished?" This question is asked at the time when it was anticipated on the contracted plan that a particular goal would be attained. In addition to this formal evaluation stage, it is possible to integrate a systematic evaluation throughout the entire General Method. Increasingly, efforts and instruments for ongoing evaluation in social work practice are being described in the professional literature.[5] The value of a concentrated ongoing evaluation is that it helps worker and system to be sensitive to movement and to the long-range goals throughout the process.

A tool may be used to assist a worker and system of contact in an ongoing evaluation process. The tool is a two-dimensional graph, which may begin to be constructed during any stage of the Method. The zero point on the graph represents the starting point when a problem is identified and a goal is first established. The vertical line of the graph intersects the zero point midway, and the line has an equal number of plus and minus points above and below the zero point. The vertical line is the goal line, which is used to chart movement toward or away from the goal as the problem gets better or worse. The highest point at the top of this line indicates goal accomplishment; the midpoint (0) identifies where the problem is when the goal is set; and the lowest point represents total failure in goal accomplishment. Each intermediate point should have some measurable descriptive criterion that indicates progression or regression. Whenever possible, all points should be described in behavioral terms than can be objectively measured.

The horizontal line of the graph is a time indicator. It may represent weeks, days, or months, depending on the nature of the problem. (For a crisis, the intervals may represent days or hours.) The line to the left of the midpoint indicates time intervals prior to the starting point, when there was no contact between worker and system. The right side of the line indicates time intervals during the course of service delivery.

Generally, the graph has four points from the midpoint on each line (see Figure 8-1). More intervals may be added as work progresses, if this appears to be appropriate for a particular situation. During the data-collection stage of the General Method, information may be obtained for plotting dots on the left side of the graph. The worker inquires about the severity of the problem prior to worker-system contact. Usually, this inquiry goes back to at least the previous four weeks. If it is a long-standing problem, a review may be made of the last four months or years. If it is a crisis that just recently began, the inquiry might cover the last four days or four hours. As the problem and goal become clear, the lines of the graph are drawn. As information is gathered about the history of the problem, person, and situation, dots are plotted on the left side of the graph. For example, if the intervals represent weeks, the worker would ask what the situation was like one week, two weeks, three weeks, and four weeks before the system began to have contact with the generalist. As the situation for each time interval is described, an effort is made to locate a point on the goal line which matches the description. A dot is plotted where the time interval and goal indicator meet. In Figure 8-1, for example, one week before contact, the problem was assessed at the -2 point; two weeks before, it was at the 0 point (same as first contact with worker); three weeks before, it was at the -1 level; and four weeks before, it was at the -1 level also. When the points are connected, it is apparent that the problem was at its worst one week before the system began to have contact with the worker. In the case of Mr. and Mrs. S, this would mean that, a week before they contacted the worker, their quarrels were moving into physical fights half the time they talked.

If the tool in Figure 8-1 is used as an ongoing evaluation instrument, each time the worker and system of contact meet, they would plot a point on the graph to show what movement has taken place each week. During the assessment stage, the graph is refined with clear descriptors to measure movement toward or away from clarified goals within an expected time

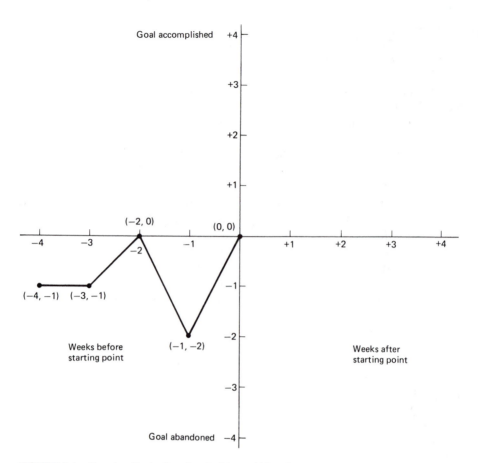

FIGURE 8-1   Ongoing-Evaluation Graph: Mr. and Mrs. S

frame as indicated on the contracted plan. As points are plotted and connected, the worker and system begin to envision the direction in which they
expect to see the connecting line move, according to time intervals and
dates anticipated on the contracted plan.

Plotting and charting movement could continue as the worker and
system go through the intervention, evaluation, and termination stages of
the General Method. During the formal evaluation stage, a thorough analysis is made of the reasons why movement has been in the directions shown
on the graph. The goal-accomplishment scale and the contracted plan may
still be used as described earlier to pinpoint the extent of goal accomplishment at the evaluation stage and to locate causal factors that resulted in
arriving at the identified point. These tools may be complemented by the
ongoing-evaluation graph, which could provide a general perspective of
movement throughout the process of service delivery.

Continuing to use the graph during termination helps the worker to detect any regression that may take place as the system begins to realize that contacts with the worker will be terminated. As shown in Figure 8-2, for example, when Mr. and Mrs. S first began to express their problems to the worker, tensions mounted between them. They accused each other of betraying confidences by talking with the worker. The problem increased (point 1, −1). Through further contacts with the worker, Mr. and Mrs. S began to grow in being able to listen to and understand each other. Progress toward the stated goal became evident. They were able to go for three weeks with open communication without quarreling. During the next two weeks of contact, some regression became apparent. The direction of the movement line went slightly downward. This regression was due to the fact that the worker began to talk about termination with Mr. and Mrs. S. They began to talk about the anxiety they were feeling as they thought about having to work on their goals without the help of the worker. A conscious awarenesss of the way they were responding to termination, with strong support from the worker, helped them to experience relief and to find strength to move to goal accomplishment.

The intervals at the right side of the graph on the horizontal line are

FIGURE 8-2 Ongoing-Evaluation Graph: Mr. and Mrs. S at Termination

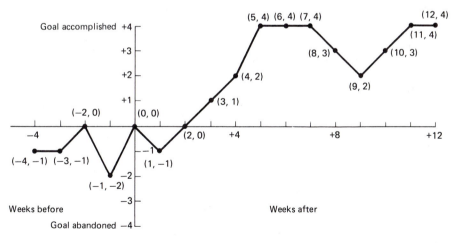

Descriptive criteria for goal line
+4 = Goal accomplished: open communication without quarreling
+3 = Communicating without quarreling most of the time (maybe one quarrel a week)
+2 = Communicating without quarreling half the time we talk
+1 = Communicating without quarreling once or twice a week
  0 = Starting point: no communication without quarreling (at least six times a week)
−1 = Quarreling moving into physical fights once or twice a week
−2 = Quarrels moving into physical fights half the time we talk
−3 = No communication without fighting
−4 = Goal abandoned: injury and separation

extended as long as may be needed to indicate length of time receiving service. Although the worker may have gathered data only on the four weeks prior to the starting point (left side of line), the service may continue even beyond a year, and thus the horizontal line on the right would be extended. In Figure 8-2, for example, Mr. and Mrs. S were seen by the worker for twelve weeks. Although there was some regression at the time of termination, they did not go back to where they were during the month before they contacted the worker. The extended graph shows that their goal was attained by the time termination was finalized.

When the ongoing-evaluation graph is used in working with a client system, it is very helpful to ask the client to keep a daily log from the time the goal is first established. If a client is asked to recall what happened over a week or a month (depending on frequency of contacts), it is very likely that there will be some error in what is said. Often, a person's memory of what happened is influenced by how the person is feeling at the time of recall. A daily log can be introduced when the graph is first formulated. The worker asks the system to indicate briefly in the log each day the extent to which the problem and the goal were present. More specifically, the system may be asked to record the number of times or the length of duration of a particular behavior or event. For example, Mr. and Mrs. S would have been asked to jot down at the end of the day in their log how many times they quarreled and also how often they communicated with each other without quarreling during each day. If they bring the log with them each time they meet with the worker, a more accurate plotting of points on the graph can take place. The worker and system need to articulate as exactly as possible the measurable behaviors that are to be recorded and used to indicate movement in goal accomplishment.

One of the main drawbacks in using the ongoing-evaluation graph is the possibility that goals may change during the course of work with a system. With a multiple-problem family, for example, a goal in one area may become abandoned or at least shifted in priority because of a crisis that arises in another area. Progress for the family is then recognized as movement toward a different goal. If more than one goal is being worked on at one time, a number of graphs may be used simultaneously. For example, a child's health problem may be the working goal for a family, when suddenly they receive eviction papers. This new problem has to be addressed immediately. The new goal is to relocate the family within 30 days. A new graph indicating progression and regression in movement toward this goal would have to be developed.

The use of groups and scales as depicted in Figures 8-1 and 8-2 is similar to that used in a single-subject research design. The research methodology includes measurement processes and statistical techniques for testing the significance of results. The short baselines and timeframes of many interventions make the use of these techniques infrequent. The graphic visual presentation of results, however, is extremely beneficial in the course of charting progress.

The ongoing evaluation process used in single-subject design and in the related variation found in Figure 8-1 is applicable to work with a variety of problems, including those of a psychosocial nature. Examples include issues of adolescence, identity, alcoholism, and loss or separation.[6]

WORKING WITH DIFFERENT SYSTEMS

No matter what type of system a worker has been working with for goal accomplishment, a time is needed to evaluate how far the system has moved toward or away from the goal. A deliberate, objective study, which includes an analysis of change, identification of impediments to goal accomplishment, and planning or reformulating contracts, may help to break through resistances and to provide direction for future interactions between worker and system of contact.

The tools and processes described in this chapter are general in nature; they may be used in evaluation with individuals, groups, families, or communities. The ten evaluation questions, the goal-accomplishment scale, the contracted plan, and the ongoing-evaluation graph may be adapted for use with any system. Even when working with teams or target systems, the generalist takes time to involve the system in an evaluation, during which the tools and processes suggested may be utilized.

When working with a team, for example, the ten evaluation questions are asked about the goals that the team identified collectively. The contract the team members developed is used to locate causal factors when goals are not accomplished. The timing, contract, tasks, problems, and goals found on the team contract are considered, along with external circumstances not anticipated by the team in planning. Internal circumstances are also considered as possible causal factors. A study would be made not only of the relationships of team members with the client or target system, but also of the relationships among the team members themselves (trust, openness) and how these relationships have affected the process of goal attainment. The goal-accomplishment scale may be used to show how much movement the team believes has taken place for each of the goals it stated. The ongoing-evaluation graph may also be used to monitor direction over a period of time toward or away from the goals.

To cite an example of evaluation in teamwork, a vocational counselor from the State Department of Vocational Rehabilitation, a social worker from the East Side Women's Center, and a child-welfare worker from the Department of Children's Services formed a team to coordinate service delivery for Mrs. Judy E and her 5-year-old daughter, Betty. Mrs. E had been reported three months previously for suspected child abuse. The child-welfare worker was monitoring the home situation. She had helped Mrs. E to reach the point where she was asking for skill training to become employed. Mrs. E and the worker developed a plan in which Mrs. E could be referred to the Women's Center and the Department of Vocational Rehabilitation. Mrs. E agreed also to have the workers from the three resources form a team to provide ongoing, coordinated services for herself and her daughter.

Once the team was formed, goals were identified, and tasks were distributed among the members of the team and Mrs. E. The vocational counselor had the task of arranging for Mrs. E to receive skill training. After completing the skill-training program, Mrs. E was to be helped by the vocational counselor to locate employment. The social worker from the East Side Women's Center was at that time leading a support group for unemployed women who needed to develop a sense of self-worth and self-confidence. Mrs. E was to be added to this group. The child-welfare worker was to help Mrs. E to locate day care for Betty. This worker also had the task of case management. She initiated the first meeting of the team and served as the team leader when it began. Rotating leadership was later used.

The main goals, tasks, and contracted responsibilities that were collectively identified by the team are summarized as follows:

1. To help Mrs. E to become employed by her going through a process of testing, training, job locating, being hired—assigned to vocational counselor and Mrs. E.
2. To help Mrs. E to grow in self-worth and self-confidence by her attendance at a weekly women's support group—assigned to social worker at the Women's Center and Mrs. E.
3. To help Mrs. E to locate appropriate, available day care for Betty through searching for a resource and completing the application process—assigned to child-welfare worker, Mrs. E, and Betty.
4. To have Mrs. E participate in the coordinated team effort by encouraging her to accept the invitation to join and become involved in all team meetings.

The contracted plan also stated the anticipated dates for completing each of the identified tasks. As interventions were carried out, the team moved into the evaluation stage. If a goal and its planned tasks were apparently the direct responsibility of one worker on the team (as in goals 1–3), this member was the one responsible for developing the ongoing-evaluation graph and/or the goal-accomplishment scale for the particular goal. This team member was asked to lead the team as members took time to assess the extent to which that goal has been accomplished. Collectively, the team reviewed the ten evaluation questions and the contracted plan. This analysis was conducted with input from the client.

The fourth goal in the team example is one of shared responsibility by all team members. Each member was expected to encourage Mrs. E to attend and to participate in team meetings. Together, the team designed a goal-accomplishment scale and an ongoing-evaluation graph for this goal. Because the goal had the distinct dimensions of (1) attendance and (2) participation in team meetings, the team decided to draw up two graphs and two scales for clarity in assessment of goal 4. For example, in Diagrams 8-4 and 8-5 (goal-accomplishment scales) and Figures 8-3 and 8-4 (ongoing-evaluation graphs), the team members—hopefully, including Mrs. E as a member—discussed and identified what they saw as criteria for identifying movement in goal accomplishment. The dual scales and graphs help to highlight the multiple options that may exist when the two variables (attendance and participation) are considered necessary to achieve the one goal (Mrs. E's participating in the coordinated team effort). In Diagram 8-4, Mrs. E is seen as attending the team meetings regularly (*4* is checked on Diagram 8-4), but she is not yet participating fully at the meetings (*1* is checked on Diagram 8-5). Both Diagram 8-4 and Diagram 8-5 would have to reach a +4 if the goal is to be accomplished totally, according to the criteria developed by the team.

It should be noted that in the scales of Diagrams 8-4 and 8-5 and in the "goal" lines of the graphs of Figures 8-3 and 8-4, there are no minus numbers and line. This is because there is no degree to which the goal of attendance and participation at team meetings can be less than the starting point (0). The *0* on the scales means "zero attendance and participation."

DIAGRAM 8-4   Attendance at Team Meetings

				X
0	1	2	3	4
Starting point: no attendance	Little attendance: one out of four meetings a month	Some attendance: two out of four meetings a month	Frequent attendance: three out of four meetings a month	Goal accomplished: regular attendance

DIAGRAM 8-5   Participation in Team Meetings

	X			
0	1	2	3	4
Starting point: no participation in meetings	Little participation: speaking up once or twice during a meeting or only when spoken to	Some participation: speaking up three or four times during a meeting	Frequent participation: speaking up and sharing five or six times	Goal accomplished: active— fully participating in flow of meetings

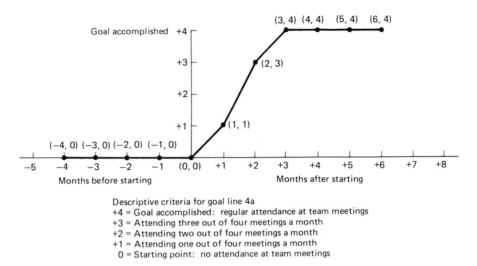

Descriptive criteria for goal line 4a
+4 = Goal accomplished: regular attendance at team meetings
+3 = Attending three out of four meetings a month
+2 = Attending two out of four meetings a month
+1 = Attending one out of four meetings a month
 0 = Starting point: no attendance at team meetings

FIGURE 8-3   Attendance at Team Meetings

The ongoing-evaluation graphs in Figures 8-3 and 8-4 show that there was 0 attendance and participation in team meetings prior to the starting point when Mrs. E was first invited to attend. The graphs also show the progress that took place as Mrs. E began to feel more in control of her life, more confidence in herself, and more comfortable with the other team members.

FIGURE 8-4   Participation in Team Meetings

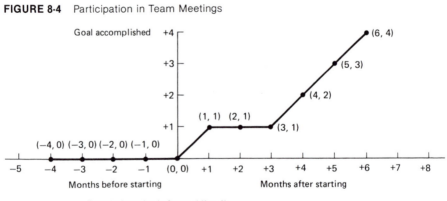

Descriptive criteria for goal line 4b
+4 = Goal accomplished: active participation in flow of meetings
+3 = Speaking up and sharing five or six times during a meeting
+2 = Speaking up three or four times during a meeting
+1 = Speaking up once or twice during a meeting or only when spoken to
 0 = Starting point: no participation in team meetings

In work with a target system rather than a team or a client system, the evaluation process may be somewhat different. Although a generalist may interact with a target system for goal accomplishment, the two may never arrive at a point where they develop a contracted plan together. A worker alone, or with a client or other resource, may initiate contact with a target system to request some assistance or change in service. The worker and other members of the action system may state clearly at that time their purpose or goals in making the contact. The target system, however, may not respond favorably. If the worker continues to try to change the target system through repeated contacts and pressures, there may be a time when the worker evaluates with the target system what movement toward or away from the stated goal has taken place since their first contact. Here, a goal-accomplishment scale or an ongoing-evaluation graph may be helpful as the worker tries to make an objective presentation to confront the target system with the reality of the situation.

For example, a generalist may speak to the landlord of an apartment complex in behalf of his tenants, to try to get him to improve the conditions of the apartment. A list is presented indicating repairs, renovations, and improvements needed. To have all 12 items on the list taken care of is the ultimate goal. The generalists and the tenants involve a Housing Code Inspector and the Housing Court in efforts to pressure the landlord to make the improvements. Periodically, the generalist meets with the landlord to continue to bring to his attention the unattended needs of the tenants. As conditions improve or deteriorate, the worker may choose to use an ongoing-evaluation graph or a goal-accomplishment scale to demonstrate what has taken place since the problems and needs were first presented to the landlord (starting point). This evaluative approach may help to create sufficient feelings for progress to be made.

As depicted on the graph in Figure 8-5, the conditions at the apartment complex had deteriorated during the weeks prior to the worker's contact with the landlord. Through various pressures and continued contacts, some improvements were made. After the fifth week of contact, however, there was a tapering off of efforts to improve conditions, and problems increased. The worker used the graph (Figure 8-5) to point out to the landlord what progress had been made, how conditions were starting to get worse, and how far they were from accomplishing the original goal (+4).

USING THE HOLISTIC FOUNDATION IN EVALUATION

The holistic foundation for general practice, as diagramed in Chapter 1 (Diagram 1-5), identifies the fundamental values, knowledge, and skills used during evaluation. The worker demonstrates care for a system and a commitment to quality service by taking time to analyze movement toward or

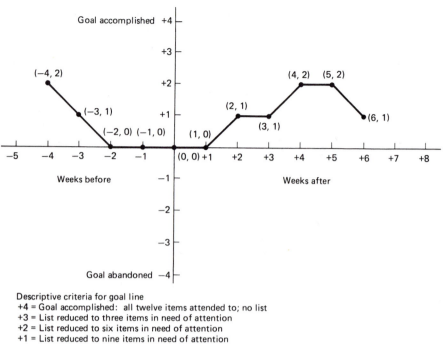

Descriptive criteria for goal line
+4 = Goal accomplished: all twelve items attended to; no list
+3 = List reduced to three items in need of attention
+2 = List reduced to six items in need of attention
+1 = List reduced to nine items in need of attention
 0 = Starting point: twelve items in need of attention
−1 = List extended to fifteen items
−2 = List extended to eighteen items
−3 = List extended to twenty-one items
−4 = Goal abandoned: housing condemned; tenants evicted

FIGURE 8-5   Case Example: Target System—Landlord

away from goals. Throughout the evaluation process, the principles of *indi-vidualization* and *self-determination* are emphasized. Any assessment of move-ment or change is strongly dependent on input from the system of contact. Any reformulation of a contract takes place only after a client system, an action system, or, if possible, a target system has spoken with the worker and has given input and consent.

In social work, the worker inquires about changes in feelings and atti-tudes as well as behaviors. The worker recognizes and encourages *purposeful expression of feelings* during evaluation. If progress has not taken place, the worker conveys a *nonjudgmental attitude* toward the system, as focus is di-rected to exploring possible causal factors and a reformulation of the plan.

From scientific research, the generalist uses knowledge and skills for measuring, graphing, and scaling during evaluation. In addition to research skills, it may be necessary to use relationship, problem-solving, and political skills. Frequently, the worker guides, clarifies, and confronts as goals are analyzed. Within the evaluation period, such problem-solving skills as prob-lem and need identification, data collection, assessment, and contracting may be reviewed and repeated.

Foundation theories used during evaluation vary according to the problem or goal that is being evaluated. In order to identify indicators of improvement or regression in a problem, the nature and dynamics of the problem must be understood.

Through holistic knowledge, the generalist is enabled to conduct a comprehensive study of causal factors. As the ten evaluation questions are raised and internal and external circumstances are considered, the worker is aided by the foundation theory base, which is integrated within the ecological perspective of *person in environment*. The generalist is sensitive to the complex and multiple factors that interact and influence a system.

HUMAN DIVERSITY IN EVALUATION

Culture

As the worker and system move into the evaluation stage of the General Method, they begin with the question, "Have the goals been accomplished?" Particularly when working with minorities, the worker must distinguish between long-range goals and short-range goals. The core problems of poverty and racism may be readily identified as basically causing a system to have unmet needs. Long-range goals may be the eradication of these two problems. Although the long-range goals may not be accomplished at the time of evaluation, the efforts made to work toward them should be evaluated. The identified immediate or short-range goals are usually articulated in more precise terms that can be measured for accomplishment. If they have not been fully accomplished, the contract review (described in Chapter 7) may help to highlight the reason why plans are not carried out successfully. Again, the timing projected for goal accomplishment may not have been in line with the time orientation of the culture of the system. The persons or resources expected to carry out the planned tasks, or the tasks themselves, may have been culturally inappropriate. It may be that the goals or the problems were not correctly understood or articulated.

As pointed out, a final question to raise during evaluation is: "Was there anything in the worker-system relationship that inhibited goal accomplishment?" To answer this question, a worker needs to ask him- or herself, "How sensitive and accepting was I toward this person, group, family, or community?" Self-awareness is necessary. If a worker has come to understand and appreciate his or her own ethnicity, it is often easier to recognize and accept the ethnicity of others. As with the systems receiving service, a worker also brings to any new relationship his or her ethnic history and personal experiences with certain cultural groups. Although, admittedly, it may be natural to transfer or stereotype, a working relationship can be very inhibited when those receiving help, or even those providing help, sense that they are not being treated as unique individuals. If goals are not being accomplished, it could be related to an absence of cultural sensitivity or of any shared cultural elements, with a resulting stereotyping by both the worker and the system receiving service. When stereotyping is present, studies have shown that participants begin to feel discomfort, and that they retreat into exaggerated behaviors that depict and confirm the ethnic-group stereotype. For example, during an interethnic study between Japanese-Americans and Caucasian Americans, it was found that in time the Japanese-Americans became increasingly quiet and aloof, while the Caucasian Americans became loud and directive.[7] An honest evaluation of the worker-system relationship can promote an increase in self-awareness for both worker and system, and it may help to break through some of the discomfort or resistance in the relationship.

Sexual Variation

In the evaluation stage, while making an appraisal of the extent of goal accomplishment and a comprehensive evaluation to locate possible reasons for any lack of accomplishment, a worker who is knowledgeable about sexual variations can better recognize dynamics and factors that may affect or prevent the attainment of goals for lesbian or gay clients. In reviewing the contract, it may become apparent that service providers or other persons who were expected to complete certain tasks may have taken longer than planned or may have changed their minds as the anticipated date arrived. The change on their part could be due to fears, threats, or insincere commitments that surfaced as the plan unfolded. Employers or landlords, for example, who said they would hire or rent to gay or lesbian persons may not have followed through when an opening actually occurred. Clients themselves may have changed their minds and plans as they began to experience pressures from family members, lawyers, judges, or others. An individual who seemed interested in joining a support group, for example, may have failed to show up for meetings because of increased fears of being identified with the group. And finally, here too, it is possible that the worker or the client may be uncomfortable with the working relationship itself and that this discomfort has interfered with goal accomplishment. Perhaps the openness or support needed did not develop, owing to hidden biases or fears. Again, an honest evaluation of the worker-system relationship at this time may result in a breakthrough so that progress can begin.

Gender Sensitivity

When it is time to evaluate goals that relate to gender-role changes, progress in personal and environmental goals should be considered realistically. Both the worker and those receiving service need to realize that only with continued efforts and much time and patience can there be any lasting change in sexist attitudes, practices, and policies. If a goal was to eliminate sexism in a target system and this has not been accomplished, progress may have been made if at least some conscious awareness of the presence of sexism has begun to develop in the target system. On a personal level, to have an individual become aware of his or her self-image and gender expectations may be a major accomplishment, even though the person may not change his or her behavior or life situation.

Here too, a major factor to be reviewed when goals have not been accomplished is the expectations and attitudes of the worker toward those receiving service. A social worker who is finding it difficult to support efforts to overcome sexism or who is comfortable with traditional gender roles may be contributing to the failure in goal attainment. As brought out by Susan Sturdevant,

> If a therapist believes that women are "by nature" flighty, irrational, narcissistic, masochistic, or dependent, etc., he/she will do little to help a client become rational, independent, or stable, since such a change is, according to his/her assumptive world, "impossible" for women.[8]

In addition to a sensitivity to culture, sexual orientation, and gender, during the evaluation stage a worker keeps in mind that goal accomplishment is related to several additional diversity variables, such as age and stages, endowment and personality, value system, social class, and geographic location.

EVALUATION IN DIVERSE FIELD AREAS

I. FIELD AREA: CHILD WELFARE

A. Agency: State Department of Children's Services

B. Client System

K, 15 years old, female, placed in group home three months ago. (For more background information, see Chapter 4, Engagement in Diverse Field Areas, I. Child Welfare.)

C. Summary of Preceding Stages

The problems, goals, and tasks identified and implemented in earlier stages are found in Diagram 6-6 of Chapter 6 and Diagram 7-1 of Chapter 7. The worker's interventions included direct work with K, the client; a referral to the group home and a court petitioning for custody continuance; and teamwork with personnel from the shelter, the group home, and the school K is attending.

D. Evaluation

Goal analysis: The primary goals of (1) obtaining and maintaining a permanent placement, (2) reentering school, and (3) personal growth were analyzed by K and the worker. They agreed that a placement had been found and was being maintained (goal 1). K was also attending school regularly (goal 2). Her personal problems (3a–3d) were beginning to surface in casework and group sessions at the home, though she was still finding it difficult to believe that she was of any worth and to talk about her sexuality. Goal 4, to obtain continuance of custody, was achieved on 3/30.

Scales were developed to assess extent to which the first two goals were accomplished. The two dimensions of goal 1 (obtaining placement, maintaining placement) were separated for greater clarity in evaluation (Diagrams 8-6 and 8-7). The goal of school reentry was expanded at this time to include optimal school performance. Two scales were also used then to evaluate goal 2 (Diagrams 8-8 and 8-9). The goal regarding personal growth (goal 3) had four subheadings (a–d). Because the child-welfare worker was not working directly on this goal with K, the four parts were reviewed in discussion and evaluated in general, on the basis of input from K, from the worker who was seeing K individually, and from the group-home worker who attended the peer-group meetings.

Goal 1a was evaluated by K and the worker as accomplished (+2). K was placed in a group home where she could stay until adulthood.

According to K and the group-home staff, K was adjusting well to the placement. They thought, however, that she could try to participate more fully in group activities. She was completing her chores and getting along satisfactorily with the other residents. Because K had only been in the home for three months and said she was not completely comfortable there yet, the worker and K evaluated the extent of accomplishment for goal 1b as +2 on the scale.

K was accepted into the local school. Goal for 2a, therefore, was accomplished, as indicated with a +2 on the scale in Diagram 8-8.

K and the worker considered ways in which they could objectively assess her progress in school. They agreed that they would look at her grades and report card from school and that they would ask for verbal assessments from K's teachers through the school social worker. At the time of this evaluation, K's performance was described by her teachers as "satisfactory." They thought she could do better, especially in her writing and class participation. They expected that K would perform at a higher achievement level as she

DIAGRAM 8-6   Goal 1a: To Obtain a Permanent Placement

				X
−2	−1	0	+1	+2
Goal abandoned	No place located	Starting point at shelter	Place located	Goal accomplished; placement obtained

DIAGRAM 8-7   Goal 1b: To Maintain a Permanent Placement

	−4	−3	−2	−1	0	+1	+2	+3	+4
							X		
	Goal abandoned: removal from placement	Marked problems: high conflict level	Increased problems	Beginning problems in adjustment	Starting point; beginning placement at new group home	Beginning to adjust	Satisfactory adjustment, but room for improvement	Marked improvement, high comfort level	Goal accomplished; stabilized adjustment

DIAGRAM 8-8   Goal 2a: To Reenter School

				X
−2	−1	0	+1	+2
Goal aban- doned	No school located	Starting point— out of school	School located	Goal accom- plished— returned to school

became more familiar with the school. K said that she liked school and her teachers and thought she was learning a great deal. She knew she could try harder and bring up her grades by the end of the semester. K did not believe that she needed a tutor or any additional help with her schoolwork at this time. The worker and K assessed the extent of accomplishment for goal 2b as +2 on the scale (Diagram 8-9).

K said she continued to find it hard to talk about herself and her personal problems (goal 3). She enjoyed the group meetings because the other residents were able to say things she couldn't. Deep down inside she knew she was feeling happier but was afraid it was "too good to be true." She said she would try harder to talk with her caseworker about herself and her feelings. K's caseworker at the group home thought that K was beginning to relax more during individual sessions and that more time was needed before K would be able to talk freely about herself, her past, or her future.

Contract review and reformulation: During contract review, the worker and K recognized the need for more time before goals 1, 2, and 3 (especially goal 3) could be accomplished. In reviewing contracted tasks, the worker and K agreed that the worker did not have to continue to follow up with K every two weeks. K knew that she could always call the worker if she needed her. They agreed that the worker would begin to visit K once a month, unless there was some reason for additional contact. The worker recorded the process of evaluation that occurred at this stage, indicating the reformulation of contract as found in Diagram 8-10.

Ongoing evaluation: At this point, the worker and K developed graphs to assess ongoing progress in (1) maintenance (adjustment) in the group home and (2) school performance. The graphs they designed are found in Figures 8-6 and 8-7. The worker and K planned to use the graphs each month when they met for ongoing evaluation and charting of progress.

II. FIELD AREA: GERONTOLOGY

A. Agency: Seaside Nursing Home

B. Client System

Mrs. J, an 80-year-old Portuguese woman in a skilled-nursing facility. (For additional information, see Chapter 4, Engagement in Diverse Field Areas, II. Gerontology.)

DIAGRAM 8-9 Goal 2b: To Achieve Optimal Level of Academic Performance

							X		
	−4	−3	−2	−1	0	+1	+2	+3	+4
	Goal abandoned; school dismissal or dropping out	Marked persistent problems	Increasing problems	Beginning to have problems in academic achievement	Starting point; beginning new school	Beginning to achieve academically	Stabilizing academic achievement, but room for improvement	Marked improvement in academic performance	Goal accomplished, optimal level of academic performance

DIAGRAM 8-10 Contracted Plan Continued

DATE IDENTIFIED	PROBLEM/ NEED	GOAL	TASK	CONTRACT	DATE ANTICIPATED	DATE ACCOMPLISHED
4/25 Evalua- tion	Evaluation of problems 1, 2, 3, 4	Goals 1, 2, 3, 4	1. Recall each goal 2. Assess extent of accomplishment 3. Reformulate con- tract	Worker and K (with input from school and group-home personnel)	4/25	4/25
Contract reform- ulation	Change in 1. Date antici- pated for task 4, goal 1; task 3, goal 3	Goal 1	Task 4—follow-up	Worker, K, group home staff	5/25 and once a month thereafter	
		Goal 3	Task 3—follow-up	Worker, K, social worker at group home	5/25 and once a month thereafter	
	2. Goal statement for problem 2; contract and date antici- pated for task 2, goals 2a and 2b	2a. To reenter school b. To achieve an optimal level of academic performance	Task 2—follow-up	Worker and school social worker	5/25 and once a month thereafter	

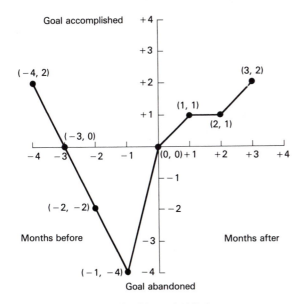

Descriptive criteria for goal line (Y – vertical line)
+4 = Goal accomplished: permanent placement maintained (stabilized)
+3 = Marked improvement: participation in group, high comfort level
+2 = Stabilizing adjustment: satisfactory, but room for improvement
+1 = Beginning to adjust
  0 = Starting point: beginning placement – insecure, withdrawn
−1 = Beginning to have problems
−2 = Increased problems
−3 = Marked problems in adjustment, high conflict level
−4 = Goal abandoned: removal from placement
Line X – horizontal line = Months in residence
  Plus numbers   = Months in new group home
  0   = Beginning placement in new group home
  Minus numbers   = Months before placement in new group home
    0 to −1   = Placement in shelter
    −1 to −3   = Months in foster home
    −3 and before   = Months in first group home

FIGURE 8-6   Goal 1b: To Maintain Permanent Placement

C. Summary of Preceding Stages

The contracted plan indicating the problems, goals, and tasks identified in earlier stages is found in Diagram 7-2 of Chapter 7. The worker's interventions were direct work with Mrs. J and teamwork with the staff of the nursing home and the pastor of the church Mrs. J used to attend. The prioritized goals for Mrs. J were the following: (1) to get to know the staff and the resources of the nursing home; (2) to work out a mutually satisfactory bath schedule with the nurses; (3) to leave room alone (at least once a day) and to attend a house activity (at least once a week); (4) to stop name-calling and yelling at residents; and (5) to share her culture with others.

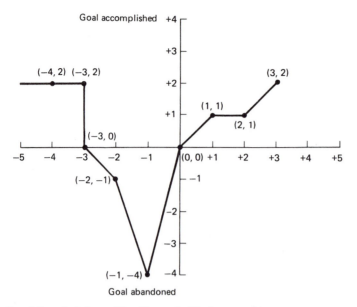

Goal accomplished

(−4, 2) (−3, 2)

(3, 2)

(1, 1)

(2, 1)

(−3, 0)

(0, 0)

(−2, −1)

(−1, −4)

Goal abandoned

Descriptive criteria for goal line (Y − vertical line)
+4 = Goal accomplished: optimal level of academic performance
+3 = Marked improvement in academic performance (writing and class participation)
+2 = Stabilizing academic achievement, room for improvement
+1 = Beginning to achieve academically
 0 = Starting point: beginning new school − insecure, withdrawn
−1 = Beginning problems in academic achievement
−2 = Increasing problems
−3 = Marked, persistent problems in academic performance
−4 = Goal abandoned: school dismissal or dropout
Line X − horizontal line = Time
  Plus numbers   = Months attending new school
  0   = Beginning new school
  Minus numbers = Months before attending new school

FIGURE 8-7   Goal 2b: To Achieve an Optimal Level of Academic Performance

D. Evaluation

Goal analysis: After three months, the worker and Mrs. J analyzed the extent of goal accomplishment for the five prioritized goals. Goals 2 and 4 had clearly been accomplished. Mrs. J's bath was scheduled earlier, and she no longer fought with the nurses. She also stopped calling the residents names and was beginning to feel more comfortable in the home as she got to know the staff and the resources available (goal 1). She met with the program planner, the director of volunteers, the head nurse and other nurses, the chaplain, and staff members from recreational therapy. Although there were occasional days when she did not leave her room, she was attending nursing-home activities with her roommate (goal 3) and appeared less fearful of having her possessions stolen. Regarding goal 5, Mrs. J's pastor and two members of the congregation came to see her. They took her to their church for a Christmas prayer service and a concert. A volunteer who spoke Portuguese visited Mrs. J for three weeks in November but then dropped out of the program.

Scales to assess the extent of goal accomplishment for goals 3a and 3b were developed and drawn on a large sheet of paper (Diagrams 8-11 and 8-12). The scale for goal 3a was expanded into an ongoing-evaluation graph, which the worker reviewed with Mrs. J each succeeding week (Figure 8-8). The nurse at the head station agreed to help Mrs. J and the worker to keep track of the days when Mrs. J was able to leave her room on her own. A small calendar was kept at the head station, and the date was circled when Mrs. J came to the station to say "hello" to the nurse on duty.

The goal does not extend to Mrs. J's going outside the institution on her own. At this time, it is not seen as a possibility. The maximum goal accomplishment considered, therefore, was Mrs. J's being able to freely and frequently go out of her bedroom on her own. The graph in Figure 8-8 demonstrates that Mrs. J was able to live alone up to three weeks before she was hospitalized. She was in the hospital for two weeks prior to her placement in the nursing home. During her first two weeks at the home, she regressed. At the time of evaluation (twelve weeks in residence) she progressed to occasionally leaving her room independently (averaging once a week), which is shown at point +1 on the goal line of Figure 8-8. With the added involvement of the nurses at the station on Mrs. J's floor, the goal reached the point +2 by one week after the evaluation, as shown in point 13,2 of Figure 8-8.

Contract reformulation: The evaluation conducted by Mrs. J and the worker twelve weeks after she began residency in the nursing home was recorded on the contracted plan (Diagram 8-13). As indicated, the task for goal 3a was expanded to include Mrs. J's saying "hello" to the nurse at the station on her floor at least once a day after leaving her room on her own. The task of having the nurse chart on the calendar Mrs. J's visit to the station was also added to the contract. In addition, the head nurse and the social worker planned to meet once a week to review Mrs. J's progress, using the charted calendar. The worker would use this information when she met with Mrs. J to chart progress in goal 3a on the evaluation graph each week. As shown in Diagram 8-13, the contract reformulation and the three-month evaluation were indicated on the contracted plan.

III. FIELD AREA: PUBLIC SOCIAL WELFARE

A. Agency: State Social Services

B. Client System

Mr. and Mrs. P and their two children (ages 2 and 4), placed in emergency shelter (Center City Motor Inn) for 44 days, currently living in an apartment. (For additional background information, see Chapter 4, Engagement in Diverse Field Areas, III. Public Social Welfare.)

C. Summary of Preceding Stages

The problems, goals, and tasks identified and enacted in earlier stages are listed in Diagram 6-10 of Chapter 6 and Diagram 7-3 of Chapter 7. The interventions of the worker were primarily (1) referral to several resources, (2)

DIAGRAM 8-11 Goal 3a: To Leave Room Alone (at Least Once a Day)

−3	−2	−1	0	+1 (X)	+2	+3
Total refusal to go out of room— goal dropped	Increased refusal to leave room (once a day)	Occasional refusal to leave even when someone offers to take her (about once a week)	Starting point: only leave when someone takes her for meals	Occasional going out of room alone (about once a week)	Increased going out of room alone (once a day)	Going out of room alone freely; maximum goal accomplished

direct work with the P family, and (3) teamwork with the income-maintenance technician and Mr. P's psychiatrist.

D. Evaluation

Goal analysis: After ten weeks of service, the worker and Mr. and Mrs. P evaluated the extent to which the goals of the contracted plan were accomplished. They agreed that goals for problems 1, 2, 3, 4, 6, 7, 8, and 9 were accomplished. These goals are the following:

1. To obtain an emergency food supply
2. To move into emergency shelter

DIAGRAM 8-12   Goal 3b: To Attend House Activity (at Least Once a Week)

	X		
0	1	2	3
Starting point: attending no house activities (program or meeting)	Attending house activity with worker or staff member (once a week)	Attending house activity with other residents once a week	Attending house activities with residents more than once a week; maximum goal accomplished

FIGURE 8-8   Goal 3a: To Leave Room by Herself

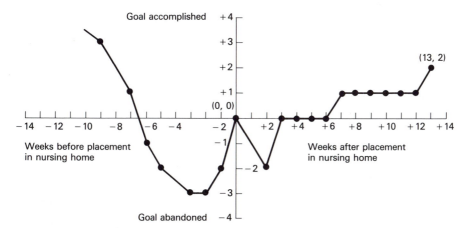

Descriptive criteria for points on goal line (Y — vertical line)
+4 = Goal accomplished: going out of room freely
+3 = Increased going out of room (more than once a day)
+2 = Increased going out of room alone (once a day average)
+1 = Occasionally going out of room alone (once a week average)
 0 = Starting point: placement in nursing home; leaving room only when taken to meals
−1 = Occasional refusal to leave room even when someone offers to accompany her (once a week average)
−2 = Increased refusal to leave room even when someone offers to accompany her (once a day average)
−3 = Repeated refusal to leave room even when someone offers to accompany her (more than once a day)
−4 = Goal abandoned: total refusal to leave room
Line X — horizontal line = Weeks before and after placement in nursing home

DIAGRAM 8-13 Contracted Plan Continued

DATE IDENTIFIED	PROBLEM/ NEED	GOAL	TASK	CONTRACT	DATE ANTICIPATED	DATE ACCOMPLISHED
12/8 Evaluation	Evaluation of problems 1–5	Goals 1–5	1. Review each goal 2. Evaluate extent of accomplishment for each goal 3. Reformulate contract	Mrs. J and worker	12/18 and 12/20	12/18 and 12/20
Contract reformulation	Change in tasks, contract, and dates anticipated for goal 3a	3a. To leave room alone (at least once a day)	(3a) 1. To leave room alone and walk down to nurse's station and say "hello" to nurse on duty	1. Mrs. J	12/21 and each day thereafter	
			2. To circle date of visit on calendar	2. Nurse on duty	12/21 and each day thereafter	
			3. To meet to discuss Mrs. J's progress	3. Head nurse and worker	12/27 and each Thursday thereafter	
			4. To evaluate progress toward goal 3a using graph	4. Worker and Mrs. J	12/27 and each Thursday thereafter	

3. To receive a food supply until AFDC check and food stamps arrive
4. To move into an apartment for long-term residence of family
6. To have children examined at the health center
7. To obtain fuel assistance
8. To receive AFDC check and food stamps
9. To have the refrigerator repaired

Goals 10, 11, and 12 were not accomplished by the time of the evaluation. These goals are:

10. To receive Supplemental Security Income
11. To receive a Thanksgiving food basket
12. To receive Christmas gifts for the children

No goal was ever stated on the contracted plan for problem 5 (poor money management) because Mr. and Mrs. P refused to recognize this problem. They continued to blame others and to deny that their evictions from past apartments were related to their poor management of money.

Contract review: In reviewing the goals that were accomplished, the worker asked if the attainment of goals was a result of the plan contracted. With the exception of goals 4 and 9, goal attainment directly followed the completion of planned tasks. The contract for goal 4 stated that the P's and the worker would collaborate on locating an apartment. For goal 9, the worker and the P's planned that Mr. P would contact the Salvation Army for financial assistance to pay for repairs. Instead, the P's contacted their income-maintenance technician directly, and she arranged for them to receive a new refrigerator.

In analyzing goals that were not accomplished (goals 10, 11, 12), the worker noted that the arrest in the process of goal accomplishment for each of these goals could be pinpointed to tasks contracted to Mr. P that he failed to complete. He did not follow up on his application for Supplemental Security Income, nor did he contact churches for a Thanksgiving food basket or the Salvation Army for Christmas presents for the children.

Even with goal 9 (refrigerator repair), instead of Mr. P's getting estimates on repair costs and contacting the Salvation Army, he and Mrs. P called the income-maintenance technician and requested a new refrigerator. (The worker and the income-maintenance technician realized that they should have communicated with each other about this new request before either one enacted a plan—teamwork breakdown.)

The social worker did not use scales to assess extent of goal accomplishment during the evaluation stage because of the basic nature of the identified goals and the interventions utilized. Although the primary needs for housing and food were being met for the present, the worker realized that there were two continuing problem areas: (1) poor money management and (2) excessive dependency on others to meet their needs. At the time of the evaluation, the P's were not recognizing these problems and did not want to work on either of them. When the worker pointed out that the tasks assigned to Mr. P had not been accomplished, he said he planned to do them when he felt up to it.

Since the P's were not asking for help from the worker with the two cited problems or with any additional problems or needs at the time of the evaluation, and because the worker did not want to continue unnecessary dependency, he began to talk about terminating with the family. Both the P's and the worker agreed that they would begin the process of termination.

E. Charted Progress

The worker recorded the evaluation process on the contracted plan as found in Diagram 8-14.

In the worker's discussions with the P's, their income-maintenance technician, and Mr. P's psychiatrist, the worker shared his continued concern regarding the family's management of money and dependence on outside resources to meet their needs. The problem of the family's poor money management had been recorded on the problem list earlier. During evaluation, the family's problem of dependency became more obvious to the worker, and it was added to the problem list when he recorded the evaluation (see Diagram 8-14). The worker expected that the case of the P family would possibly need to be reopened at a later date, and he thought it would be helpful to have the basic problem of dependency highlighted in the summarized chart.

IV. FIELD AREA: COMMUNITY SERVICES

A. Agency: Clayton Neighborhood House

B. Client System

Four Hispanic families who needed heat in their apartments on the second floor of 33 L Street. (For more background information, see Chapter 4, Engagement in Diverse Field Areas, IV. Community Services.)

C. Summary of Preceding Stages

The problems, goals, and tasks as identified and contracted in earlier stages are outlined in Diagram 6-12, Chapter 6, and Diagram 7-4, Chapter 7. The worker's interventions were direct and indirect, with residents and their landlord. By the third meeting of the worker with the residents, they were ready to move into the evaluation stage of the General Method.

D. Evaluation

Goal analysis: After the residents monitored the heat in their apartments for a week, they met to share their findings with the worker. Each family reported that the heat was adequate, ranging from 65° to 70° each day. At night the heat went down to 63° to 65°, and this was acceptable to the families. The residents expressed relief and gratitude to the worker. They were hopeful that the heating would continue throughout the winter.

As the worker and the residents began to recall their identified goal, she presented a scale (as found in Diagram 8-15) for goal analysis.

DIAGRAM 8-14 Contracted Plan Continued

DATE IDENTIFIED	PROBLEM/ NEED	GOAL	TASK	CONTRACT	DATE ANTICIPATED	DATE ACCOMPLISHED
12/4 Evalua- tion	Evaluation of problems 1–12	Goals 1–4 and 6– 12 (no goal for problem 5)	1. Review goals	1. Mr. and Mrs. P and worker	12/4	12/4
			2. Assess extent of accomplishment	2. Mr. and Mrs. P and worker	12/4	12/4
			3. Analyze progress	3. Mr. and Mrs. P and worker	12/4	12/4
			4. Reformulate con- tract or begin ter- mination	4. Mr. and Mrs. P and worker	12/4	12/4
Contract reform- ulation	Add problem 13: family's depen- dence on out- side resources					

DIAGRAM 8-15   Goal 1: To Obtain Consistent, Adequate Heating

								X
30	35	40	45	50	55	60	65	70
				Starting				

The families agreed that at this time their heating during the day is checked as averaging 68° (see the X in Diagram 8-15). The goal of adequate heating was being accomplished. The continuation of heating throughout the winter remained in question. They wanted to continue monitoring the heat throughout the winter and asked how they could show it on the scale each week. The worker introduced the ongoing-evaluation graph found in Figure 8-9. She explained that the horizontal line represented weeks and that the vertical line indicated temperature. She showed them when and how to plot their findings on the graph. They agreed to meet again the following week to plot their findings.

Contract review and reformulation: In reviewing the contracted plan, the worker reminded the residents that she had never met with the janitor (no entry in "date accomplished" for Task 1, Goal 1, in Diagram 6-12, Chapter 6). They agreed that there was no need for anyone to say anything to him now that the upstairs was being heated adequately. The residents knew that they continued to have a problem communicating with the landlord, but they didn't want to do anything about it for the present.

At this time, the worker and the residents agreed to extend their contact for another week. If there was no further problem with the heating and if the

FIGURE 8-9   Temperature Monitoring

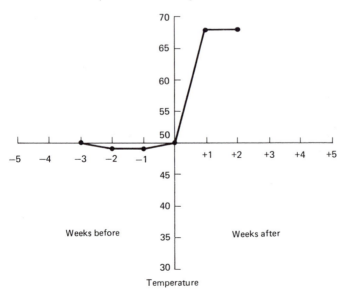

residents had nothing else they wanted to work on with the worker, she would terminate with them during the next meeting.

E. Charted Progress

The evaluation and contract reformulation by the worker and the residents was recorded on the contracted plan as indicated in Diagram 8-16.

V. FIELD AREA: EDUCATION

A. Agency: Keeney Elementary School

B. Client System

Mr. and Mrs. G and their 8-year-old son, Jim, in the third grade, who was showing regressive behavior in school and at home in reaction to his parents' strained relationship. (For additional background information, see Chapter 4, Engagement in Diverse Field Areas, V. Education.)

C. Summary of Preceding Stages

The problems, goals, and the tasks that were identified in earlier stages are outlined in the contracted plan found in Diagram 6-13, Chapter 6. After the joint session with Mr. and Mrs. G, Jim, and the worker at school, Mr. and Mrs. G followed through with going for marital counseling at a local family counseling center, and Jim began to show improvement in his school work.

D. Evaluation

Progress in school performance was evaluated by Jim and the worker as they met twice a week in her office. When the worker called Mrs. G each week, they would evaluate what progress had been made. During the last home visit, the worker, Jim, and his parents reviewed the contracted plan and analyzed the extent of goal accomplishment for all four problem areas.

Goal analysis: As the worker and Jim met together and focused on his school performance, they looked mainly at the extent to which Jim was (1) paying attention (showing interest in learning), (2) participating in class (raising hand to give answers or ask questions), and (3) bringing his grades up in math and spelling. These were specific areas in need of improvement identified by Jim's teacher. Each week, the worker met briefly with Jim's teacher to receive a report on his progress in the classroom. The teacher showed the worker Jim's weekly test scores in math and spelling. When Jim met with the worker, the teacher's report was reviewed, and scales to evaluate goal accomplishment were used (see Diagram 8-17).

By the end of the second week after the meeting with Jim and his parents, Jim's academic performance was assessed as +3 on the interest scale ("much interest") and as +3 on the scale for class participation ("raising hand five or six times a day"); his grades in math jumped from an average of 40 to 90, and his spelling grades went from 50 to 100 (see Diagram 8-17). There was obvious progress in Jim's investment in school. His school attendance was no longer a problem. He arrived on time each day and was back to walk-

DIAGRAM 8-16 Contracted Plan Continued

DATE IDENTIFIED	PROBLEM/ NEED	GOAL	TASK	CONTRACT	DATE ANTICIPATED	DATE ACCOMPLISHED
12/12 Evaluation	Evaluation of problems 1 (heating) and 2 (communication with landlord)	1. Adequate, consistent heating (no goal set for problem 2)	1. Review goal and problems 2. Evaluate extent of goal accomplishment 3. Reformulate contract	Worker and residents	12/12	12/12
Contract reformulation	Drop task 1, of goal 1, add tasks 6 and 7 for goal 1		6. Continue to monitor heat daily 7. Meet to review findings (and possible termination)	6. Mr. T, Mrs. V, Mr. A, and CR 7. Worker and residents	12/12–12/19 12/19	

DIAGRAM 8-17 Goal 3: Improved School Performance

INTEREST LEVEL (PAYING ATTENTION)				
			X	
0	1	2	3	4
Starting point; no interest	Little interest	Some interest	Much interest	Totally interested
CLASS PARTICIPATION				
			X	
0	1	2	3	4
Starting point; not raising hand	Little raising hand (once or twice a day)	Some raising hand (three or four times a day)	Much raising hand (five or six times a day)	Frequent raising hand (seven or more times a day)

MATH GRADES
X (above 90)

0	10	20	30	40	50	60	70	80	90	100
				Starting point					X	

SPELLING GRADES
X (above 90)

0	10	20	30	40	50	60	70	80	90	100
					Starting point				X	

ing to school with the neighborhood children. Mrs. G also reported that he was sleeping better at night. When talking with Mrs. G on the phone, the worker learned that Mr. and Mrs. G were not finding the counseling sessions easy, but Mrs. G did think that they were helpful.

Contract review and reformulation: In the last planned visit with Mr. and Mrs. G and Jim, the worker and the family recognized that all of their goals were being accomplished. More time was needed for Mr. and Mrs. G to work on their relationship, and they planned to continue in counseling for as long as was needed. Jim's problems had apparently subsided and he was back at his earlier functioning level (above average academically). Mr. and Mrs. G agreed that there was no reason for them to meet with the school worker again unless additional problems developed with Jim.

Jim said he liked to meet with the worker in her office and he didn't want to stop seeing her each week. They agreed that their visits would be reduced to once a week (instead of twice) for two more weeks (once before Christmas and once after he came back from vacation). During these sessions, they said they would talk about ending their work together.

Ongoing evaluation: Since the worker and Jim would meet to review his progress, ongoing-evaluation graphs were drawn and hung on the worker's wall (see Figures 8-10 and 8-11). The graphs indicated Jim's progress in math and spelling from the time he began school in the fall. Each point on the horizontal line indicated weeks before or after he started working with the social worker.

The vertical lines indicated grade averages each week, with the center point at the grade Jim was averaging when he first met the worker.

E. Charted Progress

The evaluation of grades and the additional tasks planned at this time were recorded by the worker on the contracted plan as shown in Diagram 8-18.

VI. FIELD AREA: CORRECTIONS

A. Agency: Juvenile Court

B. Client System

A group of six male youths, all age 14, on probation and attending weekly group meetings led by co-workers at Juvenile Court. (For further back-

FIGURE 8-10   Spelling

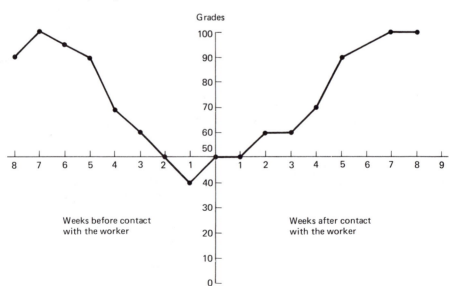

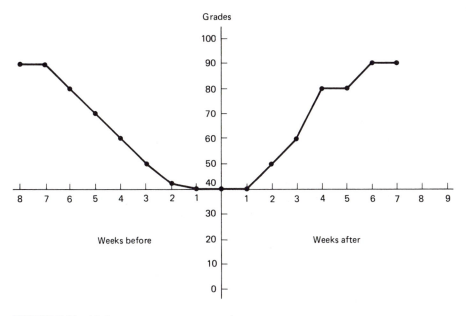

FIGURE 8-11 Math

ground information, see Chapter 4, Engagement in Diverse Field Areas, VI. Corrections.)

C. Summary of Preceding Stages

The problems, goals, and tasks contracted in earlier stages are outlined in Diagram 6-15, Chapter 6, and Diagram 7-7, Chapter 7. Attendance and participation in group meetings and weekly behavior reports from home and school were charted on graphs from every member of the group at the end of each meeting. Issues of interest or "changes" for the members were selected and discussed each week. After three and a half months (fourteen weeks), the workers began to go through a formal goal analysis with the youths. They also talked about the group process and progress. The ongoing-evaluation graphs and weekly charts that were developed and used earlier (Figures 6-1, 6-2, 6-3, and 6-4 in Chapter 6, and Figures 7-5 and 7-6 in Chapter 7) were helpful in the evaluation process.

D. Evaluation

Goal analysis: Since the four-month probationary period would be over in two weeks, all of the youths were eager to know if they would be getting off probation and if the group would be ending at that time. In evaluating goal 1 ("to get off probation in four months"), the members were reminded by the workers of the criteria that had been stated earlier for achieving this goal.

DIAGRAM 8-18 Contracted Plan Continued

DATE IDENTIFIED	PROBLEM/ NEED	GOAL	TASK	CONTRACT	DATE ANTICIPATED	DATE ACCOMPLISHED
12/4, 12/6, 12/13 Evaluation	Evaluation of problems 1, 2, 3, 4	Goals 1, 2, 3, 4	1. Review and evaluate goal 3 (school performance)	1. Jim and worker	11/27, 11/29 12/4, 12/6	11/27, 11/29 12/4, 12/6
			2. Review and evaluate goals 1, 3, 4 (Jim's school functioning and sleeping)	2. Mr. and Mrs. G, Jim, and worker	12/17	12/17
			3. Review goal 2 (Mr. and Mrs. G's relationship)	3. Worker, Mr. and Mrs. G	12/17	12/17
			4. Reformulate contract or terminate	4. Worker, Mr. and Mrs. G, and Jim	12/17	12/17
Contract reformulation	Change task and date anticipated for task 4, problem 3 (see contracted plan, Diagram 6-8, Chapter 9)		4. Meet once a week	4. Worker and Jim	12/20 and 1/8	

1. To maintain a score of 2 for group attendance—present each week unless excused
2. To maintain an average score of 3 ("much") or higher for group participation
3. To maintain an average score of 3 ("good") or higher for behavior at home
4. To maintain an average score of 3 ("good") or higher for behavior at school
5. To obey the rules of society (no further law-breaking)

Each of the group members was asked to look over his graphs and to assess the extent to which he met the criteria for accomplishing goal 1. It was obvious that four of the youths (MK, ML, B, C) could be recommended for a reduction in probation from six to four months. One member (A) had already left the group and had been sent to a correctional center. The other two (J and T) had failed to attend and to participate in meetings regularly. J's home reports averaged "poor" to "fair," and T had "poor" school reports because he continued to get into fights at school. J and T realized that they had not accomplished goal 1 and, therefore, would need to continue to meet with the workers each Monday. They were told that if they brought their scores up in all areas during the next six weeks, they could have their probation reduced by a month. They also knew that if they continued to do poorly, their probation period would be extended.

In evaluating goal 2 ("to control tempers"), each of the youths reviewed his scores on the weekly chart (Diagrams 7-5 and 7-6, Chapter 7). All agreed that they had grown in recognizing when they were beginning to feel angry and it was time to "cool it." They verbalized ways they had learned to handle their feelings instead of "blowing up." In looking at the progression of their weekly scores, improvement in temper control was apparent for all of the youths except T.

In analyzing the third goal (to learn more about "the changes" of teen-agers), the youths reviewed the topics that had been covered during group meetings. They indicated which issues or speakers they thought were the most interesting. They described the film on human sexuality as "kind of stupid," but the talk by the ex-prisoner and the trip to the vocational training school were "great." They all agreed that they had grown in understanding some of the changes they were going through.

After the evaluation, it was clear that four of the group members would probably be leaving the group in two or three weeks. Although the co-workers would continue to meet with J and T, the plan was made to begin to discuss in the following meetings "what it is like when you're off probation and there's no more group."

E. Charted Progress and Contract Reformulation

The worker recorded the group evaluation and contract reformulation as outlined in Diagram 8-19. The outline indicates that the anticipated dates for group meetings would be extended to at least six additional weeks for J and

DIAGRAM 8-19 Contracted Plan Continued

DATE IDENTIFIED	PROBLEM/ NEED	GOAL	TASK	CONTRACT	DATE ANTICIPATED	DATE ACCOMPLISHED
1/14 Evaluation	Evaluation of problems 1, 2, 3	Goals 1, 2, 3	1. Review goals 2. Evaluate goal accomplishment 3. Reformulate contract or introduce termination	Members and co-workers	1/14	1/14
Contract reformulation	1. Add goal 1a, task 1, contract date anticipated to reflect plan to extend group meetings for J and T for at least 6 more weeks 2. Add beginning termination plan, tasks 1 and 2	1a. To get off probation by March 1	1. To attend weekly group meetings	J and T and co-workers	Up to 2/25	
			1. Introduce termination	1. Co-workers	1/14	
			2. Discuss being "off probation"	2. Co-workers and group members	1/22	

T. Also indicated in the record is the plan made by the group to begin to discuss group termination and being off probation at the next meeting.

SUMMARY

In this chapter, the meaning and process of evaluation in general practice were presented. Evaluation was recognized as a particular stage in and as an ongoing dimension of the General Method. The need and values of evaluation in social work practice were emphasized.

Tools and processes were introduced that may be used during evaluation with any type of system. Various examples were given to demonstrate their applicability. The art and the science of practice are very apparent as a worker objectively and sensitively tries to assess progress and direction in each individualized situation.

As pointed out earlier, evaluation may lead to a reformulation of the contracted plan with additional interventions, or it may serve as a bridge to cross into the final stage of the General Method. Evaluation is a necessary prelude to termination.

NOTES

[1]Edward J. Mullen and James R. Dumpson, "Concluding Note," in Edward J. Mullen, James R. Dumpson, and Associates, eds., *Evaluation of Social Intervention* (San Francisco: Jossey-Bass, 1972), p. 244.

[2]Martin Bloom and Joel Fischer, *Evaluating Practice: Guidelines for the Accountable Professional* (Englewood Cliffs, N.J.: Prentice-Hall, 1982).

[3]Man Keung Ho, "Evaluation: A Means of Treatment," *Social Work* 21, no. 1 (January 1976): 24–27.

[4]Thomas J. Kiresuk and Robert E. Sherman, "Goal Attainment Scaling: A General Method for Evaluating Comprehensive Community Mental Health Programs," *Community Mental Health Journal* 4, no. 6 (December 1968): 443–53.

[5]For examples, see Bloom and Fischer, *Evaluating Practice;* Richard H. Ellis and Nancy C. Z. Wilson, "Evaluating Treatment Effectiveness Using a Goal-Oriented Progress Note," *Evaluation*, Special Monograph No. 1 (1973), pp. 6–11; Tony Tripodi and Irwin Epstein, *Research Techniques for Clinical Social Workers* (New York: Columbia University Press, 1980), pp. 208–29.

[6]Ruth Grossman Dean and Helen Reinherz, "Psychodynamics Practice and Single System Design: The Odd Couple," *Journal of Social Work Education* 22, no. 2 (Spring/Summer 1986): 73.

[7]Colleen Johnson and Frank Johnson, "Interaction Rules and Ethnicity," *Social Forces* 54 (December 1975): 452–66.

[8]Susan Sturdevant, *Therapy with Women* (New York: Springer, 1980), p. 27.

9

Termination

For everything there is a season, and a time for every purpose under heaven.

—Ecclesiastes 3:1

Human beings need to form attachments. Through an exchange of feelings, thoughts, and actions, trusting relationships develop that may be identified as attachments. There is a natural season for the separation of human systems and for the termination of attachments. Although it is natural for systems to become separated, the process of coming apart may be very painful, even traumatic. As a person anticipates the grief for the loss of a meaningful other, separation anxiety may develop. If the anxiety and feelings around separation are not expressed, there may be a change in behavior and a withdrawal from possible future attachments.

Termination in social work practice is often a time of heightened anxiety for both a worker and a client system, particularly when they have developed a trusting relationship. It is the time to end their ongoing contacts and to plan for the future. Even when working with target or action systems, once goals have been accomplished, a worker needs to take time to end ongoing contacts.

When a social worker begins to disengage with a system, time, skill, and understanding are needed for an effective closure of services. The art of termination involves skillful interactions and procedures with honest sharing in an atmosphere of realistic hope. Although each system is unique with its own individual pace and method of responding to loss, some general patterns of grief reactions are often present during termination and need to be identified.

In this chapter, the knowledge, values, and skills utilized during termination will be presented. The need for a social worker to develop the art of termination cannot be overemphasized. A poorly timed or poorly executed termination may result in marked regression or failure in goal accomplishment. A meaningful, growth-promoting termination experience can stabilize progress and serve as a support and model for a system as it faces new attachments, separations, and losses in the future.

THE MEANING OF TERMINATION

In this chapter, *termination* means the ending of contact between a worker and a system. As the last stage of the General Method, termination comprises the time taken and the process used when a worker and a system begin to plan the ending of their contacts with each other. Even when there has been only brief contact or little emotional sharing, a time is needed for worker and system to recall goals and evaluate progress, as well as to clarify the reasons and plan for termination, prior to the ending of contact.

Central to an understanding of termination is an awareness of the possible feelings and reactions that may take place as two systems separate. For some systems, the recognition and expression of these feelings may come quite easily at this time. For others, however, strong defenses against these feelings may come into operation. Disguised reactions to particular feelings can make termination a time of confusion and frustration for both client systems and workers.

Children, for example, have been found to experience such feelings as fear, anxiety, sadness, loss, rejection, guilt, helplessness, and cultural shock when they are separated from significant others or familiar surroundings. Instead of being able to express these feelings, some react with such behaviors as hostility, acting out, lack of trust, bed-wetting, poor schoolwork, destructiveness, lying, and running away. Rather than acting out, some children become extremely withdrawn and refuse to form new attachments. In studying this reaction, Ner Littner writes:

> To the degree that he cannot master these feelings and must repress them, the child will need to fend off close relationships, using the various techniques previously mentioned, and suffer the painful consequences of this self-imposed emotional isolation. He will keep bottled up within him an enor-

mous desire for closeness, which he cannot allow himself to really satisfy. It is noteworthy too, that his impaired ability to relate to people may also influence his capacity to be close to his own children, and therefore sometimes directly affects their ability to be close to others.[1]

The clients of social workers have often experienced painful separations and terminations in their lives. They are often guarded and fearful of forming a trusting relationship with a worker. If an attachment is formed, when it comes time to terminate with these clients, strong feelings from past separations may emerge along with feelings over the anticipated loss of the worker. A variety of defenses and reactions may be displayed to ward off past and present hurts and anxieties. The feelings that are avoided often include a sense of abandonment, fear of being unable to cope alone, helplessness, guilt, failure, and holding oneself responsible for the felt rejection. These feelings may be covered up through one, several, or a sequence of reactive behaviors.

REACTIONS TO TERMINATION

The defenses and reactions of a system during termination may fall within a five-stage termination sequence that is similar to the stages of the grieving process.[2] Although not necessarily in every case, nor in the exact order described below, reactions to termination are often identified as falling within one or all of the following stages:

1. *Denial.* The client may ignore what the worker is saying or avoid any discussion of termination. This may extend to the failing to keep appointments, coming late or leaving early. In a group, individual members or the group as a whole may isolate themselves, refuse to participate in the conversation, or attempt to change the topic of discussion.
2. *Anger.* There may be outbursts of verbal or physical assaults. These may be directed toward the worker, toward other members of the system, or toward a person who is expected to take over the worker's role after termination. Anger may also be turned inward as the client displays a lack of concern or care for self, including possible personal injury. There may be regression to earlier problematic behavior in order to be punished or to punish the worker.
3. *Bargaining.* The client tries to negotiate an extension of time or a modified cutback in contacts. Promises of "being good if" are presented. Gifts or rewards may be offered.
4. *Depression.* The client manifests listlessness, little energy, withdrawal, sadness, helplessness, despair, no motivation to go on. Pain is real and evident. There is regression in accomplishments. Time is needed to mourn. Beginning resignation is apparent.
5. *Acceptance.* With the acceptance of the termination, there is an increase in energy. The client is able to talk about the good and the bad times and to think about the future. There is a "quiet expectation"[3] as the client begins to

show interest in forming new attachments. The client returns to the level of functioning prior to the depression and moves away from self-pity or self-centeredness.

During termination, there may not be a clear transition from one stage of the sequence to the next. Frequently, there are signs of regression in the process, and a discussion of fears and feelings will have to be repeated. A worker who is aware of the natural process and reactions found during termination is less likely to take what is happening personally or literally and then react inappropriately.

THE DECISION TO TERMINATE

After a worker and a system of contact have completed an evaluation of goal accomplishment, they may conclude that the purpose for their coming together has been attained. The scales and graphs suggested in Chapter 8 may have helped to demonstrate the movement and progress that have been made. In addition to these indicators, a worker can assess the appropriateness of moving into termination with a system by (1) reviewing with his or her supervisor the work that has taken place with the system, (2) observing and talking with the system itself, and (3) talking with other knowledgeable sources about the system's readiness to terminate with the worker (with informal consent of system).

If there is some hesitancy to move into termination on the part of the system or the worker, the cause for holding back needs to be identified. A supervisor can help a worker to let go of a system when there may be strong attachment because there has been progress and the worker gets much satisfaction in working with the system, or because progress has been minimal and the worker has feelings of failure.

If the system of contact is holding back from facing termination, this could be caused by the feelings identified earlier or by other problematic areas that the system would like to face with the worker, even though there has been avoidance and fear up to this time. The supervisor might help detect this and might suggest that the worker explore this possibility with the system before moving on to termination.

It may be that a worker wants to terminate with a system even when there is insufficient evidence that goals have been accomplished. Through supervision, the worker may be helped to recognize feelings of anger or helplessness in working with the system, which are causing the desire to terminate prematurely. If a system wants an early termination with a worker, it may be (1) because the worker is beginning to touch on conflict areas that the system does not want to face; or, as brought out earlier, (2) because the system is anticipating the worker's leaving and wants to be in control by initiating the termination; or (3) because the system is taking flight from having to face any of the other feelings already identified (rejection, anger, grief, etc.). Here, too, the worker may need help through supervision to discern the dynamics of the situation.

In observing and talking with a system or other resources about possible termination, the worker assesses the extent of goal accomplishment and also the current functioning level of the system. The questions to be asked are:

1. Have the goals been accomplished according to the contracted plan?
2. Can the system go on functioning at least at the level attained at this time without continued contact with the worker?
3. Although the identified problems may have been resolved and the goals accomplished, if a similar need or problem develops, will the system be able to handle it or, at least, know how to get help?
4. If additional supports will be needed after the worker terminates, are they available?

A worker continues to work with a system beyond the point of achieving contracted goals only for the length of time needed to stabilize goal accomplishment and to go through the process of termination. If the questions above are answered affirmatively, then the system is ready for termination to begin.

Sometimes a system gives the message to a worker indirectly that it is ready to terminate. Perhaps even before a worker begins to discuss the issue, a system may give indicators that it is able to handle problems on its own. Since systems often internalize the coping patterns a worker has demonstrated and, with experience, develop problem-solving skills that are transferable, there may be an apparent decrease in dependency and a desire to handle things independently. When the system is a group or community, attendance may become irregular as members no longer feel the need to meet with the worker or with one another. New sources of support and involvement may have been found by members of the system. Indirectly, the system may be showing a readiness for termination. These behaviors are different when a system reacts to termination by breaking off in anger or as a means to regain control. There is little effect connected with behaviors that indicate a readiness to terminate. Even when a system demonstrates this readiness, some of the feelings and reactions to loss described earlier may become apparent as the worker begins to talk about termination. The thought of not having the worker available for ongoing support may stir up earlier feelings of loss of a significant person. There may be some regression in functioning in order to keep the worker involved and to avoid dealing with fears or feelings of loss. The worker and system may both recognize that it is time to terminate, but opportunity will be needed to identify and express feelings and to plan for termination.

Sometimes a worker has to terminate with a system before goals have been accomplished. This could happen because of the worker's lack of skills to help the particular system or because of an inappropriate emotional involvement. When the decision to terminate is not based on evaluative evidence of the system's readiness, the worker and his or her agency have the responsibility to see that the system continues to receive help from an appropriate resource. Also, time should be given to explain to the system why there has to be a termination and to give the system the opportunity to react to the unexpected closure.

A LIFE-CYCLE APPROACH TO TERMINATION

Throughout the process of terminating with a system, the social worker may use a life-cycle approach. Basically, the worker tries to help the system to step back and review the life cycle of their work together. Initially, as the concept of termination is first introduced and early reactions of the system to the idea may include denial, anger, or bargaining, the worker helps the system to express the feelings underneath these reactions through a review of the *past.* They recall why they first came together and consider how they have moved to the present point in time. Recalling what they have been through together can help to bring out feelings of fear, anger, closeness, or loss. It can help to identify the nature and strength of the current relationship.

As the worker and system move from focusing on the past to the *present,* it can become clearer that goals have been accomplished and that the earlier needs or problems that necessitated help from the worker no longer exist. The instruments used earlier to evaluate progress during the stage of evaluation may be recalled. As the system begins to face the reality that termination is imminent, an attempt may be made to bargain for more time or to locate new problems. The worker may sensitively point out that the system has demonstrated an ability to handle such problems at this time and then begin to talk about the feelings that are making it difficult for the system to terminate. Signs and feelings of depression may begin to appear as the system becomes resigned to the termination. Strong feelings of fear, loss, or grief may emerge. Independently, the system may begin to ask about the *future* and what will happen when he, she, or they will have to manage without the worker. At this point, a plan for termination may begin to be formulated. Much time may be needed before the system has the energy ready to invest in planning for the future. Feelings may need to be expressed repeatedly before a plan is completed. If the system is not ready to move into considering the future, the worker will need to stay with the present, even though this may call for great patience on the part of the worker. In time, a system will move from mourning over the anticipated loss to an acceptance of termination.

When the system begins to accept the termination, more investment in developing and implementing a termination plan can be expected. As the worker discusses the future with the system, frequent reference is made to the needs that were identified in the *past* and to the strengths that are apparent in the *present,* in order to give hope for the *future.*

The life-cycle approach is a dynamic process used throughout the termination stage. Although the three focus points of *past, present,* and *future* are not addressed necessarily in an exact sequence, the framework offers some direction and guidance for the worker to help a system move through the process of termination.

PLANNING THE TERMINATION

As soon as possible, an ending date for the final planned contact between worker and system should be set. Ideally, both the worker and the system should mutually agree upon this date and on the extent and times of contacts they will have prior to the termination date. Meetings between worker and client may be gradually tapered off until the closing date, or they may continue on a regular basis until final termination. The termination plan developed by worker and system should be individualized according to the needs and circumstances of the system. The point to be emphasized is that for an effective termination, a plan has to be articulated, understood, and implemented. If it is apparent that a system is ready to terminate with a worker but will need additional supports or services, the process of referral or transfer should be included as an essential dimension of the termination plan.

As brought out in Chapter 7 in the discussion on referral, when resources are being mobilized for a client, every effort should be made to have the client system initiate and follow through on contacting the resource on its own. During termination, unless direct involvement by a worker is absolutely necessary, the worker should try to negotiate a plan in which the system itself establishes linkages with the resources needed. This is particularly the case when resources are informal, such as family members, church, or neighborhood. Having the system make its own contacts fosters self-confidence and provides the worker with an opportunity to see if the system can develop new relationships independently.

If a worker is terminating with a system that is unable to sustain itself without continued professional help, the worker first tries to transfer the system to another worker in the same helping agency. If the agency already in contact with the system has no workers with the time or skills needed, then the worker locates an appropriate outside resource and makes a referral (see the process for referral in Chapter 7). If a referral (outside resource) or a transfer (inside resource) is needed, a client may have feelings about being referred or transferred that need to be expressed, and there are ways to proceed that can help to insure a smooth transition as a system moves from an old worker to a new service provider.

When a system experiences the loss of a worker, particularly if a trusting relationship has developed, it can be very difficult for the system to begin to bond with a new provider of services. The former worker can help to facilitate the transition process. Generally, only after having expressed some of the reactions to termination, such as denial, anger, bargaining, and depression, can the worker and system begin to rationally consider establishing contact with a new resource. The system in need of continued service may have strong feelings of loyalty to the former worker. There may be a fear of appearing ungrateful or disloyal if the system begins to relate positively to a new resource. The former worker needs to clearly sanction the system's involvement with a new worker. This can be demonstrated in meetings that should be planned for all three parties (former worker, system in need, new worker) prior to the final termination date. At these meetings, the former worker participates in a hopeful and supportive manner. He or she conveys a sense of trust in the abilities of the new worker and of the system in need of continued service to work constructively with each other.

It is necessary for all three parties to know exactly when the former worker is going to terminate with the system and if there is any plan for a follow-up. If there is some expectation of contact after the final termination date, it needs to be clear whom the former worker will contact, when the contact can be expected, and why it is necessary. If the door is left open for the system to reestablish contact with the former worker, there may be a holding back from investment with the new worker. The system itself may contact the former worker unexpectedly by a phone call or a letter. The former worker can be most helpful by acknowledging the contact when received but then directing the system back to the new worker for continued help.

Even when a new resource has entered the termination process, there should be time on the final date for only the former worker and the system to meet together. During their last contact, there is often a planned expression of the significance of the meeting. If the system is a group or community, there is generally a party or some type of ceremony. Pictures may be taken or exchanged. This time provides the opportunity for the final expression of feelings and hopes.

Stating the termination plan in writing helps to avoid manipulation or misunderstanding. A separate format or instrument does not have to be drawn up. The contracted plan that was introduced and developed during assessment, intervention, and evaluation may continue to be used. As the worker and system arrive at a final date and make plans for the intervening period, entries are made in the contracted plan to indicate the what (tasks), who (contract), and when (dates anticipated) of the plan. If it is agreed that new resources will be needed to support the system after the worker leaves, the plan for initiating contact with these resources is included in the written statement. As the termination plan is carried out, dates of accomplishment for each of the tasks are entered on the contracted plan. An example is given in Diagram 9-1 of a termination plan for a group of young adolescent girls called "the Angels." This group was one of many offered at a neighborhood center each year. All groups terminated at the end of June and began again in September. The worker knew who was expected to take "the Angels" the following year. The new worker was, therefore, invited to meet with the group as part of the termination plan.

REACTIONS OF SERVICE PROVIDERS

As human beings, providers of service become attached to others. Social workers, teachers, child-care workers, nurses, and other professionals suffer from feelings of loss when they are separated from systems that have been meaningfully involved in their lives. If there has not been the opportunity to anticipate the loss, move through the reactions, or express the related feelings prior to final termination, a service provider may demonstrate depression, withdrawal, or burnout after one or several terminations of this nature.

In addition to the need for systems receiving services to have time to express feelings and plans prior to termination, social workers and those in collaborative service provision need time to anticipate and express their possible emptiness when a system no longer needs their assistance. A double energy is often used by a service provider in termination: (1) that of helping a system to move away, and (2) that of moving away him- or herself. A provider may deny, become angry, or become depressed during or after the energy drain. Through supportive supervision, peer meetings, and other available environmental supports, a provider may find a place, persons, and convenient time to work on what is happening inside of him or her.

When a provider is employed in an emotionally charged service, such as child protection or work with the terminally ill, the need for supportive outlets is especially apparent. For example, in a residential setting for disturbed children, the child-care director became the main significant other for a 5-year-old boy. The child progressed remarkably and was moved into a foster home. Following his placement, the director became obviously antagonistic toward the social worker and increasingly irritable toward the other children. It wasn't until the worker and the director took time to look painfully at what was happening that the director began to touch her feelings of depression due to the loss of the young boy. If the worker or others at the facility had been more sensitive to the natural feelings of the director, more time could have been given to deal with termination prior to the child's discharge, a step that would have prevented some of the reactions that followed.

A social worker who serves as a case manager for a team that is about to terminate with a system can show sensitivity to the needs of the team members by building in a time to talk about the feelings they might have as they anticipate closing the case. Supervisors and administrators also have a major responsibility to help prevent burnout in their employees. If they understand the significance of termination in the provision of services, they can find various ways to assist their workers. For example, in a hospice facility where service providers were repeatedly experiencing the deaths of their patients, an administrator not only set aside times for peer support meetings, but also designated a room on the top floor as "the Tower," where staff could go whenever they felt the need "to yell, cry, or pray." Unless a service provider can reach a point of acceptance with a termination, he or she will not be able to have the anticipation, hope, and energy necessary to invest in new clients, patients, or work assignments.

DEVELOPING SENSITIVITY AND SKILL

The ideas about termination that are presented in this chapter are often rejected as an overexaggeration. New workers, in particular, find it difficult to believe that their leaving a system can have an impact on the system or on their own selves. A verbal presentation on the dynamics of termination may be only an intellectual consideration unless some aspect of experiential learning can be included. Three basic exercises may be used to help students or service providers to grow in sensitivity and skill for working with termination.

EXERCISE 9-1   USING IMAGERY

In this exercise, all the individuals participating in the experience are asked to close their eyes and to picture a significant person in their lives. They are then asked to imagine that this person is talking with them and saying that he or she is going away and does not plan to return. Participants are then asked to identify their immediate feelings. They are next asked to imagine that they express these feelings to the person, but that the person repeats his or her plan to leave. They then imagine the person getting up and walking out. They are asked to let

DIAGRAM 9-1 The Contracted Plan Continued

DATE IDENTIFIED	PROBLEM/ NEED	GOAL	TASK	CONTRACT	DATE ANTICIPATED	DATE ACCOMPLISHED
5/3	21. Funding for trip to beach	21. Raise $50 for trip	1. Explore ways to raise funds; begin to plan	1. Group and worker	5/3	8/3
			2. Finalize plans for bake sale	2. Group and worker	5/10	5/10
			3. Have bake sale	3. Group and center	5/15	5/15
			4. Critique bake sale; set date and plan for beach trip; begin to discuss year-end evaluation	4. Group and worker	5/17	5/17
5/24 Evaluation	Year-end evaluation of problems/needs 1–21, as cited above	1–21 as cited above	1. Recall goals 2. Evaluate extent of goal accomplishment	1. Group and worker	4/24 and 6/1	5/24 and 6/1
6/1	Termination process	Satisfactory termination (progress stabilized)	1. Introduce termination	1. Group and worker	6/1	6/1

304

Activity	Who	Date	Date
2. Discuss feelings and reactions to ending the group; clarify final termination date	2. Group and worker	6/7	6/7
3. Identify present strengths, discuss the future; plan termination	3. Group and Worker	6/14	6/14
4. Invite new worker (who will have the group after summer vacation) to the next meeting	4. Mary C (for the group)	6/15	6/15
5. Meet with new worker	5. Former worker, group, and new worker	6/21	6/21
6. Beach trip	6. Former worker, group, and new worker	6/26	6/26
7. Closing session and party	7. Former worker and group	6/28	6/28

themselves enter into what they would feel when the person has left, and to try to find words to express these feelings. Finally, the participants are asked, "What would you do next?" and then, "What do you need at this time?"

This exercise helps a person to sense some of the feelings that often emerge as one perceives the loss of a meaningful other. Talking about the experience may also lead to a discussion about what actions a person may take in trying to cope with such a loss and what resources might help the person through the experience.

EXERCISE 9-2   SMALL GROUP EXPERIENCE

In this exercise, participants are divided into small groups to discuss a topic such as "timing needed for termination" or "writing up a termination plan." The facilitator moves around to different groups and eventually asks a member of one group to leave and join another identified group. After a few minutes, the facilitator moves to the next group and again directs a member to leave and join a different group, with no explanation for the move. This procedure is continued until every group has lost one of its original members.

In the discussion that follows, participants are asked to describe any thoughts or feelings they had when one of their members was asked to leave. They usually say that they wondered why the person was removed from the group and that they felt some frustration over the departure. They are then asked how they felt about another person joining the group. Here, too, feelings of anger and frustration were often experienced over having to adjust to the entry of a new person. The leaving or entering may have slowed down or stopped the group process. In addition, participants may share feelings of anger toward the facilitator for interrupting the group. Those that were directed to leave a group may disclose that they felt disoriented, isolated, rejected, or perhaps withdrawn as they entered a new group.

EXERCISE 9-3   ROLE PLAY

The third exercise is a role play between a worker and a client system. There is a partial script, which is given only to the actor who plays the role of the client system. The person in the role of the worker is directed to begin the play by saying, "I will be leaving the agency in May." To what the worker says, the person playing the client system is directed to feel free to respond as he or she feels like responding. Eventually, however, the "client system" is expected to make the statements (in whatever order seems appropriate) identified in the script.

TERMINATION SCRIPT

Worker:	I will be leaving the agency in May.
Client System:	Will I be seeing someone else?
Worker:	(?)
Client System:	I had a fight with that neighbor again.
Worker:	(?)
Client System:	What did I bother coming here for anyway? You're not really helping me.
Worker:	(?)
Client System:	I'll come to see you where you are going—maybe just for a few months.
Worker:	(?)
Client System:	Nobody cares about what happens to me anyway.
Worker:	(?)
Client System:	May I take your picture before you leave?
Worker:	(?)
Client System:	Thanks for everything.
Worker:	(?)

This exercise may also be done as a "fishbowl" experience. Here, anyone watching the role play who believes he or she may have a more appropriate way to respond to the client may come in back of the person playing the role of the worker and tap him or her on the shoulder. The worker then exchanges places with this person, and the new response is given.

In the discussion that follows the role play, the facilitator asks the participants to consider what both actors were feeling as they made different statements. A basic question asked is, "Was the worker responding to the content literally, or was he or she tuning into the feelings of the client system?" The participants are asked to consider other responses the worker could have made to particular statements by the client system. The most important question is, "What does the client need to hear at this time?"

By using these three exercises, workers can become more aware of the following central ideas:

1. Terminations may cause a variety of feelings and reactions that lead to a need for help from others.
2. Departures may cause disorientations and frustration, leading to an arrest in progress, or to withdrawal or anger toward the person who initiated the separation.
3. There are ways to respond to people who are facing terminations that can help to let them know that you understand what they are going through.
4. Workers themselves may have feelings and reactions that they need help with during terminations.

There are other exercises and activities that can enhance a worker's knowledge and skills in the process of terminating with a particular system.

For example, process-recording an individual interview on termination and then reviewing the recording by oneself or with one's supervisor or peers can help a worker to better understand the dynamics that are taking place and to locate where the system and the worker are in the termination process. During this last stage of the General Method, a worker's feelings may be so intense that it is difficult to maintain an objective perspective. Using such exercises as process recording, role play, and imagery can help strengthen the worker's comprehension and self-control.

WORKING WITH DIFFERENT SYSTEMS

Feelings and concerns of systems during termination differ according to the unique circumstances and perspective of each system. Feelings of loss may extend beyond the loss of a worker to the loss of a support group and its members (group), the loss of an external control system (institution), or the loss of a secure nurturing environment (agency). In trying to identify the feelings a system is experiencing during the termination process, a worker needs to be aware of these variations and other types of feelings frequently felt by systems of particular size or purpose.

When a worker is terminating with a community, for example, members may be planning to continue to work together on issues by themselves, or they may be breaking up because they were a short-term organization with a task focus. Continuing without the worker may be somewhat fearful for them because they depended on the worker's leadership and support. Dissolving this organization may also cause some fears over losing a structure that gave them a sense of power and protection. These feelings will need to be clarified and expressed.

Diversity in reactions to termination also depends on the extent of investment made by each system in the relationship with the worker. This may present a challenge to a worker when the system is a family, group, or community and the extent of investment differs among the individual members of the same system. Although those with little investment may have minimal feeling about ending contacts, others in the system may have strong feelings, with much difficulty in accepting the termination. In this situation, it may be helpful for the worker to plan to meet with each member individually, as well as with the whole system, to work on termination. It is probable that the meetings with the less invested may be light and brief, whereas the meetings with those more invested may be intense and lengthy. Planning to meet with every member individually avoids singling out certain members and yet allows more time for those who need it. Even when an individual has developed no attachment, the worker and this person need to overview the past (purpose for beginning contact), the present (extent of goal accomplishment), and the future (plans for when all contacts are over).

In addition to a review of past, present, and future with members of a system individually and collectively, the worker may ask all of the members share together how each one perceives the termination. Many times, members are surprised to hear, perhaps for the first time, that they have meant something to one another. Individuals who are hesitant to admit that they have some feelings about the termination may begin to feel freer to talk about them when they hear others openly express their feelings. Also, the sharing may bring about some final efforts to clarify and heal any misunderstandings the members may have had with each other or with the worker.

USING THE HOLISTIC FOUNDATION IN TERMINATION

As stated earlier, there is an art to termination that calls on the values, knowledge, and skills of a worker. The social work generalist demonstrates this art as various elements from the holistic foundation for general practice (Diagram 1-5, Chapter 1) are selected, integrated, and applied throughout the termination process.

As a worker and a system begin to bring their working relationship to an end, all of the value principles of individualization, acceptance, self-determination, nonjudgmental attitude, controlled emotional involvement, purposeful expression of feelings, and confidentiality are utilized. The timing, planning, and processing of termination have to be *individualized* according to each system's unique circumstances. If a system is avoiding or denying the termination, the worker patiently *accepts* the defense. Keeping in mind the principle of *controlled emotional involvement,* the worker honestly shares his or her feelings about terminating and artfully encourages the *purposeful expression of the system's related feelings.* If a system does not choose to identify new problem areas or to be referred for additional support, the worker maintains a *nonjudgmental attitude* and respects the system's right to *self-determination.* When a referral or transfer is made or data are collected from an outside resource, all information about the system is treated as *confidential* and released only with the informed consent of the system.

Theories on human development, group dynamics, organizations, and ecological systems are among the theories that give direction and understanding to a worker in the termination stage. In human development theory, the worker learns about the natural needs all human systems have for attachments throughout the life cycle. The trauma of separation and the impact of an abrupt termination on a human system is also presented.

Through theories of group dynamics and organizations, the worker learns about the conflicts, tasks, and processes a group, community, or organization undergoes when a person who was seen as the leader (or someone with power and control) leaves the system.

Using ecological-systems theory, the worker perceives the interdependence that develops between a client system and its service-providing environment. The theory helps workers to understand that it may not be feasible to expect an organism to maintain its functioning level when a major nurturer in its environment is removed. The need for a careful assessment of a system's available internal and external resources after termination with a worker is, therefore, highlighted.

In addition to values and theories from the holistic foundation, a worker uses a range of general skills, particularly problem-solving skills, during the termination process. For example, as a worker begins to introduce the idea of termination to a system, skill is needed for a clear identification of what it means to terminate (need-identification skills). In reviewing the past, data collection and evaluation skills are used. As focus is given to the present, a worker uses assessment skills in appraising the strengths and readiness of a system for termination and in locating appropriate supportive resources in the environment. Planning skills, including the sequencing of tasks and contracting, are used as a worker and system begin to plan for the future. Recording skills are needed for writing the termination plan. A variety of interventive skills, including referral and transfer, may be needed in the implementation of the plan. Listening, responding, and clarifying are among the communication skills that are demonstrated repeatedly throughout the entire termination process.

Essentially, the three primary skills needed during termination may be described as (1) sensing skills (recognizing feelings and reactions), (2) timing skills (knowing when to identify, wait, or stop), and (3) processing skills (moving from past to present to future). The art of termination rests in a worker's demonstrated sensitivity to the time and movement needed for a system to be ready to accept termination. All of the actions of a social worker, throughout the process, reflect an artful integration and application of values, knowledge, and skills.

HUMAN DIVERSITY IN TERMINATION

Culture

During the termination period, as stated, basic questions asked include: (1) Can the system go on functioning at the level attained at this time without continued contact with the worker? (2) Although the identified problems may have been resolved and the goals accomplished, if a similar need develops will the system be able to handle it or, at least, know how to get help? (3) If additional supports will be needed after the worker terminates, are they available? In working with minority ethnic groups, a central need has been described as empowerment. Rather than doing for a system, the worker tries to prevent dependency and to encourage self-help and autonomy. The reality is, however, that the needs of oppressed groups are often multiple and pervasive. A worker and a system may frequently feel overwhelmed or discouraged because little progress is apparent. The worker or the system, or both, may have a strong inclination to terminate, even when goals have not been accomplished and when regression will obviously take place after the worker leaves. Particular care has to be taken by the worker when planning a termination to insure the stabilization of change efforts and the availability of ongoing supports as needed.

Termination, as brought out in this chapter, is a stage when skills in timing and sensing of feelings are especially needed. Again, knowledge of a culture's orientation toward the expression of feelings and the meaning of time is imperative. If a worker has played a meaningful role in the life of a client, he or she will naturally have some feelings and a sense of loss when the worker terminates. The reactions and defenses used by the system will be culturally derived. A skilled worker will understand and enable the system to find the time and the opportunity to express feelings and to prepare for the termination. Expressions of denial, bargaining, anger, or depression may vary according to cultural orientation toward separation and death. The process of moving from past to present to future may also be influenced by the time orientation of one's cultural background. As indicated earlier, members of Asian Pacific, American Indian, and Afro-American cultures lean toward emphasizing the past, whereas Mexican-Americans are more concerned with the present and Anglo-Saxon Americans are more future-oriented. Recognizing such differences enables a worker to have more realistic expectations of the pace needed by a system to move to the point of acceptance in the process of termination.

Sexual Variation

After an evaluation, the worker and a gay or lesbian client system may decide to terminate, even though long-range goals for social change have not been achieved. With personal, interpersonal, or short-range goals attained, they may decide to continue to address the need to change target systems on their own or in other ways. The worker may continue to advocate equal opportunities and services for gay and lesbian persons through introducing or supporting related legislation, policies, programs, or practices. Gay or lesbian clients may choose to continue their efforts to achieve social change goals through active involvement in ongoing political action groups or movements. When the decision to terminate is reached by both worker and system, it is important for the gay or lesbian client to feel that he or she is welcome to return to the worker or the agency for additional services after termination, if needed.

If a group for gay or lesbian persons is terminating at an agency, individual members generally need to have other formal or informal networks available. This is particularly true for those who have not "come out" and joined the extended gay/lesbian community. As presented earlier, maintaining a hidden identity can be extremely draining emotionally and psychologically. Planning for the future should include thoughtful consideration and efforts to build in appropriate resources for these individuals.

As with any working relationship, a deep attachment may develop between worker and client system in the course of their working together. For lesbian or gay clients, it may be the first time they have met someone who has been able to listen to their questions and concerns and able to accept and respect them as unique individuals. For workers, it may be the first time they have had the opportunity to get to know and to work with a gay or lesbian individual or group. Terminating the relationship may evoke feelings for both worker and client system that are difficult to face and to express. Again, time is needed for them to overview the life cycle of their relationship and to honestly discuss their feelings, such as anger, fear, loss, and love. It will be easier for both the worker and the client system to accept termination, if a sense of acceptance has existed throughout the time they have been together. If there has not been acceptance, either one may continue to feel a need to try to prove something to or to change something in the other.

Gender Sensitivity

As a worker and a system of contact move into the termination stage of the General Method, a key question to be asked is: "Will the progress that has been made be sustained and developed after the worker leaves?" The tendency to regress to gender roles that existed for years before the worker became involved is very strong after the worker terminates. Again, if change is to remain stabilized, it may be imperative that support networks be located and activated before final termination.

As stated earlier, during termination, individuals are encouraged to express their feelings and fears surrounding the anticipated loss of the social worker and perhaps other members of a group. Here too, men who hold back from expressing feelings may not be able to admit that they will miss the worker or the group. Even though, by this time in the process, male clients may have begun to find it somewhat easier to express feelings, there may be a tendency to regress, as generally found before termination. Women, if they have been in the traditional dependent role, may also find it particularly difficult to accept termination and become independent of the worker and the group. If a bonding of mutual respect and support has developed between the client system and the worker or other group members, this experience may serve as a model for the system in future relationships and interactions.

Thus, each stage of the General Method calls for a sensitive application of values, knowledge, and skills as a worker interacts with systems of diverse cultures, sexual orientation, or gender. As brought out in Chapter 3, a worker is sensitive also to diversity in age and stages, endowment and personality, value system, social class, and geographic location. A knowledge of human diversity and an awareness of one's own human responses to various individuals, cultures, life styles, roles, and environments are essential for an effective application of the General Method.

TERMINATION IN DIVERSE FIELD AREAS

I. FIELD AREA: CHILD WELFARE

A. Agency: State Department of Children's Services

B. Client System

K, 15 years old, female, placed in group home six months ago. (For more background information, see Chapter 4, Engagement in Diverse Field Areas, I. Child Welfare.)

C. Summary of Preceding Stages

The problems, goals, and tasks identified and implemented in earlier stages are found in Diagram 6-6 of Chapter 6 and Diagram 7-1 of Chapter 7. A summary of the evaluation of goals and contract reformulation may be found in Diagram 8-10, Chapter 8. Basically, progress was identified during evaluation for all of the stated goals. The goal related to personal growth was the slowest in achievement, and more time was recognized as needed for progress in this area. The contract was reformulated to extend goal 2 to include optimal academic performance, and to change the frequency of worker contact to once a month rather than once every two weeks.

D. Termination

After K had been in her group home for six months, the worker began to terminate because she was leaving Children's Services. K's first reaction to the termination was total indifference. She said she didn't "need the state any more," and hoped she would not have to get another state worker. She was helped to express anger and fear of being abandoned. She admitted that she liked the worker and would miss her very much. She was assured that the worker would miss her also.

As the worker and K began to review the life cycle of their work together, the ongoing evaluation tools described in Chapter 8 (Figures 8-6 and 8-7) were used. Her academic performance and group home maintenance were assessed as +3. They recalled what the past was like for K and how far she had progressed, particularly in her present group home and in school. K knew that she continued to need help with her personal problems (goal 3).

In considering the future, K said she wished to remain in her present group home and school for at least another few years. Her long-range goals included returning to live with her real mother some day. K knew that this was not possible in the near future.

K's case was transferred back to a worker (recently returned from sick leave) who had originally worked with her. K remembered her original worker and said she was glad she didn't have to start all over with someone new. Two weeks before termination, K and the two state workers had a meeting, at which time goals and progress were reviewed. For their last meeting, K and her worker went for a walk. They took and exchanged pictures of each other. K asked if she could write the worker after she left Children's Services, but this continued contact was discouraged.

E. Charted Progress

The termination plan that was developed and implemented by the worker and K is found in Diagram 9-2. In recording, this plan was added to the contracted plan that was used during assessment and evaluation.

II. FIELD AREA: GERONTOLOGY

A. Agency: Nursing Home

B. Client System

Mrs. J, an 80-year-old Portuguese woman in a skilled-nursing facility. (For additional information, see Chapter 4, Engagement in Diverse Field Areas, II. Gerontology.)

C. Summary of Preceding Stages

The problems, goals, and tasks identified and contracted in earlier stages may be found in Diagram 7-2, Chapter 7. The evaluation process and contract reformulation of the preceding stage are outlined in Diagram 8-3, Chapter 8. At the time of evaluation, progress was noted for all of the stated goals. The least amount of progress was shown for goal 3a (to have Mrs. J go out of her room on her own at least once a day). Additional efforts to work on goal 3a were developed and contracted during the evaluation stage. These included the creation of an ongoing evaluation graph (Figure 8-8, Chapter 8) and more involvement by nursing staff in helping to chart the frequency of Mrs. J's leaving her room by herself. Mrs. J and the worker agreed to assess progress in goal 3a weekly.

DIAGRAM 9-2 Contracted Plan Continued

DATE IDENTIFIED	PROBLEM/ NEED	GOAL	TASK	CONTRACT	DATE ANTICIPATED	DATE ACCOMPLISHED
7/26	Termination process	Satisfactory termination	1. Introduce termination	1. Worker	7/26	7/26
			2. Discuss feelings and termination	2. Worker and K	7/26 and 8/5	8/5
			3. Life-cycle review	3. Worker and K	8/15	8/15
			4. Meet with transfer worker	4. K, worker, and transfer worker	8/22	8/22
			5. Final session	5. Worker and K	8/30	8/30

D. Intervention

After working with Mrs. J for seven months, the worker began the process of termination because she was leaving the agency. When the worker informed Mrs. J that she would be working at the nursing home for only four more weeks, Mrs. J repeated, "No, you won't" or "You won't go" and refused to discuss it any further. Mrs. J would turn on her television whenever the worker tried to talk about her leaving. One day, the worker went to see Mrs. J at their regular meeting time and Mrs. J was not in her room. She was later located walking on the floor downstairs by herself. She said she didn't know why she was there.

The worker told Mrs. J that she could see that she was upset and angry with her because she was leaving. Mrs. J said she could not understand why the worker had to go. The worker tried to review the progress Mrs. J had made, but Mrs. J said she didn't want to talk about it. She became very silent and refused to speak at all after the worker said she would not be coming back, even to visit Mrs. J. Mrs. J was told that the worker's supervisor would come to see her occasionally and would be available if Mrs. J needed to talk to a social worker. Mrs. J did not respond and remained withdrawn throughout the remainder of the time the worker was at the home.

Realizing that Mrs. J was finding it difficult to accept the termination, the worker's supervisor agreed to see Mrs. J at least once a week for a while after the worker left. During the second-to-last meeting of the worker and Mrs. J, the supervisor dropped in, but Mrs. J said very little to her.

E. Charted Progress

The termination plan was drawn up by the worker, who kept trying to get Mrs. J involved in the process. The plan was recorded as found in Diagram 9-3.

As apparent in Diagram 9-3, tasks 2 and 3 (discuss feelings, review life cycle of working relationship) of the termination plan were not accomplished. No dates are entered in last column ("date accomplished") for tasks 2 and 3. The worker was not able to engage Mrs. J either in a discussion of feelings about the termination or in a life-cycle review. In the termination summary left in the record, therefore, the worker emphasized the fact that the termination process had not been attained. The worker's supervisor planned to focus on tasks 2 and 3 when she met with Mrs. J after the worker's termination.

III. FIELD AREA: PUBLIC SOCIAL WELFARE

A. Agency: State Social Service

B. Client System

Mr. and Mrs. P and their two children (ages 2 and 4), placed in emergency shelter (Center City Motor Inn) for 44 days, then relocated in an apartment; family receiving AFDC because of Mr. P's mental incapacity. (Additional background information may be found in Chapter 4, Engagement in Diverse Field Areas, III. Public Social Welfare.)

DIAGRAM 9-3 Contracted Plan Continued

DATE IDENTIFIED	PROBLEM/ NEED	GOAL	TASK	CONTRACT	DATE ANTICIPATED	DATE ACCOMPLISHED
4/29	Termination process	Satisfactory termination	1. Introduce termination	1. Worker	4/29	4/29
			2. Discuss termination and feelings	2. Worker and Mrs. J	5/1 and 5/6	
			3. Life-cycle review	3. Worker and Mrs. J	5/1 and 5/6	
			4. Meet with supervisor	4. Worker, Mrs. J, and supervisor	5/15	5/15
			5. Final session	5. Worker and Mrs. J	5/22	5/22

C. Summary of Preceding Stages

The problems, goals, and interventions of earlier stages are outlined in Diagram 6-10 of Chapter 6 and Diagram 7-3 of Chapter 7. A summary of the evaluation that was completed is charted in Diagram 8-14 of Chapter 8. The basic goals for food, housing, medical examination, fuel assistance, AFDC payment, and a functioning refrigerator were accomplished mainly through extensive involvement by resources outside of the family. The goals of obtaining Supplemental Security Income, a Thanksgiving food basket, and Christmas gifts for the children were not accomplished (to date) because of Mr. P's failure to complete contracted tasks. The problems of poor money management and excessive dependence on outside resources were identified by the worker but left unresolved because Mr. and Mrs. P refused to recognize them as problems in need of attention. The evaluation culminated with both the worker and the family agreeing to begin the process of termination.

D. Termination

Although the P's said they had no immediate need for continued social services, they appeared a little angry with the worker when the idea of termination was first introduced. They were able to admit that they were disappointed when the worker did not take care of fixing their refrigerator and also when the worker didn't get them a food basket for Thanksgiving. They knew that they should try to do more for themselves and said it was easier for a worker to deal with other programs and services. The worker reminded them that when they really had to get something done, they were able to work it out (such as locating an apartment). At this point, they admitted that Mrs. P's father was actually the one who found the apartment for them. They asked if the worker couldn't come by at least once every month to see how they were getting along. The worker did not agree to this, because he felt it was better for the family to try to solve their problems as they arose and not to hold them until the worker came each month. Again, the worker cautioned them about their need for careful planning in money management and said that if they ever wanted help in developing their skill in this area, they could bring this to the attention of their income-maintenance technician or they could call the Social Services Department directly.

The worker planned to meet three additional times with the family before their final termination. During these last visits, the family continued to complain about how hard it is to maintain a home and raise children these days. They repeated their desire for Christmas presents for the children, and the worker reviewed the tasks identified in the contracted plan. Mr. P did call the Salvation Army (task 2, problem 12, Diagram 7-3, Chapter 7) on the day of the worker's last visit.

E. Charted Progress

The termination plan carried out by the worker and the P's is recorded in Diagram 9-4. In the closing summary for the record, the worker emphasized that although problems 5 (poor money management) and 13 (excessive dependency) were never recognized by the P's, these were assessed as continuing and serious by the worker.

DIAGRAM 9-4 Contracted Plan Continued

DATE IDENTIFIED	PROBLEM/ NEED	GOAL	TASK	CONTRACT	DATE ANTICIPATED	DATE ACCOMPLISHED
12/4	Termination process	Satisfactory termination	1. Introduce termination	1. Worker	12/4	12/4
			2. Discuss termination and feelings	2. Worker and P's	12/11	12/11
			3. Life-cycle review	3. Worker and P's	12/11	12/11
			4. Final session	4. Worker and P's	12/21	12/21

IV. FIELD AREA: COMMUNITY SERVICES

A. Agency: Clayton Neighborhood House

B. Client System

Four Hispanic families who needed heat in their apartments on the second floor of 33 L Street. (More background information is available in Chapter 4, Engagement in Diverse Field Areas, IV. Community Services.)

C. Summary of Preceding Stages

The problems, goals, and tasks identified and enacted during early stages are described in the contracted plan found in Diagram 6-12 in Chapter 6, Diagram 7-4 in Chapter 7, and Diagram 8-16 in Chapter 8. Although the families initially felt victimized and helpless, they expressed feelings of relief and gratitude during the evaluation stage. There was adequate heating in their apartments, and they were actively monitoring the temperature daily. They knew that they continued to have a problem in communicating with their landlord, but they did not want to try to improve their communications at this time.

D. Termination

When the worker returned to meet with the families and review the heating situation, she learned that consistent heat had been provided throughout the week. This finding was charted on the ongoing-evaluation graph given in Figure 8-9, Chapter 8. The worker had mentioned to the families the previous week that if there didn't seem to be any remaining problems to work on when she came for this meeting, she would talk with them about terminating her contacts with them.

Residents first expressed a wish that the worker would continue to visit with them at least once a week. Comments were made, such as "Don't you like us any more?" One tenant said that he had heard that the landlord was selling the apartment building and that maybe they all would be put out on the street. The worker assured the residents that if they received notice that they had to leave the building, they could contact Clayton House for assistance with relocation.

In reviewing the life cycle of their working together, the worker recalled their first meeting and the way in which they worked on the heating problem. The families were happy to know that they could drop into Clayton House if they ever wanted help with any problem. They were also informed of the regular community meetings and activities that went on at Clayton for children and adults.

The tenants decided that they wanted to continue their daily monitoring of the heat in their apartments throughout the winter. Mrs. T offered to keep track of their findings by marking temperature points on the graph (Figure 8-9, Chapter 8) once a week. If there was any marked regression, she would contact the worker and call a meeting.

The worker shared how much she had enjoyed working with them, even though their contact had been brief. She was invited to drop in any time she was in the neighborhood.

E. Charted Progress

The termination plan was carried out and recorded as outlined in Diagram 9-5.

V. FIELD AREA: EDUCATION

A. Agency: Keeney Elementary School

B. Client System

Mr. and Mrs. G and their son Jim, 8 years old and in third grade, who was showing regressive behavior in school and at home in reaction to his parents' problems with their relationship and Mrs. G's threat to abandon the family.

C. Summary of Preceding Stages

The contracted plan developed and implemented by Jim, his parents, and the worker is found in Diagram 6-13, Chapter 6. During evaluation, progress was noted for all four identified goals. The goal to improve Mr. and Mrs. G's marital relationship was recognized as needing more time before its accomplishment. Mr. and Mrs. G were motivated to remain in counseling at the family counseling center.

D. Termination

During the last interview with Mr. and Mrs. G and Jim, termination was introduced and discussed. Although it was agreed that the worker did not need to meet with Mr. and Mrs. G again, the contract with Jim was extended to include two additional sessions at school.

As the worker and the G's recognized the progress that had been made, Mr. and Mrs. G expressed gratitude to the worker for her interest in Jim and in them. They said it was good to know that the worker was at the school to help the children and their families. They admitted that they probably would not have gone for help for themselves if it hadn't been for the worker. They were reminded by the worker that it was Jim who was feeling their pain and reacting to the situation. It was Jim who led them to look closer at what was happening to them and to their family. Using the life-cycle approach, the worker moved from the past to the present and then to the future. In considering the future, the worker strongly encouraged Mr. and Mrs. G to continue their work at the family counseling center, even if it got rough at times. They were assured also that they could contact the worker at school if she could be of any further assistance.

When the worker began to talk with Jim about termination during their last two meetings, he said he didn't want to stop coming. He liked to play with the toys in the office. He liked talking about his grades and keeping track of his improvement on the graphs.

During these sessions, Jim repeatedly asked if the worker had started to see some other child in his place. He was assured that no one could take his place. Jim said he was happy about home, but he was sad that he couldn't

DIAGRAM 9-5 Contracted Plan Continued

DATE IDENTIFIED	PROBLEM/ NEED	GOAL	TASK	CONTRACT	DATE ANTICIPATED	DATE ACCOMPLISHED
12/19	Termination process	Satisfactory termination	1. Introduce termination	1. Worker	12/12	12/12
			2. Discuss termination and feelings	2. Worker and residents	12/19	12/19
			3. Life-cycle review	3. Worker and residents	12/19	12/19
			4. Final session	4. Worker and residents	12/19	12/19

continue to see the worker. He told the worker that he might "surprise" her and drop in to see her on his own sometime. Before leaving, he took the graphs that were hanging on the wall with him. He brought the worker a drawing he had made of himself and his family and hung it on the worker's wall. He said that she could keep it—for a while.

E. Charted Progress

The plan for termination was recorded on the contracted plan as outlined in Diagram 9-6.

VI. FIELD AREA: CORRECTIONS

A. Agency: Juvenile Court

B. Client System

A group of six (originally seven) male youths, all age 14, on probation, attending weekly group meetings led by co-workers at Juvenile Court. (For additional background information, see Chapter 4, Engagement in Diverse Field Areas, VI. Corrections.)

C. Summary of Preceding Stages

The group met weekly and focused on the three prioritized goals of (1) to get off probation in four months, (2) to control tempers at home and at school, and (3) to learn more about "the changes" they were facing as teenagers. After three and a half months, the group evaluated their progress in goal accomplishment. Four of the members were achieving the staged goals as planned. They were being recommended for termination of probation. One youth was sent to a correctional center after he had attended six meetings, because he was found breaking into a store. The remaining two members were not meeting the requirements for a reduction in probation. Group meetings were extended for at least an additional six weeks for these two members. After the evaluation, the group begin to focus on termination.

D. Termination

As the group began to discuss what it would be like to be off probation, MK and B said that they were glad they were getting off probation but that they would miss seeing everyone in the group. They asked the group leaders to let them know if the leaders were going on any trips that they could join too. J and T expressed anger over having to come back for group meetings. They began to blame the co-workers for not recommending that they get reduced time, but other group members reminded J and T that they themselves didn't keep up their scores.

As the group discussed the life cycle of their working together (i.e., past, present, and future), they began to recall what it was like when they first started attending. Most of the youths admitted that they didn't think that they could trust the workers and doubted that they would give them time off. C

DIAGRAM 9-6 Contracted Plan Continued

DATE IDENTIFIED	PROBLEM/ NEED	GOAL	TASK	CONTRACT	DATE ANTICIPATED	DATE ACCOMPLISHED
12/13	Termination process	Satisfactory termination	1. Introduce termination	1. Worker	12/17	12/17
			2. Discuss termination and feelings	2. Worker, Mr. and Mrs. G, and Jim	12/17	12/17
			3. Terminate with Mr. and Mrs. G	3. Worker	12/17	12/17
			4. Further discussion of termination and feelings	4. Worker and Jim	12/20 and 1/8	12/20 and 1/8
			5. Final session	5. Worker and Jim	1/8	1/8

reminded the group about A, saying he was sorry A didn't make it but he should have listened to the probation officers. C also shared how excited he was because his mother and little sister and brother were coming from Puerto Rico to live with him and his father.

All of the youths said that they thought they were doing better than when they first were put on probation. They didn't know if they would be able to stay out of trouble once they were off probation. J and T said they probably would never get off probation. They knew that if they began to do better they still could have a probation reduction of one month (rather than two). In looking toward the future, J and T were told by the workers that if they continued to fail to meet the requirements, the group would stop at the end of its fifth month, but J and T would be expected to meet individually with a worker each week for as long as they remained on probation.

In talking about the future for those who were leaving in two weeks (MK, B, ML, and C), the leaders encouraged each of them to try to get active with local churches or recreational centers. Specific places were identified for each of the youths. They were encouraged also to ask to see the school social worker if they started to have any problems in school.

At the end of the last meeting with all six members, the group had a pizza party. In the following weeks, J's behavior markedly improved at meetings, at home, and in school. He was recommended to be removed from probation one month early. T continued to come late to meetings. His fighting at school continued, and he was not obeying his grandmother. His probation period was extended beyond five months, and he was required to come to see the male worker once a week.

E. Charted Progress

The termination plan was recorded as outlined in Diagram 9-7.

CONCLUSION

In reviewing the content of this chapter, it may be perceived that the process of termination includes all of the stages of the General Method. The six-stage nature of the Method (engagement, data collection, assessment, intervention, evaluation, termination) is contained within the last stage. During termination, the worker and system begin with an identification of the meaning of termination (engagement). They proceed to gathering information as they move from past to present (data collection). They move on to assessing and planning for the future (assessment). The plan is then implemented (intervention) and evaluated (evaluation). Finally there is closure (termination). As diagramed in Figure 4-1 of Chapter 4, the General Method is a cyclical process. In the termination cycle, the process is repeated and completed.

The opportunity for the identification and expression of feelings has been emphasized as essential to the termination process. In this chapter,

DIAGRAM 9-7 Contracted Plan Continued

DATE IDENTIFIED	PROBLEM/ NEED	GOAL	TASK	CONTRACT	DATE ANTICIPATED	DATE ACCOMPLISHED
1/14	Termination process	Satisfactory termination	1. Introduce termination	1. Co-workers	1/14	1/14
			2. Discuss termination and feelings	2. Members and co-workers	1/21, 1/28	1/21, 1/28
			3. Life-cycle review	3. Members and co-workers	1/21, 1/28	1/21, 1/28
			4. Final session for MK, ML, B, and C—pizza party	4. Members and co-workers	1/28	1/28
			5. Continue weekly meetings for a month	5. J, T, and co-workers	2/4, 2/11, 2/18, 2/25	2/4, 2/11, 2/18, 2/25
			6. Evaluation of progress of J and T	6. J, T, and co-workers	2/11	2/11
			7. Final session for J	7. J, T, and co-workers	2/25	2/25
			8. Continue to meet once a week	8. T and worker (M.S.W.)	3/4 and each week until off probation	

approaches and exercises for understanding and working with termination feelings have been suggested. The reactions of a system to ending a relationship were described in terms of the five-stage sequence of denial, anger, bargaining, depression, and acceptance. A life-cycle approach containing the three focal points of past, present, and future was offered as a guiding framework for workers during the termination process. Attention was also given to the possible feelings and reactions of service providers as they go through repeated termination experiences. Examples were included to demonstrate a worker's sensitivity to human diversity in the final stage of the General Method and to show how termination is carried out in diverse areas of practice.

New workers frequently say that the most difficult part of working with a system is getting started. In time, workers generally say the most difficult part is the ending. At the beginning, there may be some fears and emptiness because of little experience or knowledge of a system. Seasoned workers know, however, the awesome reality that the emptiness after termination may be filled with memories of the experience, particularly the final stage, that live on.

NOTES

[1]Ner Littner, *Some Traumatic Effects of Separation and Placement* (New York: Child Welfare League of America, 1981), p. 22.

[2]Elizabeth Kübler-Ross, *On Death and Dying* (New York: Macmillan, 1969), pp. 34–121.

[3]Ibid., p. 112.

10

Identity and Integration

*I say this, knowing that the art of doing cannot be taught in any
complete sense. Only the principles by which it may be guided, the
dynamic elements that operate in "doing," the general nature and
direction of the process of being professionally helpful—only these
can be taught and learned for the practitioner's creative use.*

—Helen Harris Perlman[1]

THE GENERAL METHOD—
A PURPOSEFUL PROCEDURE

As brought out throughout this text, the General Method of social work
practice is a purposeful procedure. Respecting the right of a human system
to self-determination, the generalist follows the lead of the system receiving
service and offers an approach that is a planned problem-solving procedure. A sensitivity to human diversity enables the worker to be skillful in
timing the process and in selecting interventions, tools, and techniques.
With the identification of mutual goals, the worker and the system of contact proceed with interactions that have the purpose of goal accomplishment.

The method presented in this book is not actually new to social work.
When enacting the traditional methods of casework, group work, and community organization, social workers have often used a problem-solving approach. As articulated and organized in this text, however, the General

Method builds on ecological-systems theory and partializes the problem-solving approach into six identifiable stages.

The ongoing, dynamic nature of the Method does not restrict a worker to following a set sequence according to a fixed pattern. The stages of the Method are presented sequentially for conceptualization, but they are not necessarily irreversible. As pointed out earlier, elements of each stage are often observable in every stage. Frequently, there is a returning to an earlier stage as problems or needs evolve. In addition, the general nature of the Method does not restrict a worker to working with systems of a particular size. It may be used with individuals, groups, families, communities, or organizations. Interventions are selected to match the individualized needs of the system receiving service at a given time. A plan to work with members of a system, for example, may include seeing them individually, as a family, and in groups. The Method blends general and individual conceptualizations. A holistic perspective that recognizes individuality and interrelatedness, therefore, is fundamental to the Method.

For beginning workers, the General Method is a guiding framework. Rather than learning about a variety of skills to be applied eclectically, the worker who learns the Method has an organized body of skills. He or she is enabled to be process-minded and to recognize movement in problem solving. The Method guides the generalist and the system receiving service in their collaborative effort for goal attainment.

CLASSIFICATION OF METHODS IN HUMAN SERVICES

The terms *methods, models, approaches, modes,* and *processes* are frequently used interchangeably to refer to the organized use of techniques and skills by helping professionals. In addition to the General Method of entry-level social workers and the traditional methods of advanced social workers, numerous other "methods" may be utilized by advanced practitioners from social work or other helping disciplines. Depending on theory and value foundations, different interventions are enacted; these are described in professional literature. Various methods may be different or essentially similar. Frequently, diverse helpers use the same techniques and skills as well as the same terminology and theories. Some approaches, however, are based on contrasting theories and therefore do not work well together. To avoid confusion and increase comprehension, a means of categorizing various helping methods is needed. A systematic framework for distinguishing methods would not only provide a broad overview of different approaches but would also provide greater clarification of the place of the General Method in relation to other methodologies.

There is a way to cluster methods according to their essential characteristics. Basically, all methods may be seen as falling under three major headings: client-focused, problem-focused, or worker-focused. *Client* may be defined as *client system*. As defined earlier, a *client system* means "people who sanction or ask for the change agent's services, who are the expected beneficiaries of service, and who have a working agreement or contract with the change agent."[2] The word *problem* means the issue, need, question, or difficulty facing the client system and being brought to the attention of the worker. And the *worker* may be any one of the helping professionals found within the field of human services (as described in Chapter 1). The central consideration in the classification is the role of the worker in the triplex of client system, problem, and worker.

In the first category of methodologies, the *client-focused* cluster, the worker assumes a limited role, giving support mainly through listening and reassuring the clients of their potential for coping with difficulties. There is minimum structure, leadership, and control on the part of the worker. The worker's direct intervention with the problem itself is minimal, if present. The client is seen as strong and well able to deal with his or her problems with a little help from the worker. The methods of Carl Rogers and Robert Carkhuff would come under this category. Consultation and some locality development may also fall into this category. Developmental, client-centered, and other basic counseling approaches are the types of interventions appropriately clustered in this grouping. As shown in the "Methods A" representation in Figure 10-1, the worker using these methods may be depicted as working directly with client systems, who in turn are enabled to work out their problems or needs themselves.

In the second major category of methodologies, the *problem-focused* cluster, the worker and the client system work in a more balanced and collaborative effort. Structure, leadership, and control are shared. The nature of the problems or needs is recognized as calling for the involvement of both the professional worker and the client. Although there is belief in the potential

FIGURE 10-1   Classification of Methods

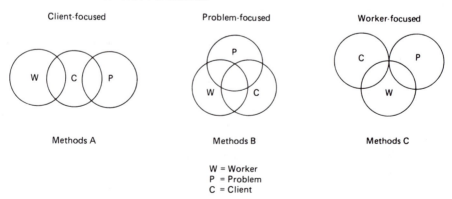

Client-focused	Problem-focused	Worker-focused
Methods A	Methods B	Methods C

W = Worker
P = Problem
C = Client

of the client system and the hope of eventual withdrawal of the worker, the method is identified as initially calling for some direct intervention by the worker as well as the client. These methods convey the notion of teamwork, as both client and worker focus on the problem in need of resolution. The methods of intervention described in the works of William Glasser or William Reid and Laura Epstein come under this category. Task-centered, problem-solving, functional, and rational approaches and some locality development may be identified in this group, as illustrated in "Methods B" of Figure 10-1.

The third and final cluster of methods is described as *worker-focused.* In these interventions, the worker plays a major directive role, assuming clearly the responsibility for bringing about goal accomplishment. Modifying models and aggressive change models calling for specialized interventions by workers are classified here. Behavior modification, class advocacy, gestalt therapy, psychoanalysis, psychotherapy, and social planning may be among the models of this group. The works of B. F. Skinner and Fritz Perls would contribute to this category of methodologies. As represented in "Methods C" of Figure 10-1, in these methods the worker carries the burden of planning, directing, coaching, and structuring for the client.

For further understanding, the categories of methods may be conceptualized as falling at different points on a circle. Usually, in the process of helping, workers move along the line depending on the progress of the service. Ideally, a worker who begins with a worker-focused method would work toward developing a more problem-focused or collaborative relationship and eventually a more client-focused approach followed by termination, with the client becoming self-actualized (see Figure 10-2). Unfortunately, at times the worker who begins with a less directive approach may see the need for greater worker involvement. If he or she is not qualified for more advanced or specialized interventions, a referral may be necessary.

FIGURE 10-2 The Methodological Process

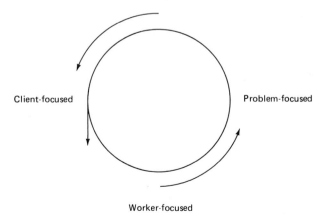

Client-focused

Problem-focused

Worker-focused

THE GENERAL METHOD IN THE CLASSIFICATION

In considering the range of methods and the three basic categories, it is easy to find the place of the General Method as a problem-focused methodology. The worker and the client work together in each stage of the General Method. The skills of the generalist may allow for the use of a client-focused method when the client has the strengths, with support from a professional, to work out his or her own problem. Moreover, the generalist has skill and knowledge to use the General Method when direct problem-intervention by the worker in collaboration with the client system is needed (see Figure 10-3). If the method needed is of the worker-focused type, the generalist has the skill to refer or transfer the client system to an advanced worker. The beginning generalist is not expected to have developed in his or her generalist education the knowledge and skills for worker-focused interventions. The beginning generalist, therefore, is not eclectic when it comes to choosing specialized methods. To practice with these approaches, the entry-level generalist would need further education and supervised experience.

For B.S.W. generalists to have the competence to use client-focused and problem-focused methods, their professional programs would have to include content and field experiences for the development of both types of methods. For advanced workers to have expertise in all three types of methodologies, curriculum content on the three types would have to be addressed in their graduate programs, unless they came to graduate school after having completed an accredited baccalaureate social work program. Presently, skills and techniques used in client-focused and problem-focused methods are found in such baccalaureate programs and also in some graduate social work programs.

THE ECOLOGICAL GENERALIST—A BASIC IDENTITY

The theoretical and experiential preparation for beginning general practice as described in this book prepares the new worker to be an ecological generalist. This person is a human service provider with broad-based skills and foundation knowledge of persons, environments, and the interactions

FIGURE 10-3   The Scope of Methodology

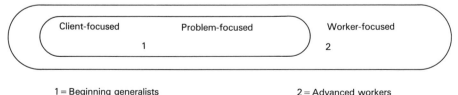

1 = Beginning generalists   2 = Advanced workers

that take place at the interface between person and environment. He or she has a commitment to social work values, as well as basic competence for working with individuals, groups, families, communities, and organizations. As described in this text, the ecological generalist is a person grounded in the use of the General Method of social work practice.

According to the latest Curriculum Policy Statement of the Council on Social Work Education, beginning social workers are prepared primarily for direct practice with a variety of client systems.[3] In addition to direct interventions with client systems, the ecological generalist may use indirect interventions with various systems in the extended environment. As stated earlier, indirect interventions refer to the efforts made by a worker to inter-act with a system that has the power or potential to respond to problems or needs and to contribute to goal attainment, even though that system itself may be neither experiencing the problem or need nor asking for help from the worker. The indirect interventions of a generalist relate to the needs and goals of particular client systems receiving services (as described in Chapter 7).

The work environment of the generalist described in Chapter 1 includes the five major systems of (1) client, (2) agency of employment, (3) client resources, (4) the profession, and (5) society at large. As depicted in Figure 10-4, ecological generalists (EG) function within an agency structure and, as such, interface primarily with client systems in direct service. The scope of their work, however, as seen in the figure, includes moving out to related resources, the social work profession, and organizations or institutions in society at large. To be true to their identity, ecological generalists see and respond to the interdependence that exists among the systems in their work environment. Although most of their formal work time (agency hours) may be used in providing direct services for client systems, generalists take time to be politically and professionally active. Involvement with the extended environment may include serving on boards or committees, giving testimony, having personal contact with legislators, and participating in political campaigns or political action groups. Unless ecological generalists maintain an awareness of and some involvement in the development of policy and services in their extended environment, they run the risk of dichotomizing their basic identity.

THE EXTENDED ENVIRONMENT— A FORGOTTEN COMMITMENT

As a profession, social work has a history of demonstrated commitment and concern for the poor and the underprivileged. Today, social work generalists and specialists continue to be needed to speak out against social injustices and unmet human needs. As the numbers of people without employ-

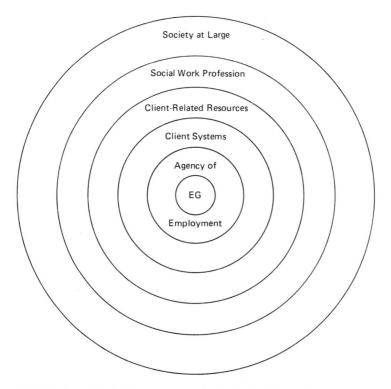

Society at Large

Social Work Profession

Client-Related Resources

Client Systems

Agency of

EG

Employment

FIGURE 10-4   Work Environment of the Ecological Generalist

ment or adequate housing, food, and care increase, social workers are greatly needed to be present once again in the extended environment as advocates for social change. Unfortunately, some workers have moved away from active societal involvement outside of direct work responsibilities. The "social" dimension of their name and profession has become obscure and perhaps forgotten.

A growing shortage in social work personnel to work with and for the poor has become increasingly evident in the profession.[4] The formal recognition and increase in the number of baccalaureate social workers since 1974 has been seen as one possible way to provide social workers for servicing the poor.[5] Addressing the broad and multiple needs of the poor, however, often calls for political skills and strategies. Although basic political skills have been identified as fundamental to practice at the beginning level (see Diagram 1-4, Chapter 1), new workers will need to have models and supervisors in their agencies who promote and demonstrate the use of these skills. If there is little activity by advanced workers in the extended environment, new generalists may also lose sight of their commitment and ecological identity.

The call for renewed and intensified involvement by social workers with the disadvantaged in American society today is very clear and urgent. Robert Stewart writes:

> If social work abandons its traditional commitments, there will be no ethnically pluralistic professional group in society concerned with poor and disadvantaged populations. Social work is the last hope for a professional societal bastion for all economically exploited and disadvantaged groups in America.[6]

Bertram Beck extends the need to a global perspective when he writes:

> Adherence to the interest in social issues and social action that characterized our forebears and still characterizes social work leadership is the right direction and the only direction that can ultimately bring about a world order characterized by peace and justice.[7]

As finite resources are becoming depleted and inaccessible, human service consumers and providers are beginning to witness a movement from a concern with quality to a concern with survival. Social welfare programs and policies that took years to be developed are being modified or eliminated in order to save on federal funding. To combat this regressive process, social workers are urged to sharpen and demonstrate political expertise. Ron Federico describes future social workers as follows:

> The professionals of the future must be astute political actors, who can work within the existing social structure to utilize available resources, and still find and use opportunities to affect social policy.[8]

Current changes that are taking place in social policy and programs call for an updating of curriculum and learning opportunities for social work students. As the implications of new legislation and policy changes are being studied, social work educators, students, and practitioners need to have ongoing communication, with opportunity for observation and validation of what is happening in the field.

Legislation, such as the Omnibus Budget Reconciliation Act of 1981, for example, is having a profound impact on human service delivery. Through the creation of block grants, programs have had to be consolidated, with a reduction in their funding. The 1981 act gives states increased flexibility in deciding how to use block-grant funding. As a result, there is growing competition among programs and special-needs groups as they vie for limited resources.[9]

For legislators, decision-makers, and groups with needs, social workers with research and political skills can assist in identifying and documenting priorities. In addition, a worker with an understanding of policy development and with relevant political skills can contribute to the introduction and passage of legislation that reflects human priorities. Because of their theoretical foundation and identity, ecological generalists understand and can help explain the strong correlations that are emerging between program cutbacks and increasing social problems in society. Anne Minahan comments:

> Social work perspectives on the interaction of person and environment and on interdependence can help us demonstrate that the intertwined factors of inflation, unemployment, and reductions in income maintenance, health and support programs have a direct relationship to hunger and pain and poverty and alcohol and drug abuse and despair and violence against people.[10]

Although social workers do engage in some political activities, they are found generally to be ineffective in the political arena. One reason for their limited success has been identified as "insufficient skills for political action," particularly "overt political behavior." For increased effectiveness, the skill development of workers may need to be expanded to include such "overt" activities as lobbying, campaigning, negotiating, boycotting, testifying, and conducting sit-ins.[11]

In the area of interpersonal communication, as brought out by Specht, "the management of interpersonal processes in sociopolitical interaction differs from the management of other professional interaction." When working with policy makers, funders, landlords, or employers, the worker needs to find ways to interact selectively in order to gain the attention and support of the sociopolitical other.[12]

Curriculum content for social work students could include guidelines for giving testimony and other techniques and tactics for legislative advocacy. For example, Cecilia Kleinkauf has developed a "Guide to Giving Legislative Testimony," in which a basic process may be identified as (1) research the bill, (2) analyze the committee conducting the hearing, (3) prepare the testimony, (4) give the testimony, (5) deal with questions, and (6) conduct a follow-up.[13]

Using this process in researching a bill, the worker begins with finding out about related existing statutes and studies them in relation to the proposed bill. The strengths and weaknesses of the bill and of suggested amendments are explored. Information about the bill's history, cost, supporters, and opponents is collected. The worker also needs to know about the procedures, composition, and members of the committee conducting the hearing. Knowledge about committee members includes their voting records, philosophy, interests, and constituencies.

Testimony is prepared orally and in writing. The testimony should be brief, and its content should be accurate. The worker, or the person selected as witness, should address the issue as well as the bill itself. Copies of the testimony should be given to committee members, because legislators are often distracted or called out during the hearing. It is important for the worker or other witness to state clearly who he or she is and what position he or she is taking on the bill. Legislators frequently ask questions of the witness. If answers are not known, the worker should not attempt an answer, but rather should say that the information will be obtained for the legislator. Workers must be sure that they follow up with information promised to legislators. After the hearing, workers need to keep track of the progress of the bill. It may be necessary to give additional testimony if the bill is passed on to another committee.

Before introducing or advocating for legislation to develop new social programs, workers should be sure that they are aware of already existing programs that attempt to meet the identified need or problem. To analyze existing social welfare programs, various frameworks are available. For example, Winifred Bell has outlined eight basic criteria for evaluating program effectiveness. They are (1) objectives, (2) legislative authority, (3) source of funding, (4) administrative structure, (5) eligibility requirements, (6) coverage, (7) adequacy, and (8) equity.[14] Workers could use a similar approach to compare proposed new programs with those that have been or are in existence. Legislators are usually very interested in seeing the comparison and in learning how the new program would be more advantageous.

Research by Ronald Dear and Rino Patti has shown that certain political tactics have been particularly effective in influencing the passage of legislation. Essentially, they identify the following seven tactics:

1. Introduce the bill early in the season or, ideally, before the session has begun.
2. It is advisable to have more than one legislator sponsor a bill.
3. The advocate of social legislation should seek to obtain the sponsorship of the majority party. . . . It is even more beneficial to obtain meaningful bipartisan sponsorship. . . .
4. Whenever possible, the advocate should obtain the support of the governor and of relevant state agencies.
5. The advocate should seek influential legislators as sponsors of proposed legislation, provided that they are willing to exercise their influence in promoting the bill.
6. The advocate should press for open committee hearings on the bill and, when such hearings are held, attempt to arrange for testimony in behalf of the bill by expert witnesses.
7. The advocate should use the amendatory process as a strategy for promoting a favorable outcome for a bill.[15]

The overt skills, list of tactics, and testimony guide are all helpful tools for social workers as they become involved in the legislative arena. An adaptation of the General Method may also serve as a helpful framework for workers as they engage in political activity in the extended environment.

USING THE GENERAL METHOD
FOR SOCIAL DEVELOPMENT

A social worker who perceives needs on the broader societal level may wonder where to start and how to carry through with efforts to bring about
social change or development. Time and energy limitations of the worker
should be realistically recognized, with activities carefully planned to avoid
wasted effort. The method of the ecological generalist offers a process that
may be adapted for use by workers as they engage in work with diverse
structures and systems in society.

For social change or development, the General Method is somewhat
modified, because usually the system of contact does not have the identified
need, or does that system see any reason to respond to the need, even
though it has the power to do so. Although the Method has been described
repeatedly as a collaborative process between a worker and a system, in this
type of work the worker often executes the process alone. Sometimes the
work involves advocacy for particular clients. In these cases, every effort is
made to involve and to empower the clients in each step of the process. At
times, however, a worker is advocating for a class of people or for a policy
change that affects people in society at large. Although a worker may try to
join with others in coalitions or teams to bring about the desired change, it
is possible that the process will have to be initiated and perhaps completed
by the worker alone. Whether alone or with others, the procedure for work
in the extended environment can be guided by the six stages of the General
Method.

An outline of the General Method as designed in this text is repeated
in Diagram 10-1. Having first identified both a need in society and the systems primarily responsible for meeting the need, a worker can follow the
outline as a guide for action. The questions raised during each stage of the
Method may be modified or expanded for greater relevance.

For example, the three main components of the first stage are shown
as "problems," "feelings," and "goals." In beginning to engage in the process, the worker first studies the problem, need, or issue in the extended
environment by asking the following:

1. What is the problem or need as perceived by
   a. Me (worker), my agency, my profession?
   b. The systems with the power to respond to the problem or need?
   c. Others
      i. The group of people feeling the problem or need?
      ii. People in society at large?

The worker then proceeds to an inquiry about feelings and goals as
the following questions are asked:

DIAGRAM 10-1   The General Method

I. Engagement
   a. Problems
   b. Feelings
   c. Goals

II. Data Collection
   a. Problems
   b. Persons
   c. Environment

III. Assessment
   a. Assessment statements
   b. Problem prioritization
   c. Contracting (plan)

IV. Intervention
   a. Direct
   b. Indirect
   c. Teamwork
   d. Referral

V. Evaluation
   a. Goal analysis
   b. Contract review
   c. Goal reformulation

VI. Termination
   a. Decision: transfer, refer, terminate
   b. Plan: timing, follow-up
   c. Termination: feelings, life-cycle approach

2. What feelings surround the problem or need as felt by
   a. Me, my agency, my profession?
   b. The power systems?
   c. Others: those with the problem or need, society at large?
3. What goals related to the problem or need can be identified by
   a. Me, my agency, my profession?
   b. The power systems?
   c. Others: group in need, society at large?

Moving into data collection (stage II), the worker gathers information about problems, persons, and environment. Questions to be answered in this stage are:

4. What is the scope (number of people), the duration (length of time), and the severity (degree to which it is a life-or-death issue) of the problem or need?
5. Who are the persons suffering from the problem or unmet need? What is their motivation and capacity to work on the problem or need?

6. Who are the people in the power systems (titles, roles, personal characteristics)? What is their motivation and capacity to work on the problem or need?

7. What are the power systems—structure, channels, lines of authority, processes, rules of procedure? How are decisions made?

Question 7 is extremely important if a worker is to intervene effectively in a power system. If, for example, a worker enters the legislative arena with the intent to have a bill introduced or passed, it is imperative that the worker have knowledge of the legislative process, as well as of the legislators themselves. A diagram of a state's legislative process, such as that provided in Figure 10-5, may help a worker to visualize the complexity of the procedure.[16]

Supplementing information about the identified power systems, the worker needs to know:

8. Are there any other systems with the potential for meeting the identified need or for resolving the problem?

9. Are there other systems that could influence or put pressure on the power systems?

10. Are there other resources to support, or to collaborate with, the worker in his or her efforts?

On the basis of the data collected, the worker is then in a position to make a clearer assessment of the problem or need and to plan interventions. The questions raised in the assessment (stage III) include:

11. *Who* has *what* (problem or need) *why?*

12. If more than one problem or need has been identified, how should they be prioritized?

13. What is the most effective plan to work on the problems or needs as prioritized?

As a plan is developed, the worker would recall and may plan to use the political skills, program analysis, tactics, and testimony guide suggested earlier. As tasks are listed sequentially on a contracted-plan sheet, a worker might include efforts to mobilize other individuals, groups, or organizations to work with him or her on mutual goals stated on the contract. If others become involved in the action, the tasks may be distributed and contracted among the participants. As pointed out, however, it is possible that all of the tasks will have to be carried out by the worker alone.

In intervention (stage IV) during indirect work, a worker may have face-to-face contact with the power systems and use various political skills and tactics. (Because a power system is not a client system, such intervention is not considered direct intervention, as defined in Chapter 5.) The worker may act as a team member in a coalition or may refer the issue to another resource for action. Throughout the intervention stage, the worker (team) asks:

14. Am I (are we) completing the tasks as planned?
15. Am I (are we) ready to move on to the next planned task?

As the worker moves into evaluation, the questions asked are:

16. To what extent has (have) the goal(s) been accomplished?
17. If there has been goal accomplishment, was this the result of my (our) efforts? If there has not been goal accomplishment, why not?

Here too, the contracted plan developed during assessment is carefully reviewed if goals have not been accomplished. Timing anticipated, resources contracted, and tasks sequenced along with stated goals and problems on the plan are reconsidered.

The worker (team) asks:

18. Is there a need to reformulate goals or any other dimension of the plan? Are more overt political behaviors needed?

In the final stage, the worker (team) makes the decision regarding termination of his or her involvement in the issue with the identified power systems. Questions raised in this stage include:

19. Is it time for me (us) to refer, transfer, or terminate my (our) efforts to bring about change in the extended environment in relation to the identified problem or needs?
20. How do I (we) plan to terminate?
    a. When?
    b. Will there be a follow-up?
    c. In terminating, are there feelings that need to be expressed? by me? the power systems? others?
21. Using the life-cycle approach, what is the past, present, and future of my (our) involvement in working on these problems or needs in the extended environment?

If the worker is a beginning generalist, the time may come in the process when a referral or transfer needs to be made to a worker with advanced expertise in political strategies or policy formation. Systems with greater legal access and authority may need to step in and take over the role of advocate. Social problems in society at large are seldom resolved fully. Even

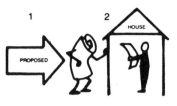

1
PROPOSED

2
HOUSE

3
SENATE

4

5
TO COMMITTEE

Introduction in the House

First reading in the House

Sent to Senate for first reading

Bill title, number and sponsors printed in the House and Senate Journals

Bill sent to one of the joint standing committees of the General Assembly

18
HOUSE

17

16
SENATE

15

14
HOUSE

Returned to first house for concurrence if amended by second house; if not amended, sent to the governor

Other house votes on bill

A "yes" vote sends bill to other house for second reading and placement on calendar

Vote on bill

Third reading. Debate and amendments

19

20

21
HOUSE   SENATE

22
HOUSE   SENATE

If House and Senate cannot agree, bill sent to special joint conference committee

If conference committee reaches agreement, report sent to both houses

If one or both houses reject changes, bill fails

If both houses pass the bill, it is sent to the governor

FIGURE 10-5   How a Bill Becomes a Law

when legislation is passed and programs are initiated, ongoing monitoring of change is usually needed. Workers may, therefore, build in a role of monitor as part of their follow-up plan for the future.

Although beginning generalists may not possess advanced, sophisticated political skills to work in complex political structures, they are the ones most likely to be aware of the pulse and the pain of the disadvantaged

6

Committee may 1) hold bill as is for public hearing; 2) combine with others and have drafted as a committee bill; 3) take no action ("box"). (Committees may also write new ("raised") committee bills)

7

Committee holds public hearings for public, legislators, state agency representatives on all bills still under consideration

8

Bills requiring appropriations are referred to Appropriations Committee for approval (Bill can die here)

9

Committee acts on bill (reports favorably, unfavorably or "boxes" with no report)

13

Final printing of bill

12

HOUSE

Second reading. Bill is assigned a calendar number

11

Office of Fiscal Analysis adds fiscal note

10

Bill sent to Legislative Commissioners to be checked for accuracy)

23

GOVERNOR

24

If governor vetoes, bill is returned to house in which it originated

25

LAW

Bill becomes law if 1) governor signs it; 2) governor fails to sign within 5 days during legislative session or 15 days after adjournment; 3) vetoed bill is repassed in each house by a ⅔ vote of elected membership

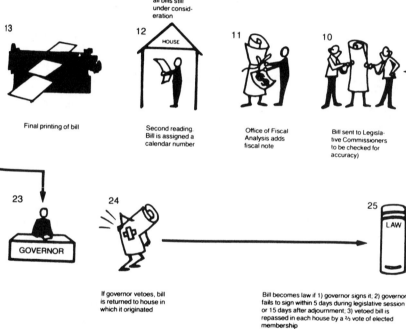

Prepared by the League of Women Voters of Connecticut
Graphics Courtesy of Ætna Life & Casualty
Published by the Joint Committee on Legislative Management

in society. Their firsthand experience and documentation, with a strong sense of commitment and perseverance, may be the most valuable forces to bring about change in the extended environment. Ecological generalists, therefore, are prepared primarily for direct practice with client systems, but they do not forget that efforts for social change in society at large are also essential to their holistic identity.

A PLACE FOR RADICAL SOCIAL WORK

Social workers who have worked primarily on social justice issues to bring about institutional change have been called "radical." In recent years, radical social workers have begun to express the need for a holistic conception of their practice. Rather than limiting the focus of their attention to issues of social justice, they are recognizing the need to understand and to work with psychological problems. Instead of identifying themselves as working only with groups, communities, and institutions, they are finding appropriate roles within their practice for developing relationships with individuals. For example, Peter Leonard writes:

> A radical perspective which ignores or argues away the psychological effects of experience and the need at times to respond to these effects individually, as well as through group, community or organizational action, is in danger of failing to consider others as a whole person, of perpetuating in another form, a fragmented, dehumanized view of men and women. Radical social work must therefore encompass direct work with individuals and families as well as with the wider group and collectivities to which they belong, and must seek to relate organizational and individual action.[17]

Although the primary method of radical social workers involves education through group dialogue, there is a growing awareness that radical workers need a range of skills for working with a variety of systems. Leonard supports the notion of shifting the focus of social work from pathology to interactions and from problems related to personal attributes to problems related to social situations. He considers pioneer works on a generalist concept of practice to be groundbreakers for expanded holistic models of social work practice.[18]

The General Method of social work practice as developed in this book provides an organized procedure that may be used by radical social workers. Throughout the General Method, an ecological perspective is used that sensitizes the worker to the impact of the environment on the individual as well as the individual on the environment. The worker using the General Method is aware of the strong possibility that efforts may need to be directed toward bringing about changes in environmental structures and systems. As radical social workers grow in their search for holism and a balanced perspective in their practice, they may find that the General Method is a relevant guiding framework for their entry-level practice.

A HOLISTIC VISION—OUR FUTURE CHALLENGE

As radical social workers move more into direct work with individuals and families and as direct-practice workers become more involved (by choice or necessity) with political or power systems, the quest for holism is becoming an apparent reality in our profession. Social workers are extending their activities to include a broader range of skills and systems. General practice for beginning and advanced workers is becoming more clearly understood and appreciated. The content of this book demonstrates another attempt within the profession to bring together various components of practice into a unified whole.

In addition to breadth, there is an ongoing search for greater depth and height in the profession. We are striving for an understanding and mastery of concentrations and specializations in practice. As pointed out in Chapter 1, further work is needed to develop and articulate the knowledge and skills for advanced practice in specialized areas. The holistic foundation (Chapter 1) and the General Method (Chapters 2–9) described in this book serve as a base on which to build, refine, and extend our efforts to arrive at a holistic conception of all of social work practice. The beginning worker depicted in this text represents the entry level in our profession. To complete the picture, extensive work is needed to identify and integrate the advanced and beginning levels of practice into a holistic conceptualization. As we grow in sensitivity to the interdependence of persons and environments, we are also becoming increasingly aware of the interdependence and complementarity that can be envisioned among practice levels in the profession.

A skeletal framework for initiating a holistic perspective of social work practice at all educational and practice levels is proposed in Figure 10-6. The inner circle depicts the center of practice, which is foundation knowledge, values, and skills (outlined in Diagram 1-5, Chapter 1). The circle surrounding the foundation indicates beginning general practice (explicated throughout this text). The next circle is divided into sections to highlight the various types or areas of concentration found within the profession. This circle also reflects a place for advanced general practice. Practitioners at this level would have M.S.W. degrees. The final outer circle represents the doctoral level, where social workers are engaged in education, research, administration, or advanced specializations. More specific content for the advanced levels, as well as the interrelatedness among various levels and concentrations, has yet to be explored and articulated.

CONCLUSION

I have found it difficult to write a social work textbook that conveys the warmth and depth that I know exists in the profession. Unfortunately, professionals sometimes seem to lose the heart of what they are about as they become engrossed in objectifying their work through scientific or technical language and documentation. The qualities that are not measurable are often described in professional terms that may confuse the student or lose

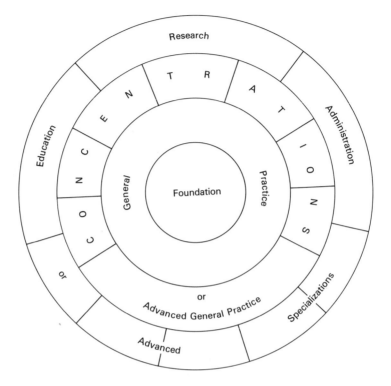

FIGURE 10-6   A Holistic View of Social Work Practice and Education

the essential meaning of what is being said. For example, instead of talking about love and compassion, we talk about acceptance and empathy. The desirable qualities of a social worker are often described in terms, for example, of knowledge, skills, dependability, adaptability, and responsibility. Little has been stated about that "special" quality that draws a person into social work and keeps him or her going even when, after repeated efforts, there is no obvious success. It may be a religious, spiritual, or humanitarian call or commitment. It may be an inner "goodness of person" that has not been defined and is seldom recognized.

To me, social workers are like the person in the Bible who kept on knocking at a neighbor's door until bread was given to another in need.[19] The person knocking did not break the door down, but neither did he or she go away. Social workers are often unnoticed, but they are there—listening to needs, calling on resources, visiting homes, and waiting at capitol buildings or legislative hearings to speak about realities that have to be addressed.

Today, there are doors of complex and powerful systems that need to be opened. There is great need for "whole" social workers—those with vision of what could be as well as what is and has been, workers with sensitivity, warmth, and hope—as well as purpose and skills.

In ending this book, it is time to recall the passage, "To everything there is a season" (Eccles. 3:1). The season has come for social workers to "get it together," to move tradition into contemporary action as we develop holistic conceptualizations and relevant methodologies. But I would not be faithful to the concept of season if I maintained that what has been presented in this text is above change. Beginning professionals are encouraged to take what is here as a proposed guide and not as infallible doctrine. Newly developed frameworks will continue to be in process as long as we have a dynamic, responsive profession. We in the profession need you, ecological generalists, with your vitality, creativity, and unifying perspective. We welcome you and encourage your full participation in our vital and growing profession.

NOTES

[1] Helen Harris Perlman, *Social Casework: A Problem-Solving Process* (Chicago: University of Chicago Press, 1967), p. vii.

[2] Allen Pincus and Anne Minahan, *Social Work Practice: Model and Method* (Itasca, Ill.: Peacock, 1973), p. 63.

[3] Council on Social Work Education, *Curriculum Policy Statement for the Master's Degree and Baccalaureate Degree Programs in Social Work Education* (New York: Council on Social Work Education, 1982), p. 7.

[4] Miriam Dinnerman, "Options in Social Work Manpower and Education," *Social Work* 20, no. 5 (September 1975): 348–51.

[5] Ibid.

[6] Robert P. Stewart, "Watershed Days: How Will Social Work Respond to the Conservative Revolution?" *Social Work* 26, no. 4 (July 1981): 273.

[7] Bertram H. Beck, "Social Work's Future: Triumph or Disaster?" *Social Work* 26, no. 5 (September 1981): 371.

[8] Ronald C. Federico, *The Social Welfare Institution*, 3rd ed. (Lexington, Mass.: Heath 1980), p. 327.

[9] Bonnie Brown Morell, "Comments on Currents, ABC's of Block Grants," *Social Work* 27, no. 2 (March 1982): 126–27.

[10] Anne Minahan, "Editorial Page, Social Workers and Politics," *Social Work* 26, no. 4 (July 1981): 371.

[11] James S. Wolk, "Are Social Workers Politically Active?" *Social Work* 26, no. 4 (July 1981): 268.

[12] Harry Specht, *New Directions for Social Work Practice* (Englewood Cliffs, N.J.: Prentice-Hall 1988), p. 251.

[13] Cecilia Kleinkauf, "A Guide to Giving Legislative Testimony," copyright 1981, National Association of Social Workers, Inc. Reprinted with permission, from *Social Work* 26, no. 4 (July 1981), 297–303 (adaptation).

[14] Winifred Bell, "Obstacles to Shifting from the Descriptive to the Analytical Approach in Teaching Social Services," *Journal of Education for Social Work* 5, no. 2 (Spring 1969): 5–11.

[15]Ronald B. Dear and Rino J. Patti, "Legislative Advocacy: Seven Effective Tactics." Copyright 1981, National Association of Social Workers, Inc. Reprinted with permission, from *Social Work* 26, no. 4 (July 1981): 289–96 (adapted).

[16]"How a Bill Becomes a Law." (Diagram prepared and published by the League of Women Voters of Connecticut, Education Fund, and the Joint Committee on Legislative Management of the Connecticut General Assembly, August 1975.)

[17]Peter Leonard, "Toward a Paradigm for Radical Practice," Roy Bailey and Mike Broke eds., *Radical Social Work*, (New York: Pantheon Books, 1975), p. 51.

[18]Ibid.

[19]Luke 11: 5–8.

Index